Begin

An Anatomy of Leadership

Sasson Sofer

Basil Blackwell

Basil Blackwell Ltd
108 Cowley Road, Oxford, OX4 1JF, UK

Basil Blackwell Inc.
432 Park Avenue South, Suite 1503
New York, NY 10016, USA

British Library Cataloguing in Publication Data
Sofer, Sasson.
Begin: an anatomy of leadership.
1. Israel. Begin, Menachem – Biographies.
I. Title
956.94′04′0924
ISBN 0–631–16363–8

Library of Congress Cataloging in Publication Data
Sofer, Sasson.
Begin: an anatomy of leadership / Sasson Sofer.
p.   cm.
Bibliography: p.
Includes index.
1. Begin, Menachem, 1913–   . 2. Prime ministers – Israel –
Biography.   3. Revisionist Zionists – Biography.   4. Irgun tsvai
le 'umi.   5. Israel – Politics and government.   I. Title.
DS 126.6.B33S64   1988
956.94′054′0924–dc19
[B]   88–3785 CIP
ISBN 0–631–16363–8

C1029480
115   3|89

Typeset by Joshua Associates Ltd., Oxford
Printed in Great Britain by
T.J. Press, Padstow

Contents

Preface

On June 20, 1977, the leader of Herut and former commander of the Irgun (*Irgun Zvai Le'umi*, national military organization), was sworn in as sixth prime minister of Israel. One of the more unlikely heirs of Ze'ev Jabotinsky, the founder of the Revisionist movement, was about to take up the mantle of power.

Menachem Begin's political activity in the Land of Israel spanned forty years. However gauged, it was an extraordinary career. In January 1944, less than two years after arriving in the country, he proclaimed the "revolt" led by the Irgun against the British mandate in Palestine. That organization and its leader soon achieved hegemony over the Revisionist movement. Almost four decades were to elapse, however, before Begin was to assert his hold over the masses and become Israel's prime minister. Two years later he would sign a peace treaty with Egypt, having in the meantime been awarded the Nobel peace prize.

In the spring of 1981 he sent Israel's airforce to bomb Iraq's nuclear reactor. Within a few months he had won an election in which he had appeared to face certain defeat, and went on to proclaim the annexation of the Golan Heights. In 1982 he launched what he termed one of Israel's greatest military operations, the Lebanon War. No one could have foreseen that little more than a year would elapse till the day he reached the end of his road. It was a broken man who withdrew, without a word to his nation, to the seclusion of his home on the outskirts of Jerusalem, close to Mount Herzl cemetery, and not far from Givat Shaul, formerly Deir Yassin.

The four decades between Begin's proclamation of the revolt and his resignation in August 1983 form the greater part of the setting for an examination of Begin's world view, political thought, and political activity, which constitutes the most significant attempt made to put the ideology of the Revisionist movement into practice. The history of Revisionist political thought is personified by a handful of individuals, and Begin's rise to leadership cannot be comprehended apart from the tragic selection process enacted by history. Jabotinsky had died in the summer of 1940. David Raziel and Abraham Stern had been killed during the early 1940s. For various reasons, other Revisionist leaders found themselves shunted to the margins of Israeli politics. It is notable that the intellectually and ideologically lackluster elements of the Revisionist leadership achieved greater organizational and political success.

This work is not a history of Revisionism, nor is it a political biography of Menachem Begin. Rather, it is an analysis of the world view, political methods, ideological teachings, and perceptions of reality that came to expression in Begin's life and political career. It is not yet possible to write a full biography of Begin. On the other hand, the historian of ideas has already all he needs to reconstruct Begin's political thought. Begin himself has written an enormous number of articles, pamphlets, speeches, and two books, which form the principal source for a study of his world view. On the theoretical level, this work intends to consider the relationship between *Weltanschauung* and the shaping of foreign policy, since we have here a striking instance of ideology narrowed down to the political sphere, and especially to the sphere of foreign policy. Future historians are not likely to have more than is presently available for an analysis of Begin's world view. Sources unavailable at present may contribute to a study of Begin's political decision-making, but not to a study of the fundamental assumptions employed by him in examining reality and making operational decisions.

This work consists of three parts. Part I examines the life and political career of Begin up until his accession to power in May 1977. This section deals with the early days of Begin's political career in Poland, his relations with the founding leader of the Revisionist movement, Ze'ev Jabotinsky, and the mystery surrounding his appointment as commander of the Irgun. The operations carried out by the Irgun, which occupy a central place in most works on Begin, are described primarily to shed light on the ideas and conceptions that lay behind the "revolt," and to enquire into Begin's qualities as a leader. Finally, the struggle for the succession with its various ramifications, until Begin remained as sole heir, is here described for the first time. Part II examines Begin's political world view – his historical vista, view of reality, and strategic conception. His attitude to the Palestinian problem, the origins of the autonomy idea, and his international orientation and images of the world order are also examined. Part III is devoted to the period after May 1977 in which Begin was put to the test of history as a politician, diplomat, and national leader. The discussion here is focused around the peace with Egypt, the war with Lebanon, and Begin's resignation. Of necessity, it is also a discussion of Israeli society in one of its most dramatic periods.

A discussion of the political philosophy of one of the two main ideological streams in Israeli society poses a particular difficulty in preserving objectivity, above and beyond the difficulties and shortcomings of any interpretation of ideas and the failings of the methodology available to us. At the very least, such an analysis must strive for truth, to the extent possible, and present all its arguments and conclusions openly, *sine ira et studio*.

A reason for studying a conception or policy of an earlier period is that a nation's behavior in the realm of foreign policy is never entirely divorced from past events, or from the conclusions drawn from them, which in time become a more permanent tradition. Our view of the history of Palestine has become increasingly flawed, though the question of how ahistorical trends have developed in the collective thought of Israeli society is beyond the bounds of this work. Those trends are not to be ignored.

No other Israeli political figure has received such unbalanced treatment from writers – mostly journalists – as Menachem Begin. No other Israeli politician of the last generation has had his outlook, mental condition, and physical health subjected to such close scrutiny. But few books or biographies have been written about him, and virtually nothing has been done in the way of research. In following the tracks of Begin's political life and legacy we must be wary of uncritical admirers and sworn opponents; but, no less, of the traces Begin himself left in an attempt to direct others to the image he hoped to be accorded in history.

I owe a great debt to a number of friends and colleagues whom I wish to acknowledge adequately. I am most grateful to Professor Nissan Oren for guiding me through the byways, and sometimes the culs-de-sac of academia, and no less for his remarkable intellectual courage. My warmest thanks to Professor Norman Rose for his encouragement, inspiration, and unfailing assistance. I have profited greatly from the generosity as well as the incisive mind of Professor Moshe Lissak and I am thankful to him. I also wish to thank Professor Jonathan Frankel for his expert advice and constructive comments, though, naturally, he bears no responsibility for any errors that may remain in this work. It is a pleasant duty to thank the Warden and Fellows of St Antony's College, Oxford, for electing me to a research fellowship. I am particularly grateful to Dr Roger Owen and Dr Avi Shlaim for their invaluable help, beyond the normal call of duty. My thanks are also extended to Professor Gabi Cohen, Professor Albert Hourani, Professor Yehoshafat Harkabi, Professor Ellis Joffe, and Professor Adam Roberts.

I recall with gratitude the courtesy and assistance extended to me by the archivists, librarians, and staff at the Jabotinsky Institute Archives; Israel State Archives; the National Library, the Library for Humanities and Social Sciences, and the Department of Oral Documentation at the Institute of Contemporary Jewry, all at the Hebrew University of Jerusalem; the Knesset Library, Jerusalem; and the Kressel Collection at the Oxford Centre for Hebrew Studies. I am also pleased to acknowledge with gratitude the financial assistance granted by the Leonard Davies Institute for International Relations and the Research Fund of the Faculty of Social Sciences at the Hebrew University.

I should also like to thank Mr Arnold Schwartz for his competent translations and editorial expertise. In the same connection, thanks are also due to Mr Peretz Kidron. Mrs Yehudit Cohen-Shor has typed the manuscript with the utmost diligence and care. Ms Connie Wilsack has been a courteous and indispensable copy-editor, saving me from many inconsistencies and obscurities of language. Finally, I must recall my indebtedness to all those at Basil Blackwell who helped in the preparation of this book, particularly Mr Sean Magee and Ms Kate Chapman. I am, indeed, most grateful for their meticulous and unremitting care in preparing this book for publication.

Sasson Sofer
Oxford

The author and publishers are grateful to the Jabotinsky Institute in Israel for permission to reproduce plates 1–11, 14 and 15, and to Popperfoto for plates 12 and 13.

Abbreviations

HCNL	Hebrew Committee of National Liberation
ICJ	Institute of Contemporary Jewry, the Hebrew University of Jerusalem
ISA	Israel State Archives
JIA	Jabotinsky Institute Archives
NZO	New Zionist Organization
WZO	World Zionist Organization
ZRO	Zionist Revisionist Organization (also, World Union of Zionist Revisionists)

Part I

The Man

1
From Brisk to Jerusalem, 1913–1942

A scarcity of biographical details about a political leader does not necessarily signify an intention to deceive. In general, however, the few facts that are made much of tend to correspond to a specific image accorded to the man *post factum*. Indeed, we know little about Begin as a young man in keeping with the insignia of a man destined from youth for greatness.

Attempts to analyze Begin's personality have generally seized upon prominent, seemingly one-dimensional features. At first glance, his strengths and weaknesses appear to be in plain view. Actually, however, his personality has profound contradictions. He is a divided figure: first, popular orator, underground leader who challenged both the British mandatory regime and the Zionist leadership, chivalrous parliamentarian; and then, a grotesque, almost hapless figure. It remains to be seen whether this schism between the heroic vision of a historical hero and a helplessness ending in depression and flight from reality is also found in Begin's inner world.

Brest-Litovsk, the staging post

Menachem Begin was born in August 1913,[1] in Brest-Litovsk (Brisk), Lithuania, the youngest child of Ze'ev Dov and Hassia (née Kosovski) Begin. In many ways, the time of his birth – the eve of the First World War – was of crucial importance. The war would mark a historical divide between two worlds and two generations. It would change the face of Europe. For the Jewish communities of Europe, the territorial changes engendered by the war determined national allegiances. The war also determined the educational system, the culture and values within which the new generation of young Jews would be brought up. It is perhaps significant that a few years later at Brest-Litovsk, Leon Trotsky, the Commissar for Foreign Affairs of the new Soviet republic, would present his negotiations with Germany as an example of the "new diplomacy," which briefly challenged the forms and foundations of traditional European diplomacy.

In 1913, Begin's year of birth, Brest-Litovsk lay within the Russian Empire. The border town was a staging post to Warsaw in the west and to the Russian steppes to the east. That was a fact of strategic importance that had influenced the lives of its citizens for generations. For the Poles, the fortifications of Brest-Litovsk constituted an outpost of European civilization against the Asiatic east. In the course of the First World War and the subsequent Russian–Polish conflict, Brest-Litovsk changed hands six times. Nonetheless it was an ordinary provincial town, not particularly well developed, its economy based mainly on timber trade and petty commerce with the nearby villages.[2]

The surrounding province of Polsia had been the home of Jewish communities for centuries. The Jewish community of Brest-Litovsk is first mentioned in a charter conferred by Vitold (Vitout) the Grand Duke of Lithuania in 1388. At certain periods, the community of Brisk was among the most prominent in Lithuania, a land renowned for its great religious sages.[3] At the time of Begin's birth, its population numbered some 60,000 – half of them Poles and Lithuanians, the other half Jews.

In a piece richly nostalgic, Begin wrote about his native Brisk, and his home on Sigmund Street, so renamed after Poland gained its independence.[4] He evoked images from his past, referring vaguely to his mother and more concretely to his father, always stressing his father's courage. He described the wooden structure that served as a kindergarten, the ill-lit house of learning, the clubrooms frequented by the young Jews, and finally, the Polish *gymnasium* (high school) he attended. As with so many of his writings, Begin concluded this article with a moral for the future: "I shall never return to Brisk, but Brisk will be with me always. For there are three important things I took with me [from there]: to love Jews, not to fear gentiles, and, third: it is good for a man to shoulder a burden from his youth."

It is hard to determine the precise social stratum from which Begin emerged, though lower middle class would probably not be far off. We have little information about Begin's famly. His relations with his father and mother are also insufficiently clear. Hassia Kosovski was Ze'ev Dov Begin's second wife, and there was a marked difference in their ages: he was in his early forties, she a young woman of about twenty. Begin was to be brought up by a young mother and a father advanced in years, almost elderly. As portrayed by Begin, his mother was a perfect, idyllic figure. However, like his older brother Herzl, about whom also little is known, she remains an enigmatic figure. She came from a family of timber merchants in Vohlin; orphaned in childhood, she was brought up by her grandfather. According to Menachem Begin and to his sister Rachel, Hassia exerted a powerful influence on the family. In later years, Begin said: "In my wife, I found the traits of my mother."[5]

Like Ze'ev Jabotinsky subsequently, Ze'ev Dov Begin exercised a major influence on his son Menachem. Information about the elder Begin is fragmentary. He was the eldest of nine children in a family whose livelihood came from the timber trade. He appears to have been an autodidact who, after attending heder and yeshiva, was gradually exposed to cultural influences from Russia, Poland, and Germany; according to his daughter he cultivated a special sympathy for German culture. Ze'ev Begin found various forms of casual employment, which progressively centered around Zionist and communal affairs. At one stage, he served as secretary of Brisk's Jewish community. Begin recalled his father as an observant Jew, and one of the first followers of Herzl. His most prominent trait was his courage. "My father was one of the most courageous men I have ever met."[6]

Courage is indeed the characteristic to which our attention is drawn in the family history. Participation in Jewish self-defense during the 1905 revolution; the years of suffering and tribulation between 1914 and 1920, in the course of which the family was forced to leave Brest-Litovsk and wander in search of shelter and income; defense of Jews in Brest-Litovsk against harassment by foreign soldiers; a sharp reply to Marshal Pilsudski who accused the Jews of speculation. Throughout, Ze'ev Dov displayed a readiness to stand up to gentiles, in spite of his inferior status, and an ability to withstand the sufferings of imprisonment. And finally, an event whose veracity is not firmly established: while marching with the rest of Brisk's Jewish community to their death during the period of Nazi conquest, Ze'ev Begin reportedly encouraged his fellow Jews to sing the Zionist anthem, *Hatikva*, and before his death, cried out for vengeance.[7] In many ways, the elder Begin was the embodiment of the type of Jew his son Menachem idealized: a Zionist nationalist faithful to his heritage, meeting the difficulties of the day with courage, and firm and resolute toward non-Jews.

In addition to being a border town, Brest-Litovsk was a cultural crossroads. Begin grew up at a time when a newly independent Poland was at the heady peaks of its national renaissance. Poland was a riven society contending with the existence in its midst of large national minorities, economic backwardness, and political instability. But the large Jewish community, which comprised about 10 per cent of the total population, was the birthplace of almost all of the political factions in Zionism. In every sense, the 1920s were a period of transition between two turbulent epochs. For Begin it was a placid period, the years of a relatively secure late childhood and early adolescence. In spite of his family's economic difficulties, this period stood in sharp contrast to his stormy childhood, up to the age of six or seven, when the family lived in the shadow of war, in makeshift lodgings, with his father generally absent. It is difficult to appraise the impact of these events on Menachem Begin. Shortly before his fiftieth birthday, he wrote: "I belong to a generation whose childhood was almost totally slain." He made particular mention of the curse of hunger. The First World War, he declared, was the most momentous of humanity's upheavals; it concluded the nineteenth century and destroyed respect "for the sanctity of human life."[8]

Begin grew up in a home closely linked to the Jewish heritage and to the new Zionist nationalism. The significance of the testimony that his family inclined toward German culture is not clear. For a time, Begin appears to have been cared for by a Russian nurse. He conversed in Hebrew with his father and in Yiddish with his mother.[9] We have only the most general details about his formal education; on his experiences and aspirations, his inner world as a child, and his friends we know very little.

After Begin became prime minister, Eva Pitlik, a kindergarten teacher who remembered him from those days, recalled that he was a gifted child, active and eager to learn.[10] Begin received his elementary education at the Tachkemoni School, a Hebrew school run by the Mizrachi religious Zionist movement. The school's young secretary remembers Begin standing on a chair, holding forth to his classmates.[11] At the age of fourteen he went on to high school, not at either of the town's two Jewish high schools (probably because of his family's economic straits),[12] but to Brest-Litovsk's Polish *gymnasium*, from which he was to graduate with honors. Three other Jewish pupils attended the Polish school with him.

Studying at the *gymnasium* was to have a far-reaching impact on Begin. It exposed him to the Polish school curriculum and to the country's national and cultural heritage at a decisive moment in Poland's history.[13] Writing later of his four years at the school, Begin chose to describe the pupils who harassed him as a Jew and an outsider. Later he said: we learned that the only things those thugs understood was force.[14] He also recalled the fact that he refused to write or sit for examinations on the Sabbath. That could have been a decision of crucial importance for him as failure to gain a pass in the Latin examination could have barred his entry to university.

Apart from the above, we know little about Begin's adolescence. Academically, it seems, the pallid youngster showed an inclination toward the humanities. In his early teens, he joined Hashomer Hatzair, a Zionist youth movement, and left shortly afterwards. At the age of fifteen he joined Betar, a Revisionist paramilitary youth movement.[15] This was the most significant milestone of his youth. Betar served as the cradle of his astonishing career; within a decade, he was to become the movement's *natziv* (commissioner) in Poland.

With regard to Begin's life from the time he joined Betar until his appointment as *natziv* in the spring of 1939 we know the following. He first heard Jabotinsky deliver a speech sometime in the late 1920s or perhaps in

1930. For Begin, it was an uplifting experience, leading him to dedicate himself forever to the Revisionist ideal.[16] In 1931, at the age of eighteen, he left Brest-Litovsk and began to study law at Warsaw University. However, his work at Betar headquarters appears gradually to have taken central place in his life. His rhetorical abilities began to attract attention, and his success in Betar was meteoric. Henceforth, Begin's name was to be linked with the history of the movement in Poland.[17]

Begin rose to the position of Betar commander of the province of Polsia. In the early 1930s, Begin was among the group of radical Betar leaders who supported Jabotinsky in the internal struggles within the Revisionist movement. After being placed in charge of Betar's organizational section, Begin was nominated the movement's *natziv* in Czechoslovakia. There are conflicting testimonies concerning his activities there: Aharon Propes, then Betar's *natziv* in Poland, maintained that he was a failure. Begin arrived in Czechoslovakia in February 1936 at a time of crisis for the movement. He served at one and the same time as *natziv*, as head of the organizational department, and as director of cultural training. Most of his time, however, he devoted to delivering speeches throughout the country. In the summer he left Czechoslovakia, and returned to Poland.[18] That same year, Begin completed his studies at Warsaw University. The decisive turning point in Begin's political career came with the third world convention of Betar, which was held in Warsaw in September 1938. The convention decided on the organizational unification of Betar and Irgun with a joint ideological platform. The decision was reached despite the objections of Propes and led to his replacement as *natziv* in Poland by Begin in the spring of 1939.

Flight from Warsaw

The period between 1938 and 1943 was the most dramatic in Begin's life. In that period he went from being *natziv* of Betar in Poland to heading the Irgun in Palestine. Along the way, he was to suffer the tribulations of the early war years in Europe, be imprisoned by the Russians, and arrive in Palestine with the Polish army of General Anders.

When Begin was appointed Betar's *natziv* in Poland, war clouds were already gathering over Europe and life was lived in the shadow of the approaching war. In May 1939, he married Aliza Arnold, the daughter of a Revisionist activist from Drohobycz. In *White Nights*, Begin writes that he sent her a brief letter: "I saw you, my lady, for the first time, but I feel as if I have known you all my life." He warned her of the likelihood of deprivation and imprisonment. Jabotinsky was one of the witnesses at the wedding.[19]

Early in August 1939, Begin set out for the Roumanian border, at the head of a convoy of Jews seeking to emigrate to Palestine. Under British pressure, the Roumanians cancelled their visas and they were forced to backtrack to Warsaw. According to Yisrael Eldad, later a leader of the underground Lehi group, who had arrived in Warsaw that same month, Begin tried to create an atmosphere of "business as usual." With some bitterness Eldad recorded that had he been so instructed he would have left Warsaw and gone sooner to Palestine.[20]

The outbreak of war on September 1, 1939 took Begin by surprise, but his response could have been anticipated: he conducted himself as a patriotic citizen of Poland. Together with another Betar leader, David Yutan, he approached the Polish authorities and asked their sanction for the formation of a Jewish unit in the Polish army to fight the Germans.[21]

On September 5, Begin attended the marriage of Nathan Friedman (Yellin-Mor), later a leader of Lehi. That same night, the building housing the editorial offices of the Yiddish paper *Der Moment* was bombed. The following day, Begin met with others at the home of his sister, Rachel Halperin, to discuss ways of getting out of Warsaw.[22] In his eastward flight to Vilna, Begin found himself in an uncertain race against the conquering Germans. Accompanied by Yellin-Mor, Begin made first for Lwow. They traveled part of the distance by train, together with thousands of other refugees from bomb-ravaged Warsaw; later, they proceeded on foot. On the way, Aliza Begin suffered a severe attack of asthma.[23] In Lwow, Yellin-Mor was arrested, but soon released. Begin, having realized that his presence in a city where he was widely known could be perilous, or perhaps because of his wife's illness, went on with her to Drohobycz.[24]

Begin was not convinced that it had been best to leave Warsaw. He held initially that it would not be desirable to remain in a region under Soviet control. However, events unfolded at a rapid pace. The partition of Poland was soon accomplished, and by October the Soviet Union had completed its takeover of the Baltic republics. In the interim period, most of Betar's leaders had moved to Vilna. Late in October 1939, Begin too reached that city.[25]

The ensuing year, up to Begin's imprisonment in September 1940, was relatively uneventful for him. The Betar leaders practised military drill, planned ways of emigrating to Palestine, and discussed their future course.[26] Begin's departure from Warsaw would continue to haunt him. He refrained in subsequent years from touching on the subject, but in a letter dated February 4, 1940, he replied in a tone both impatient and apologetic to accusations directed at him by Dr Shimshon Yuniczman, a colleague from Betar and a personal friend.[27] Writing to Begin from Palestine, where he now lived, Yuniczman argued that "the captain and officers are not the first to abandon a sinking ship." Begin retorted that "even if I left behind thousands of Betar members, when I left Warsaw – on the last day, of course – I was certain that I was *fulfilling my duty*" (emphasis in the original). He wrote that there had been reports that the German army would enter Warsaw within a day or two. For that reason, and for reasons "unknown to you," he left the city.

According to Begin's account, he wanted to transfer Betar's headquarters to the east because he expected that Poland would hold out. In any event, he was almost arrested in Lwow, being freed by "a miracle"; he did not make use of the immigration certifice he held that guaranteed him admission to Palestine since to do so would have conflicted with his obligations towards Betar. Begin found it necessary to correct Yuniczman's analogy to a sinking ship. On a ship, the captain has a special boat at his disposal; but in the present case, he pointed out, a boat was available for the crew, for a course now open but which might close, whereas for the captain the gates were already locked.

Yuniczman's charges appear to have struck home, for in this letter Begin twice reiterates his desire to return to Warsaw. "I corresponded on this mater with the *shilton* [Betar's senior leadership] which agreed with your view. I notified them that, if such is their view, I shall draw far-reaching conclusions, i.e., *I shall return to Warsaw*" (emphasis in the original). It should be pointed out that such a step would have been unreasonable under the circumstances prevailing at the time.[28] Begin also totally rejected Yuniczman's proposal that he enlist in the Finnish army. He regarded the notion of individual Jews joining the allied armies as worthless from a national viewpoint. The decisive aim should be an independent national Jewish unit. He indicated to Yuniczman that the situation had been discussed in Vilna and decisions had been reached about courses of action for the future; in Europe of 1940 virtually nothing could be done. We are left in the dark as to the content of these decisions.

Yuniczman's reply was no less sharply worded.[29] Representing the traditional Revisionist viewpoint he wrote: "I get the impression that you are now much more remote from realities than you were in the past," and charged Begin with holding "cabinet-like" deliberations as though nothing had happened. Yuniczman rejected Begin's reference to Britain as "occupier," refuted the analogy with Ireland and Garibaldi, and dismissed Begin's affirmation that there was a broad sphere for possible action apart from enlisting in armies that were fighting the Nazis. "What is this war, and between whom is it being waged? Do you think it is only between England and Germany, or do you also agree with my view that it is a war between Jewry and Germany?" Finally, Yuniczman reverted to the matter of the departure from Warsaw. He was convinved that even if not Begin himself, the other Betar officers ought to have remained "not fortuitously, but by command," with the rank and file "till the last moment." He refused to abandon his analogy. "I should remind you that, in most cases, captains do not take advantage of the boat at their disposal;

in many instances, they go down into the depths with the ship. But that is just an analogy."

In his letter to Yuniczman dated May 8, 1940, Begin renewed the argument on both topics: his departure from Warsaw, and the future course to be followed.[30] Expressing his doubts that Zionism could achieve its aims in collaboration with Britain, Begin in effect rejected the policies advocated by the Revisionist party and the Irgun at that time. He again dismissed "individual enlistment" in the Allied armies, as well as the idea that the Revisionists should rejoin the World Zionist Organization (WZO). What would happen, Begin asked, if the Powers were to reach an agreement within three months? Zionism would gain nothing. Begin insisted that this was not "our war." "In what way it is 'ours'? By virtue of the other side being Jew-haters?" Begin sounded convinced that he was right. In his view it was necessary to wait patiently, until such time as it would be possible to act independently. Begin also returned to the issue of his departure from Warsaw, though this time in rather more measured tones. The course adopted, he wrote, was decided upon after deliberation and serious thought. At the time he believed that Poland would hold out, and that the Betar leadership could continue to function a hundred kilometers from Warsaw. Apart from the poet Uri Zvi Greenberg, no one had foreseen that Poland would fall so swiftly. Now, the Betar leadership also concurred with his view.

In captivity

During the summer of 1940, Begin's mood was extraordinary. He wrote to Yuniczman: "I am totally stoic ... Fate has pronounced that I should sit here and suffer, in the spiritual sense, first and foremost because I do not suffer ..."[31] Begin found himself in the predicament often shared by leaders of national liberation movements at certain moments of crisis. At a time of great responsibility, he was unable to act and unable to reach any decision, his powers of leadership to no avail and his frustration compounded by feelings of guilt. Imprisonment by the NKVD may have been a personal calamity but Begin was to accept it with relief.

In Vilna, Begin and his wife lived with his brother-in-law, Dr Arnold, his childhood friend Yoel Kalerman, and the Eldad family. Yisrael Eldad and Begin spent their time in casual jobs, such as extending railway lines, collecting firewood, and in playing chess. The turning point came early in August with the news of Jabotinsky's death. Begin appears to have eulogized Jabotinsky at two ceremonies: one at the Vilna cemetery, the other at Kovno's central synagogue. Fully aware of being under surveillance by agents of the NKVD, he transferred his residence to the nearby township of Pavlinius. He decided to conduct his life as usual and not make use of the immigration certificate for himself and his wife that he had received a few days before his arrest. He decided to wait for the Russian agents to come for him at his home. He was arrested on September 20, 1940.[32]

Begin's attitude towards his detention was unusual and intriguing, and offers a clue to his personality. Describing his feelings at the moment of his arrest, he wrote: "There was no anxiety in my heart; on the contrary, the predominant sensation was one of profound relief."[33] He was later to recall, after becoming prime minister, that he had been ready to be arrested and was glad when the agents came for him. It was a period of despair, he added, and there was a need to bear suffering. "For me and for my family, the whole world was plunged into darkness."[34]

Like Jabotinsky's descriptions of his own brief periods of imprisonment in Russia and Palestine, Begin's portrayal is suffused with a patient, almost heroic endurance of suffering. Like his father when Polish detectives had come to arrest him, Begin demanded to see an arrest warrant. His demand caused them some embarrassment, according to Begin, whether out of a sense of "juridical" propriety, or in a "display of atavism." Begin's account of his arrest fully accords with Eldad's direct testimony. The scene as described is surprisingly like the play-acting of a stage hero who knows how things will turn out or like the behavior of a literary protagonist confident that he will survive until the end of the story.

Eldad described the scene Begin created from his arrest as "a concert." He gave his shoes a thorough polish, treated his captors with chivalrous courtesy and offered them tea, and took a Bible and André Maurois' biography of Disraeli with him to captivity. Ever the gracious host, he ushered his captors before him as he left, not forgetting as he did so to remind his wife to concede defeat to Eldad in their chess game. It was an elaborate ceremony in which Begin unhurriedly made the most of every possible gesture. It is doubtful that many others would have acted this way in the Europe of September 1940.[35]

Begin was taken to the Lukishki prison in Vilna.[36] On a par with the "revolt" he was later to lead in Palestine, this was one of the two most formative events in his life. He wrote about both episodes in *White Nights* and *The Revolt*, which he started in the late 1940s and completed in the early 1950s. His *White Nights* is the most personally revealing and literary of his works.[37] In this book, he honed his talent for allusion and sarcasm, taking evident pleasure in depicting his bearing during an experience that was by nature traumatic. In retrospect, he asserted, it had strengthened him for what was yet to come.

On arrival at NKVD headquarters in Vilna, Begin relates that he became not only a prisoner, but also a "spectator–student" of the new world he encountered. The account of his interrogation is instructive, as it presents Begin in the characteristic role of polemicist and diplomat. He managed to throw his interrogators off balance by his feigned innocence and his irony, the proud defense of his convictions, and his juridical hair-splitting. It was soon evident that the externalities of the interrogation and the rules of etiquette were of supreme importance to Begin to the point that he told himself: "If I have to suffer for my beliefs, I shall do so uncomplainingly; but as long as I am able to do so, I shall not put up with insults."[38]

At times, Begin resorted to legalistic arguments. One of these was his reference to the article in the Soviet constitution that guaranteed asylum to foreign nationals suffering persecution due to the conduct of a war of national liberation. Begin's rhetoric, his attempt to give a comprehensive explanation for every charge made by his interrogators and to enter into subtle analysis, only made his predicament worse. He added unnecessary points that were open to hostile interpretation or simply irritated the investigators. Such was the effect produced by his demand for an interpreter, to ensure that his meaning be understood thoroughly and precisely. His interrogators responded disparagingly, possibly with some anxiety about the possibility of his being provided with a platform to expound his views.[39]

The climax of the interrogation was Begin's stubborn refusal to sign a statement that contained the sentence: "I admit I am guilty of having been the chairman of the Betar organization in Poland." It is not known to what extent Begin was aware of the arbitrary nature of the Soviet system, which would not put him on trial, but he clearly considered himself to be facing a supreme and crucial test: should he fail, "there will be no point in living." In the wearying exchange that ensued, his stubbornness won out. The words "I am guilty" were deleted from the statement before he signed it – an unprecedented achievement. He was sentenced to eight years' imprisonment in a labor camp. Hearing the sentence, he muttered: "That's a fine *prima Aprilis*."[40]

From the prison where he had endured lack of sleep, confinement in a punishment cell, and sixty hours seated facing a wall, Begin was taken to the frozen Pechora region in the northern tundra where he was to work at porterage and dismantling railway tracks. Fortunately for him, the date of his release was advanced when the German attack on the Soviet Union in June 1941 totally transformed the situation in Eastern Europe. Begin was freed as a Polish citizen, following an agreement between the Soviet Union and the free Polish government.[41]

What were Begin's principal conclusions from this episode, as he looked back on it ten years later? His taste of the Soviet system inspired him with a degree of skepticism about institutions of repression and the arbitrary stupidity with which they are administered. It would be going too far to imply that his experience of Soviet prisons shaped his political attitude toward the Soviet Union. His experiences undoubtedly left their mark on him, but their impact was far from unambiguous.[42] In considering the confrontation between the revolutionary and his captors, he drew conclusions about the decisive importance of a platform from which the former could address the world about the ideals for which he was fighting. Denial of such a platform was, in Begin's view, one of the means whereby the individual is broken under the Soviet regime.[43]

Confronted with immeasurable human suffering, Begin came to the conclusion that faith is the sole spiritual mode of withstanding it. In *White Nights*, as in *The Revolt*, he devotes much space to Garin, the Jewish Communist whose life was wasted and distorted under the influence of the Communist mirage. Garin, a party loyalist, ended up in a Soviet labor camp. In Begin's description, he comes to symbolize the Jew who makes a last desperate bid to return to his people before his death. There is also a parallel Jewish character: the interpreter summoned to his interrogation, the Jewish informer who fawns on his gentile bosses.[44]

However, the main lesson Begin appears to have drawn from that period is his perception of the fragility and fortuitousness that are part and parcel of human existence. Who can guess what will befall a man, he muses; can he know "what is 'good' for him, and what is 'bad'? . . . If that great factor in life, known as 'fortuity' does not help you, you will find nothing. But fortuity helps."[45] What Begin presents in *The Revolt* as "an instructive lesson, perhaps for as long as I live," is his conviction that human life is subject to fortune, but there is always a chance; "the sun will yet rise." There is always hope, even when matters are at their most desperate. History does not unfold in accordance with any preconceived human plan; one must be tranquil and optimistic in one's sufferings, things may yet work out. For an ordinary person, conducting one's life in accordance with this fatalistic philosophy may perhaps offer hope; for a statesman and political leader, it is liable to invite surprise and calamity.

2

Begin and Jabotinsky

Heir apparent in disguise

One of the most crucial turning points in Begin's life was occasioned by an event that occurred overseas, far from Vilna. On the evening of August 5, 1940, at a Betar camp at Hunter, near New York, Aharon Propes turned to the pale figure slumped in his armchair and asked: "Vladimir Yev-genievitch, does his honor feel unwell?" That same evening, Ze'ev Jabotinsky died.[1] His final year had been particularly trying: the separation from his wife, whom he had left behind in London in the blitz, his son imprisoned in Acre. He also suffered a sense of guilt and failing at having erred badly in his predictions about the war.

Jabotinsky's death was tragic for the Zionist movement, and especially for the Revisionists. He had left no obvious successor, and the Revisionist movement's organizational structure was flimsy. Its Palestinian section was racked by crisis, control over Betar and the Irgun was feeble. The Irgun itself was effectively split. Eight turbulent years later, Menachem Begin alone survived as the inheritor of the Revisionist movement tradition and course of action.

When Ze'ev Jabotinsky's coffin was brought to Israel in July 1964, the leading pallbearers were Aharon Propes and Menachem Begin, the two men who had occupied the post of Betar *natziv* in Poland. In his eulogy, Begin addressed Jabotinsky as: "Your honor the head of Betar, our father, teacher and mentor . . . our commander."[2] On the hundredth anniversary of Jabotinsky's birth, Begin declared: "After your demise, we continued to tread the path you set before us, and we made a supreme effort to implement your teachings."[3] Seemingly, then, Jabotinsky was "the living teacher": the teachings that had guided his followers uninterruptedly from the Revisionist party (officially, the Zionist Revisionist Organization (ZRO), and also known as the Zionist Revisionist Union) and Betar to the Irgun continued to guide the Herut movement.[4]

One thing Begin shared with the old Revisionist leaders was unqualified admiration for Jabotinsky. On the tenth anniversary of Jabotinsky's death,

Begin enumerated his contributions to Zionism.[5] First, setting the establishment of a Jewish state as the prime objective of Zionism. Second, a political doctrine in which rebellion and military strength are permanent features. In Begin's presentation, Jabotinsky emerged as the father of the revolt. Begin went on to list the traits he admired in Jabotinsky: love of nation and homeland, self-sacrifice, a joyful acceptance of suffering, and the ability to fight for an ideal even as a member of a persecuted minority. One year before he became prime minister, Begin compared Jabotinsky, with typical exaggeration, to humanity's greatest figures: Aristotle, Moses, Maimonides, Leonardo da Vinci.[6] He spoke of Jabotinsky as poet, social reformer, orator, but above all, as the standard-bearer of the revolt, the Hebrew army, and national independence. We shall try to determine whether the portrayal of Jabotinsky and Begin as bound by a common vision, tradition, and political course stands the test of history.

Menachem Begin regarded himself as heir to two chains of leadership. One was that of the Zionist movement as a whole. In his presentation, the first leader was Theodore Herzl, who was followed by Ze'ev Jabotinsky. Begin expressed admiration for both of them, depicting them as the founders of political Zionism and paragons of their time.[7] In addition, Begin saw himself as successor to the Revisionist leadership, after Ze'ev Jabotinsky and David Raziel, who had commanded the Irgun from 1938 to 1941. At turning points in his political career, Begin invoked Jabotinsky, "the father of renewed Hebrew heroism," and Raziel, "the greatest commander of our generation"; he also did so on the day of the proclamation of the State of Israel.

Menachem Begin regarded himself as the successor of Ze'ev Jabotinsky and saw the Irgun and the Herut movement as instruments for the implementation of Jabotinsky's ideological heritage. In fact, Jabotinsky died without a successor, yet in the course of time, the unfounded notion emerged that Jabotinsky *had* designated him as his successor as far back as 1935, after having been impressed by his personality and talents at the Cracow convention. Two weeks before the first convention of the Revisionist party – after the War of Independence in 1948 and at the height of the struggle for primacy between the party leadership and the Irgun command headed by Begin – the daily *Yediot Aharonot* was to report that, at a celebration at Brest-Litovsk in 1935, Jabotinsky had proposed a toast to Begin, "my successor." The main source of this version was Shimshon Yuniczman. In a private letter written in July 1958, he noted: "After all, I am the only one who heard the head of Betar [say] that Menachem is his successor."[8]

At the fourth Betar convention held in 1949, Propes expressed the hope that no one would suggest choosing a new head of Betar: "There was one

and he still lives for us. There is no other."[9] In a farewell address tinged
with bitterness, Propes, the most prominent figure in Betar between the
two world wars, expressed concern for the future of the movement.
Cautioning against extremism, he stressed the value of moderation and
adaptation to the newly established state. He warned of the danger of a
political movement dominating Betar. As for Jabotinsky, Propes expressed
a fear "that the name of the head of Betar will serve only at festive gather-
ings," but he would not be "the source of our ideas."

In fact, Jabotinsky was to be transformed from founder of a political
movement into a symbolic father figure, the source of legitimacy invoked
by each of the various claimants to the succession, in spite of their conflicting views. In this struggle, Begin was obliged to present himself as
Jabotinsky's heir.

In the Revisionist creed, one role awaited its hero: that of leader of the
national uprising that would bring about the creation of a Jewish state. No
historical figure exemplified that role better than Garibaldi.[10] The "march
of the thousand" and the subsequent reunification of Italy served both
Jabotinsky and Begin as paradigms of nationalist action. They exemplified
faith in the decisive power of a revolutionary minority that sacrifices itself
for the nation in an act believed to have fundamental moral legitimacy but
lacking institutional sanction. They embodied the historical lesson that
there are fateful moments in the life of every nation when everything must
be flung into the balance, when hesitation and excessive prudence spell
danger. Jabotinsky and Begin found inspiration in Garibaldi for their
common belief that every consideration and action must be subordinated
to "the supreme interest of the homeland and the nation."

In one of his early articles, Jabotinsky reflected upon the relativity of
historical judgment, using Garibaldi and the way he was assessed in his
own time to illustrate the point.[11] Jabotinsky wrote that every historical act
must be performed at the appropriate time, adding that it was doubtful
whether Garibaldi would have been regarded in the same way at the beginning of the twentieth century. The nations whose situation resembled that
of Italy were now termed "reactionary and chauvinist." Asking whether
Garibaldi's actions should be considered misguided and a poor model for
these nations on the strategic plane, for example, Jabotinsky replied
resoundingly "No!" For him, Garibaldi remained the shining example for
his elevation of nation and homeland to the peak of human endeavor and
happiness no less than for the postponement of all internal disagreements
until the national ideal had been achieved. Elsewhere, Jabotinsky wrote:
"The renaissance of the Italian kingdom is of a value exceeding all the
sacrifices, and this was how Lincoln also perceived the ideal of the United
American republic."[12] Jabotinsky presented Garibaldi as exemplifying the

monist ideal he himself advocated, where all men and every consideration are subordinated to the national interest.

When Begin took up the analogy of the reunification of Italy, he made reference to three figures: Mazzini, "the mind and heart" of young Italy; Garibaldi, "the heart and hand" of the Italian war of liberation; and Cavour, the political strategist.[13] In his address to the third world convention of Betar, Begin spoke of the Zionist movement's struggle for national liberation, and its need to combine the endeavors of Cavour and Garibaldi. In other words, to complete Jabotinsky's political achievements, military acts were called for. At the time, Jabotinsky himself rejected the Italian analogy. It is doubtful whether he considered himself capable of discharging the double role of Cavour and Garibaldi. After Jabotinsky's death in 1940, Begin was to regard himself, the commander of the Irgun, as playing that double role.

Crossroads: Warsaw, 1938

The third world convention of Betar, held in Warsaw in September 1938, was the central assembly mounted by the Revisionist movement in the prewar period. It represented a political and ideological turning point and marked the inauguration of a new era: Revisionism would never again return to the traditions that had shaped its political and ideological path since its inception.

The Revisionists attended the convention in full force. Ze'ev Jabotinsky and Menachem Begin were there, as were the men who would later command the Irgun and Lehi (*Lohamei Herut Yisrael* – Fighters for the Freedom of Israel), the leaders of Betar, the future heads of The Hebrew Committee of National Liberation (HCNL) and leaders of the Revisionist Zionist party. When they left Warsaw that autumn of 1938, each set off in a different direction – to Palestine, Europe, or overseas. Their paths would cross again after the war. In that sense, the convention was a milestone. It also offered an instructive insight into the schisms of the years to come, as it was here that an unbridgeable ideological chasm was to open between Ze'ev Jabotinsky and the principal claimant to his ideological and political heritage, Menachem Begin.

The convention marked a clash between two generations at a moment of truth: the Arab revolt in Palestine had not yet subsided; new trends were emerging in Britain's Middle Eastern policy; and the destiny of the existing world order, and of Europe's Jews, hung in the balance. The debate was over the most fundamental issue: the ways and means of attaining the Zionist movement's ultimate aim, a sovereign Jewish state. Jabotinsky faced an ideological and organizational challenge; his leadership was questioned, forcing him for once to consent to painful compromises. The convention highlighted the predominant position Betar had come to occupy within the Revisionist movement and revealed the consolidation of a radical grouping that would forge the core of historical continuity from Betar to the Irgun and the Herut movement.

The split within the Revisionist party in the early 1930s and its secession from the World Zionist Organization left Jabotinsky dependent on a youthful radical wing, without any political formation or organizational structure to counterbalance it. Everything depended on the authority of one man. That should have served as an ominous warning for the leaders of the Revisionist party. Jabotinsky's error, which was fatal for the movement he had founded, was his disregard for, or perhaps incomprehension of, the historical process whereby Betar indoctrination, and the tempo of events in Europe and Palestine, would inevitably generate a revolutionary outlook that would diverge from the basic principles of traditional Revisionism. Jabotinsky was always confident that, by virtue of his powers of leadership, he would manage to steer the movement's course while maintaining a balance between its wings. However, from the mid-1930s onwards, in effect only the radical wing existed. Jabotinsky's influence had waned even before his death; after his demise, the balance was completely upset, and the decline of the movement he had founded became inevitable.

The first time Jabotinsky had faced criticism from the radical wing within his party was at the Vienna convention in 1932. But at that time he was supported by all the maximalist sections of the party, and they were to stand by him again when he found himself in a minority on the world Revisionist executive, whose views were more moderate than his. When the world council of the RZO convened in Katovice in March 1933, the radical wing in Poland submitted a memorandum notable for its extremism. While it did express vague support for existing policies, the paper's substance and conclusions were far from favorable towards diplomatic means of implementing the movement's ideals. It called for noncooperation with the British authorities in Palestine, civil disobedience, organization of a standing military force, and militarization of Jewish youth. The memorandum expressed support for the leader principle:

The movement must be unified, discipline should be enforced within it and it should be brought under the direct *diktat* of the leader. Our movement was born as the result of the deeds of the genius of the epoch of our national renaissance. The leader should be the sole decisive factor in our movement ... Postwar youth desires to be commanded, and will obey.[14]

The signatories of the memorandum included Menachem Begin. After the split in the Revisionist movement, and the secession of the moderate wing, its members now grouped in a new party (the Hebrew State party),

nothing remained to shield Jabotinsky from the criticism of the maxim-
alists.

In the autumn of 1938, Menachem Begin emerged not only as the
standard-bearer of an outlook and political conception at odds with
Jabotinsky's, but also as the representative of a distinct political faction.
The Revisionist movement faced an imminent crisis; Betar looked less like
a youth movement under the aegis of a political party and more like the
power reservoir of the Irgun. The group that had regarded such a symbiosis as vital emerged victorious. Betar's *natziv* in Poland, Aharon Propes,
who opposed this development, was forced to resign. He was replaced by
Menachem Begin.[15]

The records of the Betar world convention do not fully illuminate the
drama surrounding that gathering. The stenographic record of the convention differs from the official transactions published in 1940,[16] in that the
contest bewteen Betar and the Irgun, as well as particularly harsh critical
comments, were deleted from the latter. While there is a generally complete record of the speeches and their substance, and the speeches of
Jabotinsky and Begin were only lightly edited, Aharon Propes' criticism of
relations between Betar and the Irgun do not appear at all.

The marginal notes added by the stenographer – for example, instances
when applause was noted – convey something of the atmosphere and
general tone. On one occasion, there was "stormy applause": this was when
Menachem Begin, who was chairing one of the sessions, welcomed the
Irgun commander, Moshe Rosenberg, on the latter's entry into the hall.
The chronicler also found fit to add "Applause" in brackets in the middle
of Begin's speech, after which he cried "Death or victory!", as well as at the
conclusion of his address. Applause also interrupted the words of Yisrael
Eldad when he expressed his support for Begin. At the conclusion of
Eldad's speech appears the remark: "The head of Betar [Ze'ev Jabotinsky]
leaves the hall."

Begin's address to the convention was delivered on behalf of a new
generation of Revisionists. He depicted a new phase in Jewish history:
"military Zionism," which was diametrically opposed to the Labor movement's "practical Zionism." It was zealous in spirit and aimed at channel-
ing all the resources of Zionism to "the fighting bloc."[17] Begin's views on a
war of liberation, which could only be directed against Britain, and his
comments on the moral dimension in international relations, were in total
contradiction to Jabotinsky's political views and world view. Begin proclaimed his disillusionment and doubts with regard to current diplomatic
demarches. As Betar's *natziv* in Czechoslovakia, he had learned a lesson
that formed a central tenet of his political outlook: the implications of
appeasement, compromise, or surrender in foreign policy.

In the ensuing general debate, Begin rose to expound his political and strategic views. First, he remarked that in spite of the Revisionist movement's historic achievements, its political assumptions were no longer adequate for achieving the objective. If they were retained as guidelines, he said, the implementation of Zionism would be delayed by many decades. "The entire system of Herzlian politics" – moral pressure, community of interests with Britain, the League of Nations, and the conscience of the world – all these were of no value in his eyes. The League of Nations was bankrupt and "the conscience of the world has ceased to respond." In Palestine there was a glaring imbalance. Britain was taking account of the Arabs because they were fighting for their national ambitions, and the feebleness of the Zionist leadership was demolishing any prospect of Britain taking account of the Jewish side.

Begin was leading up to his main message. There was only one way – "We want to fight, to die or triumph!" – and the means was a war of national liberation. He again drew the analogy with nineteenth-century Italy. There was a need for both a Cavour and a Garibaldi. Zionism was on the threshold of a revolutionary phase. This would be the third stage in its history, which had commenced with practical Zionism, and advanced to political Zionism. It now stood on the threshold of military Zionism, "and afterwards there will be an amalgamation between military Zionism and political Zionism."

Jabotinsky contested the validity of Begin's Italian analogy in view of the balance of military force and the fact that Betar soldiers could not enter Palestine without outside aid. Begin retorted: "I am only proposing an idea, its implementation should be discussed by experts." He added, "We shall triumph by our moral force." As an expression of his views, Begin submitted an amendment to section four of the Betar oath. Instead of "I shall prepare my arm for the defense of my people, and I shall raise my arm only in defense," he proposed the text: "I shall prepare my arm for the defense of my people and the conquest of my homeland." This formulation was ultimately approved by the convention.

Begin's speech as recorded by the stenographer differs from the official version, in some places significantly, particularly with regard to the Arabs and the British. "We should recognize the Arabs' war as a national war. We regard it with respect, even though it is barbaric." He saw no possibility of equating "the tribulations of the Jews" to the Arabs' war. We must conclude, he said, that "there is no hope of a moral war in the course we have adopted." A subsequent section of his speech was also deleted: "A mighty empire can be coerced at the expense of another people if the threat of force is employed. To those who say it is impossible, . . . [the example of] CSR [Czechoslovakia] is proof . . ."[18]

In the 1940s, Begin sought to implement the "miliary Zionism" he had conceived in 1938. Thus, for all the historical, moral, and political arguments he gave to justify his proclamation of the revolt in January 1944, the inescapable conclusion is that they were not decisive: the fundamental directions had already been fully determined by the autumn of 1938.[19]

Jabotinsky responded to Begin's challenge and rejected his contentions one by one. He termed Begin's words "the creaking of a door," adding that "the words uttered here by Mr. Begin are such a creaking, and it is vital to repress ruthlessly all such creaking."[20] Jabotinsky agreed that Betar should be imbued with the spirit of Garibaldi, but he did not concede the analogy between the Italian people, living in their own country, and the Jews, who were dispersed the whole world over. Even at that, he characterized Garibaldi's deeds as a "gamble" that could also have failed. The decisive difference lay in the consequences of failure in the two cases. Jabotinsky did not abandon his view that Jewish immigration to Palestine, and the creation of a Jewish majority there, must precede "an eruption of heroism." He described the strategic advantages the Arabs would enjoy in the event of a military confrontation:

No strategist anywhere in the world would say that, in such a situation, we can perform the exploits of Garibaldi and De Valera. That's idle chatter. Our situation is so different from the situation of the Italians and the Irish, and if you think the only way is that proposed by Mr. Begin, and you have weapons – commit suicide. If there is no more conscience in the world – there is the river Vissla or Communism . . .

Jabotinsky overrated the importance of the moral dimension in politics, and in Zionism in particular. No other issue so divided Jabotinsky, brought up in pre-First World War Europe, from the generation that had grown up in the turbulent period between the wars. No less a challenge than Begin's statement, Jabotinsky's words expressed hope for the political future of mankind. These were bold words, stated as they were at the height of the European crisis of the late 1930s. In fact, he saw no salvation outside the assumption that conscience does exist in the world:

An eruption of Hebrew heroism in the Land of Israel helps greatly. But how does it help? It helps to arouse the crucial factor, conscience . . . To state that there is no more conscience – that is despair. We shall take a broom and sweep away that view. Of course, we all are permitted to express views. But there is a limit. What rules the world is conscience.[21]

One year before the outbreak of the Second World War, Jabotinsky remained faithful to the normative view by which he assessed the diplomacy of his time. His outlook was diametrically counter to the idea of military Zionism, which prepared itself for a show of arms. With that, this aspect of

Jabotinsky's view was incompatible with the Betar principles he supported
– discipline, militarism, and realpolitik.

Jabotinsky appears that year to have stretched his faith in the moral
factor in international relations to its outer limit. In January 1938, in
addressing the opening session of the Revisionist national convention in
Prague, he dedicated some remarks to the memory of Thomas Masaryk.
He called Masaryk "the mentor of our youth," who taught that justice will
ultimately prevail; even a disadvantaged people will in the end be aided by
all. Addressing the Czechs he said that, as the representative of an ancient
people, he believed that "the League of Nations is immortal, and at the end
of its development, will be almighty." Jabotinsky did not believe that the
Great Powers would renege on their promises to the small states; he
assured the Czechs that "the Great Power presently in all our minds will
not betray you, any more than [it will betray] us. Her word is steadfast, and
she will keep it."[22] In historical perspective, it is the Czech model which
divided Begin from Jabotinsky.

Jabotinsky's speeches at the Betar world convention – his opening
address and his eulogy of Shlomo Ben-Yosef (the first Revisionist youth
executed by the British authorities for an act of terrorism) – were both
aimed at curbing the spirit of extremism he had discovered in Betar. In his
opening address, he said that the "gentleman's agreement" between Betar
and the New Zionist Organization was now confronting a new generation,
a generation that had matured beyond its previous status as a youth movement but had not yet become an integral part of the party. Jabotinsky trod
the narrow path between praise for the rebellious spirit of Betar, to which
he assigned the role of catalysts of the Zionist revolution, while at the same
time striving in effect to dampen their revolutionary ardor. He wanted
Betar to be "humble as a slave, and proud as an emperor."

The delicate balance he was obliged to maintain is evident in his eulogy
of Shlomo Ben-Yosef. There can be no doubt that Ben-Yosef's death had
shaken him profoundly. He had come to the convention after failing in his
efforts to save Ben-Yosef's life. In his commemorative address, which was a
response to the mood of the convention, he gave his deeds retroactive legitimacy: "As head of Betar, I give you, Ben-Yosef, and your two companions,
the order to go out on the highroad and do what you did!" But above all, he
endeavored to present Ben-Yosef's deed as model and symbol, rather than
as the platform of a political movement.[23] In his references to *hadar*
(dignity), weapons, and military force, Jabotinsky was aiming for a change
of values for the ghetto Jew, rather than a war of national liberation.

Jabotinsky's closing address, the convention's resolutions and the new
appointments all reflect the turnabout which had taken place in Betar. The
movement's center of gravity had been transferred to Warsaw. Menachem
Begin had been appointed *natziv* in Poland. Aharon Propes had been left

without any official post. Benyamin Akzin, Jabotinsky's political secretary, had resigned from the party's presidium. The Betar oath had been amended in accordance with Begin's proposal. Betar members were forbidden to belong to any other grouping without permission from the movement leadership, but the ban was modified by decisions about "defensive training." According to the latter, every member of Betar should be equipped with the skills necessary for fulfilling his duty "in the sphere of Jewish security and defense of national honor in the world and conquest of the Land [of Israel]."[24]

In his final address, Jabotinsky spoke of the new challenge history had placed before the movement: to blaze new trails for the nation, "This Hebrew revolt elevates us shoulder high above everyone." Jabotinsky chose to conclude the convention with one of his harsh, accusatory poems that were to provide Begin with the titles of so many articles and pamphlets during the stormy 1940s: "Fructifying dew, the dew of life, the dew of revolt . . . We shall indeed yet repay you, Cain; we shall take the souls of your young men . . . We shall proclaim the revolt . . . God, You have chosen us to govern, over white-and-blue-and-red."[25]

Uriel Halperin (the poet Yonatan Ratosh) submitted a draft resolution of his own to the convention.[26] What appeared to be a marginal matter in effect represented a basic ideological departure by the radical wing of Revisionism. It was a revolutionary document that was before its time and contained some of the ideas which would later take root in Lehi, the Hebrew Committee of National Liberation, The Committee for Unification of Hebrew Youth (the so-called "Canaanites"), and the Irgun. Ratosh's document saw Betar in the role of an autonomous revolutionary army, obedient only to the imperatives of its destiny; its task was to bring about immediately, by use of force, the rebirth of the Land of Israel as "a sovereign Hebrew state."[27] As the Irgun and Lehi were to maintain subsequently, Ratosh held that the decisive factor would be the armed strength of the Jews of Palestine. He perceived the Arabs as a factor of no independent viability, and urged the party to relinquish its British orientation. He dismissed the Balfour Declaration and the British mandate as "supplementary documents for diplomatic tables." His demand was immediate sovereignty: "The basis of our right to the Land [of Israel] is that the Land is *ours*, and our strength is mainly *our strength*" (emphasis in the original).

The principles of a war of national liberation as Ratosh elaborated them were to be reiterated in similar form by the Irgun and Lehi, that is, along the lines of the deterministic assumption that such a war follows a regular pattern. It begins with the self-sacrifice of a minority while the self-indulgent majority joins forces with the alien rulers, and it culminates in a civil war. In 1938, Ratosh formulated one of the basic principles of Begin's conception of revolt, whereby "the Hebrew liberation movement, although it is a minority and *will remain* [emphasis in the original] a minority, nevertheless alone represents the will of history, the interests and the full vital powers and the fighting strength of the Hebrew Nation." The rebellious minority will ultimately conquer the masses; national unity will be forged in war and solidified in victory.

"Father of the revolt"

Begin dedicated *The Revolt* to "The memory of Ze'ev Jabotinsky, the father of the Hebrew revolt, and to the warrior family, with a humble heart and an adoring spirit." Surprisingly, Jabotinsky is scarcely mentioned in the book itself, where the Irgun features in splendid isolation; no space is allotted to the Revisionist party, to the Hebrew Committee of National Liberation, or to Lehi, other than as marginal factors in the annals of the war of liberation waged by the Irgun.

Revisionist literature presents Jabotinsky as the progenitor of the revolt. Begin declared that Jabotinsky was the father of the revolt in three respects: he called for liquidation of the Diaspora, revived the vision of a Jewish state, and created the idea of a Hebrew armed force. Writing in the early 1960s, Begin claimed that the revolt drew sustenance from "the bond with the Land [of Israel] ... the annihilation of the [Jewish] people in the Diaspora," and "Jabotinsky's teachings."[28] Begin's claim is contradictory. He ascribes the revolt to the Jabotinskian heritage but also presents it as an original idea arising from a rational and realistic examination of the international political scene in the 1940s. The leaders of the Revisionist movement also adopted, *post factum*, the idea that Jabotinsky was the father of the revolt. In their struggle to gain control of his political legacy, they crowned the leader of their movement with this title and claimed for themselves a part in the historical process that led to the revolt.

The idea of the revolt, as conceived by Begin from the late 1930s onwards, distinguished him from Jabotinsky more than it united the two men. A distinction must be drawn between Jabotinsky's ideological rhetoric about the spirit of rebellion in history and his unwillingness to support an overt military revolt against British role in Palestine.[29] During the 1930s the Revisionist movement developed two distinct trends; over the emergent radical revolutionary element Jabotinsky had no more than partial control. He himself never restricted the Revisionist ideal exclusively to underground activity and was always hesitant with regard to overt military action. He objected to some of the Irgun's operations but saw fit to support the organization as a rational consequence of his patronage of all the groups confederated in the Revisionist movement, and as a vital necessity for preserving his authority as leader.

The exploits of Brit Habirionim (a semi-secret Revisionist organization, in the early 1930s) induced Jabotinsky to clarify his views on illegal activities. In 1932, Jabotinsky kept to his understanding of *aventura*, which amounted to support for the spirit of protest. These were acts that demonstrated the potential of the Yishuv (the Jewish community in Palestine) for resistance, even civil disobedience; he advocated, however, that such actions be reserved for "special circumstances." Up to the mid-1930s, illegal activity could have been said to be in the service of the notion of political pressure. Jabotinsky was convinced that infractions of discipline could be overlooked as long as such activity was not carried out in the name of the political movement. Revisionism rested on a legalistic view, and for most of its history strove for the creation of a Jewish legion under British patronage. Jabotinsky was not really intent on rebellion; it is doubtful whether he intended a general civil uprising, and he certainly did not favor the bloodshed that would accompany continuous underground activity.[30]

The activities of Brit Habirionim waned after the assassination of the Socialist leader Chaim Arlosoroff. Its members carried out symbolic acts of protest while expressing a view that was radically revolutionary before its time. But the 1936 Arab uprising, the Irgun's defiance of the policy of *havlaga* (self-restraint) at the end of 1937, the partition plan, and international circumstances all combined to undermine some of the Revisionist movement's most basic political axioms and created fertile ground for the subsequent radicalization of Betar and the Irgun. Jabotinsky acted against this trend in a number of ways. He tried, unsuccessfully, to reach an agreement with the Hagana; he sought to redefine his authority over the Irgun; finally, he came to a partial accommodation with the new trend, confident of his ability to continue to steer the movement's course. The question that remains is whether or not, in his final years, particularly from 1938 onwards, Jabotinsky supported the notion of a military revolt against Britain.

There is no testimony that Jabotinsky ever abandoned the basic principles of his political or ideological outlook, though he did adopt a more extreme position vis à vis Britain. His attitude toward a policy of restraint was also ambivalent. For a time, he believed that such a course would facilitate the creation of an independent military force by the Yishuv. After the Irgun breach of the policy of self-restraint in November 1937, he protested against attacks on innocent women and children. At a later stage, in the summers of 1938 and 1939, he held talks with Eliyahu Golomb, the head of the Hagana, in an attempt to reach agreement with the Hagana. He was troubled at that time by the possibility of armed conflict within the Yishuv. Jabotinsky had in fact progressively lost his influence over the Irgun.[31]

The belief that Jabotinsky came to support an anti-British revolt as the Second World War approached lacks foundation. In spite of the eclectic nature of his utterances, no significant shift of values can be discerned. Some point to his article "Amen" as evidence; in fact, it contains no such proof, and, moreover, the article was substantially rewritten by the radical poet Uri Zvi Greenberg, then editor of *Der Moment*.[32] It appeared in *Der Moment* on July 9, 1939, the day Jabotinsky concluded his second talk with Eliyahu Golomb. The two men also discussed the feasibility of an agreement between the Revisionist movement and the World Zionist Organization. The article was published when the so-called Arab revolt was at its ebb and before the outbreak of the world war which was to transform Jabotinsky's assessment of the international situation and bring him closer to the mainstream of Zionism.

The article examines the Yishuv's response to the White Paper and to Arab acts of hostility; mainly, it weighs the moral aspects of reprisal when the act of reprisal is liable to injure innocent bystanders. Jabotinsky deplored the moral and political shortcomings of the policy of restraint; he belittled the importance of cooperation with the British in putting down the Arab revolt and stressed the need for "direct response against the assassins." Jabotinsky drew on a precedent to which he reverted repeatedly: British attacks on the civilians of Karlsruhe in response to German Zeppelin raids during the First World War. He concluded that the British reaction had been justified, but added that such justification existed only under special historical circumstances.

These views were formed in response to the Irgun's breach of the self-restraint policy; they were not related to Jabotinsky's international orientation, to the revolutionary principles and modes of action of Lehi, or to the revolt of the Irgun. The execution of Shlomo Ben-Yosef in June 1938 had shocked Jabotinsky profoundly and induced him for a time to adopt a harder line toward Britain. But even in the turbulent year before the outbreak of the world war, he remained hesitant and undecided on the nature of anti-British action.

His plan, never implemented, for a sporadic uprising timed for October 1939, is described in various versions as close to "the Irgun's line of thought."[33] A ship carrying immigrants was to anchor off the Tel Aviv shore, the Irgun was to safeguard the passengers' disembarkation while at the same time taking over a government building in Jerusalem and hoisting the national flag over it. The Irgun fighters were to hold the building for a full day, during which time they were also to prevent Jabotinsky's capture. Proclamations would be issued in Europe and the United States announcing the formation of a provisional government that would function as "the embodiment of Jewish sovereignty in the Land of Israel." The plan took the Irgun command by surprise. They saw it as lacking logistic rationale and of no real political value, and it was not implemented. If there was one strategic principle Begin stressed, it was the notion that the revolt was not a one-time operation; it rested on the continuous actions of an armed organization. The contention that had Jabotinsky survived he would have supported the revolt is the kind of speculation that history can never verify.[34]

At the beginning of September 1939, Jabotinsky was confronted with his greatest error of political prediction: he had predicted there would not be general war in Europe. In effect, he returned to the main principle that had guided the Zionist movement during the First World War: cultivating relations with the Allies in an attempt to become a partner to the peace talks that would follow the hostilities. Jabotinsky also revived the idea of the Jewish Legion, and again devoted most of his energies to the formation of Jewish units. The Irgun called a halt to its "warlike activities."[35]

When the "phoney war" ended and Germany launched an offensive on the Western front, Jabotinsky toyed with the idea of bringing Revisionist activity in Palestine to a total standstill and casting responsibility for the situation on the leadership of the Yishuv. In any case, he saw no prospect of influencing the policy of the World Zionist Organization. He wanted to focus Revisionist political endeavors on Western Europe and the United States. Jabotinsky reaffirmed his faith in the pro-British orientation and enlistment in the Allied armies. It was an admission that the Revisionist movement was left with the same old formulas which had characterized it ever since its inception.

Jabotinsky's situation was analogous to that of Chaim Weizmann. Each man faced a growing rift between his own outlook and policies, and the modes of action his political allies in Palestine were willing to take. Jabotinsky espoused the spirit of *aventura* and rebellion, he never committed himself to an anti-British revolt as conceived and later executed by Menachem Begin. Jabotinsky's basic error lay in his inability to fully comprehend the historical process that had led members of Betar and the Irgun to active revolt. They were restrained from taking action by his personal authority, but that was undermined even before his death. Jabotinsky remains the originator of the spirit of rebellion in recent Jewish history, but he was not the father of the revolt against Britian.

Between Odessa and Brisk

Ze'ev Jabotinsky and Menachem Begin belonged to two different generations; in effect, to two different worlds. The image of Begin as Jabotinsky's ideological heir is a distortion of historical fact. Ironically, this image has been reinforced by Begin's political adversaries in their desire to create historical continuity in the criticism directed against Revisionism and the Herut movement.

One of the more obscure portions of Begin's political biography is his relationship with Jabotinsky. In particular, we know nothing about Jabotinsky's opinion of Begin. There is fragmentary testimony, oral for the most part, and Begin's own assertions, but the factual foundation is flimsy. It has been said that Jabotinsky regarded Begin as the embodiment of provincial fanaticism and pietistical sentimentalism. In *White Nights*, Begin recalled the excitement of his first face-to-face encounter with Jabotinsky, at the Brest-Litovsk provincial theatre. Begin's Russian interrogator heard him affirm that in the immediate prewar years he had met with Jabotinsky "and conversed with him several dozen times." As prime minister he later made the same assertion.[36]

The followers of Jabotinsky's who were of Begin's generation inhabited a world very different from that of their mentor. Eldad, whose memoirs commence in the autumn of 1938, noted the difference between Jabotinsky – a man immersed in nineteenth-century Russian literature, familiar with Italy's skies and melodies, an advocate of individual liberty and parliamentary government – and the agitated interwar generation that thirsted for action and revolution: "We didn't care whether the Fascist regime was aesthetic or not." In comparison with Jabotinsky, Eldad portrays Begin as the

enfant terrible of Polish Betar, a rare blend of lawyer and romanticist. Vis-à-vis Jabotinsky, Begin resembled a Roman student facing his Greek teacher, attempting to emulate his mentor but by nature incapable of attaining the latter's genuine gentility and nobility, since he, the student, was closer to drama than to tragedy. Jabotinsky was a man of refined tragedy, his pupil more simplistic, both in thought and in mode of expression. Jabotinsky would frequently shut his eyes the better to see, and close his mouth firmly the better to think. His pupil acted otherwise. The teacher was more handsome than his pupil, but the real world exceeded them both in its ugliness, and it was there they were called upon to act.[37]

Eldad was to be less sparing in his remarks about Begin's lack of intellectual depth after Begin had stepped down from power.

When Begin was prime minister, Eldad would not be alone in questioning whether he was in fact implementing the Revisionist heritage; after all, he had brought about no change in the conduct of society or government. Profoundly disappointed, Eldad wrote that Begin had chosen neither of the two courses open before him: a revolutionary change in Israeli foreign policy along the lines of the Revisionist tradition, or reform of society and government as a preliminary to a change of direction on the external front. Setting peace as the principal objective struck Eldad as an ideological deviation from the Betar tradition which taught that the Land of Israel would be conquered and liberated by recourse to war. Eldad wondered whether Revisionism had not erred in its criticism of the Labor movement, in view of the fact that when its representative took the reins of power he failed to accomplish any change.[38]

Jabotinsky and Begin formed their views of the world in different cultural settings, of which the differences in origin and age were just one element. The difference was that between Odessa and Brest-Litovsk; between Warsaw and the grim visage of Polish nationalism and a blend of Russia, Italy, and Central Europe; between a many-sided man of multiple talents and the one-dimensionality of a man who was essentially a political being; between the world of *fin de siècle* Russian intelligentsia and the romantic nationalism of Poland; between a scion of the educated, assimilated bourgeoisie, for whom Zionism was only one of many possible courses, and a man who represented the narrower Jewish world. In the one, the impact of European civilization was real and variegated; in the other its influence was weaker, more superficial and oblique. With a measure of sarcasm, Dr Yohanan Bader, perhaps the shrewdest among Herut leaders, notes: "Begin is not a citizen of the world. He is a remote provincial town boy who made it to Warsaw . . ."[39]

One of the salient differences between Begin and Jabotinsky is in their attitude to the Jewish religion and heritage. Jabotinsky's "Story of my Life" is the confession of a man brought up without any close bonds to Judaism. Until his twenties, he knew no Yiddish. His first encounter with the Jewish ghetto left him depressed and downcast. Jabotinsky's attitude towards the notion of "gentiles' was one of unconcern. Basically, he was an atheist. There is no mention in his will of religious imperatives. The attempt to ascribe some religiosity to Jabotinsky, or a return to religion in his later years, has nothing on which to base itself. While paragrah 7 of the Proclamation of the Revolt ("Implant the holiness of the Torah in the life of the liberated nation in the homeland"), and the wording that appears in the Herut movement's platform in the elections for the first Knesset do indeed resemble the resolution of the New Revisionist founding congress in 1935, that formulation was drafted with an eye to helping the party meet its political needs.[40] By contrast, Begin was born into the world of Jewish faith and suffering. Paradoxically, Jabotinsky appears as an outspoken rebel against the Diaspora, while Begin, who had been instructed in Betar to be the spearhead of a revolution that would forge the new man of Zionism, did not move away from the customs and heritage of Judaism.

Jabotinsky's view of reality was eclectic, hovering between two worlds: the heritage of the nineteenth century merging with the crises and challenges of the twentieth. He belonged to the so-called "generation of 1914" and shared most of the characteristics of that generation whose members were born at the end of the nineteenth century.[41] Begin was born in 1913, on the eve of the great crisis of the century. He grew up in the 1920s, "the era of illusions," which gave way to a decade of chaotic cruelty. Begin belonged to the post-revolutionary generation which, having found no salvation in socialism and faced with the weaknesses of democracy, found refuge in the discipline and order of a rigid organizational structure. However, while his world view was largely molded in the interwar era, Begin also exhibited an almost mechanistic rationalism and an inclination to martyrdom characteristic of the late eighteenth century.[42]

The difference between Jabotinsky and Begin is that between the molder of the Betar ideal and one who grew up under its influence. The Betar ideal was Jabotinsky's most inviolable dogma, freest of doubt. It rested on discipline, hierarchy, and military values. The individual voluntary will found expression in total identification with the organization and its objectives. The difference is that between the freedom of one who shaped an ideology and that of one who adhered to it; between a more open belief system, and a dogmatic one. Politically, Jabotinsky was a relativist. Begin believed almost simplistically in the absolute truth of a number of fixed assumptions. Both men tended towards the manifest and the formal. They shared an attitude that regarded facts and events as symbols. Both had an ardor in their belligerence toward adversaries, but while Begin balanced his romantic ardor by juridical argument, Jabotinsky did so with the help of a rationalistic reasoning.

Although there are some points of similarity, Begin and Jabotinsky were opposite personalities.[43] In politics, both were inclined to gestures at the expense of substance. In his political discussions Jabotinsky proved to be a man of broad horizons, though he did not shine in discussions of practicalities or in the give and take of negotiations. In this he somewhat resembled Begin the diplomat as prime minister.[44]

In spite of the differing circumstances, both men acted in accord with the same heroic code of conduct when arrested – Jabotinsky in 1920 and Begin in 1940.[45] Writing in his autobiography about his arrest in Russia, Jabotinsky calls it an enriching adventure. He described the prison as "a splendid building" and his imprisonment as "one of the most cherished and pleasant of my memories."[46] Anyone reading Begin's descriptions of his own imprisonment cannot but find a similar repression of the suffering.

In "Story of my Life" Jabotinsky repeatedly refers to his weakness for striking poses, which plagued his public career, as "a trait or characteristic peculiarly capable to annoy." It is not fortuitous that Begin identified with Ibsen's Dr Stockman, the hero of *An Enemy of the People*, who had the courage to defy the majority out of moral conviction and belief in himself.[47] But whereas Jabotinsky was in the habit of breaking patterns and resuming the struggle, Begin followed a pattern of withdrawal in defeat.

As leaders, Jabotinsky and Begin displayed the same amalgam of similarity and difference. Begin's leadership, from Betar to the Herut movement, was always institutionally anchored. It always insisted on discipline and centralized control. Any questioning of his authority invariably provoked a general crisis that forced his adversary to withdraw. Jabotinsky's leadership rested on loose organizational control but unquestioned authority. Both leaders were chosen by acclamation; formal election and the delineation of authority became secondary matters. Both men were masters of rhetorical provocation – a convenient ploy and relatively economical, but one which exacts a price: an unfavorable image, and the spurring of adversaries to fight back. Both were advocates of "national grandeur" and espoused open statements and unheeding disclosure of final objectives. In appealing directly to the masses, they developed a natural preference for the superficial over structure and substance. Their formulation of ideas constitute a terrible simplification of Zionism, and this was particularly true of Begin.

One cannot overlook the disparity between the portrayal of Jabotinsky and Begin as solitary leaders vis-à-vis the masses and the inclination of their follows to describe them as "first among equals." There was a great difference between Begin the professional politician and Jabotinsky the intellectual and leader. The Revisionist "empire" shrank to the proportions of a Revisionist "township." According to his political secretary Benyamin Akzin, Jabotinsky was torn between his role as politician and his "poetic tenderness." His intimates engaged him in dialogue; Begin set unswerving loyalty above all.[48] Begin and Jabotinsky both regarded themselves first and foremost as statesmen and leaders of "exalted Zionism." But both displayed inherent weaknesses as decisionmakers and executives. Both had a natural inclination towards whatever was vigorous in style and provocative in substance. Both saw politics as being essentially struggle rather than consent, secession rather than submission to authority. Both perceived international affairs as an arena of perpetual conflict and confrontation.

The historic achievement of Jabotinsky and Begin was their success in offering continuous representation of an ideal that symbolized a political alternative to the existing order in the Zionist movement. Revisionism sought hegemony in the name of that ideal and ultimately attained it. Jabotinsky laid the ideological foundations of that alternative, while challenging the predominance of Labor Zionism. Begin personified the historical continuity of the claim to supremacy, and accomplished the canonization of Jabotinsky's heritage.

Begin's political skill was exhibited in his usurpation of the Revisionist ideal and in his creation of a new political movement, portraying it as the exclusive historical claimant to Jabotinsky's heritage. He remained at the head of his movement until Israeli society had changed sufficiently, and the Labor movement had decayed and erred sufficiently, for him to achieve power. Of the loose Revisionist triangle of political movement, military organization, and youth movement, the latter two triumphed. The story of that development began and ended with the authority of a single individual who rose from being a junior partner of traditional Revisionism to being its sole interpreter and leader.

3

The Revisionist Inheritance

Secession and schism

The history of Revisionism is much more multifaceted than is usually imagined. The claim of the Irgun, and afterwards of the Herut movement headed by Menachem Begin, to the Revisionist legacy in its entirety does not stand up to historical examination. It falls short in the political sense, that is as maintaining the Revisionist organizational framework, and in terms of ideology, as continuing the tradition of Revisionist policy and thought. Actually, conflicting interpretations of Revisionist teachings and the Jabotinskian way persisted. The nineteenth-century type liberal, the man who continuously advocated a pro-British orientation, whose activity primarily took the form of open political action and diplomacy, was also presented as a Messianic revolutionary and as "father of the revolt."[1]

From the beginning, one of the major weaknesses of the Revisionist right was its structure of authority. The Zionist Revisionist Organization as a political movement, Betar as an independent youth association, and the Irgun as an underground organization were bound only by weak organizational ties. Until 1940, authority took the form of a "personal union" embodied in one individual – Ze'ev Jabotinsky. Differences between Betar and the Revisionist party, in fact, began in the late 1920s, and the question of control over the Irgun had never been resolved: in the end, Menachem Begin totally severed the link between the Irgun and the party.

Jabotinsky's exclusive authority as head of Betar, leader of the Revisionist movement, and supreme commander of the Irgun was anchored in a personal, emotional approach, and was not always the outcome of a unity of view or of real organizational institutionalization. When he died, the party lost control of the two organizations – Betar and the Irgun – that had comprised the organizational frameworks for most supporters of the Revisionist movement. Even earlier, beginning in the early 1930s, the party ceased to express the moods and national wishes of the radical wing of the Revisionist party. The Revisionist party declined and the predominance of the leaders of Betar became an incontrovertible fact.

The fissures became apparent even before Jabotinsky's death; organizational disintegration, division into a number of centers among which there was little or no coordination, and a widening gap between the demands of the underground and the overt activity of the political movement. After 1940 came a period of fatal decline. The factions of traditional Revisionism were never to recover, suffering a final humiliating defeat when the Herut movement was established and they were routed in the elections to the first Knesset. Revisionism did not develop any further ideologically,[2] and the party's message was tiresome repetition of slogans from the past, along with an attempt to adapt them to a reality that had changed beyond recognition. The contest for the Revisionist inheritance ended in the late 1940s when the party Jabotinsky had formed met its demise, defeated by those who claimed to be its heirs both politically and ideologically. In fact, Menachem Begin sought to launch a new period in the history of Revisionism.

The Revisionist movement showed signs of schism as early as the Seventeenth Zionist Congress in 1931. The dispute between Jabotinsky and other founders of the movement led by Meir Grossman centered around the question of secession from the World Zionist Organization. Grossman was successful in lining up most of the members of the executive behind him, but did not properly gauge the strength of support for Jabotinsky in the movement nor understand the mood that underlay this support. Grossman was to some extent influenced by his control of the organizational apparatus of the movement. This control had increased after Jabotinsky had agreed at the Sixteenth Zionist Congress, held in 1929 in Zurich, to move the world headquarters of the ZRO to London, while he himself was to remain in Paris.[3]

Jabotinsky's desire to secede from the World Zionist Organization had actually crystallized before 1931. At the fourth world convention of the movement (Prague, 1930), Jabotinsky initiated an unexpected debate on the issue of the movement's independence. In the course of that discussion, he said that the Revisionists comprised a special "spiritual race" with a temperament that can find neither place for itself nor possibility for expression within the framework of the World Zionist Organization. Grossman consented to independent activity on the diplomatic front, and defended that position in public, but resisted the idea of secession.

At a meeting of the leaders of the movement in Boulogne before the convening of the Seventeenth Zionist Congress, it was agreed that if a resolution was not passed affirming that the objective of Zionism is to ensure a Jewish majority in Palestine, the world executive of the movement would propose secession from the World Zionist Organization. In the Calais agreement of September 1931, a compromise was reached between

Jabotinsky and his opponents, which did not hold for long. Paragraph 8 of the founding principles of Revisionism, which defined the status of the Zionist Revisionists as part of the WZO, was dropped. At the same time, it was agreed not to put the question of the establishment of a separate Zionist organization up for discussion.[4]

In the interim period up until the final break with the WZO, Jabotinsky's leadership was subjected to sharp criticism in Palestine and in Betar. He was aware of the decline in his status. For Jabotinsky, secession was a difficult personal decision. Now a new alliance, which lasted through 1938, was born between him and the radical wing – at the cost, however, of moving away from the platform of traditional Revisionism.

At the world council of the movement held in Katowice in March 1933, Jabotinsky's relation with the moderate faction headed by Grossman reached the breaking point. Jabotinsky was in fact in a minority position in the executive. He succeeded neither in coopting new members who supported his views nor in transferring the executive's seat to Paris. In that struggle, Jabotinsky enjoyed the support of the Palestinian section of the party. Grossman, who was present at the national council of the party held in Kfar Sava in January 1933, had been unable to block this support.[5]

Jabotinsky's Lodz manifesto is exceptional in the history of the Zionist movement. In this manifesto he proclaimed that he was taking full and exclusive charge of the management of the Revisionist movement's affairs, and that the activity of its institutions was henceforth terminated. This was striking confirmation of the organizational weakness of the Revisionist right, which lacked regulations clearly defining the authority of officeholders or specified arrangements for an orderly transfer of authority. The absolutist formulation of the manifesto gave a new coloring to Jabotinsky's leadership and to the kind of relations that had developed between him and his supporters, especially those from Betar.[6] The schism would soon move Jabotinsky away from those closest to him in the world executive of the Zionist Revisionists, such as Meir Grossman, Yona Machover, Eugene Soskin, Richard Lichtheim, and Robert Stricker. In a referendum held the following year, 93.8 per cent of those participating supported the concentration of all executive roles in Jabotinsky's hands. Such absolute support also recurred in the vote on the establishment of the New Zionist Organization (NZO), which now replaced the ZRO. In August 1934, the faction headed by Meir Grossman formed the Hebrew State party.[7]

The rift in the Revisionist movement and the establishment of the NZO in the mid-1930s were decisive turning points in the movement's history and marked the beginning of its decline. When the moderate wing left the movement, its internal balance was upset and Jabotinsky lost the freedom of maneuver he had previously enjoyed. After triumphing over his friends who had formed the movement together with him, he had sought to safe-guard his own exclusive leadership and ensure the possibility of operating outside the framework of the World Zionist Organization. It became evident to him at the end of the 1930s, however, that he had no organiza-tional or political apparatus apart from his personal authority with which to cope with the claims of the new generation and its leaders.

It is ironic that Jabotinsky's status was undermined following the rise in the power and importance of Betar, among whose ranks he enjoyed absolute support. Opposition to his policy and political views emanated from Betar, and he was left with no choice but to accept the faits accompli of the radical wing. At the time of the split at Katowice, Betar took an active role in the internal struggle, and Jabotinsky relied on its support. He preferred the Betar masses over the party apparatus, and Betar became a political factor of the first order. With this battle on the Revisionist right was decided, its fate sealed.[8]

Running through the history of the Revisionist movement is a con-tinuous dispute about control of Betar and the definition of its status. Betar was rigidly hierarchical and had a paramilitary structure. Jabotinsky was the head of Betar, but party control over it was feeble. This situation set the power base from which some of the leaders of Betar strove to achieve hegemony over all of Revisionism after Jabotinsky's death. This became a very prominent beginning with the third world convention of Betar in September 1938, which was also the occasion of the most significant opposition to Jabotinsky's leadership. The cycle was completed after the establishment of the state when Betar broke away from the Zionist Revi-sionists and became the youth movement of Herut.[9]

The real progenitor of a military approach in Revisionism was Betar, which became the major reservoir of power for the party and for the two future undergrounds of the right – the Irgun, and to a lesser extent, Lehi. Jabotinsky's decision that Betar must preserve its independence was thus to be of central significance in the development of the Revisionist right. The ideological monolithism of Betar instruction molded the spiritual character of the young generation and sustained the schism between it and the leaders of the party, who in any event differed from it in terms of culture, social class, and generation.

Jabotinsky's formulation of the Betar platform did not show the eclecti-cism or skepticism that occasionally characterized his writing. His wording was decisive, assertive, unequivocal. Everything derived from incontest-able maximalist assumptions.[10] In accord with a tendency that prevailed in Europe between the world wars, Jabotinsky attached supreme importance to youth, "the flywheel of public life." The apotheosis of youth coincided with the period's radical outlook, that "Renewal will come through youth, or it will not come at all!"[11] Ten years after Betar came into existence, there was no need to doubt that "the soul of Betar is no secret." Betar was shaped in accordance with the principles of monism, the idea of the Jewish legion, discipline, and *hadar* (splendor, dignity). Or in Jabotinsky's terse formulation: "To create the type of Jew the national requires [in order] to establish the Jewish state more rapidly and more perfectly."[12]

The debate on the place of Betar within the Revisionist movement did not come to an end in the late 1930s nor even during the period of struggle for independence. The Latvian stream, which was more pioneering and democratic, was defeated, and hegemony of the movement passed to Poland and Palestine. Jabotinsky rejected the demand to submit Betar to the political control of the ZRO and jealously guarded its independence. In that way, the party leadership and his potential heirs were deprived of the chance of imposing their authority over it. Betar itself strove for independence, and afterwards for hegemony. Its swift and ramified growth lessened the party's ability to control it. Meir Grossan protested against "autocracy without responsibility." The formation of Irgun cells within Betar was carried out independently without involving the party. In the struggle for control of Betar, neither Jabotinsky, who was the link connecting it to the Zionist Revisionist Organization, nor the moderate wing of the party was victorious.[13]

One of the outstanding features of the growth of the Revisionist right was the disparity between its great strength in Eastern Europe and its meager organizational and electoral strength in Palestine. The fact that the party played a minor role in the Yishuv facilitated the Irgun's rise to hegemony. The attempts to bring about what the leader of the party in Palestine, Aryeh Altman, called "Palestino-centrism," and to transfer the world headquarters of the ZRO to the Yishuv were unsuccessful. The party lacked the ability to hold its ground against the rising power of Betar and the undergrounds.[14]

The Revisionist movement was characterized by the dispersal of its centers. In Palestine, where Jabotinsky was forbidden entrance by the British, it was led by a committee of delegates headed by Altman that enjoyed only partial independence. There was an organizational rift between the office in London headed by Meir Grossman and the office in Paris, where Jabotinsky had made his home. The party in Palestine did not have a significant political standing. The imbalance in the decision-making structure, the dominance of Jabotinsky, and his lack of organizational skill all betokened ill for the future of the movement. Jabotinsky shrunk from anything that could be seen as symbolizing a narrow, unheroic interest and rejected the flimsy party structure of the Yishuv characterized by party hacks.

The growth in the number of Revisionism's supporters in Palestine was slow. In addition to the meager organizational abilities of the party's leaders and Jabotinsky's absence, it also suffered from the political imbalance in the composition of immigration to Palestine. In 1931 some 10,000 votes were cast for the Revisionist right in the elections to the Zionist Congress. In the elections to the elected assembly the party received about 2,500 votes in 1925, and slightly more than 10,000 in 1931. About 20 per cent of these votes went to a separate Sephardi list. The largest number of voters the party succeeded in mobilizing, 26,000, was in 1935, in the elections for the establishment of the New Zionist Organization.[15]

Neither the maximalist nor the moderate wings of the party worked to construct an institutional structure of any real substance. No organizational apparatus worthy of the name was established, apart from the National Labor Federation, which had an autonomous development. The political positions of the party were dictated to it from outside the Yishuv. Nonetheless, its position was consistently more radical than that of the majority in the world executive. The dependence of the moderate wing of the party on Jabotinsky's decisions as to how it would operate in the Yishuv impaired its development. In contrast, the party's executive encountered increasing difficulties in its attempts at controlling the radical wing. Nor did the decline of Brit Habirionim increase the influence of the moderate wing, and internal frictions prevented the emergence of a strong independent leadership. The party did not manage to widen the base of its support, nor did it expand its influence through political alliances with other Yishuv parties.[16] Revisionism assumed a mass character as a result of its expansion in Eastern Europe and the increase in Betar's strength. This was the central factor that determined Revisonism's political character up until the outbreak of the Second World War.

Ideologically no less than organizationally, the death of Jabotinsky in August 1940 symbolized the end of traditional Revisionism as it had crystallized since the mid-1920s. After the death of the movement's leader it no longer had universally recognized leadership. The party in Palestine and the two other centers of the movement, in London and the United States, now acted separately, without coordination or mutual agreement. In a last letter to Altman, written a few days before he died, Jabotinsky accepted his loss of control of a movement whose centers were so dispersed and disunited.[17]

Counter to the rising strength of the undergrounds were the institutional elements of the Revisionist movement: the Word Presidium in New York, the Administrative Committee in London, the Hebrew State party headed by Grossman, and the Committee of delegates headed by Altman. In terms of ideas, too, the party went into decline and failed in its bid to win public recognition as continuing Jabotinsky's course.[18]

Jabotinsky's last letter to the head of the committee of delegates, Aryeh Altman, is unclear on his expectations for the future and expresses his helplessness with respect to the fate of the party. He asked Altman to continue the cooperation with Great Britain, and suggested that within the Yishuv political system and in future negotiations with the Jewish Agency Altman should try to ensure a common front without abandoning political autonomy. But even in the worst case, he said, cooperate in everything but acceptance of the partition plan or a significant departure from "Herzlian Zionism."

Jabotinsky's helplessness is also apparent in his personal letter of May 9, 1940 to his former political secretary, Benyamin Akzin.[19] In this letter he contemplated the possibility of terminating the Revisionist movement's political activity in Palestine, concentrating instead in Europe and the United States while placing responsibility for what happened in the Yishuv on the Labor Zionists and the Zionist Executive. It is possible that Jabotinsky wrote this under the grave impression made by the German assault on the Western front, which had just begun at that time.[20]

The party in Palestine walked a thin line between the traditional platform of the Zionist Revisionists and tactical considerations dictated by the disparity between the radicalism of the undergrounds and the party's desire to rejoin the World Zionist Organization.[21] Ever since the split in the movement and the founding of the New Zionist Organization there had been many attempts to reunite and return to the WZO. The two goals were interrelated. From what testimony there is, it appears that Jabotinsky's position on these issues was not clear-cut.[22]

In December 1940 an agreement on cooperation during the war was drafted by representatives of the Revisionist movement, Eri Jabotinsky and Benyamin Lubotzky, and Mapai leaders Berl Katznelson and Eliyahu Golomb. The agreement was supposed to signal the return of the Revisionists to the World Zionist Organization. The agreement, which required approval by the institutions of the two parties, included a demand "to establish a Hebrew state within the historical boundaries of the Land of Israel." This initiative, however, was not successful.[23]

The Revisionist movement returned to the WZO before the convening of the Twenty-Second Zionist Congress at the end of 1946. Altman's attempt to "unify the Revisionist empire," as he called it, ended in partial success. He rallied most of the membership of the New Zionists behind the decision to return to the WZO and brought about a union with the Hebrew State party. However, he did not gain the cooperation of the leaders of the undergrounds or of the radical wing of the party. The one demand shared by all wings of the party – the establishment of a provisional government in exile – remained a slogan that did not win public support. The establishment of the Herut movement, and the Revisionist party's defeat in the elections to the first Knesset, would strike the final blow to traditional Revisionism.[24]

Each of the two undergrounds that emerged from the Revisionist right, the Irgun and Lehi, developed its own views and political outlook. Revisionism was now nurtured on new ideas and emotional impulses. The traditional conception of "pressure" was transformed into military pressure, and the pro-British orientation was converted into a conception of war against "the foreign occupier." That in effect was a new political strategy, carried out by terrorism and military means. It was a thorough-going alteration of the Revisionist platform.

The spiritual world of the members of Betar and of the undergrounds differed from that of the primarily Russian emigrants who had founded the Revisionist movement. The founders of the Revisionist movement had been born at the end of the nineteenth century or the beginning of the twentieth and had received their education and formed their political outlook and inclinations before the First World War. The Revisionist leadership was extremely homogeneous in composition. Most of the leaders were born in Russia and some in the Baltic states and Central Europe, and most had completed higher education. However, the political growth of Revisionism had begun in a Europe new in terms of boundaries, cultural characteristics, ideas, and political style.

Almost all the members of Betar and of the two undergrounds were born in the second decade of the twentieth century. Their spiritual world was formed between the two world wars, in a stormy and crisis-ridden period. Most of them were born in independent Poland at the height of its nationalism. A minority were born in Russia, the Baltic states or Palestine. Few had completed higher education, and there was a large proletarian and petit bourgeois strain among them.[25]

The cleavage within the Revisionist right is especially apparent when a comparison is made between the founders and early leaders of the Revisionists, and the leaders and commanders of Betar and the undergrounds. As opposed to the largely assimilationist and bourgeois founding group with its higher education and liberal professions, the leadership of Betar and the undergrounds were younger, of different origin, of lower socioeconomic background, lesser education, were ambivalent towards the "bourgeois orientation" that developed in the movement in the 1930s, and tended to be more militant.[26]

The gap between the generations was also apparent in the relations between the Irgun and the Revisionist party in Palestine, which ended in total rupture. If the Irgun command headed by Menachem Begin saw any justification for the existence of the party, it was as a logistic rear for the underground's activities. The Irgun had been striving for nondependence ever since the late 1930s. The party itself was drawn on to the horns of a dilemma. On the one hand, it conducted an information campaign to prove it had no formal link to the underground, and on the other hand, its standing depended on maintaining the opposite image. The fostering of that image took the form of propaganda as well as legal aid and other assistance to the families of detainees. The party's inability to control the activities of the underground in the end undermined its standing in the eyes both of the British rulers and Jewish society.

On March 30, 1944, the political office of the New Zionists, which was headed by Altman, issued an announcement condemning acts of terrorism. On that same day, the office in London, headed by Abraham Abrahams, also announced that "There is no place in the ideology of the New Zionist Organization for acts of violence. The New Zionists never viewed acts of violence of any sort as an instrument of policy. It has no connection with activities involving acts of violence." In October of that year the party again stressed that there was absolutely no connection between it and the Irgun.[27] In contrast to the troubled relations with the Irgun, a measure of understanding and cooperation was developed between the party and the Hebrew Committee of National Liberation (HCNL) in the United States headed by Hillel Kook (Peter Bergson).[28]

The revolt put an end to the façade of cooperation between the party and the Irgun. If until 1943 the party had a certain say in the selection of the commander of the Irgun, and there was some cooperation between the two bodies, relations now deteriorated towards total break. The Irgun became wholly independent. The party leadership was not interested in taking responsibility for the underground's activities and did not support its way of fighting. Specifically, the leaders of the party criticized the Irgun for narrowing the front of its fight to the military plane, for not accepting the party's authority, and for not having a political program. They challenged the claim that it was no longer possible to sustain the relationship according to which the party determines overall policy and the underground carries it out.[29]

The Irgun command regarded the party with reserve, indifference, even derision. The impression that arises from examination of fragmentary records of command deliberations between July and September 1944 is that they wanted to transform the political movement into a logistic rear for the underground, while preserving absolute independence for the Irgun. Headed by Menachem Begin, the Irgun eliminated the distinction between a political arm and military one, and saw itself as possessing overall responsibility. Begin rejected any external authority that might interfere in the underground's affairs, and regarded the Irgun as the sole element in Jewish society worthy of bearing the banner of revolt against British rule.[30]

The period of cooperation with Great Britain at the beginning of the

Second World War concealed for a while the clashing interests of the party and the Irgun. But even then, differences surfaced concerning enlistment in the British army. The end of the Irgun's pro-British orientation, however, led to a final ideological break.[31] Party activists who had been close to the Irgun and to Menachem Begin played an important role in shaping relations between the party and the Irgun during that crisis period. The most outstanding figure in that group was Dr Yohanan Bader.[32]

One of the important junctures in the development of the Revisionist right was the split within the Irgun that began soon after the death of Jabotinsky. This was both a personal dispute over control of the organization as well as an ideological schism. Some observers dismiss the ideological differences and see them as merely a cover for what was essentially a personal dispute betwen Abraham Stern (Yair) and David Raziel. In fact, however, at a later stage the two undergrounds did develop different international orientations, exclusive historiosophic approaches, and different definitions of the role and objectives of the underground and the means to be employed in the struggle for national liberation.

In the late 1930s and early 1940s, the debate focused on the nature of relations with the party and orientation toward Britain. Once Lehi developed its own political conception and an independent organizational pattern, it was no longer possible to bridge the gap between the two undergrounds. In the summer of 1940, Raziel found himself in a minority position in the Irgun command but enjoyed the support of the heads of the party, who preferred him as commander of the Irgun over Abraham Stern. The split became a fact at the end of 1940. Until Begin took over as commander in December 1943, the Irgun experienced a long period of inertia.[33]

Relations between Lehi and the Irgun were thorny and complex. During Stern's lifetime and afterward, there was disagreement on the personal level and differences of view that should not be obscured. Although Begin and the Lehi leaders, Yisrael Eldad and Nathan Yellin-Mor, held much in common, the undergrounds did not unify. Coldness, contempt, if not hostility, stood between them. Lehi's fundamental attitude toward other parties and organizations was determined by its belief that it was the sole revolutionary avant-garde capable of withstanding the trials of the national liberation struggle against British rule undeterred by any utilitarian or moral considerations. Lehi believed little in, even scorned, the ability of other organizations, including the Irgun, to endure the necessary hardships and sacrifices. On this basis, some of the Lehi leaders were convinced that Lehi would assume a major role in the late stages of the Hebrew revolution that might even lead it to power and hegemony.[34]

Whereas the Irgun, in its open interpretation of Revisionist teachings, presented itself as continuing the Jabotinskian path, Lehi regarded the political Zionism of Herzl and Jabotinsky as a stage that had already come to an end in the history of the Zionist movement and its struggle for independence. The Lehi leaders were ambivalent toward Jabotinsky. The first glimmers of a military perception could be discerned in his outlook, admittedly, but in their view these had not developed into a clear recognition of the necessity to move on to the stage of war, conquest, and final triumph. Lehi, by its own account, had parted ways on this point with the Irgun, which sought to continue Jabotinsky's course in its own way, and with the Revisionist party, which wanted to gain control of the Zionist Organization. When the Second World War broke out, the future Lehi leaders opposed enlistment in the British army and the decision by the Irgun to refrain from activity against British rule. That widened the division between Raziel and Stern concerning the role and management of the Irgun.[35]

First Tithe, Eldad's memoirs, is the work most critical of Revisionism as a political and ideological movement to come out of the right itself. Eldad berated Begin's heroic code of grandeur and gallantry, claiming it was doomed to failure. Yellin-Mor, too, thought little of the Irgun's ideological positions and of its way of fighting British rule in Palestine. They both were ambivalent, if not actually scornful, about Begin's talents and capabilities, and in particular attacked the Irgun's tendency to claim an ideological and operational monopoly for itself in the struggle against the British.

The Irgun's criticism of "personal terrorism" seemed to Eldad to be based on an illusion that war could be seen as "some sort of gentlemanly game." In Eldad's view, the Irgun's mode of struggle was no more than a continuation of Jabotinsky's "doctrine of pressure," which was in fact based on the belief that it was possible to achieve a modus vivendi with Great Britain. The path taken by the Irgun coincided with that of traditional Revisionism in viewing Britain as a strategic partner, and it was entangled in "the web of concepts of legalistic Revisionism."[36] Yellin-Mor, like Eldad, was not persuaded by Begin's views concerning the nature of the Irgun's struggle against Britain and felt it necessary to strengthen the underground's radical wing. He accused Begin of holding an "exclusivist" vision of historical mission that stemmed from a desire to put an end to Lehi's independent existence. In Lehi, he asserted, in contrast, loyalty was to an idea not to a person.[37]

The attempts to unitfy the two undergrounds, which were less intense than might be imagined, did not end in success. After the assassination of Lord Moyne and after the *saison* (open season), a Hagana initiative tacitly supported by the British which was aimed primarily against the Irgun, all chances of unification were totally lost. Two main reasons for that were emphasized in the polemic between the two undergrounds. The first was the nature of the struggle against the British. Begin was especially opposed to the definition of the struggle as a "war against British imperialism." The Irgun distinguished between British rule in Palestine and the British empire. Secondly, there was opposition within Lehi to losing its autonomous existence and ideological distinctiveness and to being swallowed up within the organizational hierarchy of the Irgun.

According to some, it was Yellin-Mor's position that decided the nature of the relations between the two undergrounds. In Yellin-Mor's view, Begin suffered the deficiencies of traditional Revisionist thinking and policy; but not only did he see himself as the sole interpreter of Jabotinsky's teachings, he also claimed for himself the authority to be the sole arbitrator should a dispute develop between the two undergrounds.[38]

Eldad holds that Yellin-Mor did not want unification with the Irgun from the outset. The reasons for Yellin-Mor's opposition at this stage were a matter of principle rather than tactical; by 1947 he had become convinced that it was necessary to bring about a leftward turn within Lehi. According to Eldad, Begin had already agreed to formulations he had not accepted in 1944, and even consented to the foreign policy principles of Lehi as formulated by Yellin-Mor. However, Eldad does not offer a reasonable explanation of Yellin-Mor's opposition to unification with the Irgun at an earlier stage, nor do we have evidence testifying to a change in Begin's outlook in 1947.[39]

Begin and the Irgun command were very suspicious of Lehi intentions, particularly in light of the relations that had developed between Lehi and the Hagana. In a letter to the Lehi leadership on September 1, 1944, Begin stated in detail their differences of opinion. From that letter it appears that Yellin-Mor was doubtful about the necessity of creating a single organizational framework and opposed a joint command. Begin protested against Yellin-Mor's "diplomatic" approach in negotiations. Privately, Begin denounced "the faction" (Lehi), for inciting against the Irgun while outwardly displaying a desire for unification.[40] It appears that there was opposition to unification within both undergrounds. The revolutionary structure of Lehi, its ideological direction, and the characteristics of its leaders propelled it away from a central role in the struggle for Jabotinsky's legacy, whose teachings it openly rejected.

The "outlier" batallion

The struggle within Revisionism was also being fought on another front, between the Irgun command headed by Menachem Begin and its "outlier" battalion – the Hebrew Committee of National Liberation in the United States whose main figures were Hillel Kook and Shmuel Merlin. Relations between the Irgun and the HCNL were not formally defined and there was no authority that could rule on them. The HCNL was originally established in the late 1930s to represent the Irgun in the United States but subsequently achieved full independence. The command in Palestine regarded itself as the supreme authority in the military, political, and foreign policy realms, with the HCNL acting as a rear providing assistance in the form of propaganda, fundraising, and political activity. The HCNL, however, regarded itself as an independent political authority, with the Irgun serving as its military and fighting arm. Most of the members of the HCNL had left Palestine before the split in the Irgun. They had a different attitude towards Lehi, and were closer to the Zionist Revisionist old guard even after the rift that had opened up between the party and the Irgun command.[41]

The disputes between the Irgun in Palestine and the HCNL about authority, division of roles, and political program intensified after the command in Palestine decided in 1946 to set up an executive delegation (the Diaspora Staff) in Europe headed by Eliahu Tavin.[42] Ideologically, the dispute centered around the distinction made by some of the leaders of the HCNL between "Hebrewness" and "Jewishness," a distinction of far-reaching significance for the nature of Jewish society in Palestine. Politically, the dispute focused on the issue of establishing a provisional government in exile, an idea that was backed by the committee as well as by some leaders of the Revisionist party in Palestine. After approval of the partition plan in November 1947 and the dismantlement of the Irgun, relations between the Irgun command and the leaders of the HCNL were to reach a breaking point that would determine their future standing in the Herut movement.

It was during the first years of the Second World War that the organizations of the second generation of the Revisionist right came into their own. The several committees in the United States, of which the main one was the HCNL, successfully utilized the uniqueness of American democracy with its social pluralism and tradition of voluntary political association. The leaders of the HCNL were especially successful between 1943 and 1947 in developing a supportive financial and propaganda structure and in lining up support within the American public beyond the traditional ranks of the Revisionist right. They exposed the weaknesses of traditional Revisionism under Jabotinsky's leadership that had failed to mobilize broad support within American Jewry. The HCNL journal *Answer* provides an impressive testimony to its activities and propaganda methods. Revisionist historiography, and especially the Irgun leadership, always downplayed the importance of the HCNL, even though in the 1940s it was the most important Revisionist political association outside Palestine.[43]

Relations between the Irgun command and the HCNL were often marred by misunderstandings because of their differing definitions of their respective roles and different ideological platform, but also because of faulty communication and personal disputes. The differences between Menachem Begin and Hillel Kook on "Hebrewness" and on the establishment of a provisional government came to an end only after history had imposed its verdict with the declaration of independence in 1948.

In a speech delivered on July 19, 1944, Hillel Kook called for recognition of the HCNL as the provisional representative of the Hebrew nation.[44] In October 1947 the committee formulated its overall political conception in a memorandum to the UN ad hoc committee on Palestine. In this memorandum the HCNL presented itself as the provisional national authority of the Hebrew nation. The HCNL rejected the recommendation to form two states, a Jewish state and an Arab state, and called for recognition of the Hebrew nation's right to sovereignty in the Land of Israel on both sides of the Jordan – to be put into effect with the help of a UN advisory council and a "provisional government of the Hebrew Republic of Palestine."[45]

The Irgun command, under the pressure of events in Palestine, complained constantly about the meager aid it was receiving from the HCNL, about the committee's excessive outlays for propaganda work and for independent political activity that obligated the Irgun to ideas it did not find acceptable. Despite attempts to arrive at an agreement regulating relations between the two bodies, the Irgun command was not able to impose its authority on the committee. At a later stage, when attempts to make the committee subject to instructions from the command had come to nought, the Irgun command helped oust Hillel Kook and have him replaced by Shmuel Merlin. Overshadowing the struggle between HCNL and the Irgun command was the Irgun's awareness that they had no alternative organizational apparatus and/or financial backing. This continued to be the situation during the critical period between acceptance of the partition plan in November 1947 and the proclamation of statehood in May 1948.[46]

In an agreement reached on May 1, 1946, the Irgun recognized the HCNL as its political representative and the HCNL, in turn, recognized the authority of the command in Palestine.[47] The division of functions between the Diaspora Staff and the committee was not clear, and their separate existence contradicted the opening paragraphs of the agreement. The designation of the HCNL as the "trusteeship institution" of the Hebrew nation is similarly unclear. Begin objected to this wording, but let it stand. In practice, the Irgun command ignored the document.

Letters by Begin and his associates to the command are replete with complaints about lack of control of the committee's activities. This bitterness increased after acceptance of the partition plan, in the period when the Irgun sought to expand its strength before the proclamation of the state. In a furious and despairing letter, Begin wrote, "When I think of the possibility of turning our war into a *war of despair* because of a lack of aid from outside, instead of making it a *war of decisive conquest*, my heart is flooded with rage. Is it possible that we will be deserted in days like these, days like these?"[48] (emphasis in original).

Hillel Kook demanded a different definition of the relations between the Irgun's command, the Diaspora Staff, and the HCNL.[49] He claimed that despite the importance of the Irgun's war in Palestine, it would lose its political significance without the activities of the HCNL. He added that the perspective gained from the underground is not sufficient to perceive the more general political picture. Kook wanted to involve the Irgun in the political struggle in the Yishuv and to transform it into the sole expression of the Hebrew revolution. Hence, the Irgun must stop its cooperation with the New Zionists and oppose the Zionist Executive with full force. What Kook wanted, in effect, was that the Irgun operate openly as the representative of a national liberation movement, with uniforms and military titles of its own. The model he had before him were the national governments in exile that acted alongside the Allies. Finally, Kook argued against the command's mistrust and demanded equal status for the members of the command in Palestine and those overseas. Apparently, he saw himself as a member of the Irgun's command.[50]

After the UN vote on partition, the Irgun had to make some fateful decisions about its future course. Time was now decisive, and aid in money and arms crucial. But now it was discovered that the rift with the HCNL was widening, both organizationally and ideologically. The lack of efficient communication and of clarity with regard to lines of authority were to be significant during the *Altalena* affair and would leave their mark on the history of the Herut movement.

The political formulations included in the agreement signed by the Irgun and the HCNL in May 1946 were unable to satisfy either Begin or Kook. The memorandum tended more in the direction of the political conception of the committee members. It spoke of the "Hebrew nation" and the establishment of a provisional Palestine government, part of which would be in the underground in Palestine and part would operate openly in the Diaspora.[51] Begin fiercely opposed this formulation. He argued that the expression "Palestine government" contained nothing of either "Hebrewness" or "Jewishness" and without the term "Land of Israel" it could be the name of any government – even an Arab government. He was particularly vexed by the fact that the British foreign minister, Ernest Bevin, used the very same expression in his public addresses.[52] Hillel Kook insisted on including the term "Palestine" in order to preserve the legitimacy of the claim to the Land of Israel on both sides of the Jordan, because "Palestine" was the name recognized in the world and expressed continuity with the historical boundaries of Eretz Yisrael.[53]

It became increasingly evident that the disagreements on the question of "Hebrewness" versus "Jewishness," the timing of the proclamation, if at all, of a provisional government, the attitude towards the partition plan, and the overall conception of a national liberation movement were no longer bridgeable. Menachem Begin rejected the concept of "Hebrewness," employed a considered tactic of postponing proclamation of the provisional government, forcefully opposed any support of the partition plan, regarded the Irgun command as the supreme authority, both militarily and politically, and viewed the committee as no more than an overseas auxiliary of the Irgun. For Hillel Kook the distinction between Jew and Hebrew became an obsession and cure-all formula solving the complicated status of the Jewish people among the nations historically and politically. He laid stress on the difference between the Irgun's struggle and the broad political objectives a national liberation movement must set for itself. Hillel Kook, apparently under the sway of the historical parallel of the governments in exile, did not appreciate the spirit or course of the Yishuv's politics. He insisted that the Irgun strive for absolute dominance of the struggle for national liberation.

This radical conception differed from the more moderate and sober position that Kook had fashioned on the political plane. He tended to support the establishment of a "Hebrew national authority" that would seek membership in the United Nations and an agreement with the British on the establishment of the new Hebrew republic. At a certain stage he did not rule out Chaim Weizmann as playing a central role in this process, whereas for the undergrounds in the Yishuv, Weizmann symbolized above all else the defeatism and flaccidity of the Zionist leadership.[54]

A few days after the UN General Assembly approved the partition plan, Hillel Kook circulated a letter among his friends in which he set out a platform that was revolutionary from the point of view of the Irgun. In contrast to his public position, Kook believed that the UN resolution should not be opposed. It contained two clearly advantageous elements – the departure of the British from Palestine and recognition of a "Hebrew sovereignty." For that reason the previous conception of the stages leading to the establishment of the state needed to be reformulated – instead of a provisional government in exile, or underground government, the road to independence now passed through a government of "partitioned Palestine."[55]

The partitioned state, claimed Kook, was a milestone toward the ultimate objective and offered an opportunity to shape the nature of the future state, to transform it from a "Jewish state" to a "Hebrew republic of

Palestine." He supposed that establishment of the state within the partition boundaries was no barrier to later changes. As in the Jabotinsky period, Jewish "evacuation" (from Europe) was still the decisive question. Before the Second World War Jabotinsky would not have opposed an offer of sovereignty that applied only to western Palestine, he said, and added that the Holocaust was a phenomenon that cannot be ignored in formulating policy. "I am convinced," he wrote, "that now to cause the partition state to fail . . . means to damage the national interest." Once the state was established, he wrote, it would be possible to disband the HCNL.

Kook did not overlook the differences of view within the leadership of the HCNL. He claimed that Eri Jabotinsky and Shmuel Merlin, who vigorously opposed partition, were in the same position Ze'ev Jabotinsky had been in after the outbreak of the Second World War, which he had believed would never happen. Kook also thought it had been a mistake not to have declared the establishment of a provisional government earlier, without concern for the wishes of Menachem Begin.

Kook's position appeared to the leaders of the Irgun, and to some members of the HCNL and the Diaspora Staff, to be a repudiation of basic tenets for the sake of political fighting and intrigues. In one place it earned the epithet, "opportunism bordering on political adventurism." It was argued that it was also tactically important that there be a national body fighting the partition plan, thereby retaining legitimacy for the claim to expand the boundaries of the State in the future. As a parallel for this position, they cited de Gaulle's opposition to the Vichy government and the gains that came to France as a result. Above all, there was also the question of "ideological purity," which Kook regarded as "dogmatism." To his opponents, however, his views on the character of the future state were an unforgivable deviation from Revisionist monism.[56]

Begin's positions between 1946 and 1948 regarding a provisional government are not clear, and his support of the idea in principle may well have been an expedient compromise meant to put off the leaders of the HCNL. His delaying tactics were sober and logical. Immediately after the draft agreement with the HCNL was signed, he qualified his support on grounds of timing, writing in June 1946 that it was necessary "to wait a bit as to real steps." There was a chance, he added, that the official representation of the Yishuv would be dismantled. The real reason for his opposition, however, was obvious – his fear of the balance of forces between the Irgun and its domestic rivals: "Our emissaries must remember that their family in the Land of Israel is advancing on a tightrope and that the danger of being stabbed in the back is always lurking. Public recognition is liable to bring out – will bring out – the knife . . ."[57]

To counter the accusations leveled against him, that nonestablishment

of the provisional government contributed to acceptance of the partition
plan, Begin again formulated his position.[58] He rejected Hillel Kook's
accusation that the Irgun's autonomous status as compared to the Hagana
and the Jewish Agency had been obscured. Begin did not accept the claim
that proclamation of a provisional government would have prevented
acceptance of the partition plan. In his view, it would not have been recognized internationally and would have been disastrous in terms of domestic
politics. The war to come would bring its own opportunities.

Hillel Kook's reading of the balance of political power in the Yishuv was
indeed unrealistic. He thought the Irgun could be made "the central core
of a people's army" in cooperation with the Hagana and Lehi. Kook
opposed participation in the government that would be formed after the
state's establishment, but thought it advisable that representatives with
views close to the Irgun's should also participate.[59]

In late 1947 the dispute between Begin and Kook became the focus of a
fateful decision concerning the Irgun's status and its role in the struggle for
independence. It was Begin's decision to seek the views of fellow members
of the command, as well as of the members of the Diaspora Staff and the
HCNL on the course the Irgun should follow if the partition plan were put
into effect.[60] Begin set out four possibilities. The Irgun could proclaim a
government for all of the Land of Israel; refuse to recognize a government
that accepted the partition boundaries, and maintain the continued existence of the Irgun as an underground; launch a battle to conquer Jerusalem;
leave the underground and form an overt political movement – Herut –
with the Irgun continuing to exist in "international Jerusalem" and overseas. The final decision was to be made by an "assembly of the 'class'
[Irgun] commanders and its representatives." Begin believed that the partition boundaries could be altered in war. That, he surmised, depended on
the quantity of arms available to the Irgun.

In February 1948, the Diaspora Staff, along with Shmuel Merlin,
decided that in light of the Irgun command's reluctance to proclaim a provisional government, a "high committee for national liberation" to be a
representative body parallel to the Jewish Agency, should be formed as a
first stage. A minority advocated supporting the state institutions within
the partition boundaries and continuation of the war against the British
and the Arabs outside those boundaries.

In his letter of reply to these suggestions, Begin was cautious, realistic,
and for once prudent. He did not totally rule out the idea of establishing
the "high committee," but saw no reason for its existence given the current
balance of forces. Neither did he reject the minority view that the Irgun
might be able to continue to exist beyond the state's borders even after the
establishment of the state. Subsequently he did rule out the idea of establishing a body parallel to the Jewish Agency. Begin renounced political

struggle by nondemocratic means. It was his assessment that "any real attempt to seize the regime means not only a bloody internal war but also the downfall of the 'class' [Irgun] and catastrophe for the nation . . ."

It was the *Altalena* affair that was to bring the Irgun to a crossroads from which there was no return – the dismantling of the underground, the founding of the Herut movement, and the cessation of the activities of its overseas extensions. For a while it was believed within the Irgun that the underground could continue to exist in Jerusalem in a diminished framework, and that the Diaspora Staff, reinforced by additional people, could serve as a basis for logistical and political support.[61] Actually, however, the demise of the Diaspora Staff was just a matter of time. It did not even figure as a real bargaining card in the Irgun's negotiations with the Hagana and the provisional government. Over the objections of the members of the Diaspora Staff, the Irgun command decided against independent activity beyond the country's borders and forbade members of the Irgun to engage in such activities without its express approval. Members of the Diaspora Staff believed that by joining the formal political system, the Herut movement would lose all influence on the outcome of the war. It appears that they also doubted Herut's chances of succeeding in Israeli politics, fearing it would become a new edition of the Zionist Revisionist party.[62]

Aryeh Ben-Eliezer, Begin's close aide, was sent by the command in Palestine to conduct talks with the members of the Diaspora Staff on its disbandment, and on redirecting it toward official, open activity on behalf of the Herut movement. Amichai (Gidi) Paglin, the Irgun's operations officer, agreed after much urging to return to Israel, but only in November 1948. Until Begin arrived, it was thought that the decision to dismantle the Diaspora Staff was not yet final. Opposition to the decision ended unequivocally when Begin visited Paris in December 1948.

As early as May 1948, at a press conference in Tel Aviv, Hillel Kook announced the dismantling of the HCNL. In mid-October, Hillel Kook, Eri Jabotinsky, Shmuel Merlin, Yermiyahu Halperin, and Aryeh Ben-Eliezer announced that the committee as a body would not be joining any political party or movement. They themselves joined the Herut movement, and apart from Halperin, were all elected to the first Knesset on the Herut list. A new era had begun. Menachem Begin and the Irgun now devoted themselves to ensuring their hegemony over the Revisionist right as a whole.[63]

Perfect usurpation

The Herut movement founded by the Irgun convened its first national council on October 19, 1948. Portraits of Herzl, Jabotinsky, and David

Raziel were hung above the stage of the Ohel Shem theater in Tel Aviv, along with the emblem of the new movement, under a banner proclaiming "Homeland and Liberty." The hall itself was covered with maps of the Land of Israel on both sides of the Jordan. The leader of Herut, Menachem Begin, made his way to the stage, holding the arm of Mrs Tamar Jabotinsky-Kopp, Ze'ev Jabotinsky's sister.

The first to be eulogized by Begin was David Raziel, whom he called "our supreme commander, the greatest Hebrew commander of our time." He then discharged any debt he might have had to Abraham Stern, founder of Lehi, calling him "the commander–poet."[64] The founding of Herut was the crowning act in the struggle for the Revisionist inheritance. Herzl, Jabotinsky, and Raziel no doubt symbolized both the Zionist and the Revisionist heritage for Begin, which was now embodied in himself as sole heir. No other figure or political faction on the Revisionist right was in a position to challenge this claim. Not the leaders of Lehi, nor the heads of the Zionist Revisionists and the Hebrew State party, nor the leaders of the Hebrew Committee of National Liberation. This was the most decisive victory in Menachem Begin's political career.

Given his political outlook, historical vision, and personal inclinations, Begin was probably not surprised by the status he attained. In his conception of political order, the nation first fights against the foreign ruler, and then, having achieved its independence, enters the stage of competition for control of the regime. The underground period restrained Begin's natural penchant for the public arena, for rhetoric and mass mobilization as the best ways for developing political power. In a speech on the eve of the proclamation of the state, Begin declared that the Herut movement, "to be established by the great fighting family that gathered from all circles, all the dispersions, all streams, around the banner of the Irgun Zva'i Leumi," would fight for its principles within the framework of Hebrew democracy. Adding a warning to the government, Begin cautioned it not to make "concessions to the outside or be despotic at home."[65]

The founding of Herut was the end, not the beginning, of the struggle within the Revisionist right. The Irgun severed its ties with the Zionist Revisionists at the end of 1943, did not unite with Lehi and prevented the HCNL from interfering in the final stage of transition from underground to political movement. Despite the contention with segments of the Revisionist party and with the former heads of the HCNL, a façade of solidarity was presented to the outside. The new inheritor of the Revisionist tradition was presented as having received his legacy in an atmosphere of unity and harmony. That legacy was depicted as the natural inheritance of the commander of the Irgun, bequeathed to him directly by the leader and founder of the movement, Ze'ev Jabotinsky.

Close to the establishment of the state, Menachem Begin was convinced that it was absolutely necessary to found a new movement separate from the Zionist Revisionists Union. The view in the Irgun was that any relations with the Revisionist party would damage the chances of broadening public support for Herut. Before the formal proclamation of the founding of the new movement, the leaders of the Zionist Revisionists attempted to dissuade Begin from carrying out his intention. Up until the elections for the first Knesset in early 1949, attempts were made to bring about a merger of the two movements. However, a final split occurred in September 1948, preventing them from appearing with a joint list in the Knesset elections.

The Revisionist leaders began to probe the Irgun commander's intentions in earnest in the spring of 1948.[66] Announcing in a speech on May 14 that a new movement would arise, Begin made no mention of the Zionist Revisionists. In early June the Revisionist party leaders invited Begin to a meeting of the party executive. At this meeting, Begin had apparently made clear his intention to form a political movement not tied to the Zionist Revisionist Union. He also refused to announce publicly that the Zionist Revisionists were about to join the new party.

On June 13, 1948, Meir Grossman sent a letter to Begin in which he spoke of the need to unify the nationalist camp. It is unthinkable, he argued, that the movement founded by Jabotinsky in 1925 would cease to exist in, of all places, the Land of Israel. He asked Begin to refrain from creating *faits accomplis* and invited him to a round of talks. At a meeting between the two men on the following day, as the *Altalena* was nearing the country's shores, Begin turned down Grossman's suggestion that the members of the Irgun join the Zionist Revisionists.

The *Altalena* affair and the ensuing damage to Begin's prestige seemed to the Revisionist leadership an opportune moment to seize the initiative. On June 17 the party published its positions. The Revisionist executive attempted to stress the unity of interests of the various segments of the Revisionist camp. The leadership presented three proposals – by party leaders Meir Grossman, Yaacov Rubin, and Baruch Weinstein, respectively – for ordering relations among the factions. When these were put before him at a meeting on July 24, Begin tended to favor the Rubin proposal with some modifications. That proposal called essentially for a division that guaranteed the Herut movement independent activity in Israel and the continued existence of the Zionist Revisionists abroad.

On September 1, 1948, Meir Grossman sent the detailed proposal of the World Council of Zionist Revisionists to the temporary center of the Herut movement. Essentially this proposal asserted that it would be best if the Herut movement were to be an organic part of the World Zionist Revisionist Union and accept its authority in fundamental matters of policy. If merger was not possible, the Revisionist leaders proposed a modus operandi based on a division of roles between Israel and the Diaspora, with a looser organizational and ideological tie. It appears that the Zionist Revisionists hoped to set up a joint temporary center composed of Herut and Zionist Revisionist members, which would approve a joint electoral list for the upcoming Knesset elections.[67]

Begin and the other Irgun leaders unanimously opposed a joint appearance in the elections with the Zionist Revisionists. They also opposed the idea of a political merger that did not guarantee them exclusive control of the new movement. In any event, they had no illusions about the party's intentions and, despite the ongoing contacts with the Zionist Revisionist leadership, made preparations both to take over the first joint convention of the Revisionist Union and to appear with an independent list in the Knesset election. Begin feared that the negotiations with the Revisionists would keep Herut from organizing in time for the elections, and was convinced that in the final analysis much more would be determined by reality than by "formalistics and juristics."[68]

At the national convention of the Zionist Revisionist Union, the Herut movement garnered the support of an absolute majority, which decided that the Zionist Revisionist Union would unite with the Herut movement. The new center, controlled by the Irgun, was empowered to carry out the unification. When it became evident to the Revisionist leaders that they comprised a minority in the new center elected by the national convention, they made it plain to Begin that the Zionist Revisionist executive would withhold recognition from the new center, and that the decisions of the convention were not binding. They in fact announced the dissolution of the institutions elected at the national convention. They also announced new elections for its own convention, in which only those declaring they did not belong to another political movement would be eligible to vote. This marked the end of official relations between the two movements. Informal talks continued until the convening of Herut's first national council, but Begin was now determined not to reach an agreement.[69]

The results became finally clear at the end of January 1949. Herut won fourteen seats in the Knesset, the Zionist Revisionists not even one. In the election campaign Begin faulted the Revisionist leaders for the insignificant role they had played in the revolt. They, in turn, accused him of destroying Jabotinsky's movement and of making a vain attempt to foster a new image that was unrelated to the Revisionist past. These mutual accusations served as preliminaries for a rearguard battle for control of Betar. The belated attempt by Meir Grossman to organize Revisionists as an independent movement also failed. By the mid-1960s most of the Revisionist leaders still in Herut had retired from the movement, and those who did not were without real influence.[70]

The fourth world convention of Betar, held in May 1949, also served as an arena for tests of strength between the Revisionists and Herut. The battle at the convention was both ideological and organizational, the issue up for debate being Betar's objectives after the establishment of the state. The Irgun's supporters sought to create a direct link between Betar and Herut, while the Revisionist supporters and a group of Betar veterans that included Aharon Propes wanted to preserve Betar's independence. Propes held that the "gentleman's agreement" that had existed between Betar and the Zionist Revisionists should be scrapped and its relationship with the two existing movements terminated.[71]

However, the real scores that had to be settled concerned the contribution of the Zionist Revisionists to the military struggle conducted by the Irgun in the 1940s. Remba's apologetic address was a feeble echo of his forceful oration at the previous convention, held in Warsaw in 1938: "Pride, glory, and dignity require of you, underground fighters, that you do not obscure the history of the Zionist Revisionists, which served as the Irgun's support," he said, "The revolt is just one jewel in the crown." Yuniczman was more to the point when he asserted that there wasn't enough living space for two Jabotinskian parties.

Before the world convention of Betar convened, Begin was somewhat uncertain and perplexed concerning his status vis-à-vis Betar. "What will be my status at the opening of the convention?" he asked his colleagues. "Shall I deliver at speech in a Betar shirt?" It was also intended to hold the convention in Jerusalem rather than in Metzudat Ze'ev, the party's headquarters which still belonged to the Revisionists.[72] In his closing address, Begin explained the logic – the inevitable logic, in his view – for the establishment of a political movement separate from the Revisionists. At the beginning of his remarks he revealed his true historical debt. He mentioned only the "class" – the Irgun – and Betar. He told his audience that Lehi had obstructed unification with the Irgun because it had refused to recognize "the head of Betar as the supreme commander."

Essentially Begin argued that once it was decided to disband the Irgun, only a new and indepenent movement was capable of uniting the members of the Irgun and of ruling with the fervor and energy characteristic of the underground. A generation later, Begin was to explain that the establishment of Herut ensured that "those fighters can continue to pursue their ideas, without arms, in the framework of democracy." Herut guaranteed the break with the idea of revolt and acceptance of a new authority. In May 1949, Begin had presented the main objective to his audience as being "to aspire to take the reins of power."[73] He completed his conquest of the "Revisionist kingdom" in May 1954. It was then that he was made supreme commander of Betar, and united in his person all the roles that had once been filled by Ze'ev Jabotinsky.

The struggle for the Revisionist inheritance was brief. The critical interim period lasted no more than a year, from the establishment of the state to May 1949. The historical weakness of the Revisionist movement in the Yishuv was apparent, but what was not known was the extent to which Herut could expand the circle of its supporters beyond the ranks of the undergrounds and Betar. As we have seen the matter was decided unequivocally with the crushing and humiliating defeat of the Revisionists when they had failed to win a single seat in the elections to the first Knesset.

Begin put his basic premise – that the legitimation of Herut as the successor to Ze'ev Jabotinsky would be decided without regard for its ties with the Revisionists – to the test. At the fourth world convention the final issue too was decided – the political affiliation of Betar. Until the mid-1960s Herut was to continue to develop in accordance with the structure laid down at that time. Herut now confined itself to the heartland; the Revisionists were left with the possibility of operating overseas. Meanwhile, a curtain was drawn on the internal rivalries within Herut. A front of unity and harmony was presented to the outside, marred only by occasional outbursts.

At the end of the 1940s Begin had completed his most important political undertaking. In the five stormy years between the proclamation of the revolt and the war of independence the Revisionist inheritance had fallen entirely into his lap.

4

Commander of the Irgun, 1943–1948

After his release from labor camp, Begin had arrived, a lone wanderer, at the Uzbeki town of Margilan. At the end of July 1941, diplomatic relations were renewed between the Polish government in exile in London and the Soviet Union, and the Polish army known as the Anders army was formed in Russia. Service in the Polish army provided physical and material refuge for those Jews who succeeded in enlisting in it. But for the most part, Jews were disqualified from service because of their origin and were subjected to coarse and humiliating treatment. Because of Begin's poor physical condition he required the intervention of his Revisionist friends, Miron Sheskin and Yohanan Bader, to be enlisted into the Anders army. His chances of emigrating to Palestine were dependent on that. Begin began his service in the Polish army, where, he writes, the atmosphere was of "anti-Semitism, insult, and pain." He made his way to Palestine with the Anders army via the Caspian port of Krasnovodsk, Pahlavi, Habbaniyya in Iraq, and Transjordan. The future commander of the Irgun did not know that he was passing near the site of David Raziel's death.[1]

Begin arrived in Palestine in May 1942. In *The Revolt* he writes that when he crossed the Jordan, he entered *Palestina Salutaris*, Eretz Yisrael of deliverance. He lay down on the green grass and drank in "the smell of the field, the fragrance of the homeland." Eldad describes his own shock upon encountering the relative serenity, complacency, and abundance that prevailed then in Palestine as compared to a Europe in flames. It is hard to know if Begin felt the same; to Nicholas Bethell he said that on arrival in Eretz Yisrael he was overwhelmed by a feeling that he had never departed from this land.[2]

In Palestine Begin served as an interpreter for the Polish army in Jerusalem. There remains a notebook from that period used by him to study civil law, based on lectures by Dr M. Zmora.[3] Begin reported to Ya'acov Meridor, the commander of the Irgun, and in the autumn of 1942 was named *natziv* of Betar. He served in that role until the middle of that year, all the while maintaining his contacts with the Irgun command. He resigned this post when it became clear to him that he could not act as *natziv* and at the same time serve in the Polish army. It seems the British authorities had approached the Polish command on that matter.

The mysteries of accession

Begin's appointment as commander of the Irgun is one of the most insistently opaque events of his political life. The versions are as many as they are conflicting. David Niv writes in the history of the Irgun that the move to name Begin for the post began with Aryeh Ben-Eliezer's arrival in Palestine in mid-October 1943 on a mission for the Hebrew Committee of National Liberation. Ben-Eliezer held wide-ranging talks with members of the underground. He found ferment and a desire for action, as well as full agreement that Begin should be appointed commander. Through the mediation of the Revisionist lawyer Marek Kahan talks were held with representatives of the Polish army, which agreed to discharge five soldiers, Begin among them. The understanding was that the HCNL would assist the propaganda work of the Polish government in exile in the United States. On December 1, 1943, command of the Irgun was transferred from Meridor to Begin. Meridor issued an announcement in which he placed himself "under the command and direction of the new commander." Begin immediately formed a new headquarters staff; at its first meeting he proposed a revolt against the British mandate.[4]

According to Meridor, the transfer of command to Begin was much more complicated. In the winter of 1941 the Revisionist party attempted to impose its authority on the Irgun. To this end, a supervisory committee had been established composed of two representatives from Betar and two from the Irgun. The fear in the Irgun command then was that the Betar executive would instruct Betar members to leave the underground. During this nadir in the Irgun's history, the commander of the Jerusalem district placed a bomb near the home of the Revisionist leader Benyamin Lubotzky. The supervisory committee appears to have fallen apart after Lubotzky left it. When Meridor returned from Iraq – after David Raziel had been killed on an undercover mission for the British army – he was offered the post of Irgun commander. Begin reported to Meridor upon his arrival in Palestine, and Meridor immediately proposed that he, Begin, be commander in his place. Meridor gives the impression that he was waiting for someone to come and take over. But after Begin became aware of the opposition to his appointment, he turned down Meridor's offer until his discharge from the Polish army. According to Meridor, Begin participated in a meeting of Betar members in the British army and "realized they would not accept his command." He was disappointed and announced he would not accept the appointment.[5]

Meridor is of the view that he is the one who came up with the idea of designating Begin as commander of the Irgun, even though he did not know him at all. Meridor had to overcome the opposition of the majority in the command. They did not believe that Begin, who lacked military expertise, was capable of leading the underground. From Meridor's account, it appears that the party backed Begin's appointment. They surmised that as a Betarist he would be loyal to the Revisionist movement. In the end, Meridor won the command's approval, and Begin was named commander of the Irgun. Meridor proposed himself as his deputy.[6]

Meridor's testimony is baffling and unconvincing. Whatever may have been Meridor's wishes at the time, his standing as commander of the Irgun was vulnerable and the underground was in a state of disarray. Shlomo Levi (Lev-Ami), a member of the Irgun's command, writes that Meridor had been compelled to resign for the first time in August 1943. On Begin's suggestion he stayed on for a while as commander, but after the failure of the attempt to kidnap the British high commissioner Sir Harold Mac-Michael he was forced to resign permanently. Begin's appointment was apparently made conditional by some members of the command on Meridor's removal. Begin was forced to forgo Meridor's services until August 1944.[7] According to Eliahu Lankin, a member of the Irgun command, Begin's appointment was clearly an expression of disappointment over the state of affairs in the Irgun. It appears from this account that the intention to appoint Begin was born as early as in 1942. Lankin himself expressed doubts about the choice. He asserts that the appointment was made without the party's involvement, and that, moreover, it was decided to loosen Begin's ties with the party as much as possible. That was one of the reasons for removing Meridor from activity for a while.[8]

Yohanan Bader, who had immigrated to Palestine at the end of 1943, mentions Begin's close friend Yisrael Epstein and Aryeh Ben-Eliezer as having played a central role in effecting Begin's discharge from the Polish army and in his selection as commander. In any event, the idea did not spring from members of the command. In Bader's view, the key factor weighing in favor of the appointment was the fact that Begin was *natziv* of Betar. At the time, Bader himself was not sure that the choice was a good one. Subsequently he arrived at the view that the fact that Begin was not a military man was what assured his success.[9]

The Zionist Revisionists' version is somewhat different. Altman did not regard Begin as a military man, but in his view the fact that he was *natziv* of Betar facilitated his accession for the command. For a while, both Begin and Meridor took part in meetings of the party. Afterwards, Ben-Eliezer and Begin approached Altman on the matter of the appointment. Begin wanted a clear division of activity between the party and the underground. In this account, Begin's appointment had not only the consent of the

Zionist Revisionists, but also the blessing of the party leaders. Because he had been *natziv* of Betar and was an adherent of Jabotinsky's course, they anticipated a measure of influence over the Irgun.[10]

Yet another version is that of the members of the Hebrew Committee of National Liberation. Eri Jabotinsky relates that after the death of Raziel, Hillel Kook was actually the most senior commander in the Irgun. Begin's release from the Polish army and his appointment were on Kook's instructions. Shmuel Merlin reinforces this account; Ben-Eliezer was sent back to Palestine to reorganize the Irgun "which will be subject to Hillel Kook's command in Palestine or in the United States." Kook himself claims that Begin's discharge from the Polish army was in his hands and he could have prevented it. At a certain stage Ben-Eliezer may have been considered for the post, but the latter wrote to Kook agreeing to the proposal to appoint Begin. In historical retrospect, Hillel Kook thought that had been a serious misjudgment.[11]

Ben-Eliezer relates that he arrived in Palestine on October 14, 1943, and held comprehensive talks with the party heads and commanders of the two undergrounds. He found the Irgun in a poor state and unfit for action. Ben-Eliezer repeated, at least in public, the customary account of Begin's release from the Polish army. Begin was supposed to leave for America with a number of Jewish soldiers, all members of the Revisionist movement, who had been released with him to assist the propaganda work of the Polish government in exile. However, the mission never departed. In fact, the way in which Begin's release from the Polish army was obtained has not been thoroughly clarified. It seems that he was merely granted leave for one year. Although Begin was not ordered to return to military service, formally he could have been considered a deserter. Had he not been released he would have been sent with his battalion to the Italian front.[12]

By all accounts, Ben-Eliezer played a key role in Begin's appointent. In *The Revolt*, Begin wrote that the plan for the revolt took shape during walks with him. Ben-Eliezer's own intentions are not clear. Conceivably he himself wanted to be commander of the Irgun but concealed that wish. He left behind a diary of sorts in which we find the enigmatic statement, "Begin, such a modest person, commander of the Irgun. Impossible. I knew him abroad too . . ." This comment remains puzzling in light of the uniformity of view about the efforts made by Ben-Eliezer to ensure Begin's appointment.[13]

In the spring of 1967 Begin provided an account of his own.[14] In April 1942, when the Polish army was encamped at Mafraq in Transjordan, he heard of the deaths of David Raziel and Abraham Stern. Reports that the Irgun had ceased its activities against the British mandate at the beginning of the Second World War had reached him while he was still in Vilna, and he had thought it was a mistake to have announced that publicly. In the autumn of 1942 he was made *natziv* of Betar. His activity as *natziv* while serving in the Polish army had led to curtailment of his activity by the Polish command. He was ultimately released from the army, after persistent intercessions by Shimshon Yuniczman, Marek Kahan, and Aryeh Ben-Eliezer in early December 1943.[15]

Begin affirms that there was a "commissary of the NZO" in charge of the political guidance of the Irgun. He participated in some of its meetings. Immediately after his discharge from the Polish army, that is, at the beginning of December 1943, Begin was appointed commander of the Irgun; he claims that he had filled that role in practice since September of that year.

The members of the Irgun command, the Revisionist party, and the heads of the Hebrew Committee of National Liberation did not share the same interests nor did they regard Begin's appointment in the same light. Subsequently, they attributed a mysterious quality to the selection and obscured the opposition to it. The intricacies of Begin's accession to the command of the Irgun was hard testimony to the frail organizational condition of the Revisionist movement, which lacked a supreme personal or institutional authority. Into this vacuum came Begin, resolute and convinced of his own ability.

Opponents of the new commander of the Irgun argued that he lacked military and organizational competence. The experience the last *natziv* of Betar in Poland brought with him had been acquired almost entirely within the framework of the movement. In fact, it was Betar that secured his rule of the Irgun, and its ethos directed his style of leadership.

The social and political climate in Poland was congenial for the growth of Betar. At the height of its strength, the movement numbered over 60,000 members organized in some 700 local cells. The movement had a popular character; the desire was for a simple, uncomplicated teaching, especially one with a martial emphasis. Eldad was sharply critical of Betar instruction and of the tendency in the Irgun cells "to shunt spiritual education aside." He thought that Betar had to be saved from domination by "the boot that kicks the 'intellectuals', which I have seen here and there among Irgun commanders."[16] Propes relates that when he arrived in Poland in the late 1920s he found a movement that lacked content and organization.[17]

Bader writes that Begin's talents and success did not endear him to the members of the Betar executive in Poland. Not finding satisfaction in his work, he tried to revive Betar in Czechoslovakia, but encountered a difficult time there. Propes claims that Begin failed on the organizational front in Czechoslovakia.[18] A report by Shalom Rosenfeld, then a member of Betar, of his visit to Poland in June 1937 is not flattering. Disorder in the office of the *natziv*, the secretariat not functioning properly, a decline of morale, cells that existed on paper only, and commanders not carrying out the instructions of the *netzivut*. Begin is mentioned in the report as visiting outlying cities at the time.[19]

The decisive moment, however, came in September 1938. The activist line triumphed over Jabotinsky's moderate position; it was decided that there would be close cooperation between Betar and the Irgun. The new merger between Betar and the Irgun was personified by Menachem Begin.[20]

The revolt

At the end of December 1943, Begin was at the threshold of a new period in his political life. For the next decade he was to act in the guise of a revolutionary and rebel challenging British rule and the hegemony of the Zionist leadership.[21] Not until the mid-1960s would he forge a new legitimacy for himself as parliamentarian and scrupulous observer of the rules of democracy. No one yet knew that Begin would prove a success as commander of the Irgun. He lacked the skills required for military management of the underground, but his caution, even courage, and natural proclivity for a historical and political point of view saved the Irgun from early disintegration and destruction. In the end, he was able to transform the Irgun into a political movement.

Begin always considered the period of the revolt as the summit of his life. The man who most perfectly epitomized the dual loyalty to Betar and to the Irgun now came to fulfill the Betar oath, or *neder*.[22] January 1944 marked the beginning of a new era in the history of Revisionism. In proclaiming the revolt, Begin chose a path of complete autonomy and total severance from the Revisionist party, while on the external front he rejected the authority of the Zionist leadership.[23]

The Irgun's proclamation of revolt is indicative of Menachem Begin's world view. Its style is that of a supreme authority entitled to guide the history of an entire nation. By including a broad range of national and political goals, it could serve as a foundation for the establishment of a new regime. In this respect it reveals the deep contradiction within Begin between a liberal-inspired romantic world view and the absolutist, radical, and messianic formulation of the goal and of the means for attaining it.

The proclamation contains a description of historical and political reality, vindication of the path of revolt, and necessary conclusions – all of which depend on a deep inner conviction regarding the inexorable course of history.[24] It is founded on a belief in historical lawfulness according to which every nation in the community of nations is entitled on the basis of its unique sovereignty to proclaim its national aspirations as a formal first step toward achieving and consolidating its rights. The primary demand, therefore, was the call for the establishment of a "provisional Hebrew government" that would be responsible for the leadership of the Yishuv and for international negotiations.[25]

The proclamation ignored the issue of whether the Irgun command had the authority to declare a revolt against Britain in the name of the Yishuv. The call could claim to express a broad collective will only on the basis of confidence and faith in the "invisible hand" guiding national liberation struggles. Begin sought to resolve that deep contradiction by repeatedly referring to concepts in international law. To Begin, when the Yishuv sided with the Allies in 1939, and "a ceasefire between the Jews and the government" was declared, a contractual agreement between the two sides was thereby reached. By maintaining its White Paper policy, and thereby actually assisting in the extermination of Jews, Great Britain provided a juridical and moral basis for the declaration of revolt – which then assumed the dual character of military uprising and civil disobedience. The Yishuv could be considered as a party to the war only through cooperation with Britain, and certainly contractual relationship cannot be attributed to the Irgun's precarious and brief liaison with the British administration at the beginning of the war.

The proclamation of revolt opens with the assertion that "We are in the final stage of this world war." This premise served as justification for an uprising against British rule in the midst of the war against Nazi Germany. This was January 1944, six months before the Allied landing in Normandy. The ultimate outcome of the war was already determined, but its end was not yet in sight. In *The Revolt* Begin writes that "This call was not supposed to appear in January 1944 but rather in the first half of 1943," but was delayed because of incidental factors within and around the Irgun; an allusion to the internal crisis within the Irgun, its poor relations with the Revisionist party, and the decision to await Begin's formal release from the Polish army. In the spring of 1967, Begin was to say that he had proposed declaring a revolt against the British as early as the summer of 1943, but publication of the proclamation was postponed because of the plan to kidnap the British high commissioner. Apparently, there was opposition within the Irgun command to issuing the proclamation because of the fear it would not be possible to back it up with real actions.[26]

The central question before us is, do the reasons cited by Begin for the proclamation and its timing – the Holocaust and the sealing of the gates of immigration to Palestine – truly account for it? Or did it not in fact derive from permanent features of his world view and the basic assumptions he used in examining history? There can be no doubt as to the influence of the Holocaust on Begin's view of reality and on the political and strategic conclusions that he drew from it, but it is doubtful whether by 1943 he was aware of the full extent of the tragedy.

Begin's conception of the revolt was not necessarily connected to the political circumstances of the 1940s. Military uprising is inevitable in Begin's historical and ideological approach, for a free nation cannot be subservient to foreign rule. Revolt appears in history as an expression of national existence, which cannot be reconciled with a reality that denies its will and goals. The choice the nation faces is sharp and clear – "freedom or death." In Begin's world view, the revolt could have established itself before the Holocaust and the world war, though they provided grounds for its legitimation to others.[27]

Begin devoted a considerable part of his writing on the revolt to explaining its ideological origins and the historical laws that rule its development. The central assumption in the Irgun's program was the concept of "pressure": a military uprising based on sporadic actions, which would provoke reaction by the British and develop into a comprehensive struggle for national liberation. On the military level, the Irgun resorted to urban guerrilla warfare; on the diplomatic plane it sought the support of foreign powers, while domestically it hoped for a civil uprising. These means rested on the three factors that in Begin's view determine the success of a revolt or national uprising – objective circumstances or a basis for action such as territory and arms, an external ally, and support at home for the rebels by the people and their national institutions. In fact, those conditions were only partially extant.[28]

The revolt was described not as a one-time action but as a continuous process with a political end, conducted by military means. The Irgun saw itself as a liberation army waging uninterrupted war. The legitimation for the use of military means originated in a highly subjective reading of the history of past wars of national liberation. The lawfulness Begin found here was essentially deterministic; the revolt was almost certain to succeed if the right objective historical conditions existed, although a will to fight and bear sacrifices was also required. Begin did not, however, discuss the social, economic, and political circumstances that can lead an entire society to rebellion, and in fact, has not differentiated between revolt and revolution. In his depiction, the revolt looks like a continous series of military attacks whose combined effect accomplishes almost any national goal.

The revolt had symbolic – almost metaphysical – meaning for Begin. He had a deep, almost mystical recognition of the sovereign right conferred upon every nation to achieve independence, a right to be exercised even by violent means. The war against the foreign conqueror was an absolute historical deduction; strategic and political considerations took second place. However, this assumption contradicted Begin's political realism and his acknowledgement of the significance of order and legality in internal political structures and in international relations. The revolt rested on the voluntary will of the historical agent and did not have to account to any external authority. In practice, the premise that objective conditions would bring forth civil disobedience, reflecting the collective will of an entire society, was refuted; all that remained was the armed struggle.[29]

Begin did not relate to the tradition of revolutionary terror in Europe. He took up the Polish concept of "patriots," which he said is what the nationalist "terrorists" in Palestine ought to be called. The Irgun did not engage in terror but in a "revolutionary war of liberation." The justification for using violent means to achieve political goals was based on the coercive logic of reality and on the general moral character of the struggle for the fate of the Yishuv, and in effect for the fate of the Jewish people as a whole. For Begin, the rebelling minority always possessed superior moral force, with which the ruling foreign power's advantage in physical strength could be undermined.[30] Military pressure was conceived by Begin as the central means for transforming the Yishuv into an independent factor and for obtaining international aid. The notions of *havlaga* (self-restraint) and *ma'avak tzammud* (selective response) were rejected as inappropriate. Begin's guiding conceptions were not seen as a tactical stage in a more general scheme of the struggle for independence, but were considered by him to be the exclusive and all-embracing strategy for achieving the ultimate objective.[31]

In Begin's view, the revolt was based on realistic calculations and on a scrupulous study of British imperialism and its patterns of government. Begin arrived at two conclusions. Great Britain could not maintain its rule over Palestine for a prolonged period with an army of occupation because there were moral limits to the repression against the civilian population that Britain would allow itself. Secondly, Begin believed that acts of terrorism would compel the British government, under pressure of international public opinion, to begin negotiations on the future of Palestine.[32]

Begin saw the revolt as a crossroads through which all of Jewish history passes. The political events of the 1940s were described as flowing directly from the actions of the Irgun. Strategically, it stimulated the taking of military and political initiative and was central in deterring the Palestinian Arabs. It was also important in establishing the Land of Israel on the international stage and won allies for the Zionist movement. Finally, it was the main factor in striking at the British regime as a stage in driving it out of Palestine. Begin's arguments, which depended more upon faith than on historical evidence, relegated other factors in Jewish history to a secondary role, or rejected them altogether as defeatist or counterproductive.[33] This claim to "totality" was directed not only against the hegemony of the Labor movement in the struggle for independence but also against the other Revisionist factions. Lehi, the Irgun's sister underground, was allowed only the auxiliary role of perpetrator of "personal terrorism"; the Hebrew Committee of

National Liberation operating overseas was seen solely as a source of logistical and political support; while the Revisionist party was held to be useless to the national liberation struggle.[34] The revolt, in fact, diverged from the Revisionist legionary tradition and the concept of "pressure," both of which served as auxiliary to public and open diplomacy.

By proclaiming the revolt against Britain, Begin forfeited all possibility of a role for the Irgun in association with the Allies. He did not believe at all in what Jabotinsky thought was possible at the beginning of the war – inclusion in the peace agreements after the war as a combatant party. In fact, Stern's pretentious plan of the 40,000 – military organization outside of Palestine, invasion of its shores and battle against the British with the help of a third country – rested on the legionary tradition more than did Begin's notion of revolt. Stern's plan was strategically irrational, and the partners he searched for, the Axis powers, were quite unthinkable, but essentially he wanted to follow Pilsudski's example.[35]

The leaders of Lehi severely criticized the concept of revolt. Yellin-Mor viewed the proclamation of the revolt as a "manifesto" resting on "more than a hint of baseless arrogance, abrogation of facts." The ceasefire at the beginning of the war was not an agreement but rather a unilateral decision by the Irgun to interrupt its struggle against the British. Yellin-Mor also rejected the inner logic according to which the revolt would become a war of national liberation. The revolt was liable to force a general struggle against the British for an unlimited period, a struggle the Yishuv would be unable to sustain.[36]

Yisrael Eldad categorically denied the suitability of the revolt to the circumstances prevailing in Palestine. For him, Begin's revolt had romantic and theatrical foundations that were not adaptable to reality. He rejected a priori the notion that it was possible in history to plan an uprising or revolution according to a scheme laid out in advance, and argued that in practice "there was no civilian uprising . . . there was no revolt and no taking over of power as found in descriptions of rebellions and revolutions." Eldad saw similarities between Begin's fervor for demonstrative and symbolic acts and Polish romanticism, with its glory and tragedy.[37]

The concept of revolt also contained a revolutionary element, although it was largely hidden. The inner logic of the revolt as an uprising that would sweep along, in wave after wave, more and more segments of society in effect describes a revolutionary process in the course of which the authority and legitimacy of the political leadership opposed to the revolt would collapse. In September 1944, Begin wrote that if the Yishuv leadership did not establish revolutionary institutions that would conduct the war against the British,

We will call upon the masses from "below," from the depths. We will call upon them to make a twofold rebellion: against the oppressive regime and against the cowardly leadership dominating the political parties in the Land of Israel. It will be a revolt against both "Berlin" and against "Vichy." And we will fight. We will fight to the end.[38]

In *The Revolt*, Begin writes that "the banner of secession rose for our nation." The struggle of national liberation can be waged only by secession, with the national institutions backing and supporting the rebels. Who would be the supreme authority for waging a war of national liberation, and what responsibility is borne by a minority that imposes its view on a society whose institutions rest on voluntaristic foundations? Begin rejected the authority of the Jewish Agency, which he regarded as a fawning body subservient to British rule. Moreover, in his view it adhered to an entirely erroneous view of both means and ends. At the same time, Begin remained firm in his conviction that the Irgun was not struggling to seize power, although he does not deny that there were opposing opinions in the underground which held that the lack of desire for power was an error.[39]

Begin's notion was romantic and altruistic: the rebels sacrificing themselves for their nation, the idea of liberty outweighing all other considerations. But from the historical parallels he uses it emerges that power should go to those who fight for it – and for Begin that meant only the Irgun, "If we aspired to power, we would have decided to fight for it; if we decided to fight for power, we would have fought for it."[40] The failings of this outlook are obvious. Begin imposed his interpretation on a tempestuous and complex historical period on the sole basis of the sincerity of his will and subjective intentions. He failed to consider the historical and political significance of secession, the influence of revolt on foreign powers, and he exempted himself from taking democratic mechanisms into consideration. Along with unshaken faith in himself, the magic of the idea of revolt overwhelmed all else.

A secondary force

Despite its small size, the Irgun has been described by its members and proponents as the main agent in the struggle for independence, a primary factor in forcing the British out of Palestine. But the true significance of the revolt can be clarified only in terms of the concept of "complementary strategy"; namely, that it played only a partial and complementary role in the struggle for independence. This of course contradicts Begin's view of the revolt as a comprehensive, exclusive, and full explanation for the attainment of all the military and political aims of the Yishuv.

Nevertheless, Begin himself explained precisely and fully why the revolt cannot stand by itself. In a conversation with Moshe Sneh, the Hagana's chief of staff, in October 1944, Begin argued that in practice there is a division of historical roles: "There is an organization that practices individual terror, and another that conducts sporadic military actions, and there is an organization that intends to throw its ultimate weight in the final battle." Begin added that even though the Yishuv leadership had no control over the activities of the Irgun, it was likely to derive political benefit from them. Sneh disagreed and remarked that since this division of functions does not stem from "a single political disposition," it is not useful. Begin viewed the Irgun as an "open underground" waging urban guerrilla warfare, which the Hagana could not conduct because of its reliance on "rural bases." He supposed that the socialist camp's concern not to endanger its achievements had sharply restricted its room for maneuver and the degree of risk it was prepared to take in the struggle against the British. The Irgun, in his view, complemented the Hagana by operating in realms it neglected.[41]

The activities of the Irgun did not stand by themselves and cannot be isolated from the general course of events. The Yishuv's struggle ended in victory and indepenence, but it is doubtful whether that outcome justified all the means leading up to it. The Irgun's contribution was a result of the fact that overall strategic determinations were not in its hands, and it acted only a secondary role in the framework of a complementary strategy. When the Irgun sought to depart from this pattern, it failed dismally. It was unable to make the transition to a broad military format and from being a small underground body become a "second military force." The structural change in the Irgun after the acceptance of the partition plan was of no value in the deployment for all-out war in 1948. At the outbreak of the War of Independence, its strength was at a very low level. Its chances of imposing a departure from the partition plan on the Yishuv were very slender, and any attempt to preserve its independence was doomed to failure.[42] Thus, in the eyes of its commander as well, the Irgun's achievement did not appear as full victory: "Our nation once more was placed at a crossroads. Downfall would mean absolute destruction. Victory would mean liberation of the entire homeland. We did not suffer downfall; we did not achieve victory."[43]

The reader of *The Revolt* is kept in the dark about the history of the Irgun. As Begin presents it, the history of the Irgun consisted of one continuous march towards victory, with little friction and no real disputes. The man whose thinking was always historical, who wanted to bring cold logic to bear on reality, left us an emotional and impressionistic account and failed to describe historical events comprehensively and accurately.

The only minutes of the Irgun command available to us, from July to

November 1944, reveal very little about Menachem Begin. He was without doubt the authority, almost exclusively, determining the course taken by the Irgun. From the brief discussions, his penchant for weighing political considerations is evident. He insisted on drawing historical parallels even in operational planning sessions. Nor is there any mistaking the far-reaching optimism coloring his descriptions and perception of the Irgun's historical importance.[44]

In October 1944 Sneh wrote that Begin "does not know how to formulate things, speaks a great deal, speaks pompously." In his meeting with Sneh, Begin spoke of the struggle for power in the Yishuv as a side issue. He wanted to see the formation of a "national liberation committee," unity on the basis of war, and if not that – then revolt. Sneh thought that Begin might have some connection with the Americans. This was the unfounded notion of a suspicious man who gathered from that meeting that "they want to impose their way on everyone."[45] Jorge Garcia Granados, Guatemala's representative to the United Nations Special Committee on Palestine, who met Begin in the middle of 1947, received the impression that before him was a mild-mannered man who spoke carefully, measuring his words like a teacher. Perhaps under the influence of the mystery surrounding the encounter and the circumstances of the time, he wrote that the contrast between Begin's fixed stare and his smile "left you with an impression of cruelty."[46]

As commander of the Irgun, Begin dealt mainly with the political and propaganda aspects of the underground's activity. Given Begin's fondness for the public realm, the loneliness imposed by being underground was another sacrifice brought to the altar of the struggle for independence: "I loved the overt not the hidden, the public not the secretive, but nevertheless . . ."[47] Begin drew most of his information from newspapers and from the radio. In 1948 he still did not know the city he lived in, Tel Aviv. He relied more on political and historical intuition than on real knowledge of the doings of Zionist diplomacy. In his meetings with journalists and with members of the UN commission, he expressed general and overly simplified assessments. Begin always left the impression, which was unfounded, that Granados and Fabregat, the Latin American members of the UN commission, were close to the Irgun's position on the boundaries of the future state, but the position taken by the Jewish Agency prevented them from supporting a different program. There is no historical eivdence to support this claim.[48] In March 1946 he told a *Herald Tribune* correspondent that he was not pleased by the fact that the Palestinian question had been transferred to the United Nations, although he appreciated the importance of discussion of the issue at an international forum.[49] Begin often claimed that at the end of 1946 he had foreseen the possibility that the British would leave Palestine, and that in the end of 1947 he had surmised that the Arab states would invade. There is no proof that he adapted the Irgun's structure in accord with these assumptions or readied it for the approaching war.[50]

Begin ruled the Irgun command by his moral authority. Actually, he was dependent on the judgement of those under him with regard to the tactical and operational aspects of the Irgun's activity. Begin's lack of military experience, and more than that, his lack of operational control, had disastrous consequences – as proven in the bombing of the King David Hotel, the *Altalena* affair, and the massacre at Deir Yassin. Yisrael Galili, head of the Hagana, said in retrospect that Begin could be relied on, but he was easily influenced by his own men, especially in operational matters.[51]

The Irgun was an urban guerrilla force that between 1944 and 1948 numbered from several hundred to close to 3,000 at the height of its power.[52] Begin was full of praise for the commanders of the Irgun. He called Meridor "one of the best and greatest military commanders in Israel," and spoke of Amichai Paglin, the Irgun's operational officer, as a military genius. In fact, the Irgun based itself on sporadic activities by small forces, and its success was in propaganda, in Begin's ability to portray the underground's actions as in the service of a political end. In reality, however, the revolution was relegated to second place; the main emphasis was on military action.[53] Begin, in fact, ascribed the Great Powers' policy on Palestine as flowing directly from the activities of the Irgun. As for Britain he was convinced that prestige was central to the stability of imperial rule, without which Britain would have lost its hold on the colonies. Begin's absolute conviction of the importance of the Irgun operations is not supported by conclusive historical evidence.[54]

The Irgun was built on the ethos of fighters' solidarity, "the fighting family" as it was often termed.[55] As in other undergrounds, Begin's authority was forged without the members of the organization knowing him at all. In his first appearance before them, he was uncharacteristically nervous. That was before the battle for Jaffa. Within a short time he was forced to yield to their desire to press the assault following a first failure and had to intervene again when it was feared that Arab prisoners would be harmed by the Irgun fighters.[56] In his memoirs Begin wrote that the only breach of order occurred when Irgun members under Paglin's command had broken into a British military camp near Rehovot, to capture arms.[57] According to many testimonies, Begin was very sensitive about human lives. The period during which members of the Irgun were executed was especially trying for him. In the same way he was reluctant and hesitant when having to order the execution of traitors.[58]

The *saison*, during which Irgun members were handed over to the British police by the Hagana, was the most serious test of Begin's leadership. It was at this time that he made what was perhaps the most important decision for guaranteeing the continued existence of the Irgun – the decision not to take any action against the Hagana. The peril of civil war was a historical lesson of which Begin was deeply aware; this was also a sober calculation since the Irgun was in no position to stand against the much greater strength of its opponents. Begin wrote that in that period there was "a crisis of trust, the first and the last, between the command and the fighters." In fact, there was real opposition within the Irgun command to Begin's decision not to take retaliatory action.[59]

In essence, Begin did not examine the threat posed by the existence of an armed organization constantly challenging the policy line and authority of the Yishuv leadership. It is hard to assess how he would have acted had the historical roles been reversed. At a meeting between Irgun and Hagana representatives in October 1944, he refused to terminate the activities of the Irgun. "Our entire existence," he said, "depends on this war." Begin opposed the political hegemony of the Labor movement, but agreed in principle to end the secession if Ben-Gurion would assume the leadership of the struggle against the British. In effect, he wanted the majority to adopt his course of action.[60] Although the *saison* did not achieve its main objective, it did set clear boundaries for the Irgun.[61] Begin, however, relied on the "invisible hand" of history guiding the struggle of the Jewish people. He believed that ultimately the Hagana would be forced to fight against the British.

The operations of the Irgun have been amply described, but there is still some controversy as to their importance in the struggle against British rule. The King David Hotel explosion and the Deir Yassin affair, which gravely affected the Irgun's image, were not carried out under Begin's full control. On the other hand, the Irgun operations described as most damaging to the prestige of the British Empire – the hanging of the sergeants and the break in to the Acre fortress – came, in effect, as counteractions. In the decision to hang the British sergeants, Begin's credibility, and that of the Irgun as a whole, were on the line. At this point, Begin hesitated. He wanted to consult all the members of the command. This was not the last occasion on which he was to take a stand against Amichai Paglin. After finally making the decision, he sank into a deep melancholy. The hanging of the sergeants, however, stopped the executions of members of the Irgun.

The Irgun did not recognize the authority of the British courts, and refused to ask for pardons for its members as this would imply recognition of the British regime in Palestine. In *The Revolt* Begin wrote that the Irgun left the matter of whether or not to seek a pardon to the discretion of the members. This is a matter of dispute. After he had resigned as prime minister, the affairs of Dov Gruner and Meir Feinstein and the options that had been available to save them from execution by the British were to surface once again. To Bethell, Begin confided that the Irgun was taken by surprise and moved too slowly in planning the rescue of Gruner. Shmuel Katz, a member of the Irgun command, confirms that any request for pardon would have been considered as abandonment of the Irgun's essential struggle.[62]

The King David Hotel explosion was evidence of faulty communication, and the conflicting interests of the Hagana and the Irgun. It also made manifest Begin's lack of operational skills. He was utterly shocked by the large number of casualties and accused the British of not heeding the warnings that had been issued and of not evacuating the building. In a meeting with Yisrael Galili he asked that a committee be appointed to investigate the affair. There were real political reasons for terminating the cooperation among the undergrounds but in practice it appeared to be the result of the Irgun's assault on the center of British government and military headquarters.[63]

Whereas in the King David affair Begin had given full backing to Amichai Paglin, in the case of Deir Yassin, Begin gave his blessing to the fighters without in fact having any control over their actions. Begin opens *The Revolt* with an introduction that includes apologetics about Deir Yassin. He never abandoned his version, according to which this tragedy was the product of circumstances: not a massacre, but losses incurred as the result of a battle. Here too we see traces of the conception of leadership he believed in – he backed all actions performed by the Irgun under his command.[64]

The importance of the Irgun operations is still a subject of historical controversy. The Irgun failed to spearhead a movement of civil uprising, did not broaden its political influence in the Yishuv, and did not develop into a force able to decide the political or strategic course of the Zionist movement. Historical evidence is inclined to confirm that the Irgun's operations had considerable influence on public opinion, but did not necessarily have any significant effect on British policy in Palestine.[65] Comparison of Begin with leaders of national liberation movements such as Ho Chi Minh, Eamon De Valera, and Jomo Kenyatta has no foundation in historical reality. Begin did not become the leader of the Hebrew liberation movement and did not take power after independence was achieved. He remained the leader of a secessionist faction.

Altalena

The *Altalena* affair was a crossroads in the history of the State of Israel, and a turning point in the contest between the Labor movement and the Revisionists. Whatever may have been the causes of the confrontation, it was an

occasion in which one party overpowered another and imposed its authority. In the first half of 1948 Begin had failed to completely submit the Diaspora Staff in Paris to his authority. Nor was he able to impose his
instructions on the Irgun command and rank and file to enlist in the Israel
Defense Force (IDF) and hand over their arms. The *Altalena* affair also
brought into the open the disagreement on the future of the Irgun among
the members of the command in Palestine, and between them and the
heads of the Hebrew Committee of National Liberation and the Diaspora
Staff. It marked the nadir of Menachem Begin's leadership of the Irgun.

The UN General Assembly's approval of the partition plan in November 1947 had altered the Irgun's situation and undermined the significance
of its independent activity. 1948 was a year of confusion and error for the
Irgun, and of excessively slow adaptation to changing circumstances. At
the end of 1947, the challenge of convincing the breakaway undergrounds
to accept the authority of the Yishuv institutions had become acutely per-
tinent. In September of that year, representatives of the Jewish Agency
executive asked the Irgun to suspend its activities until the UN had voted
on the partition resolution, but were met with a refusal. The representatives of the General Zionist party and of the religious factions, which took
an intermediate position, restrained the resolve of David Ben-Gurion and
of the leaders of the socialist camp to bring the Irgun to heel.

Begin found himself in a situation over which he did not have full
control. He had to maneuver carefully between several fronts. He was
uncertain how events would unfold until May 1948. He had to take a stand
against members of the command, such as Paglin, and members of the Diaspora Staff and the HCNL, especially Hillel Kook, who forcefully advocated an extremist position. On the other side, Begin had to conduct patient
negotiations on the future of the Irgun and its integration into the IDF.
This time he was truly unsure of his ability to win the Irgun members over
to his views.[66]

Begin was well aware of the Irgun's weakness and his ability to impose
his will on both the internal or the external fronts. At the height of its
strength, in the middle of 1948, the Irgun was able to muster no more than
a few thousand, less than half of them in the combat force, which itself was
poorly equipped and armed.[67] In *The Revolt*, Begin writes that at the end of
January 1948 the Irgun drew up four strategic plans – for Jerusalem, Jaffa,
Lydda–Ramleh, and the densely populated Arab area known as the
Triangle. It is not clear how he intended to carry them out. The only
military operation in which the Irgun took part during the War of Independence, the main source of his pride, was the conquest of Jaffa.[68]

At the end of April 1948 the Hagana and the Irgun had reached an
agreement of sorts, but the conflict of opinions within the Irgun command
did not subside.[69] On May 15, Begin delivered his first speech after leaving

the underground. He began by saying that the Hebrew revolt had ended in triumph; "only thus" had the state come into being. The Herut movement, to be established by "the great fighting family," was to fight for the principles he enumerated in his speech within the framework of the laws of the Jewish state. Begin announced that the Irgun would cease to exist within the boundaries of "the independent Hebrew state." He left an opening for the Irgun to continue its activity in Jerusalem, which had not yet been proclaimed the capital city. The State of Israel had come into being, he said, but "the homeland is not yet liberated."[70]

On June 1, 1948, the negotiations between the Hagana and the Irgun were concluded. The members of the Irgun were supposed to enlist in the IDF and the Irgun's arms and equipment were to be handed over to the army. A temporary staff was established – Begin, Meridor, and Paglin – to function until the enlistment of the Irgun members was finalized. The Irgun ostensibly ceased to exist. However, both the Irgun and Lehi still regarded Jerusalem as an extraterritorial region, and as an arena where they could engage in independent activity.[71]

The intentions in this period of the members of the Diaspora Staff, who were joined in France by the heads of the HCNL, are not at all clear. It seems that some of them, especially Hillel Kook, were for a while convinced that by declaring the establishment of a provisional government and launching "an offensive of conquest in the eventuality of a general conflagration" the Irgun could realize its decade-long aspiration to triumph in both the internal and external battle. At this critical stage, the committee had control of most of the monetary reserves financing the Irgun's operations. It was with this money that the Irgun's arms ship, the *Altalena*, was purchased.[72]

In letters to the command in Palestine on December 3 and 4, 1947, Hillel Kook told of the intention to dispatch a large ship with 6,000 immigrants that was scheduled to reach Tel Aviv at the beginning of February 1948. Kook estimated that the British army would have left the country by that time.[73] Begin was cautious. At that time, he was moving in the direction of establishing a political movement, but reinforcement of the Irgun with arms dovetailed nicely with his intentions. He, however, wanted the ship's arrival to be advanced to before the establishment of the state. At the same time, there were attempts in Paris to bring about cooperation between the Irgun and the Mosad l'Aliya Bet, a unit of the Hagana engaged, among other things, in bringing immigrants to Palestine illegally. But neither side was enthusiastic. The Diaspora Staff wanted to preserve its independence, and the Mosad refused to endanger its network of contacts and activity.[74]

On the night of June 11, 1948, the *Altalena* sailed from the port of

Port-de-Bouc in southern France, without the Diaspora Staff informing the Irgun command in Palestine. That same day a truce under UN supervision between Israeli and Arab forces was to go into effect. On the following day, Begin heard about the sailing of the ship on the BBC. This was neither the first time nor the last that he learned of a decisive occurrence in this manner. He dreaded the possible violation of the truce and of the agreement of June 1 with the IDF. Begin sought to delay the arrival of the *Altalena* and wanted to inform the government. Not everyone in the Irgun command concurred with this view.[75] When the ship set sail, writes Eliahu Lankin, the *Altalena*'s commander, the ship's radio transmitter broke down and contact between the *Altalena* and the world was severed. No arrangement had been made with the command in Israel in case of communication failure. But the *Altalena* did receive the messages transmitted to it, one not to approach the country's shores, and a second message telling it to sail towards Kfar Vitkin.[76]

Begin first informed government representatives of the arrival of the ship only at midnight on June 15, 1948. At a meeting at the Irgun headquarters, he received general consent from the government representatives Levi Eshkol and Yisrael Galili to the ship's arrival. Begin now had to work on two fronts. He had to convince the government to set aside an agreed quantity of the arms aboard the *Altalena* for Irgun members in the IDF, and at the same time to convince the Irgun members to enlist in the IDF and to accept the arms distribution as agreed. It seems that in response to pressure from members of the command, especially Paglin, Begin now asked that Irgun members participate in the unloading of the arms aboard the ship, and that the warehouses in which the arms were to be stored be placed under joint watch.[77]

The most controversial event occurred on the beach at Kfar Vitkin. Begin lost control and buckled under the pressures of the moment. The Irgun decided to unload the arms aboard the *Altalena*. Members of the Irgun at Kfar Vitkin felt besieged and began to round up reinforcements. Begin sent two aides to Tel Aviv to inform the press of what was going on. For the next two days Tel Aviv appeared to the Irgun command as "a place of refuge." On two occasions, Paglin and Meridor, fearing for Begin's life, refused to allow him to leave the beach area and meet with Yisrael Galili or General Dan Even, commander of the regiment guarding the shore.

Paglin, commander of the Irgun fighters on the beach, an energetic, impetuous, and uncompromising man, clashed with Begin over the *Altalena*. He was convinced that the Irgun had been drawn into a trap. Ever since the *saison* he had differed with Begin on a number of important issues. Now he returned an arms boat to the ship without consulting Begin. He wanted to sail out to sea with the *Altalena* and find another beach for unloading the arms. The authority of the government, the truce, and the position of the UN forces were all secondary in his considerations. After the clash with Paglin, Begin put Meridor in charge of the Irgun forces on the beach instead. Paglin's actions during the next two days are not wholly clear. It is likely that he tried to assemble Irgun fighters at the Kfar Vitkin shore and afterwards in Tel Aviv. It seems that the Irgun at Kfar Vitkin was deployed in "deliberate military formation."[78]

Begin expected that things would work themselves out and thought the army would not move against the Irgun. On June 21 he was handed an ultimatum. It was drafted by Galili and signed by Dan Even. Begin was orderd to turn over all the arms that reached the shore for safekeeping, and to begin talks with the IDF's High Command. The immigrants aboard the *Altalena* would be allowed to travel to camps designated for them. Begin was allowed ten minutes to respond. Begin apparently did not take the ultimatum seriously. The time allotted for a reply seemed ridiculous to him, and he did not respond.[79]

It is not clear who fired first. There are also different versions as to when Begin decided to board the *Altalena*. It appears that on the advice of Merlin and Meridor, Begin agreed to board the ship and to look for a way to end the crisis when it reached Tel Aviv. Begin gathered his men for a farewell muster. Just as he began to speak, they came under fire. About thirty people dashed to a nearby motor launch to escape to the ship.[80]

Begin's decision to board the *Altalena* was one of the most unfortunate decisions of his political life. Interior Minister Yitzhak Gruenbaum, a key figure at the time in the contacts between the government and the Irgun, said that by boarding the ship to try his luck with the help of the masses, Begin made himself suspect.[81] Shmuel Katz was convinced that the only explanation of the *Altalena* affair was that it was a plot devised to get rid of Begin. According to Katz, in May 1948 the Irgun was at the height of its popularity. Exploiting his unrealistic naivety and trust, a "crafty, scheming person" had set a trap for Begin. Begin, in a state of shock, was enticed into going aboard the ship, and thereby exposed himself to the charge of having led an armed rebellion. Afterwards, he erred again. Exhausted, his nerves frayed, he hurried to deliver a speech.[82] Meridor asserts that the truth will never be known. The central problem was the lack of direct communication with Ben-Gurion. Increasingly the main culprit in the eyes of the Irgun people came to be the intermediary, Yisrael Galili.[83]

In *The Revolt*, Begin offered the most general account imaginable of the affair.[84] He confirms that his intention was to sail to Tel Aviv in order to save the situation, and that the Irgun fighters there tried to force their way to the ship. He always regretted that the ship did not arrive before the establishment of the state. Only years after the event did he put forward a version of his own containing clear allegations.

The *Altalena* sailed from Kfar Vitkin to stand in the waters off the Tel Aviv shore, between the headquarters of the Palmach and of the Kiryati regiment. "Nothing is going to happen," said Begin aboard the ship. Lankin prevented him from going ashore, out of fear for his life. The Irgun began to unload the arms, and the ship came under fire. In the meantime, Irgun fighters began to pour towards the beach. Soldiers, including the Irgun battalion in Be'er Ya'acov, deserted their bases. IDF road blocks were run. The headquarter buildings on the shore were attacked. In the end, the Irgun fighters took control of a strip of beach opposite the ship. Begin shouted to the shore to stop firing, and the *Altalena* put up a white flag. The Palmach ceased firing after the unloading had stopped. Afterwards, the cannon shell that hit the *Altalena* was fired. This time Begin wanted to be the captain who is the last to abandon his ship. Lankin had to force him to get off. The man who brought him ashore said that "he looked like someone whose world had suddenly collapsed on him." Begin reached the city's shore barefoot, his hair in wild disarray, protected by his men, who brought him to Irgun headquarters.[85]

That same evening, Begin broadcast a lengthy speech in which he described what had happened, including the vicious attempt, according to his claim, to kill him. He was highly emotional and cried. That made a deep impression. At a meeting of the Herut Central Committee in February 1949, he said to his comrades: "The 'men with the Stens' didn't weep. One man cried, and he is proud of the tears he shed that night." He added that the *Altalena* affair was not what led to the decision to dismantle the Irgun. The speech reflects the great emotional stress under which Begin was operating. He admitted to fearing that the Irgun fighters might revolt against him and issued a clear threat: "anyone who does not immediately release our officers and soldiers – his doom is sealed."[86]

At a news conference he called that night he confessed that "Today is one of the rare days in my life in which I do not know what exactly it is we must do." He confirmed that IDF soldiers who belonged to the Irgun, had deserted their camps. Their continued enlistment in the IDF was not guaranteed. A public statement issued subsequently by the Irgun asserted that the Irgun did not recognize the provisional government.

That same night, Ben-Gurion decided to take vigorous action against the Irgun. A curfew was imposed on Tel Aviv. An unsuccessful attempt was made to discover where Begin spoke from. Metzudat Ze'ev, the Revisionist headquarters, was attacked, and an assault on Irgun headquarters was also planned. In the morning it was decided to cease all actions against the Irgun. The General Zionists, but mainly the religious cabinet ministers who resigned, prevented the confrontation from worsening. Ben-Gurion was not interested in a government crisis at the end of the truce period.[87]

Rebellion had not been Begin's intention, but he was a party to a situation of mutiny which put the democratic structure of the new state to a severe test. The Irgun command and Begin appear to have stood helpless in the face of the swift pace of events and were not immune to the temptations offered by the approaching independence. Above all, the *Altalena* affair bared the fact that political rivals cannot act only on the basis of their interpretation of the other side's intentions. That was Begin's principal error. It was not intentions that were important, but the dangers and opportunities created by the historical situation. The provisional government, or to be more exact, the leaders of the Labor movement, were aware that the Irgun posed a threat and challenge to government and democracy and were ready for a final showdown, at whatever cost.

The *Altalena* affair ended in a moral and political victory for the socialist camp. The disbandment of the Irgun was now only a question of time. Within the Irgun itself there was anxiety and opposition to the dismantling of the underground. Begin had to restrain his men. Until September, the Irgun concentrated its activities in Jerusalem. However, there was only the slimmest of chances that the government would allow the Irgun to operate there on the claim that Jerusalem was outside the bounds of the state's sovereignty. There was still a chance that the Irgun would be dismantled as part of an agreement with the government. Minister of the Interior Yitzhak Gruenbaum conducted the negotiations with Begin. The main point of the agreement was supposed to be the final disbandment of the Irgun, enlistment of the Irgun fighters in the IDF, and a general pardon for all those held in detention. But on September 17, Jerusalem was shocked by the assassination of Count Folke Bernadotte, United Nations envoy to the Middle East, by Lehi operatives. The government's reaction was swift and decisive. On September 20, Shmuel Katz, the Irgun's representative, was handed an ultimatum to disband the organization. On the following day, he announced the end of Irgun activity in Jerusalem as well. All that remained now was to get the members of the Diaspora Staff to accept the judgment. This time, Begin was determined.[88]

The *Altalena* affair continued to churn up political life in Israel, especially in the Ben-Gurion period. Begin's requests to set up an inquiry commission were rejected. There were few issues that so enraged Begin as the accusations leveled at him in this affair. Ultimately, he contented himself with the conjecture he heard from Shimon Peres, who refused to make it public, that Ben-Gurion had been misled. The wheel of history again came to a halt pointing at Yisrael Galili. Ben-Gurion, however, rejected the contention that Galili had acted contrary to government guidelines.[89]

5

Leader of the Opposition, 1949–1977

The "fighting family"

Begin entered Israel's political scene as a nationalist revolutionary. Years would pass before he would change his image – the parliamentarian who observes all the rules, the gentleman who awaits his turn, was a much later arrival on the scene. Following the *Altalena* affair, Begin was to achieve one of his most important political accomplishments. After a bout with the Revisionist party he was to become the sole heir of Ze'ev Jabotinsky.

In August 1948, Begin announced the formation of the provisional center of Herut, which made hasty preparations for the first Knesset election campaign. In these elections Begin made a final effort to conclude his historical debt to the various segments of the Revisionist camp. He placed Hillel Kook, Shmuel Merlin, and Eri Jabotinsky, all of the Hebrew Committee of National Liberation, on the Herut election list. He himself was followed on the list by the radical poet Uri Zvi Greenberg. Begin compiled the list of candidates by himself, and the party's center approved it. The negotiations with the leaders of the Zionist Revisionists on a joint appearance in the elections came to naught. In the first test of strength they crumbled, gaining as we have seen no more than a fifth of the delegates in the elections to the Revisionist national convention, and failing to win even one seat in the elections to the Knesset. Begin's leadership of the "fighting family" appeared to be incontestable. Henceforth, any challenge to Begin's leadership was to lead to a crisis in Herut. The first such crisis was already at the threshold. Despite a great deal of optimism in Herut about the upcoming elections – so much so it was even thought there was a chance to form the next government – Herut won only fourteen seats in the first Knesset. It began its parliamentary life as part of the opposition.[1]

The principles espoused by the Herut movement in those early days were radical. First and foremost, it asserted that "The Hebrew homeland, whose territory extends on both sides of the Jordan, is a single historical and geographical entity." The movement's platform included the essence of Begin's foreign policy outlook. It referred to the very same powers he was to refer to in his first speech as prime minister. The Herut movement, it was said, "will fight to foster relations of friendship and understanding between the Hebrew state and the United States." The Soviet Union appeared in the same category, and a special appeal was directed to "the great French nation." In domestic policy, Begin was thoroughly eclectic – both populist and liberal. Herut called for war against all forms of "trusts and monopolies" and for nationalization of basic industries and public utilities, for land reform, progressive taxation, and guaranteed housing for every citizen. The platform called for the drafting of a national constitution. The structure of government he proposed resembled the American system. Education was to be provided by the state free of charge and was to be based on the indivisibility of the homeland, love of the homeland, and military training. Another element in education would be "the sacred values of the nation, its past and tradition." Sabbath observance would be obligatory. All the citizens of the country would comprise the army's reserve force: "Every citizen – a potential soldier."[2]

In August 1948, Begin declared that Herut is "a popular, fighting, progressive and creative movement." In its struggle against the government in Israel it was not fighting against socialism, because the government was not socialist. "It is a regime," said Begin, "whose fascist nature is most prominent." It was a regime of one party only that seized all the key positions for itself, bringing other parties in only as camouflage. Let us not be afraid, he added, to stand up against it "in one front with the Communists, and even with Mapam."[3] But domestic policy was always secondary to Herut's aspirations on the external domain. At the opening of the first national council of Herut, Begin said that Herut's only orientation was liberation of the homeland, and that this policy had to be backed by military strength. He accused the "official" statesmen of not readying a military force for the coming battle. He then said that foreign policy and domestic policy should not be separated.[4]

In 1950 the first crisis in the Herut movement began to come to a head. Begin's leadership was challenged on two fronts: by the Revisionist veterans headed by Grossman and Altman, and the former leaders of the HCNL – Merlin, Kook, and Jabotinsky, who organized into an opposition faction. Begin tried to give the new movement a popular character and to get away from the stigma of continuous political defeat that attached to the Revisionist party in the Yishuv. After the Revisionists' rout in the first elections, an agreement crystallized according to which the Zionist Revisionists would continue to operate in the Diaspora and the Herut movement in Israel. The Revisionist leaders were not all of one mind concerning the agreement; Meir Grossman opposed it.[5]

In the 1950s, Begin spent long periods abroad. Merlin and Kook tried to widen their support in the party and to isolate Begin as much as possible. In fact, an opposition faction called Lamerhav arose, headed by Merlin; Shmuel Tamir was one of its major activists. This faction contended that Herut was concentrating on foreign policy issues and neglecting issues of central concern for the society and state – economic affairs, the religious domain, relations with the Arab minority, and the state's relations with the Diaspora. Hillel Kook was particularly critical of the hierarchical structure of the party and its ideological narrow-mindedness.[6] Begin was attacked for suppressing all independent thought in the movement. Begin succeeded in blocking Merlin and his faction at the national council that convened in December 1949, and packed the executive with his supporters. In 1950 municipal elections were to be held. Begin was characteristically optimistic. He declared that Herut was on its way to taking over the regime. The election results fell far short of expectations, and served as a basis for a sharp attack on Begin. The opposition prepared for a decisive contest at the second national Herut convention, which was to be held in February 1951.

The Herut movement now reached one of its low points. After the establishment of the state there had been several waves of departure – by Revisionist activists and also by a number of former Irgun commanders.[7] In 1950 Eri Jabotinsky and Hillel Kook left the party's Knesset faction. As demands to remove Begin increased, he apparently decided to resign at the party convention along with Landau and Meridor. In the meantime the internal power struggle continued, and before the convention veteran Revisionist activists were enlisted as a counterweight to Merlin's faction. All were preparing for the anticipated confrontation at the beginning of 1951.[8]

The second Herut convention was held in February 1951 in Netanya. At the convention there was organized opposition, headed by Merlin, to the chairman of the movement. Begin's opening address failed to still the opposition. On the next day he announced that he was not a candidate for the movement chairman. He later retracted this statement. Bader weighed the balance of forces and discovered that the Lamerhav faction did not have a majority. The party came to the elections held that year divided and in disarray. Merlin was removed from the Knesset list. Herut's candidates were now for the most part loyal supporters of Begin, with a sprinkling of Revisionist leaders.[9]

Herut suffered a humiliating defeat in the Knesset elections of July 1951. Its Knesset strength declined by half, from fourteen to eight seats. The number of voters for the party declined, even though the overall number of voters participating in the election had nearly doubled. That was a blow too hard for Begin to bear. The elections seemed to confirm the charges of his opponents. Begin relapsed into one of his black moods and resolved to

82	*The Man*

leave political life. He had never been as close as he was in that year to
retiring from politics. He left with his wife for Italy, as in other instances
leaving the political wrangling to his followers. He also left a letter of resignation from the Knesset and asked that it be presented before he returned
to the country.

Begin's political fate was in the hands of a master politician, Yohanan
Bader. Bader withheld the letter of resignation and saw to it that nothing
final happened in Begin's absence. He persuaded Landau and Meridor not
to resign. When Begin returned he decided to take an extended vacation
and Ben-Eliezer was named acting chairman of the movement. Begin
registered as a clerk in the law office of the Irgun's former attorney, Max
Kritchman, and began to prepare for his bar exams. He was not sworn in as
a Knesset member.[10]

What brought Begin back to the Knesset was the campaign against the
reparations agreement with Germany. The day he took his Knesset oath was
perhaps the stormiest day in the Knesset's history. It was on that day,
January 7, 1952, that he delivered his fiery speech at Zion Square in Jerusalem, after which the crowd assembled there stormed the Knesset. Scores of
policemen and even more civilians were injured. In his Knesset address,
Begin clashed with Knesset Speaker Yosef Serlin after an exchange of harsh
invectives with Ben-Gurion, whom he called a hooligan. The speaker
demanded that he retract, and prevented him from continuing. Begin replied
that if he could not speak in the Knesset, no one would. Serlin announced a
recess. Landau and Bader rushed to the platform to protect their leader.
Begin was suspended from Knesset debates for three months.

Fruitless opposition

In the early 1950s Begin concerned himself mainly with foreign affairs and
defense issues. He mercilessly attacked what he regarded to be the weakness of Israeli diplomacy, its submissiveness before the superpowers, and
the strategy of "hit and run" reprisal actions against terrorist incursions
from neigboring countries instead of exploiting the opportunity for conquest and liberation of the homeland. That was until one day before the
Sinai campaign in 1956, when he was invited to the home of the prime
minister. Ben-Gurion, running a fever, informed him of the plans for war.
As expected, Begin gave his blessing, but only for a short time. In the
middle of November 1956, after the government's decision to withdraw
from Sinai, Herut submitted a no-confidence motion.[11]

By the time Ben-Gurion resigned the premiership in June 1963, Begin
had taken his first steps towards erasing the stigma of delegitimation with
which he had been branded from the time he entered the political arena.

Instead of the revolutionary hurling challenges at the political order, on to the scene came the gentleman and parliamentarian with clemency to his rivals, advocating the unity of the nation and representation of the general interests of the people.

In the 1950s and 1960s the demographic composition of Israeli society had undergone far-reaching change as a result of a massive influx of immigrants. In the elections held in July 1955 Herut had doubled its strength. Begin felt that he had penetrated the hearts of the new Israelis in the immigrant camps and towns. In his view, his failure in the 1951 elections could be attributed to the fact that because they did not know Hebrew he had not been able to address them directly and had to use an interpreter. Herut came to rely on Begin's rhetorical powers and on the authority he projected as a leader.[12]

Begin denounced the government's selective immigration policy and at mass protest rallies called for an acceleration of immigration from Morocco. Herut's entrenchment among the immigrants was not to be effected by presenting a radical platform. It was accomplished, rather, by a combination of populism, rhetorical skill, attentiveness to the symbols of the Jewish tradition, and constant harping on the theme of the bureaucratic tyranny of the socialist regime.

The number of Sephardic candidates on the Herut Knesset list rose during the 1960s, but in most instances they were not new immigrants. For a march of veterans of the "generation of the revolt" in Tel Aviv in April 1958, Herut still assembled representatives of the Revisionist tradition–Betar units, Herut leaders, Revisionist party veterans, conquerors of Jaffa, and defenders of Jerusalem in 1920.[13]

Expedient considerations and a desperate search for political alliance compelled Herut not to abandon its commitment to the middle class, free enterprise, and some liberal principles. Herut's class orientation, and Revisionism's for that matter, was never resolved. Courting disparate classes, Herut lost elections and also rose to power. In the 1950s, the Zionist Revisionists argued that Begin erred in not basing his movement on the middle class and in not developing a clear anti-socialist front. The proletariat, they said, was in the hands of the labor movement.[14] The success of the General Zionists in the elections to the second Knesset seemed to confirm their contention.

Contrary to his usual practice, Begin opened the third Herut convention in April 1954 with a comprehensive lecture on domestic and economic issues. He said that in 1949 the nation had been promised that it would be given a constitution. Herut, he said, will fulfill that promise in order to protect the people from assaults on their liberties. In the economic realm he called for increased capital investment, elimination of foreign currency controls, an end to discrimination in tax payment – especially unfair tax advantages for kibbutzim enterprises belonging to the Histadrut (General Federation of Labor). Waste in production must be eliminated, monopolies and cartels broken, free trade unions established, and compulsory arbitration instituted for resolving labor disputes. An economy of free initiative and competition is a more efficient and cheaper economy, said Begin. He also maintained that Herut was not fighting for the interests of a particular social stratum. As a nationalist movement, it is the only movement that believes in the common denominator shared by all social strata, in the economic domain as well.[15]

What kept Begin from adopting a bourgeois orientation was his natural penchant for historical reasoning, his nationalist fervor, populist rhetoric, and lack of genuine interest in economic affairs. The view that there is a stable division in society between the bougeoisie and the proletariat, which comes to expression in respective support for the right and for the labor movement, was never substantiated in Israeli politics, but significant social changes and the degeneration of political norms were increasingly suited to Begin's style of leadership and simplistic rhetorics.

The major feature of Herut's political activity in the decade between 1955 and 1965 was to be the search for alliances that would enable it to present itself as a viable alternative to the rule of the socialist Mapai party. The potential allies were the bourgeois parties of the right. To form an alliance unifying the right – a goal the right had desired for two generations – Begin had to marshal forces for a contest within Herut. The merger with the General Zionists, who since the beginning of the 1960s had called themselves the Liberals, had been made conditional on the formation of a Herut faction within the Histadrut. However, the only substantial organizational apparatus inside Herut, the National Labor Federation headed by Eliezer Shostak, was opposed to that.

The National Labor Federation had interests of its own, and since the 1930s had developed ways of its own for contending against the left. The contest within Herut in the 1960s over the formation of a faction in the Histadrut became a general contest for control of Herut. Although the National Labor Federation politicians lost their battle in 1963, together with Shmuel Tamir and his supporters they continued to plan for a showdown with Begin and his camp until 1966.

At its seventh national convention, held in January 1963, the Herut movement approved the establishment of a Herut faction inside the Histadrut, the Blue and White faction. Begin carefully guarded his own position on the issue, but in the end threw all his weight behind the convention's decision. His victory was a condition for the merger with the General Zionists. The National Federation activists were defeated in a secret ballot. Attempts to prevent the party from forming a Histadrut faction, including a legal battle headed by Shmuel Tamir, proved of no avail.

The intention now was not to topple the queen but to take her in her own garden.[16]

Before the municipal elections of 1950, Begin had summarily rejected a proposal by Yisrael Rokah, the mayor of Tel Aviv, for cooperation with the General Zionists. After the 1955 elections, when the strength of both parties had become more or less equal, Begin called for a merger. He made public his letter to Peretz Bernstein, leader of the General Zionist party. Serlin, Bernstein's rival for the party leadership, contended that the way the call was made was an indication that Begin's intentions were not serious. Bernstein denied that talks between the two parties had been held.[17] The negotiations between the two parties were resumed in the fall of 1957. This time the tendency to a merger coincided with a test of strength within the General Zionists. A group of party activists headed by Yosef Sapir, Elimelech Rimmalt, and Yosef Serlin, wanted to oust the old guard of the party headed by Bernstein. The talks failed. Rimmalt, who was head of the General Zionists faction in the Histadrut, told the Herut leaders that if they wanted a merger they had first to form a faction within the Histadrut. Most importantly, however, the talks indicated that ideological differences took second place to a dividing up of power.[18]

Mapai made a gross blunder in the early 1960s by failing to bring the Liberals into the coalition. In November 1961, when the new government was presented, Begin said in the Knesset that the religious Zionists knew that it would be possible to form a government without Mapai. Moshe Shapira, the leader of the National Religious Party, smiled from his seat. In turning to the Liberals, Begin recalled that Ben-Gurion had said that "the Liberals should be brought into the government, for if not they will draw close to Herut."[19] That, it turns out, was a prescient forecast. In its moment of crisis at the time of the Lavon affair, the leaders of the torn and divided Mapai devoted their energies to ensuring the unity of the left and amalgamated with other left-wing parties to form the Alignment. At the same time, the Herut leadership succeeded in overcoming internal opposition to cooperation with the Liberals. In August 1961, the Liberals still resisted Begin's appeal that they form a bloc for the elections. The Liberals' attempt to adorn their list with the veteran Zionist leader Nahum Goldmann failed. Begin persisted in his appeals to the Liberals. In talks at the beginning of 1965 he offered exceedingly generous concessions. An agreement on the establishment of a Herut–Liberal bloc, Gahal, was reached in February of that year, and signed on April 25. Simcha Ehrlich, Begin's most important ally in the future, was at that time opposed to the new partnership, but ultimately it would be the collaboration between him and Begin that guaranteed the stability of the political alliance between the two parties. Even though Herut was almost twice as strong as the Liberals in the Knesset, seventeen seats to the Liberals' ten, Begin promised the Liberals a ratio of twenty-two Herut candidates to eighteen Liberal candidates in the first forty places on the joint election list. From now on the Liberals were to guard this agreement zealously.[20]

The platform of the new parliamentary bloc obscured ideological differences in matters of state and foreign policy, as well as their different approaches in the economic realm. Herut's emphatic formulations with respect to relations with Germany were softened, as was its attitude to the indivisibility of Eretz Yisrael, and its slogan about both banks of the Jordan was completely toned down. Herut now spoke instead in general terms of the Jewish right to the Land of Israel in its historical entirety.[21] The economic conception was woven of threads taken from here and there and was based on free initiative, competition, and a progressive social policy. The sections dealing with religion and state were made simplistic.[22]

During the entire period of Ben-Gurion's premiership, right up to his resignation in June 1963, he and Begin engaged in blistering and ugly verbal attacks on each other. "The clown from Herut," "silly Fascist," "demagogue"; and on the other side, "quisling," "maniac," "murderer" – were only some of the invectives they hurled at one another. It is hard to say where in those battles the personal animosity ended and political expedience began. In May 1963 Ben-Gurion charged that the leaders of Herut "glorified, lauded, and bore on high the name of Hitler, and posited him as the model of a leader of a national movement . . ." Ben-Gurion at that time was deeply anxious about the future of the state if he were to step down. In private letters he warned that the state might be destroyed if Begin came to power.[23]

Herut did not manage to turn the Lavon affair, which in the 1960s was to lead to a split in the Labor movement, to its immediate advantage. The Lavon affair was a traumatic crisis in the history of Mapai, the leading party of the Labor movement. For years, the political establishment was embroiled in an ugly struggle for power; the pretext being the accusations that Pinchas Lavon, when serving as defense minister in the early 1950s, authorized military intelligence to conduct sabotage acts against British and American installations in Egypt and cast the blame on the Egyptians.

Developments in the Labor movement clearly substantiated Begin's oft-repeated claim that rot and corruption had set in. In 1961 Ben-Gurion found it difficult to form a government and the task was handed to Finance Minister Levi Eshkol. It was hard not to sense Begin's derisiveness, and nearly exultant pleasure, at the way Ben-Gurion's last government was put together.[24] But, the results of the Knesset elections continued to delude and confound Herut, right up to its victory in 1977. Although in 1955 the party had doubled its strength, despite its earlier fear of the outcome of the election, in 1959 and in the early 1960s, it managed no more than to preserve its strength. The election outcome that proved to be of decisive importance for the future was the steady decline in the strength of the General Zionists, which forced them to grab hold of Herut's coat-tails before they went under altogether.

Ben-Gurion resigned from the government in June 1963 and the political climate in Israel underwent a total change. The bones of Jabotinsky were brought to Israel for reinterment, with government approval. For the first time, Begin found words of praise for a Mapai prime minister, the moderate and indulgent Levi Eshkol. When Golda Meir resigned her post as foreign minister in January 1966, Begin congratulated her warmly.[25] On the occasion of his fiftieth birthday, in 1963, he entitled his article in *Herut*, "How Good to Serve This People by This Movement." He was especially proud of the congratulations sent by political opponents. "Not for nothing," he wrote, "did we work to press home the difference between opponent and enemy."[26]

Self-defeated challengers

The crisis in Herut in 1966 came in the wake of unanticipated failure in the elections. The Herut–Liberal bloc (Gahal) won only twenty-five seats, less than the combined representation of the two parties in the previous Knesset. At the eighth convention of the Herut movement, held in June 1966, Begin's leadership of the party was challenged more seriously than ever before. The opposition, headed by Shmuel Tamir, came well prepared. Tamir had left Herut in 1953. In the mid-1950s he had joined a new political body called Koach Hadash (new force). The new party was not successful, and in 1964 Tamir had returned to political activity within Herut. He was a member of the election campaign staff and head of the information department. Tamir widened his influence within the party apparatus and drew close to party activists associated with the National Labor Federation. He attacked Begin loyalists and offered himself as candidate for the post of chairman of the executive.

During the convention it became evident that Begin and his supporters were in the minority. The opposition won a large majority in the elections to the presidium, and to the movement's mandates committee. Yohanan Bader suggested that the closing of the convention be postponed. Ben-Eliezer proposed an equal division of strength between the opposition and Begin loyalists on the standing committee, the key steering organ. The opposition rejected the proposal. In the end, Bader offered himself as candidate for chairman of the committee. He won by a narrow margin of

three votes, and achieved a measure of control over events at the convention.[27]

This time the opposition to Begin consisted not only of former Zionist
Revisionists and delegates associated with the National Labor Federation,
but also included a long list of party activists. Amichai Paglin, who had not
been active in the movement for years, took a last stance against his former
commander in the Irgun. Begin resigned as chairman of the movement.[28]
Begin's resignation did not cause the opposition to crumble. At the closing
session of the convention, Tamir sharply criticized the party's leadership
and picked out some senior members belonging to the "fighting family" for
special criticism. In the end, not mincing his words, he turned directly to
Begin and said: "From this moment I stand as opposition to you . . . not in
ideology but against the methods that came into view at this convention."
The convention closed without a new chairman of the movement being
elected. But a new center was chosen to the satisfaction of both camps.
Begin's departure seemed final. As in 1952, he left the wrangling to others.

Herut was run for a while by a provisional executive, leaving the field
open for a continuation of the contest. For the immediate future, Begin
loyalists agreed to share rule of the party with Tamir's supporters. In the
end, a questionable ruse was found for getting rid of Tamir. The pretext
was a letter sent by Hayim Amsterdam, a Tamir supporter, to *Ha'aretz* in
July 1966 under an assumed name. The letter was a vicious attack against
Begin. The chairman of the executive, Ya'acov Meridor, and the chairman
of the center, Dr Yohanan Bader, wasted no time. They ascertained the
identity of the real author hiding behind the assumed name and the false
address. Meridor dissolved the executive. Action was initiated against
Tamir and Amsterdam in the movement's disciplinary court. Tamir was
suspended from activity in the movement. Subsequently he left Herut and
formed the Merkaz Hofshi ("Free Center"). Tamir's entries and depar-
tures from Herut always seemed to be poorly timed.

The Herut executive convened at the end of February 1967 and
denounced the defectors. Dr Bader nominated Menachem Begin for the
chairmanship of the movement. It was hoped he would be able to reunify
the party and he was indeed elected without any opposition. There were
two abstentions. One of them was the new chairman.[29] Begin returned to
lead his party just before the Six Day War that was to change the history of
the Middle East and would be a critical crossroads in the history of Israeli
society.

When Begin returned to the leadership of his party in the spring of 1967,
all the future seemed to promise him was a permanent stature as leader of
the opposition. No one could have foreseen the twists and turns, the inter-
twining of victory and defeat, of the approaching decade. During this

decade, too, the political constellation composed of the Revisionists, the Liberals, religious Zionists, and defectors from the Labor camp began to take shape. That configuration, and the decline of the Labor movement, would secure Begin's rise to power.

In the early 1960s Begin had opposed the formation of a national unity government. Such a government seemed to him contrary to the norms of democracy.[30] However, the war crisis that developed in May 1967 led to an expansion of the government so as to include representatives of the Herut–Liberal bloc and of Rafi, a faction led by Ben-Gurion, Begin's sworn opponent. Initially, Begin thought of proposing to Eshkol that he offer the premiership to Ben-Gurion. That, however, was not feasible. Begin now insisted on bringing in Moshe Dayan as minister of defense. When he went to Jerusalem, in the beginning of June 1967, to take up his position as minister without portfolio, Begin first paid a visit to Jabotinsky's grave. Within days he would be pressing the government to hasten the conquest of Jerusalem and the Golan Heights.[31]

The period of the national unity government was one of mixed blessings for Israel. For Begin it was a period of rejuvenation. He limited his public appearances, and was careful in formulating his public utterances. For the first time, he appeared in kibbutzim. Dayan declared that in matters of security Begin was closer to him than Meir Yaari of the left-wing Mapam. Begin started to stress the similarities between the ideas of the Jabotinskian movement and those of Ben-Gurion's heirs. The field of opposition from the right was abandoned for a while to Shmuel Tamir's Free Center. Begin gloried instead in the splendor of importance. His remarks lost their bitter stinging edge. In interviews he said that residues from the past do not influence the present. In articles by journalists close to Begin it was said that he was playing a major role in shaping a policy opposed to withdrawal, and was thwarting all initiatives that entailed renunciation by Israel of territories occupied in the war.[32]

Begin's role in the national unity government between 1967 and 1970 and the positions he took will have to be carefully examined by future historians after the relevant documents and records become available. Yitzhak Rabin wrote in his memoirs, *Service Diary*, that Begin was a party to the cabinet decision of June 19, 1967, which stated that in return for a full peace agreement, Israel would be prepared to withdraw to the international boundary with Egypt and Syria; the fate of Judaea, Samaria, and the Gaza Strip, it was said, would be decided separately.[33]

The Herut–Liberal bloc formally joined the government at the end of 1969. The bloc had preserved its strength in the elections of that year and now, for the first time, it was to join forces with the National Religious Party in its claim for representation in the government. That was a sign for the future. Begin at first refused to join the government, demanding that the coalition agreement include a paragraph promising a compulsory arbitration law in labor disputes. But when the June 1970 Rogers initiative for the Middle East was made public he abandoned his opposition and joined the government.[34]

In August 1970 the Herut–Liberal bloc resigned from the government. The pretext was the acceptance of the Rogers Plan. For the first time, Begin said, Israel had undertaken to implement UN Security Council Resolution 242 and committed itself to the principle of withdrawal. At the stormy meeting at which it was resolved to resign from the government, he said that he could not be expected to renounce what he had believed all his life – "The homeland is in danger, the nation is in danger, and we are walking into a trap." No one at this time could possibly imagine what concessions Camp David would bring from Begin himself. The vote on resignation from the government revealed a clear division between Herut and the Liberals. The decision was passed by a vote of 117 in favor, 115 opposed. The Rogers Plan was undoubtedly not the only factor that led Begin to resign from the government. Apparently, the credibility of Herut as a viable alternative to socialist hegemony was tarnished in this ill-fated partnership. Begin returned to his office in Metzudat Ze'ev and to the opposition.[35]

The early 1970s were not promising for the Herut–Liberal bloc. Begin was immersed in petty matters. At the time of the internal crisis in Herut in 1972, most of the members thought the party had missed its opportunity to become a viable alternative to Mapai. They also believed there was no chance of revamping the party as long as Begin headed it. A year later, the Yom Kippur War was to carry the changes in Israeli society that had begun with the Six Day War a crucial step further. History began to beckon towards Begin, encouraging him to leave the sidelines and take up a position in the center of the field. He was not a party to the two central events of 1973 – the war and the establishment of the Likud. As head of Herut, however, he was in a position to reap the fruits of these developments. In doing so, he was to have new partners.

In 1969, General Ezer Weizman had lost all chance of becoming chief of staff, and Yosef Kremerman, a senior Herut politician, suggested to him that he join the government as a member of Herut. By means of a crafty maneuver, of which Begin was unaware, Kremerman himself was elected as a Herut candidate for a cabinet position, his intention being to relinquish his place in favor of Weizman. Weizman's nomination to the cabinet blocked the road for a natural contender to the post, Begin's old friend, Yohanan Bader, who now resigned angrily from the chairmanship of the party's Knesset faction. Other comrades of Begin also disappeared from the scene. The man thought to be Begin's heir, Aryeh Ben-Eliezer, was to die a few weeks later. Ya'acov Meridor had earlier lost his faith in Herut ever coming into power and had dropped out of political life.[36] Against this background, Begin received Weizman at Metzudat Ze'ev with open arms, "My friend, my general, my comrade," he exclaimed. With a touch of strained ingenuousness, or intentional forgetfulness, Weizman writes that he found himself in an alien world – the courtyard of what he called "the closed sect of Herut oldtimers," a place where all were blindly obedient to the commander and where the piercing glance of the leader silenced all opponents. Yet immediately after entering the cabinet, Weizman cast a vote in the government against Begin's view, in favor of Foreign Minister Abba Eban's planned visit to Germany. Begin did not forget that. On the night of the clash with Weizman at the eleventh Herut convention, he was to state that he had almost resigned from the government because of Weizman's vote. In August 1970, what was called the Kremerman faction mobilized votes against resignation from the government. Later, Weizman would write, "In the case of Begin, residues from the past have great weight in the way he regards people."[37]

After the Herut–Liberal bloc left the government, Weizman was named chairman of the Herut executive. Up until the eleventh convention, which was to be held at the beginning of December 1972, he worked to expand his influence in the party apparatus and the branches, and pushed out the Herut old-timers to the extent possible. Weizman was aiming to win a majority at the convention. At the convention itself it was apparent from the results of the elections to the presidium and the permanent committee that, as in 1966, the opposition to Begin commanded a majority. However, this time Begin crushed the contest before it took wing. He took a stand against Weizman and asked the party representatives to decide between the two factions. In an emotional speech he played on all the strings of the Herut members' loyalties and spoke of the great damage already done to the party by the contention within it: "Members of the Herut movement, who are you afraid of?" The opposition crumbled. Weizman resigned the chairmanship of the executive. He abandoned the arena before the struggle within Herut was decided.[38]

In a television interview Begin described Weizman as a "cute rascal" – everyone had been glad he joined the party, "but, in the final analysis, he lacked experience." Begin acted swiftly and resolutely. He appointed a new executive: Haim Landau as chairman of the executive, Yitzhak Shamir as Landau's deputy, and Eitan Livni as vice-chairman. It was expected that Weizman's supporters would be relieved of their roles in the party apparatus. At first, Weizman considered running against Landau but dropped the idea. The approaching elections, the damage caused by the crisis, and the pressures from the Liberals led to a compromise. Begin took Weizman's role for himself. He now occupied three posts – chairman of the movement, of the executive, and of the center. Weizman was named member of the executive and election campaign manager.[39]

The crisis in Herut occasioned a variety of responses and interpretations outside the movement. What could be detected in them was a sense of despair over the possibility of building an alternative to the Labor movement. Herut appeared to be subject to the authority of a single individual. Begin seemed so set in the past as to effectively prevent any political change. Analysts and commentators shared the view that the chances of the younger generation in Israeli politics to bring about reform in the country's political life were slim indeed.[40] After the convention Herut came under further attack for its support of the Bader-Ofer Law, which gave an advantage to the large parties in the distribution of excess votes in Knesset elections. Herut now seemed so deeply rooted in the establishment as to preclude the growth of smaller parties.[41]

Call of the times

In September 1973 the agreement establishing the Likud was signed. The new political body was composed of Herut, the Liberals, the Free Center, and what remained of the various factions that had deserted the Labor movement. The man who now stormed on to the political stage was Ariel Sharon. The ebullient ex-general had begun his talks with the leaders of Gahal while he was still in uniform. Undeniably, he was the effective force behind the agreement. In the course of the talks to form the Likud, Sharon threatened Begin, who tried at first to get out of setting up the new party, and the leaders of other factions that he would make their obstruction of the negotiations public. The agreement was reached, and Likud went forward to contest the elections. Apparently, Begin viewed initially the heterogeneous Likud as a threat to his authority, and moreover the Herut veterans had to overcome their animosity towards Shmuel Tamir.[42]

The results of the elections, held in late 1973, were received with some despair in the Likud. Begin himself was depressed. For the first time, all factions on the right had been united into a single bloc aimed at winning power, at a time as difficult to the ruling Labor party as could be imagined, but had won only thirty-nine seats. The Labor movement, which had recourse to all the tricks in its political armory, declined by only a few seats. The situation had been misread. The reaction of Israeli society simply took longer to ripen.[43]

After the Yom Kippur War, Begin changed his position on the establishment of a national unity government and called for its speedy establishment.[44] For the Labor camp the next years were to prove traumatic. For the first time, a strategic failing of the highest order combined with a crisis of leadership, an economic debacle, and moral and social malaise. Yet Begin was still not able to reap the benefits of this multiple crisis immediately. There was a fatalistic feeling in the country that he lacked what was needed to bring Herut to power. Prime Minister Yitzhak Rabin described Begin as an asset for the Labor movement, an "archaeological specimen." Begin responded sharply. He contended that Israel's credibility was being eroded because of "the prime minister's confusion" and because "vulgar comments do not comprise a program."[45] Begin was also accused of joining forces with Gush Emunim in its defiance of the government's authority and settlement policy for the West Bank.[46]

In these years Begin became ensnared in the most severe financial scandal in Herut's history, the so-called Tel-Hai Fund affair, in which party members were found to have had their fingers in the pot and taken loans at unrealistic interest rates. Herut was on the verge of financial collapse. The party leaders, and Begin foremost among them, had not kept the party's treasurers under effective accounting control. It was impossible to cover up the scandal, for the loans were taken not only from financial institutions but also from private individuals, including people of limited means whose money had been deposited in a savings fund. Begin made an arduous effort to raise money and to repay the party's debts.[47]

The election campaign of 1977 was conducted without Begin playing an active role. Management of the campaign was handed to Weizman, who had meanwhile re-established his image in the party. Before the elections, Begin suffered a severe heart attack. He came to a television debate with Shimon Peres looking frail and wan. Before the voting he called on the citizens to "free themselves from intimidation, to overcome fear, to uphold civic honor."[48] The Likud was victorious in that election.

Herut was unprepared to take the reins of power. This was an ill omen for the future. Although Begin was undoubtedly a skilled politician, he was not among the sharpest, shrewdest, or most talented people to come out of Revisionism. But the man whom all thought they knew would, in the first months of his government, surprise both followers and opponents alike.

Part II

The World View

6
Conception of Reality

Both as an inmate of Lukishki prison and in his solitary position at the head of the Irgun, Menachem Begin was aware that a man could create a reality of his own. Numerous remarks to that effect are to be found in *White Nights* and *The Revolt*. Facing the spot on the cell wall at which he gazed for countless hours, Begin wrote of the inner world of the prisoner: "By virtue of a 'self-command,' that magical creation of the human spirit, one reality gives way to another; the reality forced upon you vanishes entirely, and there appears, in all its splendor, that 'reality' for which the soul yearns."[1]

Most great political blunders stem in part from a failure to understand a given reality and are a function of the meaning the historical actor assigns to a specific event within the framework of a fixed conception. Established conceptions are slow to change, and their relative immutability renders them inappropriate and outmoded most of the time.

A conception of reality is a unique weave of various forms of knowledge and ideas into a framework of thought characteristic of a particular individual and is one of the modes whereby that individual relates to his environment. It allows him to map ideas and feelings, situations and events, within a single meaningful framework. This totality of beliefs, values, and expectations regarding "the world" or "reality" directly influences the manner in which a person's world-view is shaped. We generally assume that a person's inner world and the manner in which he acts are related. The implication of this is that an individual deals with historical events, which are by nature dynamic, with the help of a fixed conception. The conception of reality shapes the selective perception, unique to each individual that leads to differing interpretations of the self-same facts or events.

Evidently, each individual's conception of reality has a dimension of relativity, which depends, inter alia, on the structure of his personality and his personal experience. The importance of a conception of reality when studying a historical figure relates to its relative immutability. An objective perception of reality "as-it-is" is assumed to be impossible. The relationship between image and reality is all we have before us. We are concerned therefore with a phenomenon which is an integral part of an individual, and at the same time we must seek its roots in the historical and political realities of his time.[2]

Begin's perception of reality frequently reflected a quest for confirmation and validation of his world-view. When an examination of reality is transformed into an instrument in the service of an immutable policy, the chances are great that it will lead to misperceptions. Begin's romantic nationalism served to enhance reality, to glorify and ennoble it above the everyday, to sanctify it; it sought to make all actions meaningful, explaining and interpreting them within the content of historical lawfulness. In *The Revolt*, he wrote: "The voice of history is not mystical; it is a mighty factor in [shaping] reality."[3] The stress on the formal aspect – the juridical, as a rule – serves as a counterbalance for Begin, adding unity and rationality to his romantic outlook. The absolute nature of his views frequently left him incapable of distinguishing between the various shades of reality. However, his profound belief in himself, and his capacity for self-persuasion, often delayed the congruence between his views and the world about him.

Begin always contended that what is hidden behind the visible surfaces of historical events should be exposed; in perceiving realities, the roots of phenomena must be understood before reaching conclusions about courses of action. Not by chance was Ibsen's Dr Stockman his favorite hero. Recognition of the truth and a sense of justice enable an individual, or a minority, to stand up against the foolishness or viciousness of the majority, and resist illusory pleasure-seeking within a false reality.[4] Begin's inclination was to eliminate any ambiguity between realities and his world-view. Revisionism's pejorative term for an erroneous perception of reality was "impressionism," which meant being drawn into a superficial view of things; such was "the shifting calendar" – whether of the Jewish Agency or the Israeli government – which was late in comprehending realities and in applying cold logic to their analysis.

Begin tended to base his conceptions on quasi-scientific historical lawfulness that determines the behavior of individuals, societies and nations. Begin's cavalier generosity and condescending forgivingness toward his adversaries stemmed from the optimistic conviction that his beliefs would prevail in the end. In this, he was no different than a late eighteenth-century revolutionary: history and the nation will ultimately acknowledge the justice of his cause. Hence Begin's somewhat passive acceptance of reality: time, and the invisible hand of destiny, would ultimately resolve any difficulty or predicament, personal or national.

Begin always exhibited the self-awareness of a historical hero convinced of his ability to shape reality and affect its course. For Begin, the range of possibility offered by reality was wide. His inner contentment during the period of the revolt stemmed from his self-image as the leader of a national liberation movement whose triumph was assured. His period in the underground was also his most fruitful as a writer; it was during this time that he formulated most of his assumptions about policy, strategy, and the laws of history.

Begin's conception of reality exhibited a sharp duality. For him, reality existed, in effect, on two levels. One level was defined in ideal terms, the other inclined toward "empirical" proof – observation, definition of the situation, and the drawing of conclusions. These two levels rested upon two distinct forms of rationality: one was that of historical metaphysics which describes the hidden progress of national existence; the other was that of political realism. On the one hand, there was a totalistic, romantic conception of reality; on the other, a bald realism that claims to be realistic and rational. This is a profound inner contradiction, and the romantic element has frequently undermined the realistic political assumptions that Begin carefully assembled into unchallengeable axioms. On the one hand, Begin had recourse to a "voluntarist" view that rests on will, faith, and determination; on the other, action depends on a rationality derived from the given reality. At times these two elements are in balance, at other times they clash. The contradictions deepened when Begin himself ceased being a spectator and became the executor responsible for the reality in whose shaping he played a substantial, often central, role.

In September 1974, Begin declared: "In politics, as in logic, the conclusion will be correct only if the proof is genuine."[5] The kind of proof Begin relied upon can be seen in numerous citations from his writing. He laid down the principle as far back as the beginning of the revolt, in 1944:

In logic, there is a certain principle known ... as *petitio principi*. This principle requires that no supposition upon which one is about to build specific conclusions shall be considered acceptable as long as proof has not been provided that it is correct; otherwise, it would be possible to make false suppositions and build upon them a structure that will collapse as soon as they [the suppositions] are examined and analyzed.[6]

Indeed, Begin wrote, "there is no escaping the rules of logic." However, Begin's general outlook, the basic principles of the policies for which he strove throughout his life, rested upon principles of "natural right" or "historical right," which are totally beyond proof. Commonsense deduction can assist a lawyer in arguing his brief, but it is a questionable method of proving historical laws or establishing the ground for the shifting maneuvers of the politician.

Few can rival Begin's skill in taking an idea or fact and building it into a new pattern for the purpose of granting legitimacy to an existing policy or belief. On the whole, each fact or event figured as a truth in itself, but the link established between them lacks logic, or was unrelated to the reality in which policy is formulated. Formal or juridical proof was brought to vindicate an ideology which neither required nor was capable of proof. When arguments of this sort are brought forward to defend natural rights, they are intended either to mislead or as part of bargaining strategy.[7]

A rational analysis of reality served Begin as a means of reaching conclusions and undertaking a commitment to action. He attributed the aphorism "Truth implies drawing conclusions" to Jabotinsky's teachings. This truth can be deduced from history; it can be discovered by anyone as long as he employs the correct manner of proof.[8] Behind the laws governing the comprehension of reality and its interpretation lies a determinism that makes it meaningless, or even immoral, to conceal the goal towards which an individual strives, whether for himself or on behalf of a political movement or a nation. "With regard to the objective," Begin wrote "we affirmed, following Ze'ev Jabotinsky, that we must not conceal it by restricting it, or expand it by concealing it."[9] Begin, it seems, had an almost dialectic view in which true reality is concealed from sight, but at the same time he sought to present reality in a manifest and unconcealed fashion.

The method of political realism, which seemingly draws upon the Revisionist tradition, underwent a metamorphosis in Begin's world-view. It was a realism that considered reality in terms of *raison d'état*, but also in accordance with an immutable metahistorical superstructure. This superstructure is in a state of imbalance and tension with political reality, which is both concrete and in flux.

The metahistorical reality can be linked with concrete political goals only by sophistic rationalizations, and generally without specific means of attaining them. This relationship was usually absolutist, allowing choices that were sharply defined and final: defeat or victory, liberty or death. The elements of political realism were undermined by the projection upon reality of mystical and metaphysical elements. That is the "realistic reversal" of Revisionism as a whole. As an approach to international relations, political realism relates to a concrete reality. It attempts to adapt means to end and continuously assesses the balance of power. In other words, political realism constantly takes account of reality. In the Revisionist ideology, the process was reversed. Instead of careful assessment, or choosing the option promising the greatest possible gain, reality was adapted to basic ideological axioms. This illogical element was camouflaged by the use of terms drawn from the language of realpolitik. Reality was not seen as a constraint upon action. On the contrary, reality was constantly scrutinized for elements that could serve as leverage for its transformation and adaptation to the fixed final objective.

Begin had a total view of reality. By its very nature, such a view of reality as a single entity does not concern itself with details; it alters the context of facts and events, at times disregarding them completely. Instead of a detailed perception, Begin saw only generalized patterns that recur again and again. His was a "closed" vision of the world that tended towards the simplistic, but provided a sense of self-confidence with respect to its interpretation of reality, albeit at the expense of precision and comprehension.

When the conclusions of such a conception of reality are transformed into absolute imperatives for action defined in strategic or political terms, the way is laid to distorted perceptions that lead to failure. At the conclusion of a memorandum presenting the program of the Irgun, its commander, astonishingly, wrote: "This is the plan in its fundamentals. We do not go into detail, and the details which we have brought as points in the plan are not crucial. It is possible to change, to add or delete. [What is] important and decisive is the principle."[10] Elsewhere, he wrote that the order of the times was "growth and construction," to which he immediately appended another: "a war of liberation" – without noting the profound contradiction.[11] It was from such a conception of reality that the Lebanon War could be launched from a desire to wipe out a hostile entity defined as a total enemy, without examination of the logistics that would make the objective attainable. We must seek the factors in Begin's conception of reality that led to the omission of important details, thereby undermining the attainment of strategic goals of the first order.

Another expression of Begin's total perception of reality was his conception of time. His descriptions of events omitted entire periods, was general, and lacked clear chronological continuity. Begin's conception of time was "narrow." In a "broad" conception of time past, present, and future are interrelated in the individual's belief-system. In a narrow conception, there is no continuous link between times, and the stress is on one dimension of time – in Begin's case, generally the past.[12] The definition of time becomes absurd or meaningless when the terms employed are "eternity," "never," or only "forty years."[13]

In *World View and National Conception*, Begin wrote that "'realistic truth' is to be found by reversing Marx's maxim to read 'Consciousness determines existence,' which is perhaps the essence of idealist philosophy."[14] In *The Revolt*, he wrote: "Certainly the wish is father of the thought." The historical agent's consciousness determines his actions; the will is born of faith and is transformed into action; facts are less important. Begin's attitude toward reality appears to verge here on the symbolical. A fact represents a symbol or idea and appears in history in a particular form. Placing will at the center narrows the distance between what can be attained and what is mere aspiration.[15]

Begin's conception of reality was also influenced by ideological dogmatism. Dogmatism is generally related to closed thinking and to intolerance of opposing views. In this case, there is also a marked tendency towards categorization of individuals or groups according to their affiliations. Begin's images of various nations were highly stereotyped. He frequently conducted imaginary dialogues with "the Englishman," "the German," or "the Arab." Like all stereotypes, his too contained a grain of truth. However, as a basis for thought, stereotypes lead to error, distorted interpretations of phenomena, and to unfulfilled expectations.[16]

In such a dichotomous vision, the finer shades disappear.[17] The sharp choice precludes any attempt to seek the narrow outlet which can make the difference between defeat and narrow victory. An individual whose convictions are absolute and hermetically sealed tends to build up mechanisms which prevent reality from undermining his beliefs. However, when reality nevertheless breaks through and its effects are undeniable, it leads to a collapse of faith, and, at times, to a disintegration of the conception of reality.[18]

7
Historical Vista

Begin takes history and converts it into a politician's workshop, from which he is free to help himself at will, drawing conclusions from it by analogy or parallel to prove what is already part of his world-view or political disposition. There are of course lessons to be drawn from history, but the conditions for learning them are poor, the study generally fragmentary and imprecise. The attempt to understand a historical event is difficult for the professional historian, and doubly so for the dilettante one.

The failures of rulers and statesmen often stem not from a failure to learn the lessons of history, but from having drawn the wrong conclusions from it. At root, such learning from history is simplistic. It rests on superficial analogy, the use of common sense, and the drawing of parallels on the basis of crude similarity or difference. As a rule, the emphasis is on spectacular events, victories or defeats that receive a symbolic dimension in the collective memory transcending the specific circumstances that gave rise to them.

Studying the outcome of an isolated event, however momentous, and drawing conclusions from it leads to wrong judgments. The attempt to attune present policies to past events leads more to failure than to success. There is an inclination inherent in historical analogy to take account of final outcome rather than of the complex process that made the outcome inevitable. A spectacular event captures the human imagination, but it has little to teach. When translated into the language of principle or morals, it is unable to illuminate present reality, which is oblique, full of surprises, and constantly changing.

Begin was always fascinated by history. His books, articles, and speeches abound in historical analogies and examples. As described in *White Nights*, his conversations with his fellow-convicts were largely historical ruminations in which Begin interpreted the course of history, arguing with his companions' views concerning the inevitability of events. When President Reagan published his peace plan for the Middle East, Begin wrote to him: "There are cynics who sneer at history; they may sneer as much as they wish, but I adhere to the truth."[1] History, then, for Begin, was inseparable from present objectives.

Begin's view of history saw only broad brush strokes. It was selective, focusing mainly on the period of antiquity, the great revolutions of the eighteenth century, the nationalism of the nineteenth, and ultimately, as a result of his own direct experience, the upheavals between the two world wars. It appears that Begin learned from the history of that latter period, so as to learn nothing more from history. Hence the paradox: Begin's "historicism," with its eternal lessons and its fixed ideas, came to disregard facts and becomes fundamentally ahistorical. He often believed that he had understood the course of history, but history does not necessarily stand by those who claim so much from it.

Begin, it seems, was always making historical reckonings: for him, reinterpretation of the past was always a valuable exercise. He asserted absolutely, in a way that brooked no dissent, that the key role in the struggles of the 1940s had belonged to the Irgun, and that the British withdrawal from Palestine was the decisive step in the creation of the State of Israel. The entire history of Palestine was enlisted to serve this purpose. Any diminution of the contribution of the Irgun was labeled falsehood and distortion. *The Revolt*, as we have seen, begins with an apologia for Deir Yassin. In June 1955, he proposed an inquiry into the assassination of Arlosoroff, reopening an issue over which the Revisionist movement had once been defeated, and in a further effort to redeem the past during his second term of office as prime minister, he appointed a commission of inquiry. When the commission published its findings early in June 1985, he declared: "The issue was justice. It has been done."[2]

History as an idea or law of nature

To Begin, history was largely a mode of thought. In this, he was not far from the East European tradition. The wheel of history turns unceasingly in Eastern Europe, determining the destinies of individuals and nations, for better or for worse. Every event and deed has a "historical" dimension; the past invariably dominates the present. His historical thinking was generalized, simplistic, and analogical; it did not concern itself with processes, and it ignored the *longue durée* of history, preferring to attribute the greatest significance to the unique event – rebellion, war, or calamity – that changed the course of history. Yellin-Mor said of Begin that "he does not acknowledge historical processes. For him, the world stands still. He does not see the processes that unfold dynamically, like a movie. He sees the still pictures of a magic lantern, that can be passed through the projector as desired, back and forth."[3]

Begin did not assign importance only to the substance of an event; of equal importance to him was its external form, and the way it was integrated in the course of history. This is the "aesthetic dimension" of the historical act, also found among the radical right in Europe. Independence should be achieved through war, autonomously, without reliance on external powers. The notion of partition impairs the wholeness of national liberation. It not only violates the unity of the one and only homeland, which is indivisible, it is also a historical verdict that can be changed only by some extraordinary event in the future. Indeed, Begin's conviction that history can be changed by a unique, spectacular event imbued him with optimism that history would ultimately fulfil his wishes, and would do so "Only thus!".[4]

It was Begin's belief that the constantly turning wheel of history would, in some manner unknown to individuals or the nation, come to a halt at a predestined point.[5] During the revolt, he elaborated the two fundamental principles upon which he based his struggle against the British Empire: the deterministic course of a war of national liberation, and the inevitable disintegration of all empires. For his examples, he drew, selectively as ever, upon the great revolutions of the late eighteenth century, through the nineteenth century – the century of great ideals – until he reached Poland and Ireland in the First World War. "Liberation of the homeland and redemption of the nation" is the theme that runs throughout history. It is absolute redemption. It is the course that would transform the generation of extermination into the generation of national renaissance. "How? Blood and soil accomplished the miracle."[6]

There was just one way of actualizing history, in Begin's view. Should the majority be unwilling, it will be carried out by a daring, heroic minority. The political situation, as construed by Begin, was simplistic. Every nation possesses natural rights, first and foremost of which is the right to liberty; in addition, there is the historical right to a single, undivided homeland, to which it is bound by eternal proprietorship. Should the nation find itself under foreign rule which refuses to concede its natural right to liberty, its leaders proclaim a rebellion.

Such a rebellion has its own legitimacy. It begins with a few individuals, and spreads to ever-growing circles; it forges the national will, which is made ready for all sacrifice. The goal is always attained. No empire has ever withstood the moral force of a just national struggle. Nemesis, the goddess of vengeance, fixes her gaze on the enemy and brings about its downfall.[7]

Begin was always under the spell of ideas. The idea is father of the will. Identification with an idea is crucial to harnessing the self-sacrifice of the individual fighter. The idea, like the words of which it is composed, is autonomous and can unfold in different directions. Begin did not swerve from his belief in moral force and its prime role in directing the course of history, though it contradicted the concept of political realism that he elaborated concurrently.[8]

Begin believed that "ideas give birth to their executors," as part of the lawfulness of history. It was in this sense that the nineteenth century was important to him. It was the seedbed of the great ideas that fanned the flames of the twentieth century – "the century of materialism and cruelty."[9] His conviction that with idea and will-power it is possible to overcome any obstacle, gave rise to his revulsion against the concept of "compromise," which distorts and deflects history's advance to its objective. With regard to "the great [and] fundamental [matters] which shape the nation and mold the individual," Begin wrote, there can be no compromise. He supported his contention by references ranging from Socrates through Jewish teachings and Prometheus to the heroes of human history.[10]

Begin's legalistic formalism and his image as a stickler for parliamentary decorum concealed the fact that his role in Zionist politics was that of a revolutionary nationalist. He was a romantic who fused morals and politics into the broad spectrum of the new nationalism, from its romantic–progressive pole to the elements of integral nationalism.

As the standard-bearer of the national idea Begin was contemptuous of the materialist worldliness of the labor movement, which left it too enfeebled and timid to stand up to the stormy torrents of history. He invariably responded with fury to the contention that the left represent historical progress, while the right is reactionary. He argued that socialism could be either progressive or reactionary – a relativist view he rarely applied to nationalism itself. Begin found no greater rhetorical pleasure than in his sarcastic refutation of Marxist ideas and belittlement of their exponents, particularly the Soviet Union, or, in Israeli domestic politics, Hashomer Hatzair. In *World View and National Conception*, he wrote a lengthy preface refuting the premises of "scientific socialism," which he thought as unable to withstand the test of time or of human nature.[11]

"My heroes are Herzl, Jabotinsky, and Garibaldi"

Begin always regarded heroism and self-sacrifice as among the noblest of human traits. There can be no doubt that, as leader and individual, he linked himself to the line of heroic leadership in history.[12] He frequently cited Thomas Carlyle in support of his views. In *The Revolt*, he wrote: "What it all comes down to is that, in the annals of humanity, there is no force stronger than the force of self-sacrifice, just as there is no love more profound than the love of liberty."[13] Begin was always inclined to attribute mankind's past glories and greatness to the feats of historical heroes. He tended to "usurp" great leaders and apply them to the historical proofs of the justice of his cause.[14]

When Begin put forward his plan for the formation of a provisional government in the 1940s, he saw in his mind's eye the leaders of the Yishuv solemnly proclaiming independence, then going underground to supervise the national struggle; at the very least, he wrote, in such a situation, they should welcome their arrest with love, as a symbolic act inwardly and outwardly.[15] There is no reason to doubt Begin's statement that "nothing, not even becoming prime minister," could compare with the heights he reached in the 1940s.[16] During the elections to the first Knesset, when Moshe Sneh referred to him mockingly as the Jewish de Gaulle, Begin retorted that of course he was no de Gaulle, but that in France at least, everyone acknowledges de Gaulle's part in the national liberation.[17]

Heroism figured as a leitmotif of Begin's reading no less than historical subjects do:

I don't stop reading the Bible. Ze'ev Jabotinsky's books are constantly being studied, the same goes for Herzl's diaries, and the writings of Klausner ... *The Book of Faith and Denunciation* by Uri Zvi Greenberg, and Bialik's *Scroll of Fire*. I sometimes peruse the writings of Thomas Carlyle – particularly on the French Revolution. Again and again I read Shakespeare, Oscar Wilde, Tolstoy, Dostoevsky, Tchernikhovsky's poetry, and the writings of Thomas Jefferson. I repeatedly study all works by Garibaldi, who is the third of my personal mentors. Occasionally, I glance at Homer's *Iliad* ... I have totally given up German and Polish poetry.[18]

Begin is not the only twentieth-century statesman whose historical interest in heroism was undermined at some point early in the century. On occasion, he contradicted himself by voicing "Tolstoyan" doubts about the virtues of the historical hero. Addressing his fellow convicts in Lukishki prison he predicted that even Stalin's wisdom would prove inadequate, in spite of the declarations of the Red Army's political commissars. Begin returned to a similar idea after the Yom Kippur War, when he contrasted human intentions with the chaotic realities of war.[19]

The historical hero who dominated Begin's imagination during his formative years was Garibaldi. The leader of "the thousand" provided Begin, perhaps even more than Jabotinsky, with a perfect parallel for his own actions. The man who had cried "Rome or death!", "We shall prevail – or die!", "Here we shall create Italy or die!" and who really intended to conquer mountains and cities supplied the Revisionists with one of the best-known symbols of their political and military tradition: "to die or to conquer the mountain."[20]

As we have seen, Begin was fascinated by Garibaldi and "the noble secret of the homeland," by his capacity for subjugating temporary interests to the supreme interest of the nation, by his exploitation of a rare historical opportunity, by his pursuit of *aventura* and rebellion, by his efforts towards national unity for the sake of national objectives – irrespective of whether the choice was "kingdom" or "republic"; by his ceaseless activity aimed at reminding the world and the Powers of his nation's existence and importance. In Begin's view, Garibaldi's charisma was complemented by Cavour and his diplomatic genius; and he was convinced of his own fitness to fuse the roles of both men in his own person.

In an ecstatic oration delivered in September 1955, at the unveiling of a memorial to the fighters of the Irgun, Begin spoke of the wondrous Garibaldi and his "liberating vision of secession (*prisha*)." He referred to "the thousand" as "Garibaldi's secessionists." He would have liked to compare the Jewish Agency to Victor Emmanuel, but this was impossible since the official Jewish leadership never rose to the stature of the king and never summoned the Irgun to an act of "disobedience" that would totally transform "the state of affairs" in the Land of Israel. Turning his gaze to the East, Begin said that there lay the boundary of our eternal inheritance. "It is a divine, a national, [and] a human mission" not only to liberate the Land of Israel from the curse of partition but also, as the self-styled liberator of humankind, to liberate the Arabs of the Land of Israel from "tyranny, from poverty, from fear." Begin concluded by proclaiming, more firmly than ever, that "secession is the driving force of history."[21]

A twentieth-century hero who caused Begin some perplexity was Winston Churchill. Begin could not forget that the British prime minister whom he so admired had called for the suppression of the Jewish undergrounds. Notwithstanding, in November 1944 Begin had written of Churchill as "one of the greatest men of mankind," adding that his Dunkirk speech had served him, Begin, as a guide.[22] When Churchill died, Begin called him "the greatest statesman of this epoch," going to great lengths to overlook his record on Palestine in the 1940s. He focused his attention on Churchill the "Zionist," his term of office as colonial secretary in 1922, and as leader of the opposition who flayed Attlee and Bevin, and ignored Churchill the prime minister of the Britain that had ruled Palestine.[23]

When Begin resigned from the cabinet early in August 1970, drawing as ever on historical analogy, he referred to Churchill as the kind of man who is "born once in a thousand years." Quoting Churchill's characterization of the Treaty of Locarno as the most precise pact concluded after the First World War, he added: if the Treaty of Locarno was broken, could the recently concluded agreement with Egypt be expected to be upheld?.[24]

The pitfalls of analogy

Historical analogy was central to Begin's thinking. Any analogy is a selective abstraction chosen from a broad field. The selection itself is of significance in comprehending the inner world of the historical agent. The historical parallel, with all its characteristics and pitfalls, was not only rhetoric for Begin, but was often meant to underpin present action with historical lawfulness and a causal explanation. It was an attempt to invoke history as a witness for shaping the present and a vision of the future.[25]

Begin's analogies were comparisons of events and individuals rather than of historical processes. Periods and personages were linked together associatively on the basis of external similarities. In this respect, Begin's analogies were a double-edged sword, and could be turned against him no less than against his adversaries.

Begin claimed to have studied the history of underground movements – the Irish in particular – so as to avoid repeating their mistakes. However, an examination of Ireland's history, and of the Irish struggle against Britain, discloses the feebleness of Begin's analogy. The Easter revolt of 1916 was a total failure. The rebels' proclamation called for the creation of a "provisional government," but most of their leaders were killed within three weeks. Begin certainly lacked the military skills of Michael Collins. A minor parallel may perhaps be drawn nevertheless: the first offensive launched by the Sinn Fein after the release of Eamon De Valera took place in April 1920, and began with a series of attacks on income tax offices throughout Ireland. The first operations of the Irgun were similar.[26]

As a recently arrived new immigrant in Palestine in 1942, Begin considered the situation in comparison with 1917. In 1917, he wrote, the political constellation was favorable for the Jews, who were free to choose their allies. Nowadays, the powers were aware that the Jews had no alternatives. After the partition plan, and the Munich-like policy of *havlaga* (self-restraint), "we are regarded with contempt." In 1917, negotiations sufficed; in 1942, "the Hebrew army also needs *war*, a serious war, a systematic war" (emphasis in the original).[27] Even as the Irgun commander, discussing operations, Begin did not abandon his historical comparisons. He argued that all great revolutions begin in the great cities, usually in the capital. It is a general phenomenon in history that regimes cannot withstand a paralysis of population centers and of transportation. Begin thus came to the conclusion that the military options available in Palestine were superior to those in Ireland, adding that this awareness "does not stem from abstract belief, but from a logical and mathematical analysis of the facts."[28] Addressing the Irgun command in August 1944, he declared that the uprisings in Paris and Warsaw were indications that the Irgun should operate in similar fashion "and we too, if we operate in Jerusalem, that will have great value."[29] Later, when the West Bank was annexed to the Hashemite Kingdom of Jordan, Begin regarded the step as temporary, pointing to Alsace-Lorraine, to the Soviet Union's success in changing the consequences of the Treaty of Brest-Litovsk, and to Beneš and the Sudetenland.[30] During the period immediately before the Six Day War, Begin compared himself to Edward Grey warning the Egyptians – in time, not as in 1914 – of the consequences of their aggression.[31] During the Yom Kippur War, he cast the Soviet ambassador to Cairo, Vinogradov, in the role of Schulenburg, Egypt as Germany, and Israel as Poland facing the threat of annihilation and partition into spheres of influence.[32] When, as prime minister, he argued with the Egyptians over the demilitarization of Sinai, he reverted to the Yalta conference, transfiguring Sinai into Poland, and Israel into Russia unwilling to assent to a corridor that might be used for attack against it.[33]

The Polish analogy, for all its importance, remained largely implicit. Begin was certainly familiar with the trials and reversals that characterized Poland's unique history. He, in fact, borrowed some of the values, features, and style of Polish nationalism.

In February 1944, after the Irgun came under Begin's command, a letter by the Irgun commander was delivered to the Polish consul in which it was said that, "[the] fighting Jewish youth is convinced that the government of your great country, and public opinion there, being faithful to the most magnificent tradition of freedom and justice, will understand and appreciate our struggle for life and for the future of our ancient nation." Poland provides the most conspicuous example of the dualism of Begin's concept of nationalism, which combines a romantic, utopian view with radical and conservative elements. In Poland, the interpretation of national history often served as the point of departure for political action in the present.[34]

There are many elements in Poland's historical heritage that may have influenced Begin. The ambivalent relationship to the Western Powers and their role at times of crisis for Poland; the attempt to build up the Polish republic as the leading military, political, and cultural power in Eastern Europe; Pilsudski and his idea of the Polish legions; Poland's dismal failure in resolving the problems of its minorities during the interwar period; the national *hubris* of Poland as a medium European power in the wrong period; the tragic gulf between heroic deeds and their practical outcome, with Poland celebrating a national defeat as though it were a triumph; the "realistic" reaction in Poland after 1863, and particularly at the beginning of this century, in response to the romantic view, which regarded international relations as an arena in which the national interest deserved primacy.

Poland, where religious faith did not clash with national ideals and frequently served to safeguard them, was a land where "aristocratic" traits and a chivalrous style filtered down to the lower classes; where even the intelligentsia tended to support romantic idealism and the notion of decision by military force; where the right of self-determination was cultivated as a natural right of all peoples, and integrated, perhaps before anywhere else in Europe, with an international conception applicable to all mankind; where geostrategical considerations were of central importance; and, finally, where the Messianic idea mixed morals with politics in a disastrous fashion. All these elements of the Polish heritage seemed to have left their impression on Begin.[35]

The most outstanding historical analogy in Begin's view of the world was undoubtedly Munich and Czechoslovakia.[36] The 1930s in Europe were the most important years of Begin's political and historical education. The Czech analogy was a perfect historical example: a small nation crushed by Nazi Germany, betrayed by the Western Powers headed by Britain, a nation that missed the opportune historical moment to fight for its national existence. The struggle of the Czech people symbolized for Begin a national character, a historical pattern, and a political tradition to be resisted. War alone was capable of transforming this people "from object to subject of history."[37]

"The Czech example" served Begin as a sabre to be waved in political debate. From the armistice talks that followed the 1948 War of Independence, up to the interim agreements with Egypt after the Yom Kippur War – all outside pressures were depicted as reviving the "spirit of Munich." Any situation in which an Israeli government hesitated on the brink of war was presented as Munich-like indecision. Any withdrawal, or thought of territorial concession, became "capitulation" after the manner of Munich. The overriding political principle was: no surrender to threats, and no concession under external pressure. In voicing his opposition to the Rogers plan, he declared:

What is Munich? . . . There stands a cruel aggressor . . . pretending to seek peace – and threatens [to launch] a war of attrition, and a bloody war, if his wishes are not fulfilled. In the face of this aggressor stand the friends of the small state, and even its allies who are committed to its defense, and tell it: Surrender, save peace, give up part of your territory. . . .[38]

In the course of time, the second part of the Czech analogy was directed against the Arab states and their leaders. The parallel began with comparisons between Nasser or Sadat, and the dictators of the thirties; Begin mercilessly attacked anything he regarded as representing the spirit of appeasement. At a later phase, the 1930s reappeared in direct parallels between the Nazis and the Palestinians.[39] Begin abhorred concepts like self-restraint, partition, or withdrawal. In contrast to such notions, and in the wake of the Holocaust, he drew parallels with Jewish heroism of the Second Temple era.[40] The archetype of the new Jewish warrior bore aloft the vision of a renewed Jewish history – rebellion against any foreign ruler, war against any aggressor.

8

Strategic Perspective

When Menachem Begin named himself defense minister in mid-1980, he asked the Knesset rhetorically: "Why shouldn't I be minister of defense?" Stung by insinuations to the contrary, he attacked those who claimed that he lacked the competence to handle military matters.[1] When he came to power Begin had a number of basic assumptions concerning military strategy, which he had held virtually unchanged for over a generation.

Revisionism saw itself as the resuscitator of Jewish military virtues. War and offensive were concepts that featured regularly in the mental world of members of the movement. In a novel he wrote, Jabotinsky placed the first testament he bequeathed Israel – "amass iron" – in the mouth of Samson.[2] Military and security matters always occupied a central place in Begin's criticism of the Labor movement and of its leaders. Given the circumstances in which Israel found itself from the day of its establishment, and considering his standing as leader of the opposition, it might have been expected that Begin would be expert in issues concerning Israel's security. A man in his position might well be expected to have clearly formulated ideas about strategy, and about changes that ought to be made in the structure of the army and in Israel's security doctrine.

The reality was somewhat different. Since the time he had served as commander of the Irgun, Begin had acquired no firsthand knowledge either of the military field proper or in the strategic realm.[3] Thus, in September 1942 he had written that what was needed to rescue European Jewry and liberate the world from Hitler was a "Hebrew air force that will bombard Berlin, Munich, and Nuremberg in an act of vengeance . . .';[4] Begin was enthralled by ideas that could not be carried out. When he resigned from the government in August 1970 he cited every Katyusha that fell in Israel by caliber and range, as if that were the important thing.[5] And after the conquest of the Beaufort fortress in June 1982, he asked, "Did they have machine-guns?" Begin's lack of military expertise was not always a deficiency. It was always his belief that as a matter of principle military action must be guided by policy. Begin was a skilled propagandist and knew how to build up patiently the pretext and justification for a military action or war.

His knowledge of the geostrategic aspects of Israel and of the Middle East came to him second hand. His relationship to the Land of Israel was emotional and historical, almost metaphysical; it was not that of a traveler, hiker, researcher, or soldier. On the other hand, Begin had a special regard for people from the military.[6] He was proud of the fact that five generals had served in his first government. He always lauded IDF commanders as heroes of Jewish history, and except for Ezer Weizman, never subjected them to public criticism.

It was of fateful consequence that a person whose conception of national strength centered around quantitative criteria became prime minister at a time when Israel's army had vastly expanded in size. It had become an armed forces that measured its combat strength in terms of divisions, corps, and armies. Begin lacked the historical perspective shared by the founding fathers of Israel, the vision and memory of the gradual build up of the IDF from what had been a meagerly equipped defensive force.

Begin never publicly expressed the slightest doubt about the army's capability. In the same way, in his Irgun days he always had confidence in its strength and had been motivated by a sense of purpose. Although the Irgun had been a small underground army unable to be of decisive influence in war, it did not prevent him from adopting an offensive view and from loathing the more limited policies of *havlaga* (the Hagana's policy of restraint) and *maavak tzamud* (selective military reprisal for Arab attacks). He had a deep faith in the time factor and was infused with the belief that most of what is willed can in fact be attained.[7]

As commander of the Irgun, Begin had one fundamental strategic assumption: that revolt was the principal way for conducting a struggle for national liberation.[8] On the tactical level, he advocated the development of forms of urban guerilla warfare. In practice, however, he did not engage in the operational planning of the Irgun's activities.

Begin always exaggerated the role of the Irgun in the War of Independence. His description of the conquest of Jaffa is most telling. Even at almost a generation's remove from the event, he wrote that the conquest of Jaffa was "one of the fateful events in the Hebrew War of Independence." To wait for May 15, 1948, as the "official strategists" wanted, would have been disastrous; the British might not have evacuated the city at all. What is more, "Gaza is not far from Jaffa by sea. The Egyptian invading forces that landed in Gaza could also have landed in Jaffa ... The Egyptians would have unloaded tanks, cannons, mortars, troops, and Tel Aviv would have had to fight a battle launched from land, sea, and air ..." Begin concludes: "No one can say how the war would have ended under such circumstances. A shudder of fear passes through the heart at the thought that we might have found ourselves in such a circumstance. That undoubtedly would have been a terrible danger to our national existence itself."[9] Begin transformed the role of the Irgun in the conquest of Jaffa and made of it a heroic event on which the War of Independence as a whole turned.

Military obsessions

Begin's positions on strategic issues derived from his conviction that Israel has an almost permanent, historical possibility for constant offensive, dependent only on the free choice of its leaders. This assumption is a leit-motif in Begin's strategic thought, running from the War of Independence right up to the Lebanon War. This conception espouses overall offensive or counteroffensive rather than limited retaliatory actions; preventive or preemptive war in response to any offensive intention on the part of the enemy; and opposition to any tactical or territorial concession as part of a temporary rather than permanent arrangement. Finally, at least in Begin's public pronouncements, international constraints are presented not as real but as an obsessive fear gripping leadership.

Begin's attitude regarding the limits of Israel's expansion was vague. It oscillated between geostrategic considerations and the normative histor-ical definition that encompassed both sides of the Jordan. Begin thus denied that the boundaries of Israeli settlement necessarily reflected the political boundary, or that there are real limitations, moral or social, to Israel's territorial expansion. Paradoxically, it was the Six Day War that narrowed Herut's geopolitical vista and focused it on the smaller, operative goal of Judaea and Samaria.[10]

Begin did not accept the partition boundaries of 1948, and was con-vinced that nothing stood in the way of an IDF victory over the Hashemite Kingdom and the establishment of Israel on both sides of the Jordan. In a speech in early August 1948, he told his Jerusalem audience that "the State of Israel, as it is, is a narrow strip along the coast . . . we must break forward . . . The Jordan is not the border of our land and the sea is not the border of our nation.'[11] Until the Sinai campaign in 1956, Begin maintained the view that a limited response was inadequate. Ever since 1948, the approaching war with the Arab countries appeared to him not only as inevitable but also as desirable. It was necessary, he wrote, to reach a situation in which it would be possible to carry out "'fulfillment operations' at the right moment, namely liberation of parts of the occupied homeland according to a strategy carefully calculated with respect to place and time."[12]

It is possible, but only a surmise, that Begin's offensive perspective and his sharp and unprecedented attacks on the government in the 1950s con-cealed a pessimism and deep anxiety about the very physical existence of the State of Israel. The period of Sharett's premiership, like the Rabin period in the 1970s, was marked by Begin's fierce criticism of an atmosphere of appeasement and a readiness for concessions that endangered the existence of the state. Many concepts came under his whip in these attacks, among them "defensive posture," "retaliatory action," "compromise," "interim agreement," and "territorial compromise."[13] After the Gaza raid, which was a milestone on the way to the Sinai War, Begin said that the method of "hit and run," his derisive term for the retaliatory actions, was insufficient. Up until the launching of the war in October 1956, he continued to accuse the government of missing historical opportunities, of neglecting Israel's security, and of criminal misunderstanding of the international situation.[14]

In December 1954, Begin wrote a programatic article on security. He listed three factors that determine national security – manpower, weapon power, and components of the country's strategic situation (by which he meant control of territory).[15] These were followed by other factors, such as organizational ability, production capacity, scientific level, and above all, "morale."[16] Quantitative amassment seemed to Begin the key to national strength. He saw the smaller size of Israel's manpower and quantity of its weaponry as endangering the country. As early as the 1950s, on the basis of the Korean War, he concluded that the territorial factor and infantry were important even for the superpowers and even in the nuclear age.[17]

Two weeks before the Sinai campaign, Begin again attacked the "doctrine of retaliation." Actions in Husan and Qalqilya had raised doubts among many concerning the usefulness and cost of retaliatory actions, but Begin also rejected the concepts "preventive war" or "initiated war" because they cast Israel in a bad light. In the war situation prevailing between Israel and the Arab states, he argued, there is only a "war of right" – a war to liberate the soil of the homeland. In October 1956, Begin was looking to the east, not to the southern front. The collaboration between the two Hashemite kingdoms provided an opportune moment for "an advance on our part towards the Jordan if the Iraqis pour towards the Jordan from the east." Begin threatened a "war of terror" against Britain in the eventuality of a military clash with it because of Great Britain's commitments to Jordan and Iraq. But Begin was not certain that the government would take any action, in the south or in the east.[18]

In the middle of January 1957, circumstances forced Begin to change the tenor of his criticism from the government's reluctance to go to war to what he styled the "perfidy of abandonment." In a no-confidence motion he strongly condemned the government for withdrawing from Sinai. Begin truly could not understand what pressures could bring a sovereign government to evacuate territory it had occupied in a defensive war.[19] Exploiting his arsenal of legal hair splitting, Begin explained that had the government adopted a concept such as "an act of self-defense," instead of "preventive war" or "initiated war," Israel's action would have been understood as a legitimate exercise of the sacred right of self-defense, and Israel would have had "freedom of military operation." As later events were to show, Begin never abandoned the principle of legitimate territorial acquisition in a war of self-defense.

For a long time Begin had to defend himself against the charge that he was a militarist and warmonger. In the first decade of Israel's existence he advocated initiated war, carefully planned (and directed primarily to the east), a war of conquest aimed at establishing Israeli sovereignty on both sides of the Jordan. In April 1957, he called on the government to announce that the ceasefire lines of 1948 do not constitute the boundaries of Israel, and that in the event of further war, "the State of Israel will rely on this basic principle: right, not might." [20]

To Begin, the Six Day War seemed to prove the truth of his contentions concerning security; he recalled his warnings against withdrawing from Sinai. During the "waiting period" between the Egyptian blockade of the Straits of Tiran and the outbreak of the war, he was more reserved than usual. He was less enthused this time than in the past about going to a war whose expected outcome and cost in lives cast a widespread gloominess. [21] The war would soon change Israel's boundaries and the horizons of its diplomacy. Begin's historical and strategic perspectives remained unchanged, but the principles he had always advocated were now marshalled to defend the achievements of 1967.

The first principle which he had consistently held was simple; political or territorial concession leads to further concessions; worst of all is a concession granted in response to pressure. The only concession acceptable to Begin was defined normatively. It must be mutual, and its end must be the normalization of relations between countries, i.e., termination of the state of war and a contractual peace agreement. He repeated this principle, in various versions and under different diplomatic circumstances, from the Six Day War until he came to power. [22]

Begin stated that two schools of foreign policy thought had been created in the aftermath of the Six Day War: "One says that we will achieve an agreement with the Arabs and peace for ourselves only by promising concessions. The second tries to explain that the promised concessions will not lead to a peace agreement but will only invite international pressure for further concessions." Accordingly, until he himself took the reins of government, Begin opposed all peace initiatives. [23]

The Yom Kippur War provided Begin with the broadest opportunity for slamming the government and the Labor movement for its handling of security matters. He constantly admonished, "Why didn't you call up the reserves between Rosh Hashanah and Yom Kippur, and why didn't you move up the weaponry." [24] He could not, however, propose anything more than the government did to prevent the outbreak of the Yom Kippur War. He too had believed that the military option was closed to the Arab states.[25] Begin now adhered even more intently to the principle of no territorial concessions without termination of the state of war and a peace agreement. Beginning with the rescue of the Egyptian Third Army at the end of the war and up until the interim agreements with Egypt in September 1974, he saw before him a plot to abandon Israel's security.[26]

The Rabin government became an anvil for the hammer of Begin's criticism unlike any since the time Sharett had been prime minister. Not only did he reject any settlement with Egypt, up until 1977 he was convinced that Egypt did not want peace.[27] As in the 1950s, he did not acknowledge any diplomatic or military constraint as warranting withdrawal. He was not far from a position that saw concession and appeasement as a deeply embedded feature of the left, a kind of spiritual submissiveness having no relation whatever to political reality. Begin rejected the conception of "peace in exchange for territories." The harshest blows Israel had ever had to take, he argued, were suffered during the rule of a dovish government. The withdrawal from Sinai in 1975 seemed to Begin to be the height of political and strategic imbecility. It was not a corridor to peace but Israel's submission to a foreign power, part of a plan being conducted by a man of fiendish talents, Henry Kissinger.[28] Paradoxically, much of what he said between 1974 and 1977 could have equally been directed against him after he became prime minister.

The lessons of Munich

The concepts "alliance," "treaty," and "ally" were terms that constantly cropped up in Begin's political and diplomatic world. One of the most pilloried was "guarantees." For Begin, alliance was the normative situation of internatioal relations which sovereign states equal in rights try to achieve; guarantees are a cover for imminent international treachery, such as Munich. Alliance, by Begin's definition, was a mutual contractual commitment. He understood the interdependence of nations only in the strategic–diplomatic sense, not in an economic sense nor in terms of any other factor. When he spoke to President Reagan about strategic cooperation, he used the very same vague words he had used in a memorandum in the 1940s about cooperation with the Hagana; "I am speaking here only of the principle. The details will have to be worked out by the two defense ministers."[29]

Begin's conception of the dilemma in a defense treaty has Revisionist roots. The goal was to have the Jewish state be an ally and strategic partner of a great power, but there was also a desire to develop autarkic, exclusive power, that of a nation deciding its own national fate independently of the good graces of others. At the second convention of the Herut movement, in 1951, Begin had spoken against forming an alliance with, or granting bases to, a third power. That would not prevent an invasion by Russian divisions, he said.[30] Throughout the 1950s, however, he heaped praise on France, the senior and loyal ally that adhered to the sublime ideals of the great Revolution. Then, in the 1960s the United States gradually supplanted France as Israel's main ally.

Begin's attitude toward the idea of a defense treaty with the United States during his term as prime minister was vacillatory and therefore somewhat ambiguous. Secretary of State Vance wrote that when he visited the Middle East in August 1977, Begin politely but firmly rejected an offer of security guarantees by the United States, including the possibility of a formal treaty.[31] Before leaving for Camp David a year later, Begin said that he would recommend a defense treaty if the subject should come up in the talks. After the peace treaty with Egypt in March 1979, he said that if the United States were to offer a defense treaty, he would propose that the government accept it. The smaller state cannot take the initiative in this, he said, "and so we'll wait."[32]

The Americans were reluctant to give Israel guarantees, and were cool about the idea of an alliance. Dayan said that the Americans waved the idea of a treaty before Israel like a carrot, but were vague about the commitments they were prepared to undertake. Begin himself was reluctant to accept any guarantee aimed at forcing territorial concessions or at preventing a continuation of the IDF presence in the occupied territories.[33] Even though there was no defense treaty between Israel and the United States, Begin regarded the relations between the two countries as if such a treaty did exist. Nonetheless, in style, rhetoric, and the timing of Israel's actions he did nothing to expand the strategic and political understanding with the United States. More than once he publicly stated that Israel sometimes contributed more to the national security of the United States than the United States contributed to Israel's.[34]

One of Begin's favorite themes, almost to excess, was his contention after the Six Day War that by blocking the Suez Canal Israel had provided the free world, and especially the United States, with a strategic service of inestimable value. This assumption led him to imagine not only that Israel had become an international strategic factor, but also that the United States was not truly interested in a settlement between Egypt and Israel if such a settlement was to remove this anti-Soviet strategic card from its hand.[35] In December 1973, he maintained that the IDF presence on the Suez Canal had saved the lives of many American soldiers, "If the Soviets would have had direct access to the Persian Gulf and thence to Asia," he said, the balance of power between East and West would have been thoroughly upset.[36] In March 1974, he proposed demilitarization of the canal and passage through the canal by merchant ships only.[37]

During Begin's term as prime minister, and especially after Ronald Reagan was elected as president of the United States, he continued to make much of Israel's importance as America's ally curbing Soviet penetration of the Middle East. In doing so, he expressed the most far-reaching American orientation in Israel's history. It is doubtful, however, that this stance bore much fruit than the period when Israel was unwilling to commit itself to such an anti-Soviet posture. America's caution prevented the complications that might have ensued had this position been given contractual significance or made a real part of Israel's defense doctrine.[38]

The height of strategic cooperation between Israel and the United States was supposed to be the memorandum of understanding between the two countries. Begin's attitude toward the stationing of American troops, or the establishment of bases, in Israel, like his attitude toward a defense treaty, was not consistent. Before leaving for his first visit to the United States as prime minister, in July 1977, Begin did not rule out the possibility of an American naval base in Israel. Before signing the peace treaty with Egypt he said, in response to a question, that he would agree to the establishment in Israel of a permanent base for the Sixth Fleet. In the beginning of 1980, however, he vigorously rejected the contention of Shimon Peres, then leader of the opposition, that he had proposed to the United States that it establish bases in Israel.[39] Yet, in April of that year, Begin proposed to President Carter that the United States make use of services Israel could extend for curbing the Soviets and protecting oil supplies to the West. There was talk then of, among other things, landing rights, and the use of ports and maintenance installations should the need arise. Meanwhile, Washington released quiet denials that there were any real plans for a defense treaty or for the establishment of permanent military bases in Israel.

The collapse of the Shah's regime in Iran, the war between Iran and Iraq, and Reagan's election to the presidency created a more agreeable setting for the idea of strategic cooperation. Immediately after the US elections in November 1980, Begin declared that the United States should station troops in the Middle East, and that an effort will be made to conclude the memorandum of understanding between the two governments.[40] At the beginning of November 1981, the prime minister informed the Knesset that a "very thorough discussion" of this question had taken place. He stated that if an agreement was reached with the United States for countering the Soviet threat in the region and surroundings, "we will be given a free hand in all other matters." With typical hyperbole, he declared dramatically that the strategic cooperation with the United States was meant to defend the region "against a serious danger, the likes of which has not existed – I want intentionally to repeat these things from this platform – since the end of the Second Wold War, of totalitarian domination of the region and surroundings."[41]

The major innovation of the memorandum, signed by Secretary of Defense Caspar Weinberger and Defense Minister Ariel Sharon, was that its wording was pointed directly against the Soviet Union. Apart from that, it spoke in general terms about the commitment of both sides to military co-operation, the use of certain Israeli installations, coordination in the development of weapon systems, and the establishment of frameworks for consultation.[42]

After Begin brought the Golan Heights bill to the Knesset in December 1981, he parried attacks against him by noting the status Israel had achieved. He recalled sarcastically that Sharett had turned to Secretary of State George Marshall in 1950 and pleaded for food and arms in return for an Israeli promise that IDF soldiers would cooperate with the United States in the defense of democracy in the world. Now, he said, he "will insist on the idea of perfect and unqualified equality among nations."[43] Just one week later, reporters were astonished to hear the government secretary, Aryeh Naor, repeat word by word what Begin had told US Ambassador Samuel Lewis in a closed meeting: "Are we a vassal state of yours? Are we a banana republic?" And then he added: "We note the fact that you have withdrawn the memorandum of understanding. The Jewish people has lived for 3,700 years without a memorandum of understanding with America and will live another 3,700 years without it. In our eyes, this is [tantamount to] a cancellation of the memorandum."[44] Begin, it appears, was prepared to dismiss with a wave of his hand what just a few days before had been a vital strategic protection against a danger the likes of which had not been seen since the Second World War.

Begin's pronouncements about strategic cooperation and a treaty with the United States did not prevent the latter from taking unprecedented punitive measures against Israel. In the Begin period, Israel lost its battle against the first arms deal in which arms supplies to Israel were linked to arms supplies to Saudi Arabia and Egypt. The US administration, in fact, used the supply of arms as an instrument for restraining Israel more than it had in any other period. The use of cluster bombs in Lebanon prompted the administration to bring in the Arms Export Control Act. After that, Israel failed in its fight to prevent the sale of AWACS airplanes to Saudi Arabia. Following the bombing of the Iraqi reactor, the Reagan administration for the first time suspended a contract for the supply of aircraft; after the Golan Heights Law was passed, as we have seen, it suspended the memorandum of understanding.[45]

Begin had inherited the two-edged sword of strategic cooperation with a foreign power from revisionism. A formal treaty between a large power and a small state, as Begin had noted for years, had never led any power to act contrary to its interests. The shifting circumstances of international relations, ironically, make the strategic dimension a shaky and transient basis for a diplomatic alliance. Cooperation founded on shared values and moral outlook, by contrast, often has greater permanency. It appears less demanding than a formal treaty, and is less influenced by external changes.

The last resort

In September 1982, Begin said: "We have developed a deterrent force that will guarantee our existence forever." He had made few other pronouncements bearing on Israel's nuclear option. In the 1950s he had held that the nuclear age had not done away with the elements of human thinking in the realm of strategy, nor had it dispensed with the need for conventional strength. Begin supported Israel's nuclear armament. He believed that there is no relying on demilitarization or on an international agreement against nuclear proliferation. Begin rejected the argument that small states are necessarily less responsible than great powers when in possession of nuclear weapons.[46]

Apart from the Lebanon War, Begin was involved in one other decisive decision of a military nature – the bombing of the Iraqi nuclear reactor. The full strategic and international significance of that decision cannot yet be assessed. Defense Minister Ariel Sharon presented the decision as a doctrine to which any Israeli prime minister would necessarily have to subscribe – the destruction of a nuclear installation in an Arab country that posed a potential threat to Israel.[47] Public debate in Israel about the decision centered not around the strategic or international significance of the affair but around its timing: shortly before elections and just a few days after a euphoric meeting between Prime Minister Begin and President Sadat. Above all, debate was sparked by the question of when the Iraqi reactor would have become operative, because after that time such an attack would have been impossible without endangering a large civilian population.

The decision to bomb the Iraqi nuclear reactor was not taken casually, and was accompanied by strong internal debate in Israel's political and defense establishment. The decision was reached against the view of military intelligence, which gauged that Iraq would not have a bomb until the 1990s. This issue remains a matter of dispute.[48] Begin contended that the reactor would "become hot" in July or September, and if it was bombed then, "fatal radioactivity would pour over Baghdad." He minimized the influence of the bombing on relations with Egypt and dismissed world reactions to it. Begin himself issued the instructions to release the government announcement about the bombing. He denied that Israel was the first to announce the attack, but did not explain why it had not been possible to continue to maintain silence without flagrantly reacting to a vague announcement made by the Jordanian radio, that "vital targets in Iraq" had been bombed. At a press conference Begin declared that a secret installation, forty meters underground, was also damaged, a fact utterly of his own imagination. One year after the bombing, Begin declared in an address to the UN General Assembly that Israel was prepared to discuss the establishment of nuclear-free zones.[49]

9

Eretz Yisrael, the Palestinians, and the Idea of Autonomy

Begin's images of "the Arabs" and his approach to the Arab question were among the most unchanging features of his world view. He had no direct acquaintanceship with Arabs. The Arab as he envisaged him was the enemy from the East seeking to undermine and demolish Israel's independence, wreaking havoc among its inhabitants. For the most part, the Arab was seen as a stereotype expressing threat and danger and the historical possibility of the annihilation of the Jewish people.

The Irgun's position on the Arab question was contradictory, and originated in an attempt to draw an artificial distinction between the battle against British rule and the fight on the Arab front. The closer we come to the War of Independence, the more the image of the Arabs of Palestine changes from that of weak opponent to real threat, until they become the principal enemy. *Havlaga*, the Hagana's policy of self-restraint, had always been seen as a strategic error of fatal consequences resulting from a lack of understanding of political reality. However, Begin offered a different assessment in June 1947 to representatives of the UN commission:

The Irgun does not believe in this fairy tale of independent Arab opposition to Jewish immigration or sovereignty. All the Arab opposition is a product of British incitement . . . The Irgun does not believe that the Iraqis, Lebanese or Syrians will attack the Jewish state. They do not have serious armies, unless they receive foreign help.[1]

For Begin the contest between the Jewish community and the Arab population of Palestine was not about sovereignty; as far as he was concerned, that was a closed matter. The view that the Jews have an incontestable historical right to the Land of Israel and that the Palestinian Arabs are a national minority entitled to all civic rights was shared equally by Begin the commander of the Irgun and Begin the prime minister who presented a plan for autonomy. Begin repeated the traditional Revisionist blurring of the distinction between a political plan and the ideological justification offered in its support.[2]

Israel's place among the countries of the region was perceived by Begin through two opposing images – either war, or formal, contractual peace. The intermediate situation, which is what in fact characterizes the relations between Israel and the Arab countries most of the time, cannot be satisfactorily explained by the platform of the Irgun or of the Herut movement. Begin's geostrategic perception of the Middle East lacked detail. One could even say it showed a lack of acquaintance with the basic facts of the region. The recurring theme in his argument was always that of the many Arab countries, their dominions stretching from the Atlantic coast to the Persian Gulf, seeking the destruction of the one, small state belonging to the Jewish people. His view of pan-Arabism complemented his belief that the self-determination of the Palestinians is expressed in the existence of one Arab nation.[3]

Begin's monolithic perception hampered his ability to discern changes taking place in the region. In fact, he rejected the division between moderate and extremist Arab states. On the contrary, the Arab countries portrayed as moderate, such as Tunisia, Saudi Arabia, and Jordan, were denounced in the sharpest terms. Virtually every change in intra-Arab relations was interpreted by Begin as increasing the threat to Israel. After formal unions were proclaimed in the 1950s between Iraq and Jordan and between Syria and Egypt, Begin accused the government of being shackled to a status quo view of the Middle East that blinded it to the far-reaching changes taking place in the region.[4]

Begin consistently rejected all proposed arrangements or plans that entailed territorial concessions in return for anything less than formal, contractual peace. This had been his unchanging position since the establishment of the state. Begin ordinarily slashed at two opponents at the same time – the Labor party and the Hashemite Kingdom – when he portrayed the "Jordanian option" as a mountebank formula. He inveighed against the idea of a federation between Jordan and a Palestinian entity to be established on the West Bank. He ridiculed the united kingdom that would result, declaring that it would "hang in mid-air." Since the War of Independence, Begin had considered the Jordanian conquest of the West Bank an act of aggression that did not accord it any rights; the Land of Israel, he maintained, "was divided in a war of aggression, and was united in a war of self-defense." After the Six Day War he demanded that Israeli law be extended to Judaea and Samaria.[5]

No wonder, then, that Begin's attitudes and actions as prime minister came somewhat as a surprise. He did not resolve the question of sovereignty in the West Bank, and in Sinai he agreed to a compromise that involved far-reaching concessions. Only in two areas were his actions consistent with his previous statements: Jerusalem and the Golan Heights. The Jerusalem Law, annexing the entire city to Israel, was his response to the challenge set by a radical right-wing faction led by Geula Cohen. The

Golan Heights Law, which extended Israeli law, jurisdiction, and administration to the Golan Heights, was his own, and swift, initiative. In presenting it to the Knesset he said, "Historically the Golan Heights was and will remain an inseparable part of the Land of Israel." The only reason he offered for the bill was expressed indirectly, in an attack on the Syrian position in the Arab–Israeli dispute.[6] His language in response to his critics was exceptionally abusive. There had been no consultation on this matter with the United States, he said, so as not to place the US in a difficult position.

Indivisible patrimony

Begin's approach on the Land of Israel rested on three pillars: historical right, the indivisibility of the country, and Jerusalem as the nation's heart. The idea of the wholeness of the land, which first appeared in the political lexicon of Jewish Palestine in the late 1930s, does not have clear Revisionist roots. It is the product, rather, of an encounter between deeply rooted religious ideas and opposition to the partition plan of 1937. (The left wing of the socialist Zionist camp had also arrived at the idea of the indivisibility of the country, but from altogether different premises.)

The Zionist Revisionist convention in September 1948, at which the Irgun commanded a majority, resolved that the disciples of Jabotinsky would not rest "until the homeland in its entirety will be the free and sovereign State of Israel." The convention also called for Jerusalem to be included within the boundaries of the state and for it to be declared "the nation's and homeland's capital."[7] The first two paragraphs in the founding statement of the Herut movement declared, "the Hebrew homeland, whose territory extends on both sides of the Jordan, is a single historical and geographical unit"; and "the role of the present generation is to restore to the bosom of Jewish sovereignty those parts of the homeland that were torn from it and delivered to foreign rule."[8]

At a public rally in the spring of 1950, Begin declared that the task before the present generation was to demolish Abdullah's kingdom. There was nothing the least bit equivocal in Begin's statements in that period concerning the Hashemite Kingdom: "It's either Abdullah and Bevin on the outskirts of Petah Tiqva or us on the Jordan."[9] As late as 1957 he said, "So much of the land still remains to be taken possession of." Soil of the homeland that is under foreign rule does not cease being soil of the homeland.[10] At a joint meeting of the Herut movement and Liberal party centers in June 1966, Begin declared, "It is wholly inconceivable that any bit of the soil of the Land of Israel will be handed over to foreign rule."[11] After the Six Day War he asserted that Israeli law and jurisdiction must be extended to what he called the liberated territories. In January 1969 he declared that the Jewish people also had title to the east bank of the Jordan, but he would not propose "initiating a war to gain control of that part of the Land of Israel."[12] Partition, wrote Begin, is not a principle, but the outcome of a war.[13]

No notion was detested by Begin more than "partition," and later "territorial compromise". He fought all his life against the partition decision, even when the chances of winning that battle were dim. He considered the decision "a historic national catastrophe." When the armistice agreements were approved in the spring of 1949, Herut put forward its first no-confidence motion. Begin accused the government of returning to the policy of the London round Table Conferences, of legitimizing an imperialist scheme which was essentially a new Peel plan, and of making unconscionable concessions to the Hashemite Kingdom. The memory of British rule was still fresh. He envisaged Great Britain as behind the plot, and the Hashemite Kingdom as its trifling puppet.[14] After Jordan had annexed the West Bank, Begin accused the government of having allowed "an act of theft and conquest [to be transformed] into an accepted and legal political act." He said further that it was fear that was making the government rush into a peace agreement with a "vassal state," a weak kingdom that in fact posed no threat to Israel and was bound hook, line, and sinker to England. He challenged the government's right to make this historical concession. This was a problem that would not be solved, he said, by "raising hands" in the Knesset; another government, in the future, would not recognize the legitimacy of the Hashemite takeover of the West Bank.[15]

Begin never reconciled himself to partition, either as idea or as historical fact. He was on guard against any suggestion that did come to terms with it – the Allon plan, disengagement agreements with Jordan, or any federative solution. The Hashemite Kingdom, Israel's constant implicit ally, received the harshest condemnation from him, and its kings were subjected to ridicule.[16] For Begin, territorial compromise was a futile dream, and the Jordanian option, an illusion. When King Hussein pronounced his judgment, "totally unacceptable," Begin's sense of triumph was complete.[17] Until he came to power, Begin presented a front of opposition to any retreat as part of any sort of settlement on any front. This tended to obscure the distinction he in fact made between Judaea and Samaria and other territories under Israeli rule.[18]

The Land of Israel suffused Begin's thought, historical outlook, and deep nationalist fervor. However, Begin's Land of Israel was a product of the mind no less than of geographical fact. Its boundaries were based on historical right rather than on actual physical presence. Begin was less enthralled by the country's natural landscapes than were those leaders who had arrived in earlier waves of immigration. Land settlement as a practical expression of sovereignty was a late development in Revisionism, and received real force only after the Likud came to power.[19] Begin refused to accept the idea that the boundaries of settlement on the West Bank demarcated a strategic hold for the future and represented the lines of a repartition of the Land of Israel in a future political settlement.[20]

Begin never distinguished between a national historical attachment to the Land of Israel and the political claim to sovereignty. The reality of geographical and demographical data were of no significance. He was equally indifferent to the possible moral, social, or economic influences of erecting settlements in densely populated Arab areas. In the spring of 1982, in a cantankerous speech which was essentially a reply to the arguments of his opponents, he cast the settlement issue in terms of a moral argument: "Either Zionism was moral from its inception . . . and then it is moral to settle in all parts of the Land of Israel; or . . . our settlement activity today is not moral, and then we must make amends for what we did these last hundred years in the Land of Israel."[21] The past legacy of the socialist movement, which Revisionism had in the past opposed, now became proofs in the hands of Revisionism's political heirs. It was not a view shared by the radical right. Shmuel Katz accused Begin, in fact, of completely neglecting the settlement of Judaea and Samaria.[22]

The key concept for understanding Begin's approach to the Land of Israel is "historical right." This notion, which Begin formulated in a number of ways, refers to an immutable normative situation, which is a compound of natural rights and title deriving from historical heritage. All the deeds of Zionism at all times derive from this right, for Zionism is the restoration of ownership that had been taken from the nation. The nation was now returning to its homeland, to its patrimony from time immemorial, and exercising its natural right of self-determination.

The concept of right sat well with Begin's tendency to refer to the rules of international law and his normative conception of international relations. In making his claim of historical right, Begin mixed the right of primacy with precedents from Middle Eastern diplomacy up until 1922, and gave these priority over any subsequent historical development.[23] In the end, Begin arrived at a dialectical conception of right and might. A policy based on historical right, he said, would win international recognition of Israel's political justness. Above all, this notion imparted right to the means used to actualize it: "recognition of the right also engenders the power to attain it."[24]

The facts of political reality were strong enough to largely contradict most of Begin's beliefs. After he was elected prime minister, he said, "There is no contradiction between our right to the Land of Israel and Resolution 242." But he, in fact, renounced his intention to extend Israeli law to the West Bank. After the peace agreement with Egypt was signed, Begin said that annexation of the territories would have meant abrogation of the Camp David Accords, of the establishment of autonomy, and of the peace treaty with Egypt.[25] In the beginning of 1980 it was hinted that the government would soon move to extend Israeli law to the territories. Two years later it was rumoured that Begin wanted to present a draft proposal for a law preventing the dismantling of settlements as a consequence of diplomatic negotiations. This was never done, and in the meantime the settlements of the Sinai peninsula were dismantled.[26]

Begin's perception of the Palestinians reflected three different images. The first was of a national minority. The second was of a nationality demanding the right to self-determination, though in Begin's case this perception of the Palestinians can only be inferred from his rejection of it. The third image was of a social aggregate led by a terrorist organization, posing a danger equivalent to that of the Nazis.

The view of the Palestinians as a national minority entitled to full civic rights was fully compatible with the liberal outlook Begin liked to emphasize. In Greater Israel, wrote Begin in 1953, "Jabotinsky's poem 'Left of the Jordan' is not a 'song', but law."[27] The poem, in fact, described two extreme and contrary situations for the Land of Israel, whose combination in reality is highly improbable. First, "Two banks to the Jordan, this one's ours, the other too." Then, "There in abundance, reposing in joy, live [the] son of Arabia, [the] son of the Nazarene, and my very own boy."[28] Begin thought that fears of a binational state were groundless. Such fears dissolved before his formal legalism, which defined a binational state as equal sharing of rule, without considering the character and values of the society so ruled. On the contrary, Begin was fully confident about the future. In 1976, he claimed that within a generation the Jewish people would number 24 million, and in that period "between two and four million will join us here."[29]

Through the long years of opposition Begin kept an impeccable liberal façade. In 1959, criticizing the government's domestic policy, Begin said, "We believe an individual has rights that come before the form of human life called a state." He opposed the military government in Arab areas and demanded its abolishment. In February 1962, he presented a draft proposal for a bill in the name of his party abolishing the emergency defense regulations.[30] He argued that there was no relationship between the military government and the problem of internal security. The military rule was being exploited for the political interests of Mapai and it "places a question mark over the fundamental rights of every Israeli citizen." There was considerable rancor in his observation that the emergency regulations had sometimes been used against the Irgun.[31]

At the same time, however, Begin was able to present a no-confidence motion because Ben-Gurion had said that he could understand the human feeling of the Palestinian *fedayeen*: "Were I in their place I might do the same."[32] Begin marshaled a full battery of arguments against this statement, about which he said: "Words so grave for the security and future of the state . . . have never been uttered from the Knesset rostrum." Was it not obvious, he asked, that people would readily violate the law if they are humanly understood? Ben-Gurion retorted that Begin's arguments were demagogic. Begin's rise to power did not mark any significant change in the government's policy toward the Arab minority in Israel. The changes that did take place and the rise of a new extremism in the relations between Jews and Arabs were a result of internal changes in Israeli society, changing norms and values, and a different political style.

At a meeting with the press after he was elected prime minister, Begin said, "I am a Palestinian."[33] This was a way of expressing the foolishness of the idea of Arab Palestine as a historical or political concept. For that purpose Begin often recounted the lineage of the term "Palestine" since the times of the Roman Empire as applying to the place that was and always will be the Land of Israel.[34] The first to use the term "Palestinian Arab people," according to Begin, were the Communists in Israel. The Jewish supporters of Palestinian independence went further than the Arabs themselves in claiming that there exists a "Palestinian Arab people." There is one Arab nation, and it has fulfilled its nationalist aspirations in the existing Arab states.[35]

In his second period of office, Begin took public exception to the remarks of Foreign Minister Yitzhak Shamir and Defense Minister Ariel Sharon to the effect that Jordan is already the Palestinian state. First, he denied that they had ever said anything of the sort, but then he added that since most of the Palestinians are found in Jordan "it is [in that sense] a Palestinian state."[36] Begin took great care not to use the term "Palestinian people" or nation. He stubbornly resisted the term up until and including the peace agreement with Egypt, where the term used by him was "Palestinian Arabs." He wanted to employ a moral yardstick that would be satisfied by a promise of minority rights or a solution of the Arab refugee problem, which was seen as parallel to the plight of the Jewish refugees from Arab countries. Begin often noted the Arab countries that maliciously perpetuate the Palestinian problem despite their number and size.[37]

In the 1970s, especially after the Yom Kippur War, he often linked his opposition to a Palestinian state to strategic considerations. "Palestine" would be pro-Soviet, and would become a Russian base in the Middle East, a threat to Israel and the entire free world. Any Palestinian entity would end up a PLO state, and in a victory march "unlike any seen by human eye since the king of demons marched into Vienna." The debate as to whether Judaea and Samaria would come under Jordanian or PLO rule seemed to him a "moral horror."[38]

A dramatic development in Begin's conception took place in the 1960s and 1970s, namely the direct parallel he drew between the PLO and Nazi Germany, and between the Palestinian Covenant and *Mein Kampf*. "Since the days of the Nazis," said Begin, "there has not arisen an organization as barbaric, as anti-human, as that called PLO."[39] The parallel was made complete by Arafat's bunker in Beirut. Before mentioning the name "PLO", Begin always added "the so-called," or "that calls itself". He regarded use of the name Palestinian Liberation Organization as "clear moral and spiritual surrender." Every terrorist action underscored his sanguinary image of the organization and reinforced his absolute disqualification of the PLO as a negotiating partner.[40]

There was no comparison that outraged Begin more than that between the Irgun and the Palestinian organizations. He once replied at length on this allegation.[41] The Irgun, he said, fought to save our nation, they to destroy people; our struggle was to build a home for those who had none, and theirs is to dispossess the Jewish people; the Irgun fought against a foreign ruler and they fight against a legitimate regime; the Irgun fought for a state in which there would be equality, they fight for the destruction of a people and its sovereignty. Begin did not acknowledge the existence of a "Palestinian problem." He denounced Israeli leftists as well as government spokesmen for using an Arab expression, but put his signature to the very same formulation in the Camp David Accords.[42]

The idea of autonomy

The political solution that served to unify Begin's world view, his nationalist aspirations, and political reality was the idea of autonomy. It was not said so outright, but the inference was always allowed that the autonomy plan formulated by Begin in 1977 drew upon and was inspired by Jabotinsky. There was a desire to emphasize the liberal origins of the idea.[43]

Ze'ev Jabotinsky's comments on autonomy are spread over a period of four decades. At one time the idea was intended as a way of preserving the rights of the Jews as a national minority, at another it was utilized for defining the status of the Arabs in a sovereign Jewish state. He first advanced the idea before the First World War, a period when large multinational empires existed in Europe and the Middle East. It was put forward again after the war and the revolutionary changes that had taken place in the world order. Examination of Jabotinsky's writings on autonomy leaves the idea as it always was, and apparently always will be, either an empty formula serving as a screen for other intentions or a double-edged sword.

The idea of autonomy, or "cultural autonomy," is a distinctly East European notion; where citizenship and national identity did not always coincide, the existence of cultural autonomy was at times of great importance to those who were unable to actualize their right to self-determination. There may conceivably have also been some German influence in the idea that a nation can preserve its national identity through a common culture.[44]

Jabotinsky called the Helsingfors program, which was adopted by the third convention of Russian Zionists (December 1906), the "crown of my Zionist youth." It may have been a nineteenth-century breeze for him at the beginning of a new century, "that deceitful century that so disappointed our hopes."[45] Jabotinsky wrote that he was only one of those who shared the idea of "national autonomy in Exile." He regarded himself only as "redactor" of the plan. The intention of the idea of autonomy, according to Jabotinsky, was to base the Jewish national struggle on two props, "a synthesis between the fortresses built for our people in Exile and the large fortress we will capture on both sides of the Jordan."[46]

Autonomy was only a temporary solution for the plight of the Jews in light of the political, economic, and social changes that had taken place in East Europe. It was not meant to replace the national aspirations embodied in the Zionist idea. Simultaneously with his support of autonomy, Jabotinsky opposed the assimilatory and anti-Zionist autonomistic idea and engaged in intense polemic against the Bund, which was at the height of its influence at that time.[47] For Jabotinsky, autonomy was the labor of the present that did not undermine the hope for the future.

The Helsingfors program called for "the Zionist masses naturally joining the liberation struggle of the territorial nations in Russia," for the "autonomy of national regions and suitable guarantees for national minorities," and for "recognition of the Jewish nation as an entity possessing the right of self-rule in all national matters."[48] Jabotinsky was in fact more interested in "self-administration" to guarantee Jewish rights than in national–political autonomy as a permanent state of affairs. He also supported the creation of a Jewish faction in the Russian *duma*.[49]

Jabotinsky's "Letter on Autonomism" was an attempt to demonstrate the interrelationship between autonomy and the national idea and sought to show that the former does not preclude the realization of the latter. Jabotinsky's outlook was in fact oriented toward "national instinct." He regarded national character as something in a person's blood, as integral to his physical and racial type. Only total assimilation could change its balance. In the "Letter on Autonomism," Jabotinsky takes rather an optimistic view of the future of Jewish life in exile. One objective of autonomy in exile, in his view, is normal relations between Jews and non-Jews and full equality of rights, even though he was skeptical about the achievement of this goal in East Europe. But beyond that, Jabotinsky also thought that the preservation of national character was necessary for human progress, so much so that if 'one national unit passes from the world, that is in itself a loss and also an occasion for humanity's mourning."[50]

In his treatise "Self-Rule By a National Minority," Jabotinsky set out in detail his position on the question of the rights of a national minority.[51] According to Jabotinsky, the national problem has two aspects: the question of national territory – the royal route of nineteenth-century nationalist movements – and the question of the national minority. To guarantee the rights of the national minority, Jabotinsky adopted the "personal principle," which grants rights to every individual according to his national membership. But for determining national membership Jabotinsky resorted to the vague and subjective concept of "national consciousness."

Jabotinsky was not overgenerous in the rights he granted to the national minority. Apart from certain aspects of self-administration, he tied the minority closely to the territorial state. Autonomy was to be granted primarily to an ethnic community capable of establishing a central representative organization, and its significance was mainly the safeguarding of the civil rights of the members of that ethnic community. Jabotinsky did not regard the size of the territorial area as a decisive factor in determining whether a people should receive autonomy or sovereignty. To the same extent, he believed that if the national minority is the majority in a particular area, that does not alter its definition as a minority. On the other hand, Jabotinsky allowed far-reaching rights to minorities within the framework of the state. Its actualization as a "public and personal legal association" throughout the state would guarantee "the rights of the self-governing body" in civil matters, including taxation, the management of the flow of immigration, and the preservation of cultural autonomy.[52]

The principle of autonomy cannot be a universal principle, and is not applicable everywhere. It is clearly a relative notion, which is also how Jabotinsky understood it, leaving much room for maneuver to the statesman: "When it comes to sketching the form of autonomy for specific national minorities, it is important to refer to real life, to be attentive to the voice of reality."[53]

Jabotinsky returned to this subject shortly before the Second World War. The resolutions of the first national Revisionist convention in Prague spoke of granting "national–cultural autonomy" to the Arabs in Palestine.[54] The last formulation of autonomy endorsed by Jabotinsky appears in his book, *The Jewish War Front*, which was published just before he died in

August 1940.[55] Its passages on autonomy come from a draft of a proposal formulated as early as 1934. Jabotinsky wanted to demonstrate that the Arab minority that would live in a state with a Jewish majority would enjoy full rights. He wrote, "The world has no right to suppose that Jewish statecraft is unable to establish a fair regime, just like that produced by English, Canadian or Swiss statecraft."[56] Jabotinsky noted that his ideas had evolved at a time when the Revisionists envisaged independent Palestine as a dominion within the British Commonwealth, "and there are many who advocate that idea to this day."

The plan outlined was essentially a federative structure that granted preferential rights to the Jewish majority. It spoke of a Jewish community and an Arab community possessing equal rights, each with its own elected national assembly. The prime minister would be alternately a Jew and an Arab, the vice–prime minister a member of the other community. Jabotinsky's preface to the plan, however, contradicted the details. There he argued that the Jewish people can actualize their right to self-determination only in the Land of Israel, while the Arabs already have nine states of their own (a point that Begin often repeated). In essence, Jabotinsky's eclectic proposals were much closer to what Begin called a binational state: equal rule by two national communities in the same land.[57]

Begin's double-edged sword

As commander of the Irgun Begin wrote that "Rule means real rule: a Hebrew government and not religious, cultural, or municipal 'autonomy' of a 'Jewish ethnic group' under foreign rule."[58] The notion of autonomy, and the issue of the rights of a national minority, began to occupy Begin once again after the Six Day War, and especially in the early 1970s. The idea of autonomy had irresistible appeal, for it combined political practicality and the desire to weaken the Palestinian demand for self-determination with liberal generosity.[59]

The autonomy plan was drawn up by Begin in absolute secrecy.[60] But he was not the only one to probe the idea of self-rule for the Palestinians. During his first visit to Israel after the Likud had come to power, Secretary of State Vance had spoken of the possibility of an "interim settlement." Vance had in mind a UN trusteeship managed jointly by Jordan and Israel culminating after a number of years in a public referendum and self-determination. Vance wrote that this idea was one of the sources of the autonomy plan approved in the Camp David Accords. In August 1977, Begin totally rejected the secretary of state's proposals.[61]

The first to see Begin's autonomy plan, apart from his intimates, were the Americans. He then showed it to President Sadat in Ismailia. Finally, he divulged it to the Knesset.[62] The crux of the plan for "administrative autonomy" for the Arab inhabitants of Judaea, Samaria, and the Gaza Strip was abolishment of the military government's civilian administration and the election by the inhabitants of an "administrative council." The inhabitants would be given the opportunity to choose either Israeli or Jordanian citizenship. Israel would remain responsible for security and public order. Immigration matters would be decided jointly by representatives of the inhabitants, Israel, and Jordan. Jews would retain the right to purchase land and to establish settlements. Similarly, Israel would retain its right to claim sovereignty over the territories.

In December 1977 Begin said that Sadat "will not be able to say 'no' to my plan." In reality, however, the plan was only the beginning of what turned out to be exhausting negotiations. The plan contained elements that had not been given thorough consideration and were subject to conflicting interpretations. As far as can be judged today, Begin genuinely misunderstood the reaction of President Carter and his advisers. Begin, intoxicated by his plan, viewed his trip to the United States, together with Attorney-General Aharon Barak, in December 1977 as a real political success. In consequence, he totally misinterpreted the president's reaction, mistaking a polite response for an expression of support.[63]

Defense Minister Ezer Weizman thought that President Carter had encouraged Begin because of his concern for the success of the forthcoming meeting between Begin and Sadat in Ismailia. Foreign Minister Dayan wrote that the autonomy plan was intended as a counterweight to Sadat's peace initiative. He thought it unfortunate that Begin rushed to make the president's positive comments public because he thereby invited a more reserved public response from Washington. Cyrus Vance surmised that the plan drawn up by Begin was meant as an alternative to withdrawal and the granting of self-determination to the Palestinians. That, of course, did not match the intentions of the United States, which had its own objectives. The positive aspect of the plan, in Vance's view, was the recognition of the existence of a Palestinian problem. Zbigniew Brzezinski, adviser to the president, suggested to Begin that he change the name of the proposal from autonomy to "self-rule," because "autonomy" sounds as if it refers to part of a country or a region. Carter himself wrote that Begin was more flexible concerning the West Bank than he had expected, but he later discovered that "his good words had multiple meanings, which my advisers and I did not understand at the time." Elsewhere he notes that he spent an entire evening with Begin trying, unsuccessfully, to clarify what was meant by the term "autonomy."[64]

The root of the diplomatic jousting of 1978 lay in the desire of the United States to convert the autonomy into an interim settlement, a stage on the way to granting self-determination to the Palestinians. With that end in mind, they sought to exploit any point in the plan that could be used to narrow Israel's authority and control. Similarly, they tried to enlarge the inhabitants' chances of being able to decide their fate, among other ways by holding a public referendum to determine the future of the territories.[65]

After the peace agreement with Egypt, Begin slowly freed himself from the bonds of the autonomy plan. He was close to admitting that the autonomy plan had been primarily a means to achieve the peace – "Its only an idea."[66] He adhered to the Camp David Accords and insisted that they be upheld to the letter. After he visited Egypt in January 1980, his response to Sadat's request that the autonomy be applied to the Gaza Strip was polite but noncommittal. From time to time he said that progress had been made on "minor matters" in the autonomy talks. To the members of the Knesset Foreign Affairs and Security Committee, he described the situation as "constructive deadlock."[67]

Moshe Dayan began his book on the peace talks with his own resignation from the government. He had announced his intention of resigning at the end of September 1979. At that time the prime minister had told him that he would have to get his approval before expounding proposals or ideas of his own. Yosef Burg, the minister of the interior, was named head of the Israeli negotiating team at the autonomy talks, Dayan had refused this position and had not proposed anyone else for it. He thought that Begin and his supporters were aspiring to extend Israeli sovereignty to the territories but doubted that they had a clear plan concerning the status of the Palestinian inhabitants. He himself was opposed to the annexation of the West Bank, as well as to territorial compromise and the establishment of a Palestinian state. He wanted the interim situation, with the Arabs conducting their domestic affairs as they wished and Israel guarding its vital interests, to continue.[68]

In the beginning of October, Dayan informed the prime minister that he was, in fact, resigning from the government. He disagreed with the way the autonomy talks were being conducted, opposed the composition of the delegation conducting the negotiations, and thought that, to a large extent, "the negotiations going on now are pointless."[69] Begin's swift acceptance of the foreign minister's resignation was interpreted as evidence of his intention to be faithful to his ideological beliefs this time, and not to forgo control of the molding of the autonomy. Those conducting the negotiations were indeed given very little rein. A year after his resignation, Dayan tabled a motion in the Knesset which called for self-administration for the Arabs of the territories, to be established unilaterally. The source of authority would be left in Israel's hands, and negotiations parallel to the official autonomy talks would be conducted with the local mayors.[70]

The autonomy talks, which coincided with the waning days of the Carter administration, produced no results. Indeed, the role of the United States in the talks was unclear. The American delegations, headed at first by Robert Strauss and afterwards by Sol Linowitz, did not play a decisive role. The talks got bogged down in details and matters of minor importance. In the end, it was President Sadat who suspended the talks. The end of the Carter administration was another nail in the coffin of negotiations that had been destined for failure from the beginning.[71] Menachem Begin remained on guard, protecting his notion of autonomy, rejecting all attempts to interpret or to add anything to "the spirit of Camp David." He harped on his theme that the self-ruling authority was to be an administrative council. In his view, Egypt's role in the negotiations was temporary; it cannot play the role of Jordan, he said, and give Israel "peace in the east."[72]

It has been said that at the cabinet meeting that dealt with the autonomy plan in advance of the negotiations with Egypt, Begin was moved to tears and sunk at times into long silences.[73] Had the cabinet reached a decision that meant renunciation of the Land of Israel, he said, "I would have gone to the president and submitted my resignation." The meeting was described as one of the toughest of that government. Menachem Begin had no intention of altering his beliefs concerning Judaea and Samaria. The autonomy was designed to defend his principles against a reality that was threatening at home and from abroad. He was fully confident, more than was meet, that this vague term was a real political tool and would serve as a solid bridge to Israeli sovereignty in the future. The insistence on the part of the Arab inhabitants that they be represented by the PLO delayed the testing of Begin's idea and intentions in the crucible of history.[74]

Autonomy, even in its restricted sense, required historical responsibility for the nature of the relations that would develop between Israel and the new political entity; control of the social, economic, and political processes that would begin with its establishment is doubtful. Israel's power of military coercion remained the last barrier before the conversion of this corridor to self-determination into something of real substance.[75]

Both on the left and the right there were those who thought that Begin had crossed his Rubicon. Eldad wrote that the autonomy plan is a "distortion of Jabotinskian thought about the rights of Arabs under Israel sovereignty on both sides of the Jordan."[76] For Begin it was a *deus ex machina*, a political defense against an assault on Judaea and Samaria. It is doubtful whether we shall ever know if Begin had intended from the beginning to drain the idea of autonomy of content, or whether he made a policy error of gravest consequence.

10

International Orientation and Images of the World Order

Begin always viewed foreign policy, especially the diplomatic realm, as his primary field of concern and activity. Before becoming prime minister, Begin had neither diplomatic experience nor wide-ranging knowledge of the international system; instead, in analyzing and interpreting Israel's foreign policy he adhered to a number of principles, most of which had crystallized in the 1930s and 1940s. As prime minister he had a chance to test them against reality.

Few politicians have a clear view or image of the world order. Begin's conception of it can be termed "post-Continental." The conception of the international system held by the generation of the Second Aliyah, and also by Jabotinsky, was limited to Europe. Up until the 1940s, indeed, America was the only non-European country to knock against their already formed perspective. Begin, who was born close to the time of the outbreak of the First World War, fashioned his political outlook at a time when the structure and norms of the international system were in a state of flux. When Begin proclaimed the revolt, in January 1944, the presumptions underlying his activity were derived from a world order that was passing from the world. A new period was at the threshold.

In the 1940s, the decline of Europe and the diminished status of the colonial powers had become the salient feature of international politics. A new, bipolar world order was taking shape, replacing the balance of power that had characterized Europe for centuries. The rise of the superpowers, the development of nuclear weapons, the division of Europe, and the Cold War were to be the predominant features of the coming period. The economic dimension became central in international relations, and the rapid recovery of Europe emphasized even more sharply the division taking place between north and south. Colonial dependency underwent change, and was soon to appear in a new format. The number of new states that would join the international community was without precedent. National liberation movements in Asia and Africa brought their peoples to independence. A non-aligned bloc formed, and then dissipated. The norms of international relations changed. There was a brief period of harmony at the close of the Second World War, but immediately thereafter a sharp ideological and political confrontation developed between the two superpowers. The frequent crises in which the superpower confrontation erupted forced many countries into constant maneuvring with respect to their international orientation.

What of all this did Menachem Begin see? What assumptions were at the base of his conception of the world order and the orientation of his political movement? And what did he offer as an alternative to his country's foreign policy?

The apotheosis of *realpolitik*

A nation's greatness, as Begin understood it, is reflected in its foreign policy – in the active role played by the state through diplomacy and the use of force. Power is the prime value in the determination of a nation's status. Power is the key to international recognition, to the fruits of prestige, to achieving defined national objectives. That was also his view when he was commander of the Irgun. He derided the leaders of Mapai for their timidity: "Power that cannot create a hindrance is of no value in international relations."[1] In a lecture to party activists, in 1954, Begin said that "international developments should be seen in terms of national interests." The two major objectives of Israeli foreign policy – the liberation of the homeland, and peace – were to be achieved by two means, diplomacy and force:

This ought to be the rule for us: every nation should try to achieve its national goal by diplomatic means, as far as is possible. The use of force, if right is on your side, is not forbidden. At times it is even obligatory. But you should use force only when the diplomatic means available to you have disappointed or have proven inadequate.[2]

Begin believed that foreign policy, to be worth anything, must be backed by force. But he always combined this view with a moralistic position. He held that right engenders might.[3] At the height of the War of Attrition he attacked Nahum Goldmann as well as the entire left side of the spectrum of Israeli politics. He does not believe in force, Begin said; it is morality that turns the wheels of history, "You believe in *causa justa*, and justice is on your side, truth is on your side. You believe in moral force, which moves human history . . ."[4] Begin never reconciled the contradiction between his belief that force must be employed because the world's conscience is dead, and his expectation that Israel's struggle will win the world's recognition.

Begin's presuppositions about the rules guiding international relations were founded on deep logical fallacies. On the one hand, he saw force as decisive in foreign policy, which operates within a situation that is essentially chaotic. On the other hand, he believed that the international system acts in accordance with normative rules, prominent among which are the norms of international law, and that the actions of a country are judged in terms of its natural rights, justice, and the morality of its intentions and deeds. But when he asserted that every country is sovereign to determine its national goals and the means to attain them, even without domestic or external consent, he turned morality into an empty expedient.

Begin faulted Israeli foreign policy in the first years of the state, not for believing in world morality and for appealing to the world's conscience, but for not building up military strength and for unintelligent use of it.[5] He wanted Israel to have absolute freedom of action in the employment of its power, but never considered how the world order would be affected were all countries to act at the same time in accordance with that rule. In the context of Begin's political realism, the meaning of morality, diplomacy, and international law became auxiliaries to the use of power and not determinants of norms of behavior in international relations. Begin turned from the defense of a small sovereign community surrounded by enemies to "realistic" assumptions that could not serve a small country like Israel. Begin declared time and again that by telling the truth openly, and by force of Israel's historical right, it would be possible to win international consent to Israel's aspirations.[6] The open statement was always important to Begin. In the early 1950s he said, "the simple truth is that in international policy declarations are acts."[7]

Begin would later learn that the abstract formulation of rules of foreign policy, whether concerning the use of force or the importance of morality and the exposition of one's position, could not compel foreign governments to consent to his policies. He changed nothing in Israel's efforts to present its case and did not succeed in improving Israel's image or status, not even after the peace agreement with Egypt. The most striking failure was Camp David. At the most important diplomatic conclave during his premiership, Begin did not succeed in explaining Israel's demands in accordance with the criteria and principles he espoused. To succeed would have required compromise and compliance, concepts he had nothing but contempt for.[8]

The first principle on which international relations must be based, in Begin's view, is "mutuality."[9] The principle of mutuality is related to the importance Begin ascribed to national prestige. On the sway of prestige in the relations between states, Begin said, "it is the intangible, invisible factor on which empires stand and without which they crumble."[10] He firmly rejected the concept of "international guarantees," because it is an expression of unilateral protection by a foreign power, which history has shown does not stand up to the test of reality. The examples he had most recourse to were the guarantees given to Czechoslovakia and Poland in the late 1930s. He liked to recall that Winston Churchill had referred to the Locarno treaties as the "most precise international document," yet they too were violated. That was his reason for rejecting the Three Power declaration on the Middle East in May 1950, and for opposing guarantees to Israel by any foreign factor whatever. For Begin international guarantees were not only an insult to national honor, they also were an invitation to international pressure. He commented sarcastically that "there is no guarantee that can guarantee the upholding of a guarantee."[11]

Not guarantees but a true, formal alliance is the basis for relations between nations founded on mutual interest, the principle of mutuality, and the obligation to uphold all the terms of the alliance, *pacta sunt servanda*. But on this issue, too, Begin did not have a clear or consistent position. In *World View and National Conception*, he asked whether the treaty between England and Russia concluded in the early 1940s was what really determined relations between them.[12] In 1954 he held that the first consideration of the powers in preserving and forging alliances concerned manpower. That is an indication that alliances are a vital component of national strength. That same month he told Herut party activists that the concept of an alliance had altogether changed, and that now "it is possible to form an alliance without signing a treaty."[13] As an example he cited the relations that were developing between France and Israel.

In the mid-1950s Begin began to demand that "a real, formal alliance be concluded between our nation and the French nation." He saw the Herut movement as spearheading its realization. He accused Ben-Gurion's governments of "wangling for guarantees." For Begin a guarantee was a unilateral act of protection that will culminate in pressure for "territorial compromise." As used by him at that time, the term "territorial compromise" meant renouncing the claim to all of Palestine, which had not yet been conquered.[14]

In the mid-1960s Begin returned to Jabotinsky's concept, "a policy of alliances," adding to it a vague concept of his own – "juncture points." His formulation was highly simplistic: a common interest among states in the international arena.[15] With the countries of East Europe, he wrote, such a potential juncture point is opposition to Germany and its rearmament. In contradiction to the principles underlying his diplomacy of alliances he lauded the "moral reflex," a notion about which he had once fiercely challenged Jabotinsky, "That is one of the great errors that have persisted ever since the head of Betar [Jabotinsky] tried to explain to our opponents that the position of the Jewish people has a moral value, and that this moral value is of great political value." In 1966, Begin tried to direct the policy of alliances towards France, and to focus the "juncture points" against Germany. A year later, what remained of the "alliance" with France crumbled altogether, the countries of Eastern Europe severed diplomatic relations with Israel, while West Germany came to Israel's economic and military assistance.

A central principle Begin prized in considering the norms of international relations was the rules of international law. Begin had already equipped himself in the 1940s with rules derived from international law that accorded legitimacy to and provided post-factum explanations for political actions. As employed and envisioned by Begin, international law is a code used by an imaginary tribunal that metes out punishment and reward to all nations, prosecutes or defends them, on the basis of their actions. On the other hand, he also put the juridical component to what was clearly expedient use to explain or justify diplomatic and other activities serving a particular end. For the most part, however, Begin relied on "historic" or "natural" right, which dispenses with all legal apparatuses of diplomacy such as arbitration, compromise, and concurrence.

Begin appeared both as a formalist who sticks to the letter of international law and as a believer in the romanticism of a war of national liberation, in a strategy of offense, and in an absolutism resting on national will. This contradiction was never reconciled. We see rules and order, but they are employed to justify goals of revolt and war, which cannot be achieved given a normative conception of international relations. International law, justice, and morality come bound together with a war of survival by the weak who are entitled to use any means at their disposal to free themselves from the dangers to their existence.[16]

The most prominent use by Begin of the practices of international law was his conception that political relations between nations must be established through direct negotiations and the only normal relations between countries, are those set out by a peace treaty. Accordingly, he rejected any interim settlement such as a ceasefire, armistice, or non-belligerency. He viewed each of these as a continuation of the state of war.[17] Begin argued that according to international law, territory can be acquired by force if the war was fought in self-defense. Indeed, "all the territorial changes recognized by the nations came about in the wake of defensive wars." Begin turned this principle into a "just political doctrine," which explains border changes. In the early 1970s he spoke of the falsehood in the preamble to Resolution 242 that asserts the "inadmissibility of acquisition of territory by force." It was over the interpretation of this resolution that he resigned from the National Unity government in August 1970. After he became prime minister he contended that the statement in the preamble to the resolution stands by itself and does not contradict the principle of territorial acquisition in a defensive war.[18]

He found in Russia, of all nations, support for his contentions.[19] Russia, he declared, had signed conventions in the 1930s that defined who would be considered the aggressor under specified circumstances, and added his own historical assessment, "It may be supposed that Russia mainly feared an all-out attack by Estonia . . ." After the Second World War, all countries recognized Russia's territorial conquests. He also cited Grotius, Article 51 of the UN Charter, and other sources to justify Israel's retention of the occupied territories. But, of course, the division of Europe and recognition of the Soviet Union's conquests was determined not by the rules of international law but by an international reality that could not be changed. It was the same reality he believed in. Concessions were forced on Israel at Camp David not because of Israel's failure to explain the rules of international law, but because of American threats and fear of the damage that would result were the conference to fail. How different was reality from Begin's abstract conjectures.[20]

Orientations

In the twentieth century, declared Begin, no country can permit itself "splendid isolation," and every country must take a stance on matters decided upon in the capitals of the Great Powers, even if it is unable to influence those decisions.[21] Begin's view of the world order was incomplete, fragmented, and often imprecise. With all his criticism of Israeli foreign policy over the years, he was party to the ignorance of or lack of interest in tendencies developing in the international system. Begin evinced considerable curiosity but not deep understanding. Matters concerning international economics did not hold his attention; his strategic conclusions were not always precise. When he surveyed the shifting events of international relations Begin never abandoned the historical scores with the nations of the world, especially the European countries. It took many years before he overcame his loathing of England. Germany was an unremitting focus of his hostility.

In August 1950, at a mass rally in Tel Aviv, Begin shared his thoughts about the international arena with his audience, "Study of the international situation and knowledge of it is a must for everyone in Israel." There is no Cold War today, just as there is no "hot peace," Begin observed. What is being conducted now is worldwide guerilla war, one of the heights of which is the war in Korea. There, Begin said, the Americans made a sore error. To save China they had not sent even a single soldier; now, for a small peninsula, they were caught up in a bloody war. Two nations were at the focus of his hatred. Germany, whose people are no more than "a pack of mechanized wolves." He demanded that the Israeli delegation to the United Nations propose a resolution to the General Assembly preventing Germany's rearmament. After Germany came England – an active partner in the murder of Jews during the war, and the hypocritical party, in his view, to the Three-Power declaration on the Middle East.[22] The United Nations was an institution upon which Begin looked with skepticism ever since its foundation. The articles written by Begin in the 1950s are filled with derision and criticism of the UN, and especially its observers in Palestine. He was suspect of international supervision over Israel. Before the Sinai campaign he warned against "the entrenchment of the UN apparatus in Israel." On the basis of a misquotation of UN Secretary-General Dag Hammarskjold, who spoke of the armistice agreements as an "international regime," he concluded that the UN apparatus was trying to become "an international regime in the State of Israel."[23]

Begin's interest in foreign affairs was not limited solely to matters related to Israel although after 1967 his attention was increasingly focused on the future of the territories, on establishing Israel's historical and legal right to retain them, and on thwarting diplomatic initiatives that hinted of withdrawal. One of the issues he had addressed in the 1950s and 1960s was the emergence of nuclear arms and its influence on policy. In the 1950s Begin doubted that nuclear weapons had eliminated the importance of territory and of conventional weapons. What he regarded as a revolutionary historical change was that for the first time the United States faced the possibility of a direct attack on its territories; but the real danger was the numerical superiority of the Soviet army in Europe. He did not believe that talks, agreements, and treaties could solve "the fundamental problem of our times," so long as a desire to rule, imperialism, is intrinsic to Communism.[24]

He thought overall war breaking out in a way similar to the eruption of the First World War was a possibility, but thought it unlikely that use would be made of nuclear weapons, because of the danger of annihilating the human race. This, however, would allow small nations to conduct their "small" wars.[25] At the time of the Cuban missile crisis in 1962, Begin devoted more of his attention to the meaning of the concept "blockade," than to the danger of nuclear war between the superpowers. At the same time, the war between China and India led him to revise his previous thesis that war between Great Powers was inconceivable. But there was nothing of a superpower nature about this conflict – except for the size of the populations of China and India, to which he attached great importance.[26]

Begin frequently made platitudinous statements about the Third World, generally in the context of its poverty and ignorance. He also tended to wax lyrical about the historical duty of the liberation movements in Asia and Africa to learn from the experience of the Irgun. He wrote that the process of decolonization, "to which we in the Land of Israel gave serious impetus," could be used to boost Israel's name in the Third World, were it not that the government's petty internal calculations led them to conceal the

Irgun's part in the War of Independence. But as the developing countries became increasingly negative to Israel as a result of their position on the Israel–Arab dispute, and their stance vis-à-vis the Soviet Union, Begin's enthusiasm waned.[27] He certainly did not see Israel as part of the Third World. In fact, in the mid-1960s Begin was opposed to Israel being called a Middle Eastern country. Israel, in his view, is a Mediterranean country, a continuation of southern Europe. "With respect to civilization, it is not our desire to continue what had existed in the region called the Middle East. We brought European civilization here and we want to continue it and build it.'[28] This distinction was not directed against the peoples of Asia and Africa, but it should "determine the political path."

Begin was consistent in his position on South Africa. He called Israel's votes in the United Nations against South Africa unfortunate and foolish. He denounced the apartheid regime but saw no reason to exacerbate relations with South Africa. He was especially angered by the fact that in the early 1960s Israel joined its voice on this issue to that of the Communist bloc and the Third World. That was a mistaken calculation, he said. After he was elected prime minister he said that he opposed all forms of racism, but Israel would continue to maintain good relations with South Africa, and would not conceal the fact.[29]

Although Begin's international orientation ostensibly relied on "changing constellations," it was actually quite stable as it was based on a fixed historical conception. There were nations he saw as representing a unique national character, each culture represented by a corresponding foreign policy. This was especially so with regard to the European nations who were the representatives of traditional diplomacy – the English, French, Italians, Russians, and Germans. Begin constantly maintained that Israel needed allies. He described the method for selecting allies, but could not offer any alternative that was not anchored in the reality in which Israel's foreign policy was shaped.

The proclamation of the revolt in January 1944 indicated that the Irgun's platform and orientation was clearly pro-Western. Begin suggested that sovereign Israel propose the establishment of a mutual alliance with Great Britain, the United States, and France. The Soviet Union occupied a separate category as a country with which negotiations would have to be held regarding the release of its Jews. His ideological monism seemingly freed Begin from any limitation in selecting partners for diplomatic alliances. At the base of his policy was common interest, not moral support or sympathy. Begin believed that a national revolt would draw allies to it mainly for a "negative" reason: interest by countries in the battle being waged against a power they regard as hostile. The operations of the Irgun, he believed, accomplished two things: the emergence of the Palestine question as an international problem, and the acquisition of political support that made the establishment of the state possible. Begin's international orientation was, at root, thoroughly statist. In Begin's conception, the opportunity to gain an ally became something mechanistic if a display of strength by a small nation coincided with the military or diplomatic interest of another Great Power. This was a convergence of interests with no ideological basis or moral consideration, and did not even require diplomatic cultivation. It is a partnership that comes and vanishes in the changing configurations of international relations.[30]

On the day the state was proclaimed, Begin set forth more or less the same international orientation. In first place appeared the two superpowers. The call for understanding and friendship with the peoples of the Soviet Union and the United States were formulated identically. The countries of Europe were in a different category, but only France was mentioned by name.[31] Thirty years later, when he presented his first government in June 1977, he was to mention the same countries he had referred to in the 1940s. First, he said, we shall try to deepen the friendship with the United States. Israel was now an inseparable part of the free world. Afterward, he said, we will work to renew our friendship with France, to extend a hand across the Mediterranean to renew the alliance of the past. And finally, he concluded, we are interested in the normalization of relations with the Soviet Union. What had been a presumption for him in the early years had since become a fact – the great change in Russia's attitude during the 1940s was, he said, a result of "the liberation war against the British regime."[32]

In the first years of the statehood, his pro-Western orientation was somewhat qualified. He rejected the "orientation towards the United Nations," and neutralism, but neither did he propose unilateral support of the United States. In an article aimed at soldiers of the IDF, which was in fact not published, he wrote, "We will not build our land with a loan from the American Import–Export Bank that has political strings attached."[33] Begin opposed the notion of "neutralism" in vogue in the 1950s. He had scorn for what he called an "orientation of nonidentification with nonneutrality."[34] Israel cannot be neutral, Begin argued, for the simple reason that it has enemies; that is why it should be looking for allies with whom it can "go a certain distance." But, he added, "Messrs. Ben-Gurion and Sharett did not seek real alliances but vague sympathy instead." That is why they set themselves the illusory goal of achieving peace without wanting to liberate the homeland . . ."[35] At the very same time, the Herut movement denounced the government's stance of "automatic obedience" in supporting the United States on the Korean issue. An Israeli commitment on this issue, said Shmuel Katz in the Knesset, is a matter that concerns the nation as a whole.[36]

Although Begin rejected nonalignment, he said more than once in the early years of the state that the choice between East and West is not one between absolute good and absolute evil. There are Germanies on both sides of the Iron Curtain, and as far as he was concerned, England was wrongly placed. There is no East or West. The internal disputes within each bloc should be exploited: "Our orientation is towards the Hebrew homeland, honest patriotism and no principled ossification towards those who helped us in our war."[37] The orientation was still a derivative of one fundamental objective: assistance in liberating the homeland.[38]

The embattled alliance

When Begin came to the United States for the first time in Autumn 1948, he likened himself to Gulliver arriving in the land of the giants. America, for Begin, was the land of freedom and of the great revolution.[39] At the same time, he had an ambiguous attitude to the American role in the Israeli–Arab conflict. During the 1940s and 1950s he voiced sharp criticism of the United States, and of the way in which Israeli diplomacy went about fashioning its relations with the United States. Many years were to pass before the image of the United States as a permanent ally crystallized, and even when it did there were still vehement outbursts in times of crisis. Moreover, Begin always portrayed Israel as a loyal ally of the free world and never viewed America's assistance as a one-sided affair. After the Yom Kippur War his rhetoric echoed Kennedy when he asked: "Citizen of America, in these days ask not what your country has done for Israel, ask what Israel has done for your country."[40] As prime minister he told the members of the Knesset that he had made it clear to the US secretary of state Alexander Haig that he was not pleased that Israel was referred to as a "strategic asset." Haig replied that there was a "permanent alliance" between Israel and the United States. Begin added that he could not recall when agreement between the two countries had been so deep and extensive.[41]

That same year he surprised the United States with the Golan Heights Law and his subsequent extraordinary meeting with US Ambassador Samuel Lewis when he complained about US attempts to limit Israel's freedom of action. In September 1982 he complained to Defense Secretary Caspar Weinberger, "Israel has given the United States a free Lebanon, but the US also wants to take Judaea, Samaria and the Gaza Strip."[42] That was not atypical. The road to the peace agreement with Egypt was pitted and bumpy – substantial concessions side by side with unilateral actions and provocative declarations. The statement "there was no pressure and no confrontation" was repeated many times by Begin during his premiership.

In fact, American diplomacy made an unprecedented impact on Israel during that period, to the extent that the American ambassador was even nicknamed "the High Commissioner." The peace efforts, the democratic values shared by the two countries, and the mutual interests in the region prevented a crisis in the relations between them.[43]

Begin's attitude to America was rarely unequivocal. In the decade between the end of the Second World War and the Sinai Campaign, Begin did not fully understand US policy in the Middle East, did not relate it to America's world policy, and did not properly assess the complex relations between the United States and Great Britain. He saw America as containing Russia, counterbalancing and competing with England, and as a potential ally that was adopting a policy directed against Israel as the price of mollifying the Arab countries. The US participation on the Anglo-American Committee in 1946 aroused his anger; the Americans, he said, were trying to get a foothold in the Middle East, "on the backs of the Jews, but not for them; the Anglo-Saxon powers are trying to penetrate Central and Eastern Europe." He regarded the committee as a British scheme to dampen possible American support for the Zionist cause.[44]

Begin's ambivalence to the United States was at its height in the 1950s. First, he viewed the United States as "a dam holding back a flood of enslavement." Were it not for America, Germany would have conquered Europe and large parts of Asia and Africa in the First World War; in the Second World War Russia would have done so. He derided Ben-Gurion and Sharett for supporting the idea of a third force between Soviet imperialism and Western imperialism. Begin correctly surmised that US policy was two-pronged: containment of the Soviet Union, and efforts aimed at dismantlement of the old empires. But he saw that at the same time, Washington was also drawing closer to the Arab countries and disregarding Israel and he anticipated a crisis in US–Israel relations.[45] Begin assailed "filthy mouthed Mr. Ben-Gurion and the man of hollow phrases, Mr. Sharett," for bowing to John Foster Dulles and consenting to closer relations between the United States and the Arab countries. Begin's criticism of the government was so severe that it seemed as though America was conducting its foreign policy on the basis of what was said in Jerusalem. At the same time, he displayed nothing but contempt for Israeli diplomacy and those managing it.[46]

American arms sales to the Arab states in the 1950s brought Begin's attacks on the US to a new height. How did we come to such a pass, he asked, that "America will take hostile action against Israel involving a danger of death for us and our children?" His firm conclusion was that it was the result of Israel's readiness to make concessions; the readiness to repatriate refugees and to drop the demand for unification of the homeland

Plate 1: The Begin family in 1932, Brest-Litovsk. Nineteen-year-old Menachem (center) with his sister Rachel and brother Herzl; sitting are his parents Hassia and Ze'ev Dov.

Plate 2: Warsaw, the late 1930s. Ze'ev Jabotinsky, the founder of the Revisionist movement (sitting, second to the right) with Aharon Propes and Menachem Begin in Betar uniform.

Plate 3: Palestine, 1942. The soldier in the Polish army with his wife Aliza and friends.

Plate 4: Days of hiding. The commander of the Irgun as Rabbi Yisrael Sassover.

Plate 5: The *Altalena* burning in the waters off the Tel-Aviv shore, June, 1948.

Plate 6: The demolished southern wing of the King David Hotel, July, 1946.

Plate 7: Members of the Herut party with their leader at the old Knesset, 1949. Behind Begin, the poet Uri Zvi Greenberg (left) and Ya'acov Meridor. On the far right, the previous leader of Lehi, Nathan Yellin-Mor.

Plate 8: The 'faction'. Begin speaking in memory of the founder of Lehi Abraham Stern (Yair), 1964. Sitting in the center, the previous operation officer of Lehi, Yitzhak Shamir.

Plate 9: Meeting of the old rivals. David Ben-Gurion and Begin at the King David Hotel, December 11, 1967. In the center, General Ezer Weizman.

Plate 10: Leader of the opposition. Begin addressing the Knesset, 1961. Prime Minister Ben-Gurion, apparently amused, and Golda Meir listening.

Plate 12: Camp David, September 1978. Carter with Sadat and Begin, outside the president's lodge.

Plate 13: The Israeli delegation at Camp David. Facing Begin are Moshe Dayan and Ezer Weizman. Pipe in hand is Aharon Barak.

Plate 11 (*left*): The elected prime minister is greeted by President Ephraim Katzir, June 20, 1977.

Plate 14: Triumph. The Peace Treaty with Egypt, March 26, 1979.

Plate 15: Defeat. Menachem Begin announces his resignation, August 30, 1983.

had persuaded the Americans that they need have little regard for Israel's will and capability.[47] Begin advanced the thesis that a forceful verbal stance would have sufficed to change the policy of a superpower;[48] he could not see that this was implausible.

Likewise he could not see that there could be any relationship between US arms shipments to Arab countries and its concern for defense of the free world. The arms supplies, in his view, were a function of the competition between the United States and Great Britain in the Middle East. The only option that remained was war, "elimination of the fronts, abolishment of the enemy's bases of aggression, in accordance with a well-calculated strategy, choosing the right time and the right operation."[49] In October 1954 Begin appealed directly to the members of Congress, pleading for their support against Arab aggression.[50] The attempts to conclude the Baghdad Pact aroused his fears. He thought the Iraqi–Turkish agreement was the severest blow ever suffered by Israel. "Do we now face the mightiest attack on our very existence by the major Western powers?" he asked in the Knesset. Begin sharply criticized the government, which ostensibly supported the Eisenhower doctrine without manifestly declaring an anti-Soviet policy or receiving guarantees in return.[51]

At the end of 1955 it was clear that the balance of power in the region was about to shift as a result of the Czech–Soviet deal with Egypt and arms supplies from Great Britain and the United States to the Arab countries. Begin intensified his attacks on Dulles and on American diplomacy in the Middle East. In Disraelian style he declared in the Knesset, "In this place, where our feet tread, our forefathers established a kingdom long before the civilized world had heard of a continent called America."[52] He derided the government for postponing military action in the vain expectation of receiving American arms, and portrayed Ben-Gurion as a man with no strategic knowledge.[53] After the Sinai campaign he expressed his concern about American diplomacy that had strengthened the Soviet Union and turned the defeated Nasser into a victor. He was able to explain this only in terms of the dual policy pursued by the Americans – anti-Communism and anti-colonialism – and the timorousness of Israel's leaders.[54]

Begin's criticism was directed at the external aspects of Israeli diplomacy – the lack of style, honor, and rhetoric. Apart from this, however, the leader of the opposition was unable to offer much to the young state contending with severe hardship at home and grave dangers from outside. The goal on which he set all his attention – a war that would bring peace in its wake, and unification of the homeland on both sides of the Jordan – was unrealistic. Begin's imagination did not reach beyond the horizons of Israeli diplomacy.

The improvement of relations with the United States beginning with the Kennedy administration, and the war in Vietnam, opened a new channel for

Begin's diplomatic imagination – strategic cooperation between Israel and the United States. But immediately after the Six Day War he resumed his attacks on American policy in the Middle East. The interim agreement with Egypt after the Yom Kippur War, which was the first and necessary foundation for the diplomacy he was to pursue in 1977, came in for especially sharp criticism.

The apparent contradiction in Begin's attitude towards the United States was that he aspired for a strategic alliance but also wanted Israel to be allowed freedom of action, as befits a sovereign nation; wanted US military and economic aid to continue, but did not want the United States to orchestrate relations between Israel and the Arab countries in accordance with its own global interests. On the contrary, he actually insisted that the client state determine the nature of the relations between it and its patron. He sought a partnership of interests with the United States, but wanted a superpower to give secondary consideration to its overall interests in the Middle East. When he entered office, he imagined that it would be possible to achieve the maximalist objectives of Israeli foreign policy by being resolute and taking a firm stand – without a real confrontation with the United States. He saw only one obstacle standing between failure and the attainment of "the great goal": lack of talent and a defeatism that to some extent or another was intrinsic to the Zionist left.[55]

Begin's election as prime minister aroused grave fears in the US administration. It had never had to deal with a change of regime in Israel. The Carter administration was still new, but already had a well-formulated conception of an overall settlement in the Middle East. It surmised that Begin's election meant that its intention of convening a conference in Geneva in the fall would have to be postponed for an indefinite period. The administration also had difficulty assessing the reasons for the Likud victory. Was the rightward turn the result of a transient situation or did it reflect a deeper change of values in Israeli society? Begin's hawkish and nationalist image was a cause of considerable disquiet, but some reassuring voices were also heard. It was said that, like de Gaulle and Nixon, he might be able to effect a change in Israel's position. There were also voices demanding a tough policy toward Israel, something at least like that of the Eisenhower–Dulles period.[56] In a letter to Begin right after his election as prime minister, Carter noted his deep commitment to achieving peace between Israel and its neighbors and invited him to Washington.[57]

Before this first visit to the United States as prime minister, in July 1977, Begin displayed great sensitivity about his image and America's posture. He spoke of peace, appointed Dayan foreign minister, and reassured Samuel Lewis, the new US ambassador in Israel. He did everything to assure the success of his American trip.

At a gala dinner in his honor, Begin was unrestrained in his praise of the president of the United States. He said his talk with him was "one of the best days of my life." He noted that the United States was Israel's faithful ally, and that it set its sights above all on peace. Begin told his audience that the rabbinate in Israel had appealed to the people to pray for the success of his mission and had specified a particular psalm for each day of his visit. After his election as prime minister, he told them, he had said that "Carter knows the Bible, and that will make it easier for him to know whose land this is."[58] He then capped his performance with the ultimate superlative, comparing the president to Ze'ev Jabotinsky.

Carter stayed close to the business at hand, though he proved himself no less talented than Begin in dispensing empty compliments. But it was obvious that he was determined. Solution of the conflict should not be delayed, he said. He felt the hour was right for an effort in this direction. The president noted that the talks with Begin were among his most enjoyable and encouraging since taking office. The diplomatic description of the talks, however, was extremely precise: "We had incisive talks today. We clarified differences of opinion in a most open and direct manner." As was his practice, and as he would do many more times in the future, the president summarized the points of agreement and disagreement to set the stage for a new assault on his opponent in the future.[59]

The expectations that a confrontation was imminent gave way to a sense of satisfaction. The assessment of observers was that Begin had succeeded in his mission. His own feeling was euphoric: "I have ended the confrontation with the United States," he was to declare on his return. His trip to the United States was a sweet, albeit short, respite for the new prime minister. This was still the period of full-dress state ceremonies; on his return two red carpets were rolled out, there was an honor guard, and the IDF band and the entire government was out to receive him. For the first time, Begin declared, it was agreed between Israel and the United States that the goal of negotiations would be a peace treaty. Begin also announced a diplomatic innovation of his own: "We acted in accord with a new strategy," he said. A confrontation was avoided because he did not try to reach agreement with the United States on the central issues of the peace negotiations.[60] The cost of that nonconfrontation would be revealed in the course of the following year. In the Knesset Begin said that, "The president of the United States is a great man . . . He has a love for the freedom of man. Therefore he insists on human rights and I am sure that the State of Israel will give him unqualified support in this field."[61]

From here on, Begin was wide open to attacks by political opponents and allies. Shimon Peres said that the prime minister "preferred immediate relief at the cost of burdening, maybe even laying a trap for, future relations between Israel and America." Yitzhak Rabin was to write in his memoirs that Begin had destroyed the traditional understanding about consultation between the two countries before the launching of any diplomatic initiative. Begin saw himself as the victor who had saved Israel from a disaster almost brought upon it by Rabin. In so doing he created a deceptive façade that sorely damaged the credibility of the Begin government.[62] Begin had described Rabin's last talk with Carter as one of the most difficult and harshest ever held by an Israeli prime minister, but when he said this he did not know what history had in store for him. The peace plan he had taken with him to America served as a springboard for more comprehensive American plans. At the end of July 1977, it was decided to convert three military installations on the West Bank into civilian settlements. That step marked the beginning of a tortuous road along which relations between the Carter administration and the Israeli government were to travel. Just one month after his return from the United States there was already talk that the two countries were headed toward a confrontation.[63]

At the end of November, Begin assailed the Alignment for having said that America would not want to talk with the Likud and proudly informed them that he had since "exchanged fourteen important personal letters with the president of the United States . . .," and that there was no pressure on Israel.[64] In practice, the Carter administration had arrived at a fairly precise assessment of the prime minister's weaknesses and now set out to chip away at his status. Even during his first term there was talk, for the first time in Israel's history, of attempts by the US administration to topple a prime minister in office.[65] True, there was an easing of relations with Israel during Carter's last year as president, but this was not the result of a change in US policy. Rather, it was due to a combination of darkening skies in the international arena, especially the Iranian crisis, and the administration's domestic difficulties during an election year.

The election of Ronald Reagan to the presidency was welcomed by the Likud government who felt comfortable with the new administration and the ethos it brought with it. Reagan and Secretary of State Haig found in Israel a government that tended to accept the idea of cooperation against the Soviet Union. There was talk in Herut circles of cooperation with the "New Right" in the United States.[66] Visiting the White House again in September 1981, Begin said that he had never been received so warmly. One of the main subjects of discussion was strategic cooperation between Israel and the United States, which Begin for a time made an issue of central importance.[67] But after Begin's return, the tone of relations between the two countries changed rapidly.

In December 1981 Begin, in a surprise move, brought the Golan Heights Bill to the Knesset, which swiftly approved it. The plan for operation "Big Pines" in Lebanon was shown in outline to representatives of the United States. The agreement on strategic cooperation was suspended.

Secretary of Defense Caspar Weinberger began to take over Brzezinski's role as the symbol of administration hostility to Israel. In a cabinet announcement in February 1982, Begin put his sarcasm to use to attack Weinberger for having refrained from visiting Israel during a tour of the region, and expressed concern that the balance of power would be upset as a result of the administration's intention to sell sophisticated weapons to Jordan and Saudi Arabia.[68] President Reagan speedily sent off a letter to the prime minister on the subject of arms sales. The administration, aware of the plans being drawn up with respect to Lebanon, wanted to mollify Begin. In his letter of reply, Begin wrote that the arms deal was "one of the gravest potential dangers since the renewal of our independence."[69]

The Lebanon War that erupted in June 1982, what Begin called "the War for Peace in Galilee," was to badly damage Israel's image and bring its standing in American public opinion to an all-time low. But in the beginning of August an unrepentant Begin sniped at Senator Percy: "We bow only to God."[70]

Begin had been taken by surprise by Reagan's Middle East plan. The administration had not felt it necessary to consult with Israel about it beforehand, and Begin now rejected it out of hand. Israel's Lebanon War, which Begin had said would deliver important strategic gains to the United States, ended with the United States presenting Israel with a plan designed to remove the West Bank from Israeli control. In a letter to Reagan, Begin complained that the American proposals comprised a deviation from the Camp David Accords, and stressed in the sharpest terms that Israel would never give up Judaea and Samaria. Foreign Minister Yitzhak Shamir told the Knesset that he viewed the concessions made in Sinai as "the very limit of the security and territorial risks" Israel could take.[71]

During the Begin period, the tendency to kick out at Israel's main patron in order to increase self-confidence and make political gains at home intensified, but to no avail. The United States continued to see its role as guarantor of Israel's security, not of its conquests. That fact was not altered by Begin's absolute belief in his diplomatic skill, the influence of the Jewish lobby in Washington, and the strategic partnership between Israel and the United States. This, one would think, might have cast a shadow of doubt over beliefs and conceptions that Begin had held for decades.

Janus's two faces

Two contradictory conceptions vied with each other in Begin's attitude towards the Soviet Union. One was based on an analysis of the nature of communism as an ideology and regime; the other was his recognition that the Soviet state conducts its foreign policy in accord, above all, with its national interest. Begin always distinguished between "leftism" as an intellectual and historical phenomenon, and the behavior of Russia as a superpower.

Begin had begun to probe the Russian phenomenon at an early stage. *White Nights* is full of statements that attempt to analyze the character of the Soviet regime and the fate of the individual caught in its jaws. He devoted the last chapter to speculation about what was likely to occur in Russia after Stalin's death. He imagined that domestic struggles and nationalist tendencies would one day give birth to an altogether different sort of state.[72]

In the 1940s he presented the revolt as the principal factor influencing the Soviet Union's attitude towards the Zionist movement. This "realistic" view was the source of attacks on the pro-Russian orientation, which Begin attributed to all sections of the Israeli left. In explaining the Soviet position, Begin did not relate it to ideology, or to the changing will of its rulers, but to the laws of a mechanistic model according to which states' movements are dictated by the rule "the enemy of my enemy is my friend."[73] The point at which Communist and Zionist interests converged was the fight against imperialism and Russia's desire to oust Great Britain from the Middle East. Yet Begin contradicted this observation when he attributed the Soviet Union's policy to its view of the role Jews play in European society. The Jews had once served as leverage for penetrating the heart of Europe. In many countries they had been a fomenting agent serving Russia's objectives. But the conquest of Eastern Europe had changed that situation. They were now a factor to be minimized within Soviet society. On the basis of that analysis, Begin called for a "policy of alliances" – an overall agreement with Russia for the mass departure of the Jews from Europe.[74]

Begin had always objected to the association of progress with Socialism. The belief in Communism seemed to him "imposed and voluntary slavery," a product of the weakness of the human soul and the sophisticated distortions of Russian propaganda.[75] The rise of the New Left and its support for the Palestinian organizations in the 1970s stirred Begin to a renewed attack on revolutionism founded on tyranny and reaction, a barbaric leftism that possesses weapons but not morality.[76] But, as to the Soviet Union's behavior in the international arena Begin had an unchanging belief: Communist foreign policy was essentially expansionist and Russia constantly wanted to extend its rule wherever it could. Begin had supported a strategy of "containment," especially when he still doubted the likelihood of a world war.[77] As early as May 1943, when the Comintern was dissolved, Begin wrote that in dismantling the Third International, the Russians were shifting their gaze to Eastern and Central Europe, "They believe only in physical force. They want to rule and seek to expand the boundaries of their rule as far as possible." As to the Middle East, "Communism divides and must divide the peoples of the East . . ."[78] In the early 1950s he noted that while Communism as an idea and social order changes, Russian imperialism persists, and it supports dictatorships of the right as well as of the left.[79]

In the early 1960s he relished the fight between China and the Soviet Union for hegemony over the Communist world. That not only accorded with his assumptions about the realistic behavior of nations, but also showed that Marxism's pretensions about changing man's nature and the relations between nations do not meet the test of reality. World Communism now stood stripped bare of all pretence, China having made it patently clear that revolution can be spread throughout the world only by force.[80] After the Yom Kippur War, Begin was to say that Moscow carries out its expansion in three ways: war by proxy, the selection of a principal enemy and focusing the struggle against it, and the opportunistic adoption of a policy of détente.[81] Despite this dogmatic view, Begin's conception of the nature of the relations between Israel and the Soviet Union was complex and contradictory. This complexity derived from Soviet policy during the 1940s – the war Russia waged against Germany, and its support of the establishment of the State of Israel. On the diplomatic plane, Begin's realistic dimension sought to overpower the ideological dimension.

The other side of Begin's views was manifest in his ferocious attacks on the Israeli left. In the early 1940s there seemed to be nothing Begin enjoyed more than mocking the attitude of the left-wing Hashomer Hatzair toward the Soviet Union. Before proclaiming the revolt, he had called the pro-Russian orientation "one-sided Jewish love." Soviet Russia, he wrote then, "is an active enemy of Zionism and will remain so in the future as well." Russia was not interested in the exodus of its Jews, he said, and did not need a "philanthropist" in the Middle East to eliminate poverty and hunger; in fact, they served its purposes.[82] Begin continued to admonish Hashomer Hatzair in the 1950s, at the time of the Prague trials, for its adoration of a "second homeland." When Mapam changed its position, he asked with derision, "What would have happened, comrades, if Stalin would have lived another five years?" In debates with Mapam leader Meir Yaari after the Six Day War, he reminded the latter that the positions taken by Hashomer Hatzair since the 1930s expressed the tragedy of "historical contradiction."[83]

On the diplomatic level, Begin declared, relations between countries do not require friendship. He ridiculed the importance Moshe Sharett had placed on the renewal of diplomatic relations after the Soviet Union had severed them in 1953 in the wake of a bomb blast in its embassy. At the time of the Sinai campaign he attacked the government's panic in the face of Russian threats, calling the latter "one of the biggest bluffs in history." In 1960, he derided Ben-Gurion for his desire to meet with Khrushchev and for his attempt to add Russian guarantees to those given to Israel by the Western powers. In the diplomatic world, wrote Begin, one does not risk being refused.[84]

Soviet arms supplies to the Arab states, its nurturance of the PLO, and the Soviet attitude towards its Jews, once again reinforced Begin's negative attitude towards the USSR. He compared the defense treaty between the Soviet Union and Egypt to the Ribbentrop–Molotov agreement, and saw it as an expression of expansionism and the division of spheres of influence under the guise of socialism and progress. The Russians, he claimed, would expand into the Middle East regardless of Israel. Toward the end of the 1960s he saw the Suez Canal as the focus of its strategic aspirations. If a Russian army were to get past the canal, "the entire world strategic alignment would be fundamentally altered."[85] Despite the Soviet Union's hostility to Israel, Begin insisted that hostility should not be increased and an effort should be made to improve relations with the Soviet Union, "at least to diminish its hostility to us."[86]

Begin's rise to power did not change Soviet policy towards Israel, but it did facilitate its propaganda work in the Arab countries. The Soviet Union softened its stand on Israel before the announcement of the joint US–Soviet statement in October 1977, but was nevertheless distanced from the diplomatic process. The Soviet exclusion was especially clear after the Sadat visit to Jerusalem. After the Camp David Accords, the Soviet position on the Middle East was endangered by the possibility that other Arab countries would join the peace agreement. But that did not happen, and the Soviets could continue to fan the confrontation front to their hearts' content.[87]

Begin's position as prime minister was that Israel was interested in normalization of relations with the Soviet Union, but the initiative must come from the Soviet side.[88] The invasion of Afghanistan changed his view on the possibility of normalization, however, prompting him to say that "business as usual is not possible."[89] When Russia warned Israel against attacking Syria, after the Lebanon War, Begin declared, "there is no reason to belittle [the warning], nor to panic."[90] The fact that the Reagan administration adopted a tougher stand towards the Soviets also changed the balance of Israel's realtions with the Soviet Union. Israel's might had never pointed north as it did at the end of Begin's regime.

Continent of abandon

In Begin's world, Europe remained the land of slaughter, a continent of abandon and license. His fury was obsessively directed to the once great powers of Europe, England, and Germany, invoking the trials and calamities of European history. He never reconciled himself to the "dark chapter" in relations between Great Britain and the Jewish people.[91] When the nine members of the Common Market sought to grant the PLO a standing in the peace talks, his rhetoric went back to Vichy, to collaboration with the Gestapo, to the Sudetenland, "Europe has not written such a disgraceful and shameful chapter since the days of Munich in September 1938 and the Ribbentrop–Molotov agreement or the Stalin–Hitler pact of August 1939," he declared.[92] He appealed directly to the peoples of Europe and warned them that their governments' policy endangered the Jewish state, the surviving remnant.

Begin's most caustic outburst against the Europeans was in the spring of 1981. It began in response to a statement by German Chancellor Helmut Schmidt in Saudi Arabia to the effect that Germany has a moral commitment to the Palestinians. Begin called Schmidt a "greedy braggart who sells arms dear in order to buy oil cheap." He accused him of being present at the execution of the German officers who had attempted to assassinate Hitler in 1944. Subsequently he put Schmidt in one category with French President Valery Giscard d'Estaing and said that they both were greedy and heartless, without memory or humanity. Begin later said that every sentence of his was carefully considered: "There are moments when diplomacy is a sin, and clear open statements are called for."[93] He did all he could to exclude Europe from the peace agreements – out of suspicion and political interest, but also out of moral and historical revulsion.

Great Britain

With Britain and the British, Begin conducted a long historical monologue. In his publicist writings during the underground period, he addressed John, Sir John, or Lord John as the personifications of British national character.[94] Begin's ambivalence towards the gentile world was most marked in his attitude towards Britain, which combined features he admired with others he despised. In Begin's world Britain appeared as "treacherous Albion," a nation murderously hypocritical towards the Jews when its empire began to crumble. Britain violated its historical commitment to the Jewish people, and completed the work of appeasement in Europe with its scheming and incitement in the Middle East. In 1943 he wrote that the British always find a way to link a "bookkeeping interest that guarantees a profit" to lofty ideals. There wasn't a country in the world, Begin contended, that did not want to expel the British or abandon Britain.[95] But to Bethell he confided that he was brought up by his father to admire Britain and it was the Britain of the Balfour Declaration, the liberal tradition, and the parliamentarian debate that he attempted to imitate.

In the 1940s and the early years of Israel's existence, Britain dominated Begin's thoughts on international politics. He regarded Britain as lording over a historical situation that would soon dash the hopes of the Jewish people. He saw it as a country that acted guilefully and deceitfully, blocked Jewish immigration to Palestine, sealed the road to Jewish sovereignty, and incited the Arabs – all out of selfish interests. The factors shaping British policy in the Middle East led Begin to one conclusion: bitter war and an assault on its imperial prestige. Great Britain resembled Rome.[96] But, unlike *Lehi*, Begin drew a distinction between the British Empire and British rule in Palestine. He did not rule out ties with Britain after independence was achieved.[97]

Begin could not comprehend the complex relations between Great Britain and the United States. For a long time he supposed that there was total commonality of interests between them. The Soviet Union was striving to oust Britain from the Middle East, and America was trying to assure that she remain there permanently. Begin considered the Anglo-American Committee a plot by the two powers, rather than as an opening for a change in the American position.[98] Later, he reversed his conception. Beginning in the late 1940s the assumption that a clash of interests divided the United States and Britain became a central axis around which his interpretations of diplomatic events in the Middle East turned. Begin did come to the conclusion, as did other radical segments of the Revisionist movement, that Britain was in the process of losing its power and international influence. In this they were far ahead of the socialist Zionists. Such certainty as to Britain's impending decline was shared only by Mussolini, whose foreign policy in the Middle East was aimed against "Anglo-Saxon tyranny."[99]

Begin's hatred for Britain remained unchanged into the 1950s. It linked up with his obsessive hatred at that time for the Hashemite Kingdom. Britain's treaty with Jordan appeared to him a way for it to continue its struggle against Israel, a base for the unfolding of its schemes. In January 1950 he told the Knesset that the three powers with influence in the region other than Great Britain – the Soviet Union, the United States, and France – all opposed Britain's interests in the Middle East. But instead of trying to block a British settlement for the region, he said, the Israeli government in its great blindness was helping to secure Great Britain's hold and buttress Abdullah's rule in the Land of Israel.[100] At the time of the Sinai campaign, Begin's attitude toward Great Britain was in strong contrast to the praise he had for France as an ally. He called on the British not to try to deprive Israel of the fruits of its victory: "if it [Britain] does us harm – we will do it harm; if it treats us well, we will treat it well."[101]

Later, Begin would meet with disappointment from Britain. Perusal of the British press at the time of Begin's first visit in January 1972 shows the British losing their usual reserve. If Begin expected to be treated like Kenyatta and Makarios, that is not what he encountered. The British press looked back with a vengeance to the 1940s – the hanging of the British sergeants, the explosion in the King David Hotel, and Deir Yassin. A ceremonial dinner for him at the Royal Garden Hotel was canceled because of bomb threats. Begin was compelled to engage in insistent apologetics about his past as commander of the Irgun. Britain did everything it could to let him know that he was an undesirable guest on British soil.[102]

When Begin was elected prime minister, *The Times*, a newspaper he had despised since the 1940s, wrote that his victory was proof that in the end terrorism pays. Visiting Britain again in December 1977, he toasted the queen and said, as he had to President Carter, "this is one of the best days of my life." After a further visit to Britain, in May 1979, he spoke of the fairness in the relations between Great Britain and Israel that had begun during the premiership of James Callaghan and which would continue.[103] But the threshold of his suspicion of Britain always remained low, as can be seen from his reaction to Britain's participation in the European initiative for the Middle East. In November 1981 he said, "If the British want the multinational force according to the principles of the Venice Declaration, they'd do better to stay home."[104]

France

France always occupied a singular place in Begin's conception of the world order. It was always an actual or potential ally, regardless of its standing or importance in international affairs. Standing before the French National Assembly in November 1957, he proposed that a treaty be concluded between France, Israel, and the Jewish people. This treaty need not have many articles, he said. It has to include just one sentence: "France and Israel, suffused for generations with the ideas of freedom and justice, promise each other friendship and mutual assistance."[105] The idea of an alliance with France was at the very heart of Begin's policy of treaties. Underlying his conception was the disproven conjecture that a formal treaty is the cornerstone and touchstone of the relations between nations, and that if it is concluded on the basis of common interests it will last forever, as he said to the French deputies.

In the 1940s France had been a center of Irgun activity in Europe. Consent to the organization's activity was granted on the basis of the assurance that on French soil it would not take action against Britain.[106] There were real grounds of common interest then, based on France's rivalry with Britain and French aspirations in North Africa. France agreed to extend military assistance to the Irgun, though the promise given by the Irgun in exchange was vague and open to contradictory interpretation even in the written form signed by both sides.[107] Begin, true to style, always loved to compare the history of the undergrounds in Palestine to the French Resistance, and made much of this when he met de Gaulle in the 1950s.[108]

Begin made the alliance with France the issue of highest priority in his movement's foreign policy, and accorded Herut primacy in the effort to achieve it. It is likely that he was unaware of the ramified relations that had already developed between the two countries. In 1957 a committee for an alliance with Israel was formed, under the chairmanship of the French nationalist politician Jacques Soustelle. In September 1956 Begin told the French National Assembly that his party had always advocated the idea that "the enemies of France are our enemies; and the enemies of Israel are France's enemies." If Nasser was to take over Algeria, he claimed, it would be disastrous; Israel would then have another enemy on the west. But the basis of the treaty he proposed was vague: France would not have to fight for Israel, and Israel would not have to fight for France. They would have to fight only for "a matter that is just and common" to them both. A year later, in a speech in Johannesburg, he called upon the French not to leave Algeria. If Israel were to fall, he said, "the last traces of free European civilization will be erased from this vital region."[109]

The Sinai Campaign was the height of the friendship of the French people for Israel, in his view.[110] But this war was to refute the importance of the formal treaty he sought. The partnership between France and Israel in the war represented an ephemeral conjunction of interests. In the 1950s the idea of a formal treaty between France and Israel became an *idée fixe* for Begin. He could not understand why the government was opposed to establishing no more than "friendship" with France at a time when it was seeking superpower guarantees and was trying to establish diplomatic ties with Germany. The only reason he could find was the diplomatic blindness of the Mapai leadership, a petty vision that would deny any initiative begun by Herut a chance of success.[111]

Begin, who believed in the political and utilitarian basis of relations between nations, continued to call for an alliance, stressing the moral component and the common values shared with France. But after the Six Day War, de Gaulle, the man who had called Israel "our friend and ally," was to impose an embargo on arms shipments. De Gaulle had a clear view of France's role in the relations between the two superpowers and in the Middle East which left him at some distance from Israel. Begin called de Gaulle's decision "a spectacle of violated trust and ingratitude whose precedent would be hard to find in the annals of international relations."[112] Given his static assumptions, Begin could not clearly comprehend the eclipse of relations with France. But he never despaired of renewing the *entente cordiale* between Israel and France. He believed the decline was a passing phenomenon.[113]

In his inaugural address to the Knesset as prime minister, Begin called upon France to renew its friendship with Israel. France was the only country he mentioned by name, apart from the superpowers. Yigal Allon attacked the "romantic declarative appeal ... to the French government, without first preparing the diplomatic ground for it."[114] In the beginning of 1978, Begin said that he had been educated from his youth in the spirit of the French Revolution: "We are friends of France." François Mitterrand's rise to power led to an improvement in relations with Israel, which was not related to the government's policy or to any special diplomatic effort on its part.[115] But when acts of terrorism against Jews increased in France, Begin likened France to Germany on the eve of the Second World War and called upon the Jews of France to organize for "self-defense."[116]

Germany

Germany was perhaps the most striking counterexample to Begin's belief that foreign policy can be conducted on the basis of cold, utilitarian calculations. Up until the mid-1960s his attitude toward Germany was totally uncompromising. That was apparent on each of the five issues that came up for consideration – reparations, Germany's rearmament, the supply of Israeli weapons to Germany, the question of German scientists in Egypt, and the establishment of diplomatic relations with Germany.

For Begin, Germany was "the two-legged blond beast," that sallied forth to conquer the world and wipe out the Jews. At the second Herut movement convention, in 1951, he said that "atop the abyss of international relations floats the Teutonic monster," and that Germnay's rearmament would sow the seeds of the next world war.[117] A year later, Begin called for the establishment of a league to organize the boycott of German products. That was perhaps an echo of a proposal made by Jabotinsky twenty years earlier. Begin often quoted Mirabeau's statement that Prussia is an army that has a country. Begin was typically contemptuous of Clausewitz, primarily because he did not understand him. He called him "the idol of the militarists."[118]

The most emotionally tempestuous episode in Begin's political life was undoubtedly the storm that raged in January 1952, the fight against the reparations agreement. Two of Begin's speeches, one in Mugrabi Square in Tel Aviv, the other at Zion Square in Jerusalem, were astounding in their admixture of political propaganda and genuine emotional agitation. He told the Tel Aviv rally that "such an abomination will not arise and will not be in Israel." He warned Ben-Gurion, whom he now depicted not as a collaborator with the British but as a collaborator with the Nazis, that "if this is permissible in the State of Israel, everything is permissible in the State of Israel ... '[119]

The following day, the day of the Knesset debate, was the fateful day. In pounding rain, he told the crowd gathered in Zion Square to hear him, "It is going to be a fight for life or death." He spurned the talk of a different Germany – in Begin's view, all Germans are Nazis. He called Ben-Gurion "the great tyrant and maniac, who does not let himself know the depth of the Holocaust and the profundity of the danger." He pushed the opposition to the furthest limit. It may happen, he told his audience, that they will again have to be separated from their children and families before the battle begins, "We will not be brought to surrender, because there is no force in the world that can bring the soldiers of the Irgun to surrender. On that day, I inform you, there will no longer be a Jewish government, and you will not have a moral right in Israel."[120] Ben-Gurion's reaction came swiftly. In a speech the following day he said: "Yesterday a malicious hand was raised against the sovereignty of the Knesset. It was proclaimed that Israel's policy will not be decided by the nation's elected representatives but by those who wield a fist, the people of political assassination."[121]

In the debate in the Knesset, Begin tried to repair the impression made by his speeches. Reparations from Germany, he said, are intended to restore Germany to the family of nations. Adenauer's aides are Nazis. He ridiculed the amount of compensation offered as absurd. He appealed to the Arab members of the Knesset not to take part in the vote, which concerned a wholly Jewish matter. He asked the religious members to consider their position. He recited an apologia centered around the restraint he had demonstrated in the face of all the provocations that had been directed against him, "Have we no right to live as free citizens in this country? Why, we gave everything for its establishment. And have received nothing. No command, no army, no police, no government, no position – nothing." He denied any intention of attacking the Knesset, but for a just cause, he said, he would fight to the end; government force will be to no avail, "Today you arrested hundreds. Perhaps you will arrest thousands . . . They will be in prison. We will be with them. If necessary, we will be killed along with them. There will not be 'reparations' with Germany." He informed the speaker of the Knesset that to the extent that the law of parliamentary immunity was applicable to him, he regarded that law as null and void. In fact, Begin did not have any detailed plan for organizing a public protest. After a long and stormy debate, the reparations agreement was approved by a vote of 61 in favor, 50 opposed.[122]

Begin's implacable position vis-à-vis Germany remained unaltered until the mid-1960s. He regarded it through an unchanging historical prism as a factor posing a threat to world peace. There were traits that he viewed as deeply embedded within every German. Begin argued that Germany's rearmament would ignite a third world war, whether because of Germany's inability to accept the defeat it had suffered in the Second World War or because of the confrontation between the two superpowers. He opposed both the establishment of diplomatic relations with Germany and the expansion of military ties with it. On all of these issues he demanded a public referendum.[123]

In the beginning of the 1960s there arose a new issue that both confirmed his image of Germany and provided an opportunity for lambasting the government: the presence of German scientists in Egypt. In November 1962, he argued that it was necessary to create "points of juncture" with Russia and Eastern Europe for the fight against German militarism. He attacked the "Germanophilic policy" of Ben-Gurion and the government, "Jews sew uniforms for the German army [a reference to militarial cooperation at that time], and the German state places missiles in the hands of Israel's enemies." He greatly exaggerated the military danger posed by the missiles in Egypt, long after the opposite had been proven, and continued to lash out against the government for its failings.[124] But when Germany intended to halt its military assistance to Israel in response to pressure from Arab countries, Begin took up the historical score once again. Germany was striving once again to be "large, strong, and united." It did not recognize the Oder-Neisse line nor the return of the Sudetenland and pretended that the Munich agreement was still in force. If a world war was to break out, it would be over these issues. What has the government done, he asked, about the German scientists working in Egypt? Why does the government want to confront the Soviet Union and to clash with public opinion in America? Friendship between the victims and their oppressors will never be possible.[125]

In the spring of 1965 the government announced the establishment of diplomatic relations between Israel and the German Federal Republic. Begin harked back to spring 1945, to the Hitler *Jugend*, the Waffen SS; in his view, nothing had changed. He named officials and politicians in Germany and accused them of membership in a Nazi organization or the Nazi Party. He demanded a referendum.[126] The heated emotion notwithstanding, Begin had come a considerable distance from the fervor and despair of 1952. The German issue had faded, at least in his public pronouncements, like the dissipation of his anti-British obsession in the 1950s. Henceforth his statements were dressed in a responsible cover, through which from time to time erupted emotional outpourings.[127]

Begin's coming to power did not affect Israel's relations with Germany. In September 1977, he said that he had not changed his mind on the reparations, "but we have proper relations with Germany." In May 1978, he received a delegation of members of the Bundestag. A month later he met with the German foreign minister. His vehemently acid attack against Chancellor Schmidt came only in May 1981, in the heat of the election campaign.[128] There were those who thought that his resignation had to do also with the impending visit by Chancellor Kohl in Israel, but there is no proof of that.

The eternal bond

Begin's attachment to Jewish history was a central feature of his inner world, a mainspring of a fervor that heightened the legitimacy of the revolt, nationalism, and the Jewish struggle. The Jewish consideration influenced his diplomatic calculations as well as his attitude towards statesmen, nations, and countries. At the same time, there was always some inconsistency in Begin's attitude towards the Jewish people – its inherent characteristics, its behavior in times of crisis, and its power in the international arena. The belief in a Jewish nation acting as a political entity clashed with Begin's statist view of international relations and his political realism. His deep belief in Israel's right to the entire territory of mandatory Palestine, the whole Land of Israel, limited his public statements about the meaning of a "Jewish state". After the Six Day War he was to say: "The Jewish people never demanded a state in the land of its forefathers where Jews and only Jews would live . . ."[129]

In an early article entitled "How to Rescue," written shortly after the proclamation of the revolt, Begin addressed the citizens of the Yishuv: "Your brother was strangled, your mother has given up her soul, your father was killed . . ."[130] Begin, uttering this cry of despair and guilt, had in mind the members of his own family. The accusations he made against the Zionist leadership were unprecedented in their severity. He accused the leaders of the Socialist Zionists of gambling with the lives of the Jews of Europe, of criminal indifference in keeping with "the laws of proletarian selection." In 1946, after the pogrom in Kielce he voiced astounding accusations against the Zionist leaders.[131] Towards the end of the world war he asked in despair, "The historian will record and will wonder, he will look at the horrible period from a historical vantage point, and will be unable not to wonder how puny the [Jewish] leaders of that generation were, the generation of destruction? How frightening their blindness, how criminal their indifference?"[132] Yet at the same time, one of Begin's severest criticisms of the Hebrew Committee of National Liberation in the United States was its focus on propaganda and informational work for the rescue of Jews rather than putting all its efforts into getting arms and money to the fighting underground in Palestine.

Before the Lebanon War he told Secretary of State Haig how much he had suffered from the trauma of the Holocaust.[133] In fact, it was during the Lebanon War more than in any other period that he drew parallels between the Holocaust and the battle against the Palestinians. There were those who found the constant mention of the Holocaust objectionable, because it diminished its historical singularity.[134]

The decisive lesson Begin learned from the Holocaust was expressed in the conception of revolt, of the rise of a generation that would wreak vengeance and fight back. He regarded hatred of Jews as a universal phenomenon, and believed that the nations who were fighting the Nazis in the East and in the West were themselves anti-Semitic.[135] The Jews know how to revolt, he observed. The Jewish people had been a fighting people when it lived in its own land. In the homeland, Begin believed, the Jews are a different people which "knows how to water [the homeland] with sweat, and to fructify it with blood."[136] That was the basis of the distinction he made: "I think the battles in the ghettos were meant for death with honor ... In the Land of Israel, the war was waged according to ordinary concepts, a war of national liberation."[137] Begin always counterposed the "generation of rebirth" to the "generation of destruction." As opposed to the Jew who goes passively to his death, Begin spoke of the "fighting Jew." This type of Jew "has arisen and will never again disappear."[138]

Despite Begin's belief in the Jewish people he always doubted its power. This was especially notable in the early 1950s, a period of great anxiety in Begin's life. At the end of 1954 he wrote about the Jews' notion of *bitukhen*, the ability to live calmly among gentiles who would gladly see them dead. While he saw this ability as representing a greatness of spirit, it doomed the Jewish people to be an "eternal remnant," not an "eternal people."[139] That same year he said in the Knesset that if the Irish were in danger, their kin in America would demonstrate all year long, not only on St Patrick's Day, "but in our case – there is silence in the streets of New York, calmness along the avenues of Philadelphia, and complacency on the boulevards of Los Angeles."[140] Begin's method for countering criticism from the left was by diagnosing the typical Jewish trait of self-accusation. He also did that in September 1982, after the massacres in the Sabra and Shatila Camps in Lebanon.[141] The Jew appeared to Begin in several images – the cosmopolitan, the assimilator, the wanderer in the fields of others, the fighting, self-sacrificing Jew, and the religious Jew, the simple, eternal believer.

In the 1940s Begin had said that "American Jewry is a mighty political factor in the Hebrew war of liberation."[142] But the importance of "militant Jewry" in the world became fully clear to him only after the Six Day War, and now he placed an unreasonable amount of faith in it. One of Begin's unshakeable beliefs was that forceful insistence on Israel's rights, and the influence of American Jewry (which had until then almost mechanically presented a united front behind Israel), constituted a real counterweight to the power of the American administration.[143]

During his first months in office Begin awakened old strains in world

Jewry, perhaps a longing for the type of leadership the Labor movement no longer had to offer.[144]

More than any other Israeli politician, Begin believed in the great Jewish surety, which applies everywhere in the world. In the beginning of 1975 he proposed the establishment of a joint council, comprising representatives of Israel and the Jewish people, that would meet monthly in Jerusalem and would have executive functions.[145] How great an irony that Begin's period was marked by a widening rift between Israel and large portions of the Jewish people, and was a time of heightened estrangement and criticism.

Part III

The Leader

11

The Diplomat

His own diplomat

Begin's rise to political prominence began in the period when foreign relations and security matters had begun to dominate the political life of Jewish Palestine. As commander of the Irgun, however, he was removed from the conduct of Zionist diplomacy. The paths followed by Revisionism, and afterwards by the undergrounds of the right, ran parallel to Zionist policy.

At his first appearance in a formal diplomatic setting, a meeting in June 1947 with representatives of the UN Special Committee for Palestine, he displayed the traits that would be characteristic of him in the future as well – formality, a penchant for dramatic proclamations, reference to historical right as a fundamental political principle, and the volunteering of general assessments of states of affairs.

As leader of the opposition, Begin regarded the diplomatic and military realm as the focus of his concern and expertise, as well as the area of his greatest aptitude. He was highly critical of Israeli diplomacy from its inception. In one of his first appearances in the Knesset, he declared: "Our foreign policy, as shaped by the government and conducted by Mr Sharett ... swings between the vagaries of impressionism, stands on shaky legs of dilettantism, yet is also shackled to routine, bound to illusions ..."[1]

Begin's natural inclination was toward open, rhetorical diplomacy. "Not every political proclamation is a declamation," he said, but "there are proclamations that are political acts."[2] It can be said that to some extent he regarded the obfuscation of political objectives as dishonest. When President Carter told him during the Camp David talks that the harsh, unyielding Egyptian proposal was just an opening position, and that Sadat had promised he would change it, Begin's reaction was one of surprise. How can he hold two positions, a public one and a private one? That is not to say that Begin himself did not at times conceal his intentions as a statesman. That, however, was the façade he cultivated.

Shortly before the Sinai campaign in 1956, Foreign Minister Moshe Sharett asked Begin to meet with Egyptian journalist Ibrahim Izaat, who

was on a secret visit in Israel. Sharett asked him to say that the whole
political spectrum in Israel regarded the ceasefire lines as the country's
final boundaries. Begin refused, protesting that he could not openly deny
something he believed in, and the meeting did not take place.[3] His lack of
duplicity – some might say, lack of political sophistication – was also
apparent many years later, after he came to power, when he broke the
silence on Israel's assistance to the Christians in Lebanon and the Kurds
in northern Iraq. After signing the Camp David Accords, he revealed
secret details about the talks to a low-ranking official in the Israeli
Embassy. Against the opposition of the Ministry of Foreign Affairs, in
1981 he published an open letter to the American people explaining the
Israeli position after the bombing of the Iraqi nuclear reactor.[4] His self-
confidence combined with imprudence and with a failure to maintain a
clear distinction between action and the declaratory aspects of policy.

As diplomat, Begin always searched for the "grand gesture." he valued
the ceremonial dimension of foreign policy, and regarded national prestige
as an element of great importance for its conduct. In 1954 he thought it an
insult to the honor of IDF Chief of Staff Moshe Dayan that though he was
officially invited to the United States he was not flown there in an American military plane. In 1964 he complained that the president of Israel had
not received Pope Paul VI in the capital and that Israel's national anthem
was not played at the ceremonies.[5] It appears, too, that he did not always
distinguish between rules of etiquette, especially the American proclivity
for exaggerated compliments, and genuine intention. Many talks were
"good" and "excellent," even when the differences of opinion expressed in
them were substantial. When Sadat came to Jerusalem, he embarrassed him
by his insistence on being invited to the Egyptian capital. In the end, Sadat
acceded to his request and invited him to Ismailia. He tended to embrace
Sadat in public, without a thought for the embarrassment he was causing
the Egyptian leader.[6] On some occasions Begin was capable of impeccable
etiquette and decorousness; yet he was equally known for wielding an
acerbic tongue, insulting foreign leaders and domestic opponents, and
engendering unnecessary hostility.

When he criticized the government's peace gambits in the beginning of
1971, Begin said that "in policy there is no relying on guesses . . . on in-
tuitions. It is necessary to examine the facts and assess the possibilities."[7]
As prime minister he himself was prepared to launch a diplomatic initiative
and propose plans, not always after thorough study. However, when he
responded immediately to Sadat's wish to visit Jerusalem, this style bore
diplomatic fruit.

As a negotiator, Begin tended to be prolix, with a fondness for general-
ization and historical parallels. He also tended to interrupt other speakers.

At Ismailia and Camp David he wearied Sadat and Carter, as well as members of his own delegation, with his lengthy reading of political proposals and with debate over principles that led nowhere. Carter was wary of Begin's style and told him as much before the Camp David talks began. But Begin was not a man to be impressed by comments aimed at having him adapt himself to others. He felt fully sovereign over his style and rights.[8]

Begin usually pounced on the prize too swiftly, and even his concessions were not properly understood. Thus, having presented his autonomy plan to Carter and received some polite words and qualified support in return, he quickly translated this into political agreement that warranted public expression, to the dismay of Foreign Minister Dayan. One of Begin's practices as a negotiator was to ask a leading question and to interpret the reply as agreement with his positions. At Camp David he asked Sadat if the Knesset would be subjected to any pressure when it came to vote on the accords, and received a negative reply. He took this as confirmation that the Knesset could vote as it wished. Carter did not believe that Sadat had agreed to that and set about to clarify the question by himself with Israeli Attorney-General Aharon Barak, in Begin's presence.[9]

Hans Morgenthau wrote that a diplomacy that thinks in legalistic and propagandistic terms usually confounds "the shadow of legal right with the actuality of political advantage." It usually presupposes that compromise cannot be achieved and sets the legal right above all, without regard for the political and military consequences. That is a short-sighted diplomacy, because "the choice that confronts the diplomat is not between legality and illegality, but between political wisdom and political folly."[10]

Begin's political conception and argumentation embodied a fundamental misunderstanding of the role of the legal dimension. His natural tendency was to base the legitimacy of state actions and the use of force on principles of international law usually formulated in absolute, incontestable terms. There was an obvious contradiction in this. Begin usually used the rules of international law as a means to defend political objectives that derived from the national will. By their nature these objectives were not subject to arbitration or compromise. In any case, a formalistic view, which is more a matter of style, must be distinguished from a normative view that holds that international law is of central importance in international relations. One of Begin's major fears during the Camp David talks stemmed from the nonpresentation of an Israeli counterproposal to papers presented first by Egypt and then by the United States. A formal document was not required for the immediate diplomatic discussion, nor was this a lawyer's desire for a countersuit to ensure a balanced judgment. His demand reflected more the vision of a politician with an eye on the forthcoming contest for public opinion should the conference end in failure.

In some instances the legal argument was more an expedient than a principle. The legal aspect provided Begin with a defense mechanism, a code of rules for conducting negotiations. Usually, when this framework was violated, he failed to maintain his equilibrium. In practice, the prime minister's legal arguments were compatible with real interests. Any assault on the "legalistic" wall Begin erected was at once an attack on Begin's positions and on the self-defensive walls he had built. Later, even Weizman was to understand that the legal argument could also be used as a means for concealing a real change in position. Such was Begin's argument that the term "legitimate rights" for the Palestinians was no more than a worthless tautology.[11] After formal agreement was achieved, Begin tended to entrench himself behind its wording. In that way the Camp David Accords became a codex tying everyone's hands, thwarting new interpretations and impeding initiatives. At the same time, however, his tendency to package political plans in a wrapping of principles and rules also provided leverage against him, as happened with the autonomy plan.

Begin's attitude to professional diplomacy vacillated between contempt of and respect for its practitioners. On the Revisionist right, "professional diplomacy" often symbolized timidity and spineless complaisance. Yet during Begin's premiership the Foreign Ministry was not restructured in light of proposals from him or his government, even though party members complained about the political inclinations of the diplomatic cadre and its ability to represent the ideas of the new ruling party. It is notable that no professional diplomat was to be found among Begin's inner circle of advisers.[12]

One of Begin's persistent criticisms of Israel's foreign policy concerned the dissemination of the government line overseas – what was euphemistically referred to as "information." Israel's information work, he claimed, failed to provide the necessary defense for Israel's positions and rights in the world of international propaganda. He had an almost mystical faith in the power of words in diplomacy, and regarded propaganda as a substantial policy tool. It was therefore only to be expected that information work would be thoroughly restructured organizationally and substantively under Begin's government, particularly, when his rise to power met with a wave of unprecedented hostile reaction throughout the world.[13] Shmuel Katz, however, gives us a chronicle of bitter frustration and disappointment with the dilettantism of the Likud's attempt to organize Israel's information work. Begin had intended to name him Minister of Information, yet Katz was surprised by Dayan's appointment as foreign minister. Begin tried to reassure him: "Dayan will handle the diplomatic side, and you'll take care of information work, and I will oversee it all. You have nothing to worry about. I need Dayan because he is very popular abroad."[14] During Katz's first mission to the United States on Begin's behalf, the prime minister did not address a single comment, directive, or request to him. While he was still there, he learned of Begin's intention not to set up an Information Ministry. Dayan did not want information work to be removed from the Foreign Ministry, and Katz became instead adviser for overseas information. Dayan tended not to consult with him, the range of his activity was increasingly curtailed, and at the end of 1977 he resigned his position.[15]

The peace process should have led to a change in Israel's image. However, not only did the country's public image not improve, it actually declined in Europe and even in the United States. Begin, who believed he possessed a magnetic ability to explain what he took to be self-evident truths, was unable to compete with Sadat. During and after the peace talks, Begin became one of the most maligned figures in the history of Israeli statesmanship.

The failures, as well as the successes, of Begin as diplomat can be traced in large part to the basic assumptions he held, his conception of reality, and his political style. These often led him to incorrect assessments of political situations, to inconsistency, and to a policy of self-defeat. Begin acted as the supreme authority in the conduct of foreign policy, with professional diplomacy shunted aside. His authority appeared to be unrivaled and unchallenged by the bureaucracy, party, and government. But Begin exposed himself more than was necessary, and granted his opponents advantages that were not imperative. He believed that obstinacy, annealment of the national will, and placement of obstacles were sufficient means for delaying or redirecting diplomatic processes.

Begin saw himself, more than any prime minister before him, as free to take up open diplomacy and adopt a stinging rhetoric. He created a negative image of himself as an obstinate, inflexible person, even though such an image met no pressing political need. His venomous attacks on Western statesmen, who formed Israel's principal diplomatic home ground, served no end. He declared with confidence, "We don't need anyone's recognition."

In his last years in office he also adopted some of the trappings of "surprise diplomacy." In December 1981 the Golan Heights Bill was pushed through the Knesset in just one day, while military forces were concentrated in the north. The United States responded by suspending the memorandum of understanding. It was in the wake of this, on December 20, that Begin summoned Ambassador Lewis and assailed him for a full hour. "Are we your vassal state? Are we a banana republic?" Begin asked. As to the Golan Heights Bill, he said, "There is no power in the world that will get it rescinded."[16] It was a remarkable talk, the prime minister of a small country allowing himself to harangue the ambassador of a superpower on whom, in this instance, the small country was critically dependent. As Ambassador Lewis was leaving, he might have noticed the chief of staff and senior army officers arriving. A heavy guard was placed around the prime minister's building – police, border police, and the prime minister's personal bodyguards. On that day Begin revealed operation "Big Pines," the plan for a war in Lebanon, to the cabinet.

All through 1982 Begin did nothing to curb Defense Minister Ariel Sharon, who held talks of unparalleled bluntness with American diplomats, especially with Philip Habib and his deputy Morris Draper. When Lebanon's new president, Bashir Jemayel, was not enthused about making his ties with Israel public and was reluctant to sign a peace treaty, he too was summoned for a talk with the prime minister. Begin dressed him down, like a truant subaltern. Jemayel afterwards told his father, "He treated me like a child."[17]

Like other leaders who had a historical and heroic vision, Begin wanted to be his own diplomat. Dayan wrote that "it seemed to me that he was sure of his intellectual superiority over everyone else, and did not have the slightest shadow of a doubt that if he conducts foreign policy and dictates its moves, he will achieve his objectivs."[18] The foreign minister in Begin's first government did not share that assessment. There is no example in all of Israel's political history of such absolute self-belief, unsupported by similar estimation from others.

Following the tracks of Sadat

There is a measure of historical irony in the fact that the peace agreement with Egypt was signed by a government headed by Begin. It is doubtful that Sadat and Carter imagined in the spring of 1977 that Begin, with his world view, political standing at home, and talents as a negotiator, would be a key figure in achieving a true historical breakthrough.

The apparent consistency in Begin's conception of peace with the Arab countries, misled many. For years he had supported every military operation against the Arabs and opposed every peace initiative. Particularly, he detested armistice commissions and interim agreements. Partial agreements contradicted his definition of the essence of peace between nations. Carter's and Sadat's consent to full, normal relations, however, was fully consonant with Begin's world view and confronted him with a challenge from which it was difficult to escape.

From the time Sadat had come to power in autumn 1970, Begin had opposed every partial agreement, and any withdrawal from the territories, for none of these was tied to the conclusion of formal, contractual peace. He was highly suspicious of Egypt's intentions, and heaped considerable abuse on Sadat. He refused to be taken in by Sadat's peace declarations. In the spring of 1965, referring to statements by Habib Bourguiba, president of Tunisia, he had warned against "the automatic thinking in foreign policy" that views moderate declarations as in themselves positive.[19] After he left the government in August 1970, Begin had harsh words for all the attempts to reach an agreement with Egypt. He sharply criticized the reliance on UN Security Council Resolution 242, and the lack of clarity in the government's positions in consenting to renew its participation in the Jarring talks. After the Rogers Plan was announced, he maintained that "even if Israel withdraws to the lines of June 4, 1967, it's sure to face a war."[20]

Most of the positions Begin opposed in the early 1970s came up again in the peace talks, and many of his comments against the government became "self-fulfilling prophesies." Begin was emphatic about the proposals made by Sadat in his reply to Jarring in February 1971. He called Sadat's statements an "ultimatum" and termed the demand for withdrawal to the lines of June 4, 1967 and recognition of the rights of the Palestinians a call for Israel's destruction. Begin was at that time one of the fiercest opponents of reopening the Suez Canal to shipping.[21] In presenting the Herut's no-confidence motion in March 1971, he protested against Golda Meir for having said that President Sadat is the first Arab leader prepared to make peace. "Does Sadat really want peace?" he asked.[22]

The central theme of Begin's arguments was that any commitment to make a concession creates a new front line from which Israel will be called upon to make further concessions. Begin rejected out of hand any conception of "territorial compromise," depicting the idea as totally unrelated to political reality. He was deeply worried by Sadat's ability to create the image of a statesman who wanted peace, "We must see to it, through information work worthy of the name, that nothing be left of that impression except its sad remembrance. It's a deception."[23] In the middle of 1971 he once again warned the Knesset of the "Egyptian tyrant," and his ultimative language. Begin likened the defense pact between Russia and Egypt in May 1971 to the Ribbentrop–Molotov pact. He warned that opening the Suez Canal would lead to Russian domination on both sides of it. It is clear, Begin stated, "that the argument according to which the choice is between the indivisibility of the land without peace and partition of the land with peace is baseless. That is not the reality."[24]

In November, Begin moved to place the subject of "Sadat's war threats" on the Knesset agenda. He drew a strict parallel between Nasser's declarations in May 1967 and Sadat's statements about a future war with Israel. It would end in the same way, Begin concluded, with another Egyptian request for a ceasefire. But he did not propose any alternative.[25]

After the Yom Kippur War, Begin voiced his criticism with renewed force. In addition to Sadat, he now had a new target for his criticism: Henry Kissinger. In the articles he wrote at that time, Begin warned of pressure by

Kissinger, who presented Sadat as a moderate. Why, "the ruler in Egypt" even speaks of a peace agreement with Israel, but that is linked to total withdrawal and the establishment of an "Arafatite" state, which would mean Israel's liquidation. It is necessary, he said, to bare "the true face of the Egyptian tyrant," who wants peace with an Israel that no longer exists.[26] He vigorously opposed withdrawal from the passes in Sinai. He always maintained that "a state of war ends with a peace treaty, and as long as there is no peace treaty, there is no withdrawal."[27]

At the twelfth convention of the Herut movement, held in Kiryat Arba, Hebron, at the beginning of 1975, he called for taking the initiative in achieving peace in the Middle East.[28] Begin proposed a three-year cease-fire, during which peace talks with the Arab countries would be held without prior conditions, the negotiations being conducted alternately in Jerusalem and the Arab capitals. Among other things, his proposal included an effort to solve the Arab refugee question linked to treatment of the problem of Jewish refugees from Arab countries. He suggested that an official letter containing his proposals be sent to all Arab countries.

Begin's denouncement of the talks with Egypt that produced the interim agreements of 1975 were fierce. He regarded the concessions made as a "stage in a war" rather than as a stage towards peace. But even peace with Egypt was not something final for Begin. In his view, Sadat's demand for the realization of the legitimate rights of the Palestinians would lead to the next war.[29] He called on the government to resign for having violated its commitment not to evacuate the passes and oil fields without termination of the state of war. He rejected Prime Minister Yitzhak Rabin's claim that the agreement with Egypt to reach a final peace accord constituted a change on the "legal–diplomatic" plane, and called on the government not to commit Israel to withdrawals without a public referendum or new elections.[30]

There was a sharp difference between the way Begin related to Sadat before and after he became premier. In the beginning of May 1977 he still attacked the Egyptian president, whose statements were "unreasonable and foolish," as an extremist leader trying to form a dangerous strategic front against Israel. But even then he directed attention to Dayan's statement that he, Begin, had never advocated the policy of "not to give up a single inch." He hinted at his preference for cooperation with Dayan over a coalition with the Alignment.[31] The tone of Begin's statements, and their content as well, changed once he had assumed the responsibility of state power. At the end of May 1977 he declared that a compromise that would assure the signing of a peace treaty could be reached with respect to Sinai and the Golan Heights. Before his first trip to the United States as prime minister, the press was filled with Begin's peace proclamations and with reports about the peace plan he was intending to present to the president.[32]

Begin concentrated all his efforts on the attempt to get negotiations with Egypt started and to meet Sadat face to face.

Looking back today, 1977 appears to have been a decisive juncture in the peace efforts. The outcome of the Yom Kippur War and the interim agreements with Egypt guaranteed a stable transition period, but how it would end was difficult to foresee. The new US president had tremendous faith in himself and in the moral ethos of American foreign policy. He adopted the conception of a comprehensive settlement in the Middle East and most of the recommendations of the Brookings Committee for solving the Arab–Jewish conflict.[33] Carter tended to subscribe to an "all or nothing" policy, and sought to place the Palestinian question at the center of the anticipated peace talks.

The main premises guiding the administration were that the president would have greatest freedom of action during his first year in office, and that a breakthrough was possible only if pressure was applied on Israel. Brzezinski, the president's adviser on national security, believed that the American Jewish community would show more restraint than might be expected as a result of Begin's extremist positions. Like Carter, the president's adviser was sensitive to the power of the Jewish community in America. The president's position towards Israel, writes Brzezinski, was always ambivalent. Israel, although the Holy Land of the Bible, was also perceived as obstinate.[34]

President Carter's failure to reach an agreement with restrained and reticent Prime Minister Yitzhak Rabin led him to reconsider whether or not to begin a new American initiative for the Middle East. After Rabin left the United States, Carter shook hands with the PLO representative at the UN, despite his full awareness of the promises given to Israel by the previous administration that the United States would not recognize the PLO. It was Sadat's visit to the United States in April 1977 that encouraged Carter to continue his efforts. The president was captivated by the Egyptian president's manner and personality. Of the Arab leaders with whom he had met up until the end of May 1977, Sadat was the only one who agreed to publicly proclaim a readiness to begin negotiations with Israel.[35]

The new US administration learned the major lesson of the period that led to war in 1973, namely that the diplomatic initiative in the Middle East should not be left to others. By the end of 1976, Secretary of State Vance had advised the president to cooperate with the Soviet Union and to persuade it to soften the positions of the extremist Arab countries, or at least to persuade it not to sabotage the American efforts. In the beginning of 1977 Vance and his senior advisers, Alfred Atherton and Harold Saunders, undertook a thorough review of the Middle Eastern arena, and isolated four major areas of dispute: the nature of peace, the question of boundaries, the Palestinian question, and the procedural arrangements for conducting a future international conference, especially the manner of ensuring Palestinian participation. It was at this point that American policy moved onto a confrontation course with Israel. The Rabin government was the first to discern this.[36]

Begin's offer to Moshe Dayan, on May 21, 1977, to join the new government as foreign minister was the most dramatic move in the formation of the first Likud government. Before the elections Dayan had demanded, as a condition for joining the Likud list, that Begin commit himself to not extending Israeli sovereignty to the occupied territories as long as peace negotiations were under way. The selection of Dayan, which came as a surprise, inspired confidence and accorded the new government the legitimation it needed. It also had decisive impact on the policy and character of the government.[37]

The final chapter of Dayan's life and career was to be an attempt to find a solution to the Middle East conflict. Henceforth he would occupy the lead position in shaping government policy. Another person who pinned hopes on Dayan, his personal ambivalence toward him tinged with respect for the man he regarded as the IDF's best chief of staff, was Ezer Weizman.[38] Dayan himself was cautious. He was careful to clarify the agreement between him and Begin before assuming the post of foreign minister, and again before making his maiden speech in that capacity. Begin agreed to honor the agreements entered into by previous governments, to maintain the existing situation in the territories, and to attend the Geneva conference without prior conditions and on the basis of Security Council Resolution 242.[39]

Before the cabinet convened for its first meeting, Begin asked his foreign minister to prepare a memorandum about the principles that should serve as the foundation for peace negotiations. The memorandum was presented on June 24.[40] Dayan did not believe that peace could be attained in one step. He sketched the precise limits of the concessions to be made in Sinai. The border change he suggested left the airfields and the Rafah Salient settlements in Israeli hands, and advised against formulating a position in advance with respect to southern Sinai. As for the Syrian border, he regarded a military presence on the Golan Heights as vital but suggested that a demand for changes in the international boundary not be presented as an ultimatum. Dayan regarded the refugee problem and their resettlement as a key element in the Palestinian issue. He opposed the extension of Israeli law to the West Bank and the Gaza Strip. Dayan wanted a temporary arrangement for those areas, with the matter of sovereignty left open, even if peace with Egypt and Syria was to become a real possibility.

When Begin visited the United States in July 1977, the administration's attempt to clarify Begin's positions on boundaries, the need for a national home for the Palestinians, and settlements, led to an exchange of accusations that did little to defuse the tense. atmosphere. Begin instructed Ambassador Simcha Dinitz to ask the Americans not to voice their views in public.[41] According to Dayan, the meeting with the president made clear what the American position would be until a peace agreement was reached. The US interpretation of Resolution 242 virtually required a commitment by Israel to withdraw on all fronts. Second, the administration's views on the Palestinian question did not rule out the possibility of self-determination for the Palestinians. The peace plan Begin carried with him, which had been approved by the cabinet and rested on Security Council Resolutions 242 and 338, as interpreted by Israel, was highly flexible compared to Begin's past positions. It offered a readiness to withdraw in Sinai and the Golan Heights, but asserted that the West Bank and Gaza would not be returned to foreign rule.[42]

Begin's visit did not lead to a head-on confrontation; indeed, President Carter insisted on refuting the notion that his meeting with the prime minister did not go well. He spelled out to Begin the US's principles about peace – a comprehensive settlement, a broad definition of peace, Resolution 242 as its basis, and the establishment of a Palestinian entity. Carter maintained that Begin agreed to all the principles, except for the solution envisaged for the Palestinian question.[43] Presidential Adviser Zbigniew Brzezinski thought that Begin came to Washington determined not to discuss the main issues but to channel the discussions to procedural matters.[44] In the view of Secretary of State Cyrus Vance, Begin's first visit stood in sharp contrast to the president's meeting with Sadat in April. They were polite and considerate of each other, but not trusting. The Americans tried to assure Begin that there would be no imposed solution and emphasized the need to solve the Palestinian problem.

Vance, it must be said, had the most positive opinion of Begin of all the senior administration members. In his memoirs he wrote that Begin had a strong sense of history, was clear about his views, and restrained when necessary. As a negotiator he adhered to legal principles, which led him to prefer the written word over the spirit of an agreement. His precision of formulation, superb memory, and adherence to his positions made him a tough bargainer and a master of parliamentary debate.[45] Vance's view was exceptional, not only compared to that of other members of the administration but also to that of Begin's own top ministers. During his talk with Ambassador Dinitz after the visit, Vance understood that the settlements would be a major bone of contention. Begin himself returned from the United States very satisfied. He sent a personal letter to the president and asked him not to alert the Arab side to the issues in dispute. The administration regarded his request as interference in its affairs.

The second half of August 1977 was a very hectic period for Moshe Dayan. In the course of one week, he met with the prime minister and foreign minister of India, the Shah of Iran, and King Hussein. To a large extent, Begin and Dayan were following in the tracks of President Sadat. Dayan was disappointed by his meeting with the Hashemite king. Hussein rejected any compromise on the West Bank, and saw himself as bound by the Rabat resolution; at least he opposed the establishment of a Palestinian state.[46]

Dayan is very sparing in his descriptions. He does not discuss the circumstances that led to his meetings with the Egyptian deputy premier, Hassan al-Tuhami. On his first trip to Morocco, Dayan met with King Hassan. He was interested in direct contact with Egypt, preferably a meeting between Begin and Sadat. On September 16, 1977, he met with Tuhami for the first time.[47] The Egyptians wanted total withdrawal in exchange for peace, and agreement with Israel on all bilateral matters before the convening of the Geneva conference. Tuhami made it clear that Egypt would not sign a separate peace. Did Dayan undertake, in a proposal of his own or in one acceptable to the prime minister, total withdrawal from the Sinai peninsula? It seems that he did leave Tuhami with that impression. If that is so, it does not mean that he did not try to achieve a special arrangement for the airfields and the settlements.[48] The meetings between Tuhami and Dayan laid the foundation for Sadat's historic visit to Israel. Dayan then departed for the United States.

Dayan's visit, which began on September 18, was devoted to further preparations for the forthcoming Geneva conference.[49] The Americans tried to pry open Begin's peace plan wherever they could get a handhold, especially on the subject of boundaries and the composition of the Palestinian delegation to the conference. They pressed Dayan on the settlement problem. Dayan was open to compromise; he would propose to Begin that the settlements take the form of military strongholds. The American delegation headed by Vance presented two documents. One was a "working paper" about Geneva. The second – a draft of the joint US–Soviet declaration – sparked a storm of controversy. Announced at the beginning of October, the declaration referred to the legitimate rights of the Palestinians and to the participation of representatives of the Palestinian people at the Geneva conference. The Americans, Dayan wrote, tried "to bring us to concessions step by step" with President Carter taking a tough stand and trying to breach Israel's positions on withdrawal and Palestinian representation.

Begin did not like the working paper drafted by Vance and Dayan. He opposed the sections that legitimated Palestinian participation in determining the future of Judaea and Samaria. Begin believed that nonparticipation by PLO representatives in the talks had not been promised. Dayan was exasperated. He thought the working paper was an achievement and an asset for Israel.[50] But Begin was confronted with a fait accompli. Dayan believed that any retreat from what had been agreed with the Americans would undermine his standing with them as foreign minister.[51] Vance noted with irony that the statement on the Palestinian question in the US–Soviet joint declaration was similar to that which came out of Camp David. But the working paper created the impression in the Arab countries that the Americans had backed down under pressure from Israel.[52]

It seemed to Brzezinski that Dinitz and Dayan emerged from the confrontation with the administration convinced that the president, who was moving away from the US–Soviet declaration, could be pressured.[53] Then, Sadat's visit to Jerusalem confounded the administration's strategy for convening a Geneva conference. That was a historic turning point that forced all sides to reconsider their positions. For a while it threw the American administration into confusion.[54]

On November 19, 1977, Begin was to receive the ruler of Egypt, Anwar el-Sadat, in Jerusalem. He said to Shmuel Katz that after all the years during which he, Begin, had been denounced and vilified by the left, the Egyptian president "decided to come to whom? to me. Despite all their efforts, he didn't come to them."[55] Begin had a powerful desire to correct what he believed to be a long-standing injustice and distortion of his character.

In the history of the Middle East there is a great gap between secret diplomacy, which when known makes the course of events comprehensible, and official, open diplomacy. We still do not know the exact reasons for Sadat's decision to come to Jerusalem.[56] Sadat did not consult the Americans before his visit; he was convinced that he had to blaze his own path. They dissuaded him of his initial intention, which was to call for a conference of the major powers and the Arab states in Jerusalem. Now they feared that the opportunity to achieve a comprehensive settlement would be lost. Sadat forced them to guarantee him some return for his initiative and to prevent his isolation in the Arab world.[57]

At the Knesset session at which the impending visit by the Egyptian president was discussed, Begin was in high spirits.[58] He gloried in every detail of delivery of the letter of invitation to Ambassador Lewis and of the personal letter he was to send to Carter.[59] He noted that he had no intention of driving a wedge in the Arab world and called upon the presidents of Syria and Lebanon and King Hussein "to come to us and begin negotiations." The government, he said, was also prepared to hold talks with official spokesmen of the Palestinian Arabs, whom he designated Arabs of the Land of Israel.

The arrival of the Egyptian president, the man who had been responsible for the strategic surprise of 1973, aroused suspicions within the Israeli military and intelligence. These suspicions were brought to the government by the IDF Chief of Staff, General Mordechai Gur, but beyond that, this revolutionary event, with all its possible consequences for the future of Israel and the region, was not discussed in depth by the government.[60]

Sadat's speech in the Knesset was carefully crafted to serve three objectives simultaneously: an address to his own people, an address to the Arab countries and their peoples, and a frank presentation of the Egyptian position without impairing his image as a pursuer of peace.[61] He noted that, as early as February 1971, and again in October 1973, he had expressed his readiness to conclude a peace agreement with Israel. Now negotiations would be conducted with the Arab nation standing firm on the "powerful foundations of strength and stability." He vigorously opposed a separate agreement between Egypt and Israel, as well as a partial agreement. The great historical change Sadat presented was the acceptance of Israel as part of the Middle East, a readiness to live with Israel "in just and permanent peace"; but his demands were unequivocal: total withdrawal from the occupied territories including Jerusalem, and the right of self-determination for the Palestinians. In Israel, Sadat's speech gave rise to fears. It left Dayan, Weizman, and Gur somewhat aghast and Begin is reported to have described it as an ultimatum.[62]

The prime minister's speech in response was shorter.[63] He said that the people of Israel believed not in force but in right. Israel did not want to divide and rule, it wanted "absolute reconciliation between the Jewish people and the Arab nation." Begin renewed his invitation to the president of Syria and King Hussein to start negotiations, and called for cooperation in regional development. The way in which he set forth Israel's conditions was more general and vague than Sadat's presentation. He noted the eternal tie between the people of Israel and the land, and said that Israel's position with respect to permanent boundaries differed from the Egyptian position. Negotiations at the Geneva conference would be conducted on the basis of Resolutions 242 and 338, but he was also prepared to hold preliminary talks with Egypt to clarify the problems between the two countries.

Sadat's and Begin's speeches created a leaden atmosphere. They brought everyone back to the hard soil of reality. It was clear to Dayan that Egypt expected some sort of exceptional gesture from Israel, but Sadat's intentions were not clear to him. He thought that Sadat's speech in the Knesset was the major diplomatic event of the visit. Dayan commented drily that although the prime minister had stated Israel's positions clearly, Begin's speech "would not be engraved in the annals of history."[64]

Sadat's visit to Jerusalem altered the structure of Middle Eastern diplomacy. Egypt and Israel became hostage to each other. The failure of the peace process was liable to inflict heavy damage on one, or both, of them. A leap forward had been made and it required that substantial concessions be granted within a short span of time. The talks between Begin and Sadat were held tête-à-tête, and no protocol was taken.[65] It became evident, however, that the unique historical event would not be yielding equally impressive immediate diplomatic results. The agreement reached included the resounding motto of the meeting, "No more war, no more bloodshed." Sadat knew he could regain sovereignty over the Sinai peninsula, but he was not prepared yet to abandon the Palestinian problem and the search for its solution. Sadat's promise that his troops would not cross the Mitla and Gidi passes, and Begin's consent to return all of Sinai, were each interpreted differently by the other party and consequently became issues of contention.[66]

Sadat had overturned most of the premises on which Israel's diplomatic strategy had rested since 1967. He had also compelled the United States to enter deeper into the thicket of Middle Eastern affairs than it had ever done before. Sadat was now about to complete the circle he had begun in 1971.

The brief interval between Sadat's visit and the meeting in Ismailia was sufficient for relations between Egypt and Israel to worsen. The period was marked by unprecedented attacks on Begin in the Egyptian press. Sadat had expected that Begin would be munificent in his gestures towards Egypt, would give greater consideration to the time dimension, and would conduct the peace process with due discretion.[67] He now found himself isolated in the Arab world. Hussein wavered and then did not join his peace initiative. Sadat wanted to convene a conference in Cairo in preparation for the Geneva conference, but only Israel and the United States responded to his call and it therefore turned out to be a meeting of no significance.[68] Moreover, on his visit to the Middle East, Secretary of State Vance learned that Begin was not in fact interested in making the Cairo meeting a preparatory stage for Geneva. Begin was about to present his autonomy plan to Carter. Vance advised the president to avoid debates with Begin on this issue and to concentrate instead on the effort to convene the Geneva conference.[69]

In a policy statement issued by the government on November 28, 1977, Begin rejected Sadat's conditions – full withdrawal to the lines of June 4, 1967 and the establishment of a Palestinian government – "utterly and without reservation."[70] He scoffed at the demand that he should make a gesture to Egypt, "Gentlemen, policy is not gesticulation." He contended that Sadat did not have US support for his positions, and that in its platform the Democratic party has undertaken not to impose a peace formula.

In the beginning of December, Dayan met with Tuhami for a second time. He showed him the proposals for a settlement concerning Sinai and

set forth the autonomy plan. Begin and Dayan were prepared to return
Sinai to Egyptian sovereignty, despite the objections voiced by the army
and the Cabinet. When the American delegation headed by Vance visited
Israel, Dayan sought to ascertain whether his proposals to Tuhami could
serve as a basis for starting negotiations. He was given an affirmative
reply.[71]

The principles of the peace agreement were to be laid down at the
Sadat–Begin meeting in Ismailia. The meeting, however, the last between
the two leaders before Camp David, was not successful.[72] A joint declaration on the Palestinian issue was not arrived at, and the talks came to a
standstill on more or less the same issues that would be the focus of hard
bargaining at Camp David. The plan Begin brought with him did not bring
agreement on a declaration of principles any nearer. The only outcome of
the meeting was the establishment of two committees – political and
military – that were to meet for the first time in Cairo.

Dayan noted scornfully that reality did not exactly match Begin's
declaration that he returned from Ismailia a "happy man." Begin tended to
ignore Egypt's official positions. He still did not correctly assess the
importance of the Palestinian question for Egypt. Sadat rejected the autonomy proposal, but the Egyptian fear that Israel and the United States
would coordinate positions turned out to be baseless. Nor was there agreement on withdrawal from Sinai.[73]

In the government's statement to the Knesset about Israel's peace plan,
Begin said that the meeting at Ismailia had been a success.[74] The prime
minister boasted that it had taken just five minutes to reach agreement on
the most decisive matter – that the objective of the negotiations would be
the signing of a "peace treaty," not a "peace agreement." The political committee, he noted, would also deal with "the moral issue – what can be called
the Jewish–Arab issue – of the Arabs of the Land of Israel." A great effort
had been made, he said, to arrive at an agreed formulation with respect to
the Palestinian question, but the announcement on this issue had two
separate parts – a Palestinian state in the Egyptian version, and self-rule in
Judaea and Samaria in the Israeli version. The euphoria created by Sadat's
initiative had faded, and what remained were the disagreements and differences of a harsh reality.

President Carter received contradictory reports on the outcome of the
Ismailia meeting. Sadat had described it as a total failure, whereas Begin
presented it as a great success.[75] Carter clearly tended to favor the positions
of the Egyptian president. First was the Aswan declaration on January 4,
1978. That declaration included recognition of the legal rights of the Palestinian people and called for allowing the Palestinians a role in the determination of their future.[76]

Dayan saw a positive aspect to the Aswan declaration. Although it spoke both of Israel's withdrawal and the participation of the Palestinians in the peace talks, it also called for full normalization of relations between Israel and the Arab states.[77] In January 1978 there was talk for the first time within the American administration of the possibility of inviting Begin and Sadat to Camp David. For the time being, however, it was decided to invite the two leaders separately and to use arms sales as leverage. Sadat, for his part, had wanted to shake the Americans out of their repose.[78]

After he had made a substantial concession in Sinai, Begin still found himself fighting a holding battle on all the remaining fronts. Since the end of 1977 he had engaged in verbal wrangling that had contributed little to improving Israel's image. When he presented the autonomy plan in the Knesset, there was something of an apologetic strain to his words.[79] In heated debate between him and Knesset members who were among the best of his friends, he said he would accept "with love" whatever was decided. But now what was needed was "that degree of civilian courage without which political decisions cannot be made." There is "great moral support," he said, in the administration, Congress and the Jewish community for Israel's positions. He directed his criticism at officials in the Egyptian foreign ministry who were prisoners of conventional thinking, were exercising a maleficent influence on Sadat, and believed that international pressure would lead to a change in Israel's positions.

Sadat and the Egyptian press kept up their venomous attacks on Begin. He was to answer them at a meeting of the Herut center in January 1978:[80] if Egypt rejected the Israeli government's proposals now, he declared, the government would feel itself free to withdraw them. On Sadat he said, "Let us leave the monopoly on the burning of settlements to the Roman emperor Nero." Begin placed all the weight and prestige of his position behind the peace plan, and asked for a vote of confidence. He received the support he sought but nonetheless, Shmuel Katz, competing for a ministrial position against Begin's candidate, Hayim Landau, received a considerable number of votes in what was a rare expression of internal opposition to Begin.

The political committee was scheduled to meet in Jerusalem in January. As talks were going on, Sadat suddenly summoned the Egyptian mission back to Cairo. The chance of an early settlement between the two countries had definitely been allowed to slip by.[81] Dayan believed that talks held with Egyptian foreign ministry officials were sure to remain deadlocked. He also had reservations about leaving the conduct of the negotiations to the prime minister. He thought that Begin's political speech at the opening session of the political committee, in which he stated Israel's position, had constituted a breach of the promise Begin had given Foreign Minister Mohamed Ibrahim Kamel to the effect that both sides would refrain from making declarations. Now Begin called the Egyptian foreign minister "young man." Nonetheless, Dayan blamed the Egyptians for the failure of the talks.[82] Vance was surprised by Sadat's move and thought the Egyptian president had made a mistake. As a token of good-will, Sadat agreed to continue the talks of the military committee. Even so, Dayan still feared for the fate of the peace treaty with Egypt. He turned to the Americans to find out what concession had to be made on the West Bank to ensure its conclusion.[83]

On January 23, 1978, Begin mounted the Knesset rostrum to make an announcement on the diplomatic situation and to reply to Sadat's speech.[84] He accused the Egyptian president, in effect, of deception in having broken his promise that the Egyptian army would not move beyond the Sinai passes after a peace agreement; the peninsula, he said, is a *place d'armes* for Israel. He cited the vicious attacks against him and Israel by journalists Anis Mansour and Mustafa Amin. The latter had called him "Shylock." He apologized for what he had said at the opening session of the political committee, but protested the fact that Sadat had ordered his delegation back to Egypt, "without any justification, without any warning."

In February 1978 the US administration expected that Sadat would present a proposal of his own, which would be rejected by Israel, thereby giving the United States wider scope and maneuverability as an intermediary. The Americans were preparing themselves for a confrontation with Israel and were interested in shaking Israel's self-confidence as much as possible. The attempt to do so reached its height during Begin's March visit to Washington. The president was ready to abandon the diplomatic effort for a time, if that was what was needed to soften the Israeli position. To that end he was even prepared to shift the struggle to Congress, even though it was considered a bastion of pro-Israel sentiment.[85]

Begin arrived in Washington after Sadat and after the Litani operation in Lebanon. This time President Carter had little patience for Begin's wordy argumentation. He asked for substantial concessions from Israel, in return for the nonestablishment of a Palestinian state. Dayan described Begin's reaction to the president's proposals and harsh attitude as shock; his speech sounded "detached, not getting through, without resonance"; it was evident that his strength had been spent in controlling his emotions.[86]

Carter was later to write that Begin said he had been hurt to the depths of his soul by the president's withdrawal of support from his peace plan, that he regarded Sadat's visit to Jerusalem no more than a "grand gesture," and that in fact Sadat had not at all budged from his extremist positions. But to Carter, it was Prime Minister Begin with his "six no's" – from nonwithdrawal from the West Bank to not allowing the Palestinians a hand in determining their fate – who had become "an insurmountable obstacle to further progress."[87]

In Vance's view, Begin tried to be as flexible as he could, but was fearful of domestic opposition in Israel. The United Staes wanted to block a separate agreement between Israel and Egypt at almost any price. Vance also suggested that Israel be forced to provide a clear answer about its position on the West Bank by presenting it with written questions. At the same time, the administration tried to persuade the Egyptians to draw up a peace proposal of their own, parallel to Israel's.[88]

The struggle for peace was also taking place in another arena. Begin and Dayan looked with anxiety, if not resentment, at the closeness that had developed between the president of Egypt and Defense Minister Ezer Weizman. They tended to doubt the reliability of Weizman's reports of talks he held in Egypt. At the end of March 1978, Attorney-General Aharon Barak accompanied Weizman on his visit to Egypt. It appeared that Sadat was inclined to agree that a Palestinian state not be established. He wanted to link the West Bank to Jordan and the Gaza Strip to Egypt, and consented to some form of Israeli presence. Weizman himself was surprised by General Gamassi's readiness to allow the settlements in Sinai to remain in place under Egyptian sovereignty.[89]

On the following day, after he had met with a Palestinian delegation and under the influence of officials from the Egyptian Foreign Ministry, Sadat withdrew his consent to an Israeli presence in Sinai. In the meantime a storm of controversy had broken out over dummy strongholds erected in the Rafah Salient by Agriculture Minister Ariel Sharon in a rather broad interpretation of the government's decision that ground be prepared for settlement purposes. It is not certain that this action is what decided the fate of the Sinai settlements, but the government's credibility was certainly damaged.[90] In the spring of 1978, Egypt began to reap the fruits of Sadat's initiative. The rapprochement between it and the United States now became a fact that Israel had to reckon with.

At the end of April, Dayan was invited to Washington to help find a way to break the diplomatic logjam. The Americans warned Dayan that Sadat's position in the Arab world was worsening. They posed Israel two related questions: would Israel accept that the question of sovereignty be decided at the end of the five-year period allotted to the autonomy plan, and how would this be done?[91] On June 18, Israel submitted a qualified response: the nature of relations between the sides would be discussed at the end of the five-year period. Negotiations on the future of Judaea, Samaria, and the Gaza Strip would be conducted with representatives elected from among the residents.[92] On the question of sovereignty, Israel refused to commit itself.

The attempts to reach agreement between Israel and Egypt had failed; Begin's public image plummeted, both at home and in the international arena. Sadat was now able to irritate Begin openly, without having to fear public opinion. On July 10, Austrian Chancellor Bruno Kreisky and the president of the Socialist International Willy Brandt issued the Vienna Document, which was based on an agreement that had been reached between Shimon Peres, as leader of the opposition, and President Sadat.[93] This declaration included recognition of the right of the Palestinians to participate in determining their future status, solution of the Palestinian problem in all its aspects, and a readiness to withdraw on all fronts. Sadat also met with Ezer Weizman. He did not accede to a request to meet with Begin but demanded a goodwill gesture: the return of El Arish and Mount Sinai.[94]

In the light of Sadat's meetings with Peres and Weizman, it would seem that Begin had lost control. The debate in the Knesset was stormier than ever.[95] Ignoring Weizman's advice, he refused to perform a token withdrawal as a gesture towards Sadat. He aimed his criticism at the leader of the opposition, accusing Peres of having misled him by not informing him of his intention to draft a resolution for the Socialist International. He did not consent to a meeting between Peres and King Hussein.[96]

The Leeds Castle meeting was to clarify the Egyptian and Israel's positions; it was convened on July 18, 1978. Dayan regarded it as "a milestone in the peace negotiations." For the first time Egypt submitted a peace plan of its own. Dayan presented a memorandum to Vance, without government approval, according to which Israel would be prepared to discuss the issue of sovereignty in Judaea, Samaria, and the Gaza Strip if its proposal concerning administrative autonomy was accepted.[97] At the same time he threatened the Egyptians that Israel would withdraw its consent to restore Sinai to Egyptian sovereignty. Begin, who thought that Dayan should not have made the proposal without his knowledge, surprised his foreign minister when he himself adopted it and brought it before the cabinet for approval.

Two distinct positions now seemed to have emerged: Israel's peace plan as presented by Begin in December 1977; and Sadat's proposal for the West Bank and the Gaza Strip, as expressed at the Leeds Castle talks in July 1978. By August, the Americans had developed a draft of a comprehensive settlement. It was Vance's impression that the positions of the parties had drawn closer, but that a new breakthrough was still needed. The talks at Leeds Castle convinced Vance that discussion between Egypt and Israel of a comprehensive settlement was indeed possible. Harold Saunders, the assistant secretary of state, had drafted the American document, which after some changes served as the framework for the Camp David Accords. The initial intention was to present the American proposal at a meeting to take place at an installation of the American supervisory force in Sinai, but Sadat opposed this after Israel refused to return El Arish and Mount Sinai.[98]

The fruits of diplomatic blunders

In the summer of 1978, the United States took the initiative in the peace talks. The mandate of the UN Emergency Force in Sinai was to end in September, and the administration subjected its positions to thorough reexamination. It had to plan the moves it would make until the anticipated crisis with Israel, and be careful to avoid any rash action that might precipitate failure. In a talk with Brzezinski on July 20, 1978, President Carter returned to his earlier idea of a summit meeting between Sadat and Begin. Asking his aides to maintain secrecy about the moves being planned by the administration, he decided to send Secretary of State Vance to the Middle East to set the process in motion.[99]

On August 6 and 7, 1978, the secretary of state traveled to Jerusalem and Alexandria to deliver invitations from the president to the Camp David summit. On August 8, the US delegation headed by Vance met an Israeli delegation headed by Begin to discuss the American proposal. Dayan later had scorn for Begin's "treacly words of greeting," and described Begin as a victim of smug self-satisfaction who remained unaware of the approaching danger. Meanwhile, William Quandt, member of the staff of National Security Council, returned from Egypt and told of Sadat's enthusiasm about negotiations at Camp David, of his desire that the sides not lay down prior conditions, and that Begin must, like him, be empowered to make decisions in the name of the government. Dayan, unlike Begin, was skeptical, supposing that Sadat had given his consent on the basis of an American promise to support him on the issues in dispute – especially on withdrawal from the territories and self-determination for the Palestinians.[100]

Begin, according to Vance, accepted the American proposal enthusiastically. Vance feared the proposal would be leaked, but Begin promised that no word of it would be let out until the official announcement. The promise was kept. The prime minister expressed his concern that he might find himself at a disadvantage against both Carter and Sadat. He asked the United States to play a mediator role and not make proposals of its own. In any event, Begin displayed an insensitivity to the seriousness of US intentions and the nature of political bargaining itself. The American policymakers were already convinced that a proposal drawn up by them to serve as a basis for a settlement was absolutely necessary.[101]

Administration officials tended to emphasize the great risk the president was taking. They focused their criticism mainly on Begin, whose obstinacy they depicted as a serious impediment to peace. If there was an opportune time for pressuring Israel, they believed this was it. The administration's announcement of the Camp David talks was cautious. It hedged about the chances of success, but asserted that the danger to peace made a summit meeting vital.

Of the three leaders, it was Carter who came most fully prepared. Bringing the habits of a meticulous engineer to the personal and diplomatic spheres, he had studied psychological profiles of Sadat and Begin and intended making full use of them. He had met jointly with the US ambassadors to Israel and Egypt to get as precise as possible an assessment of the chances of the summit's success. He also carefully outlined the tactics that would be employed at the conference. It seemed to him that the goals sought by the State Department and the National Security Council were too modest. He raised the stakes and set it as a comprehensive settlement between Israel and Egypt. He banked on the power the Middle Eastern leaders wielded at home, and on their ability to make decisions without having to fear more than minimal "political punishment."[102]

Carter estimated that the conference would last between three days to a week, and that the relaxed atmosphere of Camp David would help bring the two sides closer together; both of these assumptions proved mistaken. His own feeling was that of a soldier going to battle; he even prepared an annotated Bible to take to the summit, feeling he would need it for his talks with Begin. The day before the opening of the conference, he went into seclusion and summed up the areas of agreement and dispute between the sides.

In his address to the nation before leaving for the United States, Begin said that Camp David would not be a "fateful meeting", because Israel's destiny did not depend on this or any other meeting. Negotiations over the Panama Canal had lasted fourteen years, and those that led to the termination of the war in Vietnam took four years, "I am not talking in terms of years, but certainly a fair number of months is required for conducting proper negotiations on peace and the conditions of peace."[103] Summing up a political debate beforehand at the Herut movement center, Begin said, "We have no reason to suppose that Camp David is a trap and that what awaits us there is failure." While clearly aware of the uniqueness of the summit about to convene, he scarcely imagined that there would be no escape from it to protracted negotiations at a later date. Perhaps this helps to explain why Begin left for Camp David unprepared, his fixed ideas and principles not backed up by more precise and systematic planning. Knesset Member Moshe Arens had proposed a minimum condition for an agreement – control over Sharm el-Sheikh and the Sinai airfields, and full IDF control in Judaea and Samaria – but that was all.[104]

Begin's entourage at Camp David did not include any senior member of his party with roots in the Revisionist movement. The absence of his long-standing political intimates clearly heightened his isolation at Camp David; the presence of his wife and his political secretary, Yehiel

Kadishai, and the encouragement of his own son, were not a real substitute.

Three years after the signing of the Camp David Accords, Knesset Member Amnon Rubinstein was to say that "those negotiations will go down in the chronicles of diplomatic history as an example of extreme negligence."[105] We can only indirectly infer how the Israeli delegation in fact prepared itself. According to Aharon Barak, the delegation arrived "without adequate preparation, without background material, and without alternative proposals."[106]

The experience and characteristics that Begin brought to Camp David prepared him only in part for the trials and difficulties of diplomatic bargaining. As far as can be seen, the prime minister had not set the boundaries of the concessions he would be willing to make. The fine nuances of the negotiations were generally lost to him in the haze of broad historical parallels. He placed too great an emphasis on the procedural side and on terminology, and less on the solutions that give shape and substance to a reality of stable peace. Specific demands directed at him were staved off with a stubbornness that was rooted, ostensibly, in immutable principles. The biased view of Brzezinski notwithstanding, he did in fact employ a store of expressions of opposition – "I will not sign it under any circumstances," "It is unacceptable," "We shall never agree," and his famed "*non possumus*" – with a wearying regularity.[107]

Had the prime minister attended the summit meeting by himself, it is doubtful that he would have come away with an agreement. In such a case, the American mediation would not have been able to be flexible, the pressure on Begin would have had to be early and direct, and failure would have been certain. The image of an authoritative leader able to make decisions on the spot did not help produce a better outcome for Israel, but reliance on it by him was inevitable.

The lack of a uniform position among the members of the delegation, and the feeling that some members took exception to the prime minister's position, weakened Israel's bargaining front. Up until the final stages of the talks, the working premise of the Americans was that Begin could be made more flexible with the help of other members of the Israeli team.[108]

In Weizman's view, the differences between himself, Dayan, and Begin attested to "insufficient preparation at home, among other reasons also because of the prime minister's work methods." He also believed the conference was overloaded with jurists.[109] Dayan wrote that "the decisive, difficult, and unpleasant part" of the peace negotiations with Egypt was at Camp David. He was annoyed by the prime minister's manner of speech, especially by his practice of angrily interrupting those who differed with him. At the same time, he praised Begin's patience and openness in managing the Israeli delegation.[110]

The view according to which the senior negotiators on the Israeli team – Dayan, Weizman, and Barak – persuaded Begin to make concessions and to sign an agreement based on principles not his own is credible only in the light of the unique structure of these talks, which allowed this mode of operation to be complemented by pressures from President Carter. They fostered the image of an Israeli delegation that was not united and offered footholds for breaching its stand. Although the change they helped to bring about was a historic achivement, it set a precedent few prime ministers could find acceptable.

Diplomatic bargaining generally consists of mutual persuasion, rational calculation of profit and loss with respect to anticipated future situations, and the complex use of threat, deterrence, and incentives. A much smaller role is played by the skills and penchants in which Begin excelled – the orator who exploits the power of words and emotions, argumentation based on historical right, a use of precedents and analogies, and reliance on principles of natural justice. The traits of the politician that were so much a part of Begin's nature acted against him, detracting from what is required of a skilled diplomat.

There was a price to be paid for the prime minister's contentious style. He had a tendency to rail against views opposed to his own, without listening to what others had to say. Sometimes his style even worked against him when he obscured fundamental concessions by wrapping them in what looked like total opposition. President Carter acknowledged in his memoirs that fatigue and the wearying debates with Begin had made reality appear darker than it actually was.[111]

Carter's attitude to the two leaders from the Middle East was unmistakably uneven. Begin appeared to him as one who saw himself as a man of destiny, a man of deep beliefs fulfilling a biblical role, a leader of the chosen people. At the same time, he was endlessly concerned with words, names, and terms, and that tended to impede free discussion. Their way of working differed and so did their personal style. The prime minister was formal, always properly attired and punctilious in the observance of protocol. It bothered him that his status was not equal to that of the two presidents, for they were heads of state. Begin, accordingly, always made sure that it was he who went to Carter and not the reverse. In Carter's opinion, Begin was a hard and aggressive bargainer, and except for his tendency to interrupt others while they were speaking, he was the epitome of propriety and good manners.[112]

It is unlikely that publication of the records of the Camp David summit will reveal the reasons for the fundamental change in Begin's positions that took place between September 14 and September 16, 1978. There is general agreement that the talk with Carter on the 16th was decisive. There is no mention in the president's memoirs as to how he won concessions from Begin. He merely notes that Begin cried "ultimatum," "excessive demands," and "political suicide." The president's adviser, Brzezinski, repeats the president's version precisely;[113] Vance makes no mention of this meeting.

The prime minister's concessions covered a broad front. Terminologically, Begin retreated all down the line on the Palestinian question. He remained convinced that the meaning of "full autonomy" and "legitimate rights" was subject to a wider interpretation than was generally conceded. The formal wording concerning Judaea and Samaria took second place this time to Begin's faith that real control over the historical process that would determine the future of the territories was still in his hands. He also agreed to vacate the settlements and the airfields. On his return from his meeting with the president, Begin appeared to Weizman "drained, distraught, and preoccupied."[114]

The acquiescence of a person who bases his opposition on principles is liable in certain instances to be more profound than that of a pragmatic person. When a breach in the wall of principles is a breach in the last line of self-defense the result is often a real concession or admission of defeat. That was the outcome at Camp David. The separation between the two agreements, the postponement of the question of sovereignty in Judaea and Samaria, and the circumvention in the sections dealing with settlements, Resolution 242, and Jerusalem, facilitated the prime minister's concessions. They enabled rationalization and self-persuasion in the face of a reality that contradicted his deepest beliefs. Afterwards he insisted that he had not been pressured. Though he had negotiated with some vigour, he was late in demarcating the bounds of concessions, letting his primary positions be eroded. Then he compromised on what he had previously declared to be impossible. Any other interpretation for Begin's stand at Camp David must assume that he had an outstanding capability of completely concealing his true intentions.

There is a measure of irony in the fact that Begin's greatest diplomatic achievement may enter the annals of history as an achievement imposed upon him. This arises from the recognition that because of his personality, his status in Israeli politics, and his shortcomings as a negotiator, he was the only one able to make the concessions needed to guarantee the peace agreement. It may be that only Begin himself can tell us which is the correct interpretation: an agreement forced upon him against his will, or the greatest gamble of his life – to bring peace and also retain Judaea and Samaria regardless of the treaty commitment he took upon himself and with which he thereby obligated Israel.

The historical importance of the Camp David Accords is not in doubt. The question up for discussion is, could a more favorable outcome for Israel have been achieved by a different bargaining method, greater diplomatic skill, preference for direct negotiations between Egypt and Israel – all this up until 1978 – and afterward different conduct of the negotiations at Camp David? A satisfactory answer to this question is not likely to be found – not now when we are still close to the event, nor from the historical perspectives of the coming generation, when all the documents and records are available for inspection by the unbiased historian.

In the government's announcement to the Knesset on September 25, 1978, Begin opened by saying that he did not intend to place the content of two documents before the house – the Egyptian document and the first American document presented to the Israeli delegation at Camp David – "for reasons I shall call psycho-political."[115] Begin wanted to emphasize how wide a gap existed between the demands Israel faced at the beginning of the summit and the accomplishment at the end.

The framework for assessing Israel's gains or failure at Camp David is itself a matter of controversy. The framework for peace was supposed to have begun a historical process which if realized would mean relinquishment by Israel of the West Bank.[116] The "Framework for Peace in the Middle East" stipulated that the basis for peaceful settlement between Israel and its neighbors is "UN Security Council Resolution 242, in all its parts." The negotiations between Israel, Egypt, Jordan, and representatives of the Palestinian people will be "on the resolution of the Palestinian problem in all its aspects." It speaks of a transference of authority, withdrawal of the military government and its civilian administration, free elections by the inhabitants of the territories to a self-governing authority, the granting of full autonomy to the inhabitants, and declares that the "solution from the negotiations must also recognize the legitimate rights of the Palestinian people and their just requirements."

Begin's broadest apologetics concerned the withdrawal from the Sinai settlements, not the Palestinian part of the accords. As to the latter, he seems to have been convinced that he had managed to arrest the processes leading to the establishment of a Palestinian state. Begin believed that the critical moment of the negotiations was the debate over the preamble to Resolution 242. The most difficult moment, he said, was on the last day of the conference, when President Carter showed him his letter on Jerusalem. The United States had restated its position that it considered Jerusalem as "occupied territory."[117]

Begin contended that the decision on evacuating the settlements in Sinai was to be submitted to the Knesset. He changed his mind about holding a separate vote on that question only after he learned of the position of the Alignment, which accused him of not taking responsibility for the decision

and threatened not to participate in the debate on the fate of the settlements. Actually, without the Alignment, the Accords could not have been
approved. Several years later he was to go a step further. On May 4, 1982
he told the Knesset: "They [the Alignment] spread the lie that at Camp
David the Israeli delegation agreed to the evacuation of the settlements in
southern and northern Sinai."[118] This statement stands in glaring contradiction to Begin's efforts to persuade the members of the Knesset to confirm the Camp David Accords in their entirety.

It was clear to the members of the Knesset, just as it was clear to the
prime minister, and in accordance with the exchange of letters with
President Carter, that approval of the decision to evacuate the settlements
was a prerequisite for negotiations on the peace treaty between Egypt and
Israel, and that if that condition was not met, the Framework Agreement
would be void and invalid. Every Knesset member had to understand,
regardless of whether the vote was separate or not, that the fate of the peace
treaty with Egypt and of relations with the United States depended on
approval of both parts of the agreement.

Begin's performance in the Knesset, especially his reply to discussants
before the vote, was one of the most impressive in his political career.[119] He
posed the choice sharply: either the decision must be accepted as is, or if
not, everything "agreed upon at Camp David will be totally nullified." He
ignored the interjection of Knesset Member Amnon Lin, who asked the
meaning of "the legitimate rights of the Palestinian Arabs." But on the
question of the settlements he allowed himself to be candid. He knew that
if the Camp David summit fell apart, "the State of Israel will not be able to
endure [the effects of] that, not in America, nor in Europe, nor before
American Jewry, nor before the Jews in other lands. It will not endure that.
It will be wholly blamed."

Some who had traveled a long way with Begin and had now become his
critics – men such as Yellin-Mor, Eldad, and Katz – once again discovered
the duality they always viewed with suspicion: as much as they esteemed
his faith and principles, they doubted his ability to translate these into
reality. In an article entitled "Open and Sorrowful Letter to Menachem
Begin," Eldad wrote that no great skill was necessary to imagine the speech
that Begin would have delivered if those same proposals had been
presented in the name of the Alignment. That was written about Begin's
autonomy plan: after the accords were signed, Eldad was less restrained in
his choice of words.[120] Yellin-Mor congratulated him on the change in his
views but doubted that Begin would be able to fulfill the agreements concerning Judaea and Samaria.[121] The most sarcastic, blistering, and
thorough in his criticism was Shmuel Katz. He focused less on the agreement on Sinai and more on the questions as yet undecided, the unguarded
front of Judaea, Samaria, and the Gaza Strip. He accused Begin

of having violated most of his principles on the Palestinian question and of intentional deceptiveness in interpreting the terms included in the agreement. He accused him, in fact of having openly adopted, in an official and contractual document, the Arab demands in their entirety.[122]

Secretary of State Vance, the least biased of the American representatives at the negotiations, wrote that the Camp David Accords were among the most important diplomatic achievements of the Carter presidency. They effected a structural change in the Middle East. Egypt was taken out of the war ring, and the chances of a general war were lessened. The Palestinian question was moved to the top of the international political agenda and a specific framework was defined for its solution. If the self-governing authority would only conduct itself responsibly, wrote Vance, the process will be irreversible. Israel will then find itself politically unable to preserve the status quo in the territories and will have no security need to justify its demand for sovereignty over them.[123]

The rapid pace of the negotiations at the concluding stage of the Camp David summit meeting brought with it a haste that would culminate in misunderstanding and disagreement. Immediately after the accords were signed, a bitter dispute broke out concerning the freeze on settlement. It had been agreed that the freeze would be in effect as long as negotiations were being conducted. Begin contended that in his understanding the freeze applied to the three months set for completing the peace treaty with Egypt. Carter maintained that Begin's understanding was not reasonable; the two agreements had not been kept separate from the beginning, and the freeze was to be in effect for the five years until the permanent arrangement for the West Bank would go into effect. As far as can be ascertained today on the basis of the testimony of all sides, the dispute was the product of a genuine misunderstanding, though the versions that try to explain it contradict each other.[124]

The secretary of state, whose accounts are generally accurate, writes that Carter won Begin's consent to a settlement freeze until the autonomy talks were concluded. Vance asked Saunders to draft the letter the prime minister was to send to the president on this subject. The fierce debate that erupted on the Jerusalem question diverted attention from the letter, which was still unsigned at the time the accords were completed. On the day after the summit had ended, Saunders asked the ambassador to the United States, Simcha Dinitz, about the missing letter. He was told that the prime minister was revising it. Begin in fact did refer to a period of three months. We understood, wrote Vance, that Begin did not intend to honor the agreement. Begin himself, addressing the Knesset, maintained that the matter had been checked with Barak and Dayan "in all the notes and documents," and that the Israeli version was the correct one.[125] It will probably never be known whether this diplomatic negligence was the result of a true absence of mind or was deliberate on the part of the Americans.

Carter denounced Begin's declarations on Jerusalem, the settlements, and withdrawal from the West Bank. He cautioned the prime minister that his pronouncements would impede other Arab countries from joining the peace process. The government then announced a policy of expanding existing settlements, and Begin declared that he would move his office to East Jerusalem.[126] President Carter proposed convening a conference at which negotiations for concluding the peace between Israel and Egypt would get started. This conference came to be known as the Blair House talks.[127]

This meeting and the round of talks that followed it were conducted in the shadow cast by Egypt's isolation in the Arab world. The revolution in Iran, and the reactions in the Arab world, impelled the United States to accelerate its efforts to conclude the negotiations. In Israel, too, the peace was losing popularity. The United States demanded that Israel return El Arish within six months and present a clear timetable for the implementation of autonomy. The atmosphere in the Israeli government was charged with suspicion and rivalries. Begin would soon tighten the leash on his senior ministers, Dayan and Weizman.[128]

Three months after the Camp David summit ended, Begin came before the Knesset and explained the difficulties that were holding up the signing of the peace treaty.[129] In pedantic style he enumerated the articles in dispute, especially Article 6, about the priority of the peace treaty between Israel and Egypt over other treaty obligations. In any instance of a conflict between Egypt's other commitments and those undertaken in the peace treaty, he drily noted, the interpretation must be clear. Begin tried to dispel the fog around the relationship between Israel's withdrawal from Sinai and the time when ambassadors would be exchanged between Israel and Egypt. He firmly opposed setting a target date for the implementation of the autonomy and for the elections to the self-governing authority. Israel was being accused of not concluding the peace negotiations on time, he said, but "piles of interpretation" are draining the peace of all content. For its part, the government had been prepared to sign the peace treaty back in November, at the Blair House talks.[130]

The American administration was forced to admit that the key to the signing of the peace treaty was in Begin's hands. They applied tremendous pressure on him to accept the president's invitation to meet with him in Washington. Initially he refused; in the end he went reluctantly. It was a tough encounter and it shook Begin. Vance wrote that the meeting between President Carter and Begin at the beginning of March 1979 was one of the harshest they had ever had. Carter fulminated against Begin's attention to details, his preoccupation with terminology, and his lack of trust for Sadat. Begin seemed to Carter more nervous than ever. He began with a statement about the strength of the IDF and its ability to defend Saudi Arabia and to help Egypt against Libya. The president's view was that Begin was less concerned with peace than in demonstrating that Israel ought to be the dominant force in the Middle East.[131]

The changes taking place in the international arena and the crisis in Iran detracted from Carter's ability to devote the bulk of his attention to the Middle East and induced him to make a last ditch effort, using coercive diplomacy, to guarantee that the peace agreement be signed.[132] Carter wrote later that his decision to go to the Middle East in March 1979 was an act of despair. He was stunned when he discovered that Begin had refused to sign the agreement without the government's and the Knesset's approval.[133] The president was to have a direct experience of the byways of Israeli politics. He participated in a meeting of the cabinet and addressed the Knesset. Carter's speech was sympathetic and cautionary. He noted the US's commitment to Israel and the little that still stood between lasting dispute and the peace both nations needed.[134]

Begin's speech was one of the most tempestuous in the Knesset's history.[135] He was interrupted time after time, and was compelled at the beginning of his address to speak out in praise of democracy. He said that "we never played with words or with what is called 'legalistic definitions'." The questions were substantive, he said. After his exposure to Carter's wrath the day before, he explained why it was the Knesset's duty to approve the peace treaty. To the nation and the Knesset he said that President Carter had not come to pressure Israel (which was not true), and if he did come to pressure us, "we would refuse him." It appears that Begin knew that the president could not leave empty-handed. Carter had already snapped at him: "You must sign." Dayan and Weizman were at the point of rebelling against his authority. Now he wanted to make the most of the opportunity that had been presented him to stand proudly and assert national honor.[136]

While the points in the peace agreement still in dispute were being reviewed in Jerusalem, Israel tried to make some gains in the memorandum of understanding with the United States concerning the aid it would receive. According to Vance, the talk he held with Dayan was one of the most decisive in the peace negotiations. It led to a breakthrough at the very last moment. It was agreed that a "memorandum of understanding" would be drawn up relating to what would happen if Egypt violated the peace agreement. The president also promised Begin financial aid to help defray the expenses entailed by implementation of the peace agreement and a guarantee to supply oil in case of emergency.[137]

On March 20, 1979 Begin delivered to the Knesset the government's announcement on the peace treaty between Israel and Egypt.[138] This was one of his longest Knesset speeches and he wearied the Knesset members with the details of legal controversies and their solutions. This time he mobilized the scathing language he was reluctant to use at the festive session that President Carter had attended. He blasted the Communist members of the Knesset, and spoke of "the insolence of subjugated slaves and foreign agents, whom we allow to sit in this house." Begin opened with the dispute over the two paragraphs of Article 6, which he called "the soul of the treaty." As far as he was concerned, any alteration of those paragraphs would empty the peace agreement as a whole of all content. Knesset members demanded that he explain the principles of the agreement, not the details. But in this instance the details were of importance. Begin was to explain what precisely was the difference between autonomy that becomes a self-governing authority on the way to sovereignty and "full autonomy" for the inhabitants. Nonetheless, he was forced to acknowledge that although the Knesset was voting on the Hebrew version, the decisive version was the one in English.

Now that the peace negotiations were completed, he could once again say that Israel would never return to the lines of June 4, 1967; Jerusalem will not be divided and will remain "Israel's eternal capital"; in Judaea, Samaria, and Gaza "there will never arise a so-called 'Palestinian' state," and finally, clutching at a ruling of Israel's Supreme Court, he promised that there would always be settlements in the West Bank.

The gap between Begin's initial intentions and the peace treaty that was signed toward the end of March 1979 was significant. Although Israel had obtained the full peace he had set out to achieve, his desire to avoid total withdrawal on any front was not realized. The IDF presence and the deadlock of the autonomy talks became the main guarantees for assuring that any historical process liable to culminate in the granting of self-determination to the Palestinians would not be fulfilled. Nonetheless, the peace agreement was the primary achievement of the seven years of Menachem Begin's premiership. The state of war with Egypt came to an end. Israel withdrew to the international boundary, and the demilitarization of Sinai was backed by real guarantees. The two countries established full diplomatic relations. The memoranda of understanding with the United States established its commitment to the peace agreement.

The framework for peace was vague concerning the West Bank, and was remote from political reality. Begin regarded that as an achievement. But it is an achievement based on a hazardous gamble, which alone permits rational explanation of Begin's concessions. If he believed that by giving up Sinai he would be able to keep Judaea and Samaria, that supposition has yet to be proven. It is more likely that he was convinced that control of the territories was the key to determining their future, regardless of what international commitment Israel took upon itself. But, indeed, diplomatic negligence does sometimes lead to historic achievements.

The waning of the peace process was inevitable. The autonomy talks were deadlocked. Although the peace with Egypt held up, no progress was made with respect to the eastern front. Slowly the Middle East ceased being the center of international attention. Reagan's election to the presidency began a congenial period for Israel. For a number of years America stopped its direct pressure on Israel and did not put forward a peace plan of its own. The central figures who had played a role in the peace process were no longer on stage. Carter failed to be reelected. Sadat was assassinated, Dayan died. Weizman was shunted into a corner, and Begin resigned the premiership.

12

The War in Lebanon

In August 1983 Begin declared, "The war in Lebanon, our great war, was unavoidable."[1] The outcome of the war was by then fully clear.

The period between the spring of 1981 and the start of the war in Lebanon in early June 1982 deserves special attention from the historian. It was a year of feverish activity. The prime minister had converted certain electoral defeat into a tide which he rode to victory. He formed his second government without the reservations and hesitations that had constrained him in 1977.

Lebanon had loomed large in Begin's calculations ever since he took the reins of power. Here was another example that when a crisis is passed from one government to the next, the legacy inherited often provides an opportunity for fateful blunders. Begin's attitude toward war contained, from time to time, what might be called a "Tolstoyan" strain. In the halcyon days of spring 1973 he had found occasion to say: "The relationship between a plan conceived in advance and the reality created on the battlefield is often no more than coincidental."[2] The Lebanon War was the failure of naked political realism that rested on the illusion that it is possible to achieve an enduring political objective by force alone, and that the *fait accompli* created that way will in the end win international support.

In the conspiracy thesis, toward which all works on the war are inclined, Begin is depicted as a pathetic hero, gulled and led astray by Defense Minister Ariel Sharon.[3] He was a statesman enticed by a simplistic strategic plan that exuded a false odor of logic. The chief sponsor of the war was the defense minister, who believed it would create a new regional balance of power based on strategic partnership with the United States. The war Sharon envisaged would destroy the PLO as an independent political factor, inflict damage on Syria, the most dangerous of Israel's enemies, and establish Israel as the major power in the Middle East. Begin became a full partner the moment he gave his backing to Sharon. There was, in effect, a *putsch*, which was carried out by diversionary tactics, by depriving the government of its ability to properly conduct the war, by intentionally keeping it in the dark about the larger strategic plan.

Although many facts support this view, there were enough permanent features in Begin's strategic thinking, world view, and decision making method to make the war in Lebanon possible without recourse to a conspiratorial thesis.

"War by choice"

An obscure conception that Begin tried to present as a precept able to guide Israel's security doctrine was "war by choice." Ever since the 1950s he had opposed intermediate situations – partial international settlements that do not culminate in a peace treaty no less than reprisals and preventive actions that do not put an end to the Arab threat. When he came to power it was not surprising that from time to time he made a point of stating that Israel had abandoned "the philosophy of reprisal."[4] Not only did he not regard the reprisal operations, which he called "hit and run" actions, a deterrent factor, but he also believed that they constituted a renunciation of the strategic initiative.

In an address at the graduation ceremony of Israel's National Security College in September 1982, Begin tried to give his conception the semblance of a military doctrine.[5] He began with a historical parallel. The analogy he chose was the outbreak of the Second World War. There was no longer any doubt, he said, that the war could have been prevented. It began in March 1936, when France chose not to attack Germany after German forces had entered the Rhineland: "That, therefore, is the international proof that explains what is war out of lack of choice as opposed to war by choice." That was one of the most inappropriate historical parallels Begin ever advanced. It contained nothing resembling the circumstances of Israel's wars before or after Operation Peace in Galilee, the name under which the Lebanon War was officially launched. Begin advanced his thesis further. Israel's wars of choice were the Sinai campaign and the Six Day War; the wars of no choice were the War of Independence, the War of Attrition, and the Yom Kippur War. In an attempt to sharpen his argument, Begin in effect invalidated most of his own arguments in the 1950s and 1960s, the years of his scathing criticism of the government. He now declared that in 1956 and 1967 Israel had not faced any danger, that no attack by Egypt was imminent. True, the closing of the Straits of Tiran was an act of aggression, "but there is always room for considerable discretion in deciding whether a *causus belli* is to be used for there to be a *bellum*." The prime minister had now flagrantly contradicted the *raison d'être* of his entire foreign policy, whereby the Six Day War was a war of defense, which according to his interpretation of international law meant that Israel could permanently retain the occupied territories.

Another fact he noted was that in wars of choice the losses incurred are relatively few, whereas in a war of no choice the losses suffered are heavy. The losses incurred until the IDF's withdrawal from Lebanon were to refute this contention; in June 1985, the losses suffered in Lebanon approximated those of the Six Day War. Beyond these premises, Begin also added a prognosis: "There are grounds to expect that we have in store an historic period of peace. Of course it is not possible to set a date. But the land may be at peace for forty years.'[6]

The war in Lebanon was indeed a war of choice. It came after a prolonged crisis, after years during which a statesman could have assuredly, not hastily, considered the range of political and strategic options available to him. Israel faced no insurmountable strategic threat, and the possibilities of response were manifold. The previous government, headed by Yitzhak Rabin, had acted with considerable caution. It had provided clandestine assistance to the Christians in Lebanon, was attentive to relations with Syria, distinguished between southern and northern Lebanon, and accused the terrorists of being the cause of divisiveness in Lebanon. For Begin, Lebanon was a clear, simplistic case of a minority facing massacre by a Muslim majority, with the minority betrayed by the entire Christian world.[7]

After he formed his first government in 1977, Begin brought Israel's aid to the Christians out into the open and made it a source of national pride. On his return from his first visit to the United States in August 1977, he said that the subject of Lebanon had come up for discussion, adding, "We do not want the events in Lebanon to lead to any war."[8] Before he left for the Camp David talks, he proclaimed in a speech to the nation that Israel would not acquiesce in genocide in Lebanon. During the first two days of the summit, he was surprised to discover that Sadat and Carter did not share his altruistic perspective, and viewed Israeli aid to the Christians not as "a noble humanitarian deed," but as a complicating factor adding to Lebanon's overburdened store of troubles.[9]

After the peace with Egypt had been concluded, Begin presented Israel's Lebanon policy before the Knesset. He invited President Sarkis "to come to Jerusalem to meet with me." Israel, he declared, recognized the territorial integrity of Lebanon and was prepared to cooperate with the UN forces. However, the Syrian army must leave Lebanon. Israel had saved the Christian community from destruction, as well as the Shiites and Muslims in southern Lebanon. Because of our assistance, he added, "we can influence our Christian friends in Lebanon.'[10]

In historical perspective, spring 1981 appears as a turning point, an omen foreboding ill. The downing of the Syrian helicopters on Mount Senin and the placement of Syrian missiles in Lebanon engendered an altogether different crisis to anything Israel had known. Begin took upon himself what was a new and far-reaching commitment to the Christians in Lebanon, although he himself thought otherwise. He contended that the Christians were at the breaking point, and that the possibility that the Syrians would introduce missiles was taken into account before Israel's air force was thrown into action. He ridiculed the "variable" red line of the previous government. But after a talk with Shimon Peres, he said there was "national accord" to remove the missiles by military means if diplomatic efforts were to fail.[11]

In the Knesset Begin said that Mount Senin was the key to all of Lebanon, and if the Syrians were to hold it Israel would face mortal danger. He mentioned, irresponsibly, precise times that had been set for the air force to attack the missiles, attacks that were called off because of weather conditions. He warned the president of Syria not to adopt a policy of brinkmanship, and effectively presented him with an ultimatum to remove his missiles from Lebanon.[12] The prime minister's speech was constantly interrupted, and there were those who said that he in effect had decided to go to war. In the middle of an election campaign, Begin's response was a sorry emotional spectacle. Only a day before he had praised the leader of the opposition for the national concurrence that had been achieved on ways of handling the crisis, but now he read at length statements by Moshe Sharett and Yitzhak Rabin denigrating Shimon Peres. In that reply he also said, "If war breaks out, here are those to blame" – Knesset Members who accuse their government and not the inhuman aggressor.[13]

In the beginning of June 1981, Yitzhak Rabin accused the prime minister of giving a delegation of Christians a commitment to activate the Israel air force if the Syrian air force acted against them. For the first time, charged Rabin, a commitment had been given to put the IDF into action against a third party who was not acting directly against Israel. The activation of the air force would, under certain circumstances, effectively be determined by the Christian Falanges, he said, and this commitment had not been brought to the Foreign Affairs and Security Committee for its information or approval. "How has it happened, Mr. Begin," asked Rabin, "that you, who are known as a veteran parliamentarian, have strayed from a fundamental principle of every democratic, parliamentary regime, and at a time when you are serving as prime minister?"[14]

Begin replied that the contention was untrue. On August 22, 1978, such a promise was indeed given, but it was qualified. It was said that "in response to a request that our air force ... intervene, if Syrian aircraft attack us [the Christian Falanges], the government of Israel will seriously and sympathetically consider such intervention by the Israeli air force, and most probably the request will be granted." Except for Begin's interpretation, this was a full admission.[15] Moshe Dayan, at the time a rank-

and-file Knesset Member, drew a distinction between what had been agreed in August 1978 in his presence, and what had actually happened. In his view, the two Syrian helicopters did not constitute a Syrian air attack against the Christians.[16]

In his election speeches Begin reinforced his public commitment to eliminate the Syrian missiles. Now he added that no Katyusha rocket fired from Lebanon would ever again fall on Kiryat Shmona.[17] At the end of 1981, Begin's threats became more real. A pretext for the war was apparently being formed. Early in November, in reply to Peres' derisory comments about government inaction, Begin announced that the Syrians will have to leave Mount Senin, and further declared that Israel had the capability of destroying the missiles within two hours. As to the terrorists' interpretation that the ceasefire permitted them to operate elsewhere in the world, he said, "A day will come and we'll also deal with that."[18]

As rumors of war increased, the denials became more categorical. Begin called the rumors "war chatter" and praised Sharon as a "skilled craftsman."[19] When ambassadors were exchanged between Israel and Egypt in the spring of 1982, Begin declared that relations with Egypt would not tie Israel's hands in Lebanon. In the middle of April he again denied that the government had decided to invade Lebanon. He dismissed the contention that Defense Minister Sharon was pushing him towards war; "there is total understanding between us," he said. "Sharon is a superb defense minister." Begin now claimed that by its actions the PLO was abrogating the ceasefire agreement. In fact, he added, there was no signed agreement, just a formula agreed to by him and the American diplomat Philip Habib.[20]

The political and military circumstances in the spring and summer of 1982 were tempting. The threat on the southern front had been removed. Iraq was involved in a costly war in the Persian Gulf. In Lebanon there was a local ally; in the United States, an administration sympathetic to Israel was in office. This time the war had clearly defined political objectives, so that the fruits of military victory would not be allowed to slip from Israel's hands.[21] In practice it would be discovered that the political conception behind the war was simplistic, and the estimation of American support inaccurate. The basic premises about the internal balance of forces in Lebanon, the possibilities for cooperation with the Christians, and the reaction of public opinion at home and in the world all proved to have been mistaken. The grand strategy planning of the war suffered from the worst decisionmaking process in the history of Israel's wars. It was a war that lurched out of control, in which the overall strategy was based on a complex tactical mosaic that never existed in reality.[22]

Ariel Sharon's appointment as defense minister in August 1981 was a turning point in the preparations for the war. Although the conditions for a military operation had ripened, the resoluteness and overall conception needed for war were still missing.[23] On December 20, 1981, the plan for operation "Big Pines" was presented to the cabinet. Sensing opposition, Begin did not put it to a vote. Syrian intentions to alter the political balance in Lebanon in the elections scheduled for the summer of 1982 were apparently a factor hastening the formulation of the military plan.

In February 1982, the head of the IDF's military intelligence, General Yehoshua Saguy, left for Washington, his mission in part to convince Secretary of State Alexander Haig that Israel would not be able to refrain from military action. The military intelligence assessment of operation "Big Pines" was qualified, even negative, with respect both to the attainment of its political objectives and the trustworthiness and strength of the Falanges, and their ability to play the role assigned to them. In mid-May, Saguy expressed vigorous opposition to going to war. The junior ally is a dubious one, he said, and might lead us into a confrontation with Syria, and the people and the army are not united behind that.[24] However, General Saguy never resolved where his duty as an officer ended and his moral duty began.

At this time, mistrust and opposition to a full-scale military operation in Lebanon was being voiced by widening circles. Warnings from Washington were now added to those of the intelligence branch. The Alignment leaders also expressed opposition to the plan in their meeting with the prime minister. However, despite a certain mistrust, it seemed to them that Begin was moving away from operation "Big Pines" and was preparing a more limited operation. Begin still appeared to be in control of the situation.[25]

Begin, as we have seen, was full of admiration for Sharon's military talents. In January 1974, when he justified having talks with a division commander who was still at the front, Begin said, "Arik Sharon is one of the greatest commanders in our army. He is my friend." In the course of time they differed on policy, and confronted each other on several occasions. Begin later said of Ariel Sharon, "brilliant general, vicious man."[26] Sharon, for his part, was unsparing in his praise of Begin. In the beginning of September 1982 he was to say in the Knesset that the achievements of the war would not have been possible "without the leadership ability and courageous decision-making of the government headed by Menachem Begin." He also lauded the cooperation between the military arm and the government: "At the same time, unlike in our previous wars, the cabinet saw to it, as did the general staff, that there not be the slightest friction, that no tension remain between the political level and the military branch. In other words, both levels worked and operated for long and difficult months in perfect harmony, striving persistently to achieve the war objectives that had been clearly defined and carried out in their entirety."[27] Whatever

Sharon's intentions may have been, there was one person who bore overall responsibility. The prime minister was the one who was supposed to ascertain the significance of the war plan and guide its execution.

One of the puzzling questions about this war was the position taken by the United States. Secretary of State Alexander Haig, himself a military man played a decisive role in this. In September 1981, when Begin was on a visit to the United States, Haig cautioned him against intervening in Lebanon. At Sadat's funeral a month later, he understood from remarks made by Begin that Israel was planning to invade Lebanon but would seek to avoid a clash with Syria. Haig reports that once again he gave Begin notice that Israel would not have outright American support. The prime minister assured him he was talking only about a contingency plan.[28] In November 1981, Sharon rejected the secretary of state's recommendations, which included, among other things, pushing the terrorists' artillery back beyond a 40-kilometer line.[29] A war of choice, launched with the balance of forces heavily in Israel's favor, did not make the matter of policy coordination with the United States critical, as had been the case in Israel's wars. Sharon was to return from a visit to the United States in 1982 determined to go to war.

On December 5, 1981, at a meeting in Jerusalem between delegations headed by Philip Habib and Ariel Sharon, the defense minister informed the Americans in general terms of the plans for Operation "Big Pines." The defense minister's intentions were now clear to the American administration as well as to some of his colleagues. For the first time in Israel's history, detailed information about war plans was appearing in the open. Near the end of his term as ambassador in Israel, Ambassador Lewis said that in the beginning of 1982 there was a war just waiting to begin.[30] In January 1982, President Reagan sent a letter to the prime minister limiting US support to a situation in which Israel was attacked in a clear act of provocation. Ambassador Lewis warned Begin not to misread American public opinion.[31]

In late May 1982, Sharon left for Washington to set out his plan for installing a new order in Lebanon to Haig and his aides. Haig relates that he made it plain to Sharon that the opening of the war in Lebanon must be a response to a clear, unequivocal provocation, but also added that every country is entitled to decide how it will defend itself. Even so, he felt it necessary to write to Begin to spell out the American position once again. In his reply, writes Haig, the prime minister said: "Mr. Secretary, my dear friend, the man has not been born who will ever obtain from me consent to let Jews be killed by a bloodthirsty enemy and allow those who are responsible for the shedding of this blood to enjoy immunity . . ."[32] Even if we take Lewis's and Haig's explanations at their word, it does not seem that the

United States acted wisely, or as a salutary ally. Had it placed impediments to the outbreak of the war, it would have spared both Israel and itself a military and political entanglement of grave proportions.

Operation "Big Pines"

On the night of Saturday, June 5, 1982, the government of Israel approved a limited military operation aimed against the Palestinian organizations, with the objective of pushing them back beyond a line forty kilometers from Israel's border. When Communications Minister Mordechai Zippori contended that the operation entailed the risk of a clash with the Syrians, Begin assured him, "I said we will not attack the Syrians." Sharon said it would be a short war, two days at the most.[33] The government's announcement charged the IDF with the task of "putting all the settlements in Galilee beyond the range of terrorist fire." It also said that "The Syrian army is not to be attacked except if it attacks our forces." Order of the day issued by the chief of staff, General Rafael Eitan, stated, "This is not a war with the Syrians." The IDF opened with "sweeping operations aimed at the terrorists and their bases."[34]

From the beginning of the war until the ceasefire on June 11, and from then until the evacuation of the terrorists in August, Begin seemed to be a person cut off from military reality, ignorant of the strategic significance of the war, chairing what became a dissolute decisionmaking process. The furthest he himself entered Lebanon was to the Beaufort. When he visited there, on the second day of the war, he knew nothing of the fatalities the battle for the fortress had claimed. Begin never set foot in Lebanon again.

When the war began, the prime minister had done nothing to verify that his government and the army had one and the same coherent and agreed plan of war. He mollified the leaders of the opposition and committed himself in public that the war would be short, of forty-eight hours' duration; the IDF would suffer few losses, and war with Syria would be avoided. The actual course of the war refuted all of these contentions.

On June 8, when Begin met with presidential envoy Philip Habib and the leaders of the Alignment, he was convinced that the end of the war was near. He knew on the basis of intelligence reports that Syria was not seeking war. Begin asked Habib to take a message to the president of Syria in which he asserted that Israel would not attack first, and that the Syrians must clear the Palestinian forces out of a 40-kilometer wide strip, which was to be "totally free of terrorists." Begin added another paragraph to the message just as Habib was waiting, the next day, to be admitted to President Assad: he wanted to preserve the status quo as it had been at the start of the fighting, which meant that the Syrians were required to remove the missile reinforcements. But in fact by that time, the Syrian missile deployment in Lebanon had already been destroyed by Israel's airforce.[35] While Begin apparently thought that the IDF's outflanking operations were intended only as support of "a diplomacy of coercion" against the Syrians, skirmishes with the Syrian army had already begun.[36]

Begin came to the Knesset on June 8 in a mood of euphoria, delighted to find the house united as it had been in every war. He read out congratulatory cables from, of all places, a Druse Zionist circle on the Golan Heights and from the Christian Embassy in Jerusalem. The significant part of his speech was his repeated declaration that Israel does not seek war with Syria. At the end of his address he said that the day was approaching when peace negotiations will be conducted with "the legitimate government of Lebanon."[37]

On June 9, the Syrian missiles were destroyed and the actions on the ground against the Syrians were expanded. On the following day the Americans issued their demand for a ceasefire. Begin requested that Secretary of State Haig come to Israel, assuming that Israel would thereby gain time. However, the ceasefire went into effect on June 11, before the army had reached its objectives.[38] It became obvious that the government and the military command had erred badly concerning time and external constraints.

On June 13, IDF troops linked up with the Falanges in Beirut. For the first time in its history, the Israeli army entered an Arab capital. This unprecedented step was taken without the government's approval.[39] That same day, Begin – totally unaware of the new situation – denied to Philip Habib that the army was in Beirut. The astounded American diplomat replied, "Your tanks are already in Ba'abda."[40] In the absence of a political settlement, Begin was, indeed, determined to go into Beirut. Only the threat of a government crisis by the religious factions prevented a breakthrough by IDF troops into the southern portion of Beirut.[41]

The siege of Beirut and the bombing of the Lebanese capital by the air force had extensive consequences. The damage to the morale of the fighting forces and to Israel's image in world public opinion was devastating. In the beginning of August, a reserve paratroop brigade refused to report for duty. In an unprecedented act, Eli Geva, the young brigade commander, challenged the intention to attack Beirut and disputed the chief of staff's estimate of anticipated casualties. He was summarily dismissed from the army without being allowed to part from his men.[42]

In the beginning of August a slow operation of conquest began hacking away at Beirut's suburbs. The number of military actions, taken without the government's knowledge, induced Begin to say, "I know about every action, sometimes before it takes place, sometimes after . . ." It seems that things had gone too far even for Begin. On August 12, the day of the heavy bombardment of Beirut, the prime minister was roused from a nap in his office in the Knesset to conduct a difficult telephone conversation with President Reagan, who demanded an immediate halt to the bombing. Only at this belated hour did Begin cross swords with his defense minister about the extent of his authority. The government retracted Sharon's authority to activate the air force, the artillery, and the navy without cabinet approval,[43] but in public Begin continued to shield Sharon from his critics. On August 21 the evacuation of the terrorists from Beirut began, and two days later Bashir Jemayel was elected president of Lebanon. What had been a political objective of the war became a corridor leading to an impending disaster.

In a letter to President Reagan, Prime Minister Begin wrote, "In a war whose aim is to annihilate the leader of the terrorists in West Beirut, I feel like one who has sent an army to Berlin to annihilate Hitler in the bunker."[44] The Nazi parallel in Begin's view of the PLO was now complete. The threat was total, almost metaphysical in nature, and had to be annihilated. As former commander of an underground organization that had declared war against an imperial army, he should have known that tying down an army to exterminate a terrorist organization is strategically foolhardy and rife with unanticipated dangers.

It is true that the terrorist shellings of northern Galilee a year before the war had become a threat to the civilian population. The agreement reached through the good offices of the American diplomat Philip Habib was not complete and did not expressly refer to terrorist actions against Israelis outside the Middle East. It is doubtful, however, that a military operation of such a scale would have been chosen as a response to the terrorist attacks alone, which between April and June 1982 included the murder of an Israeli diplomat in Paris and an attempt on the life of the Israeli ambassador in London. What complicated the strategic considerations, in addition to the PLO threat, were long-range objectives against Syria. The introduction of Syrian missiles into Lebanon sprung the latch on the attempt to realize those objectives. Lebanon became Israel's "Belgium."[45]

The Palestinians apparently expected an attack against them in Lebanon, Israel's plans having been leaked via the Falanges. They were warned by diplomatic sources in Beirut, surmised that the Soviets would not come to their aid, but thought the war in Lebanon would be a limited one. In the actual fighting, the terrorists held back the IDF more successfully than had been expected, and Israel suffered heavier than anticipated losses.[46] But the prime target of the war, the PLO, soon became secondary. Beginning in September 1982, Israel was contending with something new in Lebanon: a political morass for which it had to assume responsibility, and the defense of its fighting forces deployed in accord with a stationary, and highly dangerous, strategy.[47]

One of the casualties of the war in Lebanon was the image of the Maronites, and of Lebanon in general, in the iconography of Israeli political culture. Israel's northern neighbor had occupied a special place in the diplomacy of the Zionist movement. It was also the epitome of the Pan-Hebrew vision beginning in the 1920s, developed by circles close to the Revisionist right, and strategically offering the easiest access to the fertile Crescent.[48] Instead of Lebanon being the "second democracy" in the Middle East, the vacation land to the north, a land of Phoenicans and Christians not really a part of the Arab world – it now became a menacing image of terror, of unrelenting strife between ethnic factions and political gangs. It had not been foreseen that Israel, proud of its ability to maneuver among the superpowers, would itself serve as a tool to be manipulated by a "Falangist tail."

Of all the follies of this war, one of the more unnecessary ones was the total exposure of IDF commanders and heads of intelligence and espionage – their character, thinking, and disputes – to the Christian leadership in Lebanon. Apart from the direct political and military damage of this, it paved the way for the Christians to influence decision making in Israel at the highest level. Where in other countries such political ties would have been cultivated by a junior intelligence officer, in Israel's case, the defense minister, the chief of staff, the heads of military intelligence and the Mosad, and troop commanders all joined the fray.

Israel lost control in its relations with the Lebanese Christians. With a historic bait dangling before him, Begin was a more than willing catch. There was a sense of mission about rescuing a minority in danger that had always appealed to him. In fact, this minor and untrustworthy ally had been receiving aid from Israel since 1976. This relationship was institutionalized over the years and expanded beyond the logic of reality. Menachem Begin brought these ties into the open and abandoned the reservations and restraint of previous governments.[49] As far as can be ascertained, Israel's intervention in April 1981 on behalf of the Christians was the result of Falangist provocation. It has been suggested that they received moral encouragement from those who sought a collision with Syria.[50]

The war in Lebanon was the moment of truth for Israel's relations with the Christians in Lebanon. After the IDF linked up with the Falangist forces, the latter refused to participate in the battle for Beirut. They had their political flanks to defend. The leader of the Falanges, Bashir Jemayel, did not commit himself to action and refused to appear openly as Israel's ally. Premature exposure, he contended, would prevent him from taking political control of Lebanon, a takeover which would be to Israel's benefit.[51]

Bashir Jemayel, with Israel's active support, prepared to be elected to the presidency. But he was no less devious in his dealings with Israel than he was with other factions and communities in Lebanon. The outburst of joy in Israel upon his election was premature. After he kept sidestepping discussion of a peace treaty with Israel, he was summoned to a secret meeting with Begin in Nahariya. Begin, furious, treated the president of Lebanon like a recalcitrant underling. He demanded a definite date for the signing of a peace treaty.

Israel, it turned out, did not have a real political plan with regard to relations among the Christian factions and the other communities in Lebanon. Very belatedly, a more discerning assessment of power relations within Lebanon was formed. The major ally, the so-called "trump card," was discovered to be a smaller minority than the Shi'ites and militarily weaker than the Druse. Israel found itself hurled into the vortex of the feuds and dissension of a ruinously riven society. It had to maintain its relations within a Byzantine complex of communities, within which it had conflicting loyalties.

Israel's chance of success in Lebanon were suddenly made clear when it became apparent that the assassination of Bashir Jemayel marked the dividing line between success and failure. After Bashir Jemayel was murdered, the political agreement with Lebanon had to be rescued through talks with his brother Amin, whom Begin had called a "preening peacock." The government continued to insist on a formal agreement, despite the new circumstances, and to this end adopted a diplomacy of coercion. Months of effort were required to get the agreement of May 17, 1983 signed. A loyal ally, Major Sa'ad Haddad, the commander of the Southern Lebanese army, was shunted to the sidelines for a while. Ariel Sharon voted against the agreement. In March 1984, acting in response to pressure from Syria, the government of Lebanon suspended the agreement.[52]

Operation Peace in Galilee had disastrous consequences for the Christians in Lebanon. They lost their preferential political standing, Syria remained the principal and ruthless arbitrator of their future, and the equilibrium among the various communities comprising Lebanon was upset in their disfavor. In the long run, the Christians in Lebanon lost their alliance with Israel. Instead of ruling Lebanon, they had to defend their very existence. They remained, as they had always been, subject to the vagaries of factional fighting in Lebanon, in which they were more expert than Israel.

The leader's responsibility

Menachem Begin was consistent in his view of the responsibility of a leader, and that of a government, to the parliament and the nation. He had been categorical on this issue after the Yom Kippur War: "The government as a whole bears responsibility. That is a great democratic and parliamentary rule, and we will continue to stand by it."[53] He was proud that during the war the opposition had acted as a "patriotic party" and preserved national unity. But immediately after the war he assailed the government for its responsibility for the "blunder," and for its attempts to evade its accountability. When the Agranat Commission report was published, he wrote that the government as a whole bore "full moral, public, and political responsibility for its mistake – more than a high command subordinated to it, and certainly not less."[54]

When the government announced its resignation in 1974, Begin attacked Prime Minister Golda Meir for having created a government within a government, and for not seeing her role as first among equals. He called this "usurpation of the regime." As for the relations between the army command and the government, he said, "For three years I have observed the relations between the chief of staff and the government. Never has the chief of staff done anything on his own accord; not a thing."[55]

It was necessary to wait for the massacre perpetrated by the Falanges in Sabra and Shatila in September 1982 to judge Begin himself on a prime ministerial responsibility. He approved the IDF's entry into Beirut by telephone before the government gave its approval, though it is not likely that he knew of the exact role assigned to the Falanges.[56] But, the enlistment of the Falanges' assistance, after their leader had been murdered, was irresponsible and reflected a measure of moral obtuseness.

The government announcement on September 16, 1982 said that the IDF had seized positions in West Beirut "in order to prevent the danger of violence, bloodshed, and chaos." At a cabinet session after the massacre, Begin said, that had been "our pure and genuine intention."[57] The massacre in the refugee camps was a moment of degradation. The war that had begun as a mission to rescue a minority from slaughter ended in a bloodbath. Begin had to contend with a storm of condemnation and for once not just from overseas; a crowd of 400,000 had gathered in Tel Aviv to protest against the government's policy – the largest demonstration in the history of Israel.

The moral element struck a sensitive chord in Begin. The government announcement on September 20 concluded with a defiant statement, "no one will preach morality and respect for human life to us ..."[58] In the Knesset, Begin railed against the members of the opposition. He called them "slanderers who lend a hand to defamers."[59] He refused to set up a commission of inquiry. His refusal withstood mounting public pressure for one more week. At the end of September, he charged the Kahane Commission with investigating the massacre in the refugee camps.

Begin's appearance at the inquiry commission was somewhat pallid. He confirmed the principal facts. When the IDF was ordered to enter Beirut, no mention was made of a role for the Falanges. He referred to them as being "disciplined military units" in every respect. He had told the American diplomat Morris Draper that their commander "is a good man." The prime minister had not discussed with the chief of staff and the defense minister the precise role the Falanges would have in West Beirut. The remark that Housing Minister David Levy had made in the cabinet discussion about the possibility of a massacre had not caught his attention.[60] In its final report, the inquiry commission found Begin indirectly responsible for the Falanges' entry into the Palestinian camps.

In mid-June 1982, before leaving for the United States, Begin had said, "Operation Peace for Galilee has cured the nation of the traumas of the Yom Kippur War." He denied that Sharon had dragged the government into war.[61] While he was out of the country, Israeli control of the Beirut–Damascus road was made complete; the weeks of siege of Beirut were still to come. The war in Lebanon spawned a new trauma, and caused further damage to the IDF command. There was increasing criticism not only of the political conception that had guided the war, but also of the performance of the army on the battlefield. Forceful criticism was aired of the army's failure to achieve the objectives that had been set, of the gross use of firepower, of the failure of field intelligence, and of the malfunctioning of the general staff. Beyond that, the moral fiber of the IDF suffered severe damage as a result of having been immersed for a number of years in the slime and ordure of the Lebanese morass.

Morally, and in terms of its influence on world public opinion, the siege and bombardment of Beirut were a turning point. What came to the fore was the misunderstanding of the spirit of the fighting forces, of the ethos of the IDF. From the beginning, the elements needed to assure what was called "national consensus" were missing. The war in Lebanon stretched the relations between the defense system and the civilian authority to the limit. Some went so far as to speak of a garrison state in which the government was subject to the manipulations of the military. Neither of the two possibilities concerning the role of the military command shows it in a favorable light – either it was led to war against its will and military judgment, or it willingly agreed to a political and strategic plan that was doomed to fail.[62]

After the war, Begin said: "For the first time the IDF was not robbed of the fruits of its military victory."[63] Syria, however, continued to be the leading factor determining Lebanon's fate. The Syrian–Soviet tie was strengthened, the Syrian army increased its strength, and the fundamental dilemma of the eastern front remained unchanged. Nor did the Palestinian problem disappear from the international agenda. The IDF had to worry about new and even crueler terrorism, this time Shi'ite. Ultimately, the war did not receive the full backing of the United States, Israel's strategic partner, which afterwards suffered serious casualties of its own.

Menachem Begin emerged from the chronology of this war as a leader who was inexpert in elementary strategic details, lacked a feel for the spirit of the fighting forces, and did not control the decision-making process. To rescue Begin from blame for a disastrous war, it was necessary to detract seriously from his image as a national leader, prime minister, and decision-maker. That in fact is what his aides and intimates did. This time Begin's "political realism" did not rest on a mutuality of interests between states, but on an ephemeral tribal alliance. In Lebanon there was nothing other than ethnic and religious factions, which were of limited capability and possessed the morality of a gang. The shifting and unexpected combinations resulting from their constant jostling frustrated all rational calculations. Instead of exploiting a historical situation, what he called "the opportune moment," it was Begin who became exploited. To a large extent the war consigned to oblivion the notion of alliances with Middle Eastern ethnic minorities as a worthwhile policy for Israel. Belatedly, many came to see the deep chasms separating the minorities themselves.

The war in Lebanon was a meaningless and delusive war. After the peace agreement with Egypt, Israel was in a strategic situation it had never enjoyed before – liberation from the burden of war on two fronts. Quantitatively, the IDF was at full strength. Begin did not exploit this strategic advantage for the renewal of peace efforts or for strengthening society and state. One year before he had come to power he had written that in statesmanship a person's mettle cannot be ascertained immediately: "A ship's captain is known in a storm, a maestro in playing, and a statesman in his ability to see what lies ahead." In that he failed. With his own hands he paved the way to the end of his rule.

13

Leader and Prime Minister

The leader and the faceless crowd

Begin had a heroic view of leadership. The heroic leader acts primarily in the domain of statecraft and in military affairs. He leads the nation to grandeur, is an orator unifying the people whom he directs toward affirmation and realization of the eternal values of the nation. He is a gallant ruler – forceful, authoritarian, and at the same time also disposed to clemency. His penchant for historical parallels took him to Jefferson, Lincoln, and Garibaldi in the nineteenth century, Churchill and de Gaulle in his own time, but he himself was a typical twentieth-century populist leader.

Begin's historical achievement lay in his ability to unite within his own person the continuity of the Revisionist legacy. He fashioned a credible claim that there was a social, economic, and foreign policy alternative to that offered by the Labor hegemony. He persisted in this claim for three decades until he rose to power on the Labor Zionists' decline. Begin became a leader judged less for his deeds than for his ability to preserve the symbols and beliefs of the right. As a leader he applied Jabotinsky's principle of the "personal union" to a more centralized and homogeneous political structure, in the form of Herut. The personification of the movement in Begin exacted a price: his inability to control the structural and political evolution of Herut was apparent even before he stepped down. As prime minister he lacked the requisites to prevent decline – a commendable ruling party, talented aides, and organizational vigor.

In *White Nights*, Begin wrote, "Throughout his life, Lenin's influence on his comrades was wholly moral or intellectual."[1] The sense of identification here seems clear. Begin did not add any title or rank to his designation as commander of the Irgun. His election by his fellows since 1943 was by acclamation, not by a procedure that enabled real political contest. It was here that the myth of camaraderie was born. The "fighting family" became an instrument of political order guaranteeing unity and discipline. It was a barrier to any criticism and the ground of the ultimate punishment for any challenge to Begin's leadership – total expulsion or rejection to the periphery.

Begin bore the insignia of an exclusive heir, the man who had sat at the feet of the original leader and source of legitimation – Ze'ev Jabotinsky. Those whose political fate depended on the prestige of the leader found protection in this ambience. The leader took supreme responsibility for their deeds, and they, in return for loyalty, were spared punishment. This was a major source of Begin's ineffectiveness in implementing policy, in that he did not have effective control over the actions he authorized. At critical junctures, from the *Altalena* affair to the war in Lebanon, the same logic was operative: absolute loyalty in return for absolute protection of his followers – even when they were negligent, remiss, or guilty of unbecoming behavior and moral infractions.[2]

Begin's character as a leader was shaped, above all, in the relationship he developed with the masses. Throughout his long political career, he displayed a brilliant ability to control his followers. The direct relationship between the crowd and the leader is often a threat to the political establishment, and at the core is unstable. Begin never solved the dilemma of the conflict between satisfying the volatile will of the crowd and the institutional and political order that must guide a political party. The faceless crowd always arouses suspicion. In a rare moment of despair Ben-Gurion said, "In the deep recesses of the nation there is reaction." The emergence of the crowd as a political factor is relatively new to Jewish history, and to a large extent Begin's political career coincided with the rise of the crowd in Israeli politics. Nonetheless, an adequate explanation of Begin's appeal to the masses has yet to be offered. Was his appeal to the lower social strata, the "little man" in revolt against the establishment and the ruling elite, or was it as symbol of national grandeur and as spokesman of inherent resentment against the non-Jewish world?[3]

Begin dealt very little with social reform, or improvement of the individual's lot. Above all he sought political support. His major slogans were the nation's greatness and invective against those who thwarted its realization. He did not appeal for self-sacrifice but instead offered a promise to "do well by the people." He found unifying equality in nationalism and in the commonality of shared Jewish destiny. The tableau Begin presented was one-dimensional, with national glory, "the century of Jewish power," placed above all.[4]

Begin's most conspicuous leadership quality was the orator's skill. He brought the use of rhetoric for political ends to a great height. The great orator, he observed, "is a speaker who knows how to combine logic and emotion, mind and heart . . . and at certain moments his entire audience becomes a single entity, and he becomes part of it."[5] Begin had almost sixty years of experience as a speaker. Recalling the first speech he delivered, while still a youth, he said it had concluded "with total downfall, compassionate consolation, and biting sarcasm."[6] In Poland, with its millions of Jews, a political culture of the masses was developed, and it was there that Begin took his first steps in mastering his oratorical art.

Begin was never in greater need of his rhetorical skills than in the spring of 1981, when he had to extricate himself from what looked like certain electoral defeat. During that period he referred on more than one occasion to his talents as a speaker. In the Knesset he prided himself on the fact that he rarely used a prepared text, "I just jot down some notes and say what I have to say, which I keep stored in my memory."[7] In fact he read from a prepared text on only four occasions. The first was on the day the state was proclaimed in May 1948, and all the three other times while he was prime minister.[8]

Begin attached great importance to words. In *The Revolt* he wrote, "Don't belittle words. There are words that create facts, just as there are ideas that give rise to words."[9] Declarations and speeches occupied an important place in his political activity. Often his words were forceful and uncompromising. The personal and national boastfulness he was prone to usually paid off at the ballot box more than it provided gains for the country. Begin found many ways "to say one, small, decisive word: 'no'."[10]

When he was in the role of gentleman and parliamentarian, it was sometimes forgotten that Begin had a journalist's facility with words, or a soapbox orator's. Yet his use of radio and television was surprisingly modest and unimpressive. His main arena was the city square, the amphitheater, the political hall. Here he was able to put to maximal use his talents for ridicule and sarcasm, humor and solemn mien, and above all the drubbing of his opponents. He went to the very limit of sophistry and craftiness in surprising blends of vituperation and extreme self-satisfaction. Taking the stance of an omniscient narrator explaining history and reality to his hearers, he would repeat the same truths countless times.

Although as an orator Begin was guided by simple truisms, he assumed a number of different mantles. The most esteemed by him was as spokesman of the "great unity," envoy of shared Jewish historical destiny, and symbol of the one Israel. The speech he delivered at the opening ceremony of the Herut convention in May 1968 was typical of his pompous exaltation and praise welding together the Jewish religious heritage and Israeli national history.[11] Delivered within the bosom of the ruling establishment, on the crest of national military triumph, it began by invoking the image of the Roman Legions invading the Temple Mount and plundering the Temple. This was followed by lengthy passages from Tacitus, and a reference to the Western Wall, which perhaps more than anything else symbolized for him the redemption of national honor. Begin then passed directly from antiquity to the Six Day War: "Confronted by this danger the first thing we did was to unite. We learned a lesson from the internecine strife of ancient times ... to unite against the exterminating enemy." For Begin national unity had a metaphysical quality, but also practical significance. He noted the government's successful stance in the trial it had faced, and its decision not to return to the boundaries of June 4, 1967. He insisted on the principle of the "indivisibility of the homeland" and exclaimed: "Tonight, now, we will tell him [Jabotinsky]: leader of Betar, in your life and in your death, we have carried out your testament. After the flag slipped from your hand, after you knelt and fell ... we have taken the banner, we your disciples, and have borne it high ..." The circle closed, as always, around the one nationalist core that Jabotinsky's movement represented – triumph and the unity of the homeland. The lessons of history became a declaration of Herut policy.

Begin carried the same solemnity into the ceremonial arena of foreign policy. For special effect he always turned to the elegance of Latin. At the signing of the peace agreement in March 1979, he called Carter, "*Horribile dictu*, an intransigent fighter for peace"; he himself had emerged from the depths of the abyss and of suffering, *de profundis*, "one of the generation of the Holocaust," and had come from there to the White House lawn.[12]

Begin's florid style was most in place at eulogies and memorials. There too he had historical scores to settle. The eulogies were an occasion for a last gracious act by the leader, who parted from opponents as from admirers. Lamenting the passing of his former comrades in arms, Yisrael Epstein and Aryeh Ben-Eliezer, he spoke simply, in a language not without intimacy and genuine pain.[13] In the eulogies of rivals, pardon was at last offered and the traces of past rivalry buried. Thus in an act of belated graciousness to underground commander Abraham Stern, he devoted a few, general words to "poet and rebel."[14] As prime minister he eulogied another former rival, Nathan Yellin-Mor, as "a great fighter for the liberation of the nation from foreign yoke." Yellin-Mor was a man whose political activity had ceased in the 1940s.[15] And likewise Moshe Sneh, the Hagana leader who turned to Communism, was posthumously restored by Begin to the fold of Judaism and Zionism by means of a last *kaddish*.[16] His eloquence was often most marked for those for whom he had no real esteem.[17]

But Begin's natural environment was the public political gathering. Here he gave himself full rein. At such times Begin did not so much deliver an orderly address as let himself be swept away in an extravaganza of words and gesticulations. Here solemnity vanished, as did the rules of international law and Latin phraseology. Although the left had a place in national unity, in the city square it became a bag to be punched and punched again.

His most fiery political speech was undoubtedly that delivered in Jerusalem's Zion Square in January 1952 in opposition to reparations from

Germany. That was a masterpiece of incitement during which he himself was swept away in a tidal wave of emotion.[18] Examining his speeches along the years we see the same motifs and the same ability to rail brutality against political rivals at home and foreign enemies.[19]

Begin the mass orator used every trick in the bag. He would be defiant and entertaining, would sling mud, share a secret, promise greatness. He would exaggerate, flatter, distribute empty compliments, be sarcastic, and pummel his targets without restraint or mercy. And at the same time, he presented himself as a pious man appealing to his audience's sense of honor and common sense. Begin patiently prepared his audience for the ridicule, attacks, and psychological stabbings they were to hear. His words were more simplistic and exaggerated than precise or concerned with truth. In the pseudoreality of the public square, historical time stopped its march and possibility was boundless.

Begin tried to keep his rabble-rousing language separate from his political pronouncements. But the partition was too flimsy, even when he was prime minister. This was especially marked during his last years in office when his Knesset speeches, too, were replete with insults and unnecessary ramblings. Finally, in the "rhetorical spring" of 1981, the use of abusive language passed into the arena of foreign policy and diplomacy.[20]

Between reversal and revolution

Begin believed that the nation was guided in its survival less by the transitory rationality of its leaders than by natural instincts.[21] National unity was the condition for the nation's triumph. Lack of agreement and public criticism were a source of national weakness, and in the worst instance, bordered on treason. At the same time, he never defined the boundaries, or the meaning of national consensus.

As leader of the opposition he concurred with the government whenever its policies led in the nationalist direction. Early in 1949 Begin said that at home he would oppose the government with all his might; outside of Israel it would be presented as the best of governments.[22] In the summer of 1948 he said that when consulted he gave Ben-Gurion his consent and encouragement to proclaim the establishment of the state.[23] Right after the Six Day War he declared that the National Unity government was one of the factors contributing to Israel's victory, and that "all we have to do is stand as one people and we will hold on to the fruits of our victory."[24] After the Entebbe rescue operation in July 1976, he asserted that "It is perhaps by virtue of this unity that we have been privileged to witness this greatest of days in the history of enduring Israel . . ."[25]

The national harmony Begin had in mind did not stem from shared ideas or from a political partnership entered into willingly, or from utilitarian calculations of gain and loss. He demanded the assimilation of every individual, at all times, within an all-embracing national solidarity, in which the individual is to find satisfaction and freedom. In his view national unity stood above ideological, social, and political pluralism, and was able to subdue the latter to its needs because it was the secret of the nation's strength. Herein lies the deep contradiction in Begin's approach and in that of the Revisionist right as a whole. He posited national unity as a necessity while at the same time idealizing secession.[26] When the majority decision contradicted the national will, as defined unilaterally by Revisionism, the right refused to concur with it.

The Revisionist right was caught on the horns of the dilemma of an ideology of unity and a praxis of secession. That was not perceived as weakening the overall struggle; on the contrary, the secessionists saw themselves as acting in behalf of the overall national objective. It is not surprising that the advocate of national unity began his career in an act of secession and ended it in a war that damaged the foundations of national unity.

Begin's most systematic essay is *World View and National Conception*.[27] It was written in the late 1940s, the most fruitful period of his life. This eclectic essay starts with a refutation of Marxist ideology. Socialism, that ostensibly progressive cosmopolitanism, failed the test of history. Reality overturned its teaching. Begin used the term *Weltanschauung* to define what he meant by "world view." "Our world view," wrote Begin, "derives from and complements our national outlook"; the will of the people finds expression primarily in the foreign domain. In Begin's conception, the world view of a national liberation movement has three basic components: the freedom of the individual, social reform, and the supremacy of law. Basing himself on Jefferson and the principles of the French Revolution he asserted that where freedoms are denied there exists a "right to *rebel* against the regime" (emphasis in the original). This brought him to the crux of his criticism of socialism, and in this case of the Labor movement in Israel: the unification of ruling authority and control of labor in society is a new form of slavery; he regarded their separation as the prime requisite for guaranteeing human freedom.

The second element of Begin's world view, social reform, is merely the natural aspiration for justice. The vision of a classless society, or its permanent existence in one form of social structure, is just an illusion. Begin contended that class division will always exist in human society, and the distinguishing factor will remain property. The only possible solution is by "permanently narrowing the distance between the social extremes." This process is unidirectional, from the bottom to the top, the property-owners remaining where they are, the underprivileged moving toward them.

Begin never defined the economic or political mechanism for bringing about the division of property in society. He merely asserted that the process concludes such that "economic and social progress will not express itself as the elimination of luxury but as the elimination of the concept of luxury, by the constant transformation of luxuries into items needed, used, and acquired by all."[28] Social reform, according to Begin, is a process that begins by transposing "the point of departure from zero means to minimum means." The latter were specified by Jabotinsky as shelter, food, clothing, medical care, and education. These are base points, not end points, and are all in reach, according to Begin, when social reform and the freedom of the individual are assured. "Our world view," Begin wrote, "is social–liberal, or the other way around, liberal–social." It is opposed both to Marxism and to "arbitrary capitalism." The social reform Begin envisaged rested, then, on utopian foundations, and was related neither to a defined conception of time nor to social and economic realities.[29]

Must a political movement express the interests of only one social class? No, says Begin. The Marxist conception is baseless, "There is a national movement ... which expresses what is common to all portions of the nation. It is the carrier of the historical aspirations of the nation as a whole."[30] Begin was referring not to social or economic matters, but to national interests, which he specified as liberation of the homeland and the reassembling of the nation on its own soil. The definition of national objectives and the way to achieve them, as Begin presented it, was not related to the individual freedoms he enumerated. Ultimately, everyone and everything is subjugated to the "national will"; the perfection of human existence is expressed through nationalism.

The vision that dominated Begin's view of the world and of society most of his life was that of a large Israel, squarely in the Middle East on both sides of the Jordan, but with a culture, society, and laws that draw upon the highest attainments of European nationalism. Its society upholds the freedom of the individual and social justice, and the "invisible hand" guiding it engenders a reality that is both utopian and attainable.[31]

Herut, the party's newspaper, bore the movement's motto, "For the indivisibility of the homeland, the ingathering of the exiles, social justice, and human freedom." On his first trip to the United States in 1948, Begin said that the views of his movement are nationalistic, but the movement has "a social platform that pays great attention to the workingman and is traditional in its approach to the Jewish religion."[32] It is not by chance, he said, that Herut was the first to demand an open proclamation on civil and human rights in the state. Against those who derided the Herut movement for not representing the working class, he said, "We are the workers . . . Workers stood behind us in the War of Independence."[33] As prime minister, he said that in contrast to the Labor movement, "We are soft toward the inside and tough toward the outside."[34]

In the election campaign of 1973 Begin declared that there is a marked contrast between "the socialist–bureaucratic school and the nationalist–liberal school."[35] On the social and economic plane, Begin for the most part maintained the internal contradictions of the right. The attempt to adopt the interests of the middle class while relying for support on a populism addressed to the lower social classes was inherently discordant. The liberal economic outlook always contradicted the social objectives Herut set for itself. National unity was supposed to eliminate class conflict, while at the same time the economic system was to be open to competition and free enterprise, moving it automatically towards utopian harmony, "social peace and social justice"; not strikes but arbitration, the elimination of poverty and the renewal in Israel of "simple living."[36]

Begin did not bring to office a desire for radical social change. He wanted, at the same time, economic and social stability, an effortless burgeoning of material abundance, and maximum leeway in conducting foreign policy. He never understood the close interrelationship of these realms. Begin's national priorities were clear. They had been shaped over an entire generation. He handed management of the economy over to the Liberal party. The economic "reversal," marked first by the elimination of foreign currency controls, complemented the desire "to do well by the people." Yet Israeli income data for 1980, the apogee of his stewardship, showed greater inequality in the distribution of incomes than in West European countries and greater even than in the United States. By the time he stepped down from office, inflation had sky-rocketed and the banking system was on the threshold of collapse.

Begin's lack of interest in and knowledge of social and economic affairs, and his astounding incapacity in controlling decisionmaking, exacted an immeasurable price. The moral bonds of society were loosened and the economy neared bankruptcy. Begin was apprised of the severity of the economic situation on more than one occasion, but did nothing.[37] Although he wanted a policy that would combine national grandeur and the well-being of the individual; a large army, expansionist desires, and the waging of a war of choice, along with a stable peacetime economy, he never showed any real interest in the social and economic area.[38] However, even as defeat was overtaking him in these realms, Begin was able to redirect social criticism onto the Labor movement. He sharpened that criticism into a political weapon of unrivaled efficacy.

In November 1959, *Herut* reporters described Begin's visit to various underprivileged Tel Aviv neighborhoods at the culmination of the election campaign.[39] The motorcade left Herut headquarters at Metzudat Ze'ev with twenty motorcyclists dressed in Betar shirts leading the way. Begin and his entourage followed in an open vehicle, with dozens of cars of supporters, journalists, and friends closing up the rear. The motorcade toured some ten neighborhoods, Begin delivering a speech at each. When the roar of the motorcycles beacme audible a cry went up from the crowd – "Begin's coming!" The biggest rally was in the Hatikvah quarter, where 15,000 people cheered his arrival. By the evening, about 40,000 inhabitants of Tel Aviv neighborhoods had hailed Menachem Begin.

Begin proclaimed that the Hatikvah quarter was the first to topple Mapai to the rank of second-place party.[40] In the summer of 1948 he had said, with reference to the Sephardic Jews, that every citizen is to be regarded "as a brother and friend. Do not place yourself above your friend but love him with a sense of absolute equality between you and him."[41] The symbiosis that developed in the 1950s between portions of the Oriental community and Herut and its leader would one day be the road to power. Begin brought the "truth" about how the homeland was liberated to the immigrant camps, repeatedly reminding that "those who won are subject to a regime of poverty, patronage, and abuse of individual freedom."[42] Begin called for a supreme effort to rescue "the multitude of our brethren" in North Africa.[43] In a Knesset debate about integration of the ethnic communities, he said "Shame on anyone who, because of European origin, is at all arrogant in his heart, in public or in writing, to those of our brethren, our people, whose ancestors were expelled from Spain . . ."[44] Mapai, which represents only a third of the population, he said, had taken over the state's apparatus; it was important to ensure that the Sepharadim – the Jews of non-European origin – got increasing representation in all state and political party institutions. In March 1973, he demanded that a Sepharadi be chosen as president. Begin always continued to work toward the aim he had spelled out so bluntly in the early years of the state: "Mapai will not destroy the state, but we will see the destruction of Mapai rule."[45]

Begin did not change his accusatory rhetoric after he became prime minister. At the fourteenth convention of the Herut movement in 1979, he said that 300,000 "were left to live in substandard housing by a regime that called itself socialist . . ." Rehabilitation of those neighborhoods would be the cornerstone of a new policy, Project Renewal. That same year he described Israel's economic situation as "one of the best in the world." There would be no more running from country to country to get short-term credit, "Those dark days are gone, never to return. The country's foreign currency reserves are substantial . . ."[46]

Speaking in the Knesset debate in the fall of 1981, Begin told of a visit he had made to Yavneh, a town near Rehovot formerly with a large underprivileged population. The government's Project Renewal for neighborhood rehabilitation, he said, has begun a new era in Israeli society, "crime has disappeared, a new life" has begun. At the same time, he continued to attack the "monopolists" of the Labor movement and the "kibbutz millionaires."[47] Even in the 1980s, when the economic crisis had become a palpable reality and the statistics showed a rise in poverty and widening differentials in the distribution of income and property, Herut was still able to convert feelings of ethnic deprivation into political gains at the polling booth.[48]

The rightward turn had begun in the late 1950s and continued without interruption until Herut's accession to power.[49] However, demographic data and the changes that were taking place in social structure, education, and economy had never provided an adequate explanation of the change in Israel's voting patterns. The support Herut and Begin achieved also involved deeper chords, related to radical change in values and beliefs among growing sections of Israeli society.

It was apparent in the area of religion and state where Begin fulfilled a historical commitment to his beliefs and put his criticism of socialism into practice. In *White Nights* we find him observing that, "In his hour of misfortune man has nothing to lean on, no consolation, save faith."[50] It is not the relationship between man and his Creator that is our concern here, but how religion and its symbols were incorporated into Begin's nationalist thought and utilitarian considerations. He accepted the notion that in Judaism religion and nationality are inseparable. He was close to the view that the establishment of the state and the liberation of the homeland, after the Holocaust, marked the beginning of Messianic redemption. He did not at all distinguish between the symbols of the religion and the demands made by nationalism.[51]

The principle that freedom requires a separation between state, nationality, and citizenship does not hold in Judaism, Begin claimed. The uniqueness of the Jewish people was determined by the way it appeared in history. In the history of other peoples, said Begin, religious faith did not evolve but was imposed on savages by foreign rulers. No one imposed a faith on the Jews and from that day "our nationality is uni-religious, and our religion uni-national. They are inseparable." In America, too, professed Begin, there is no separation between religion and state; by "religion" the Americans actually mean "church" in the sense of a social institution, not a faith. Separation of religion from state means the extirpation of faith, as is done in socialist regimes. To reinforce his claims, Begin would quote from Jabotinsky's writings and statements, but in fact, there was little resemblance between Jabotinsky's conceptions on matters of faith and religion and his own.[52]

In September 1981 Begin said that he had always objected to Ben-Gurion's dictum that Israel is a state of law, "We are both a state of law and a state of *halakha* (Jewish religious law).[53] Notwithstanding ideological premises which at times were clearly anticlerical, rightist regimes entered easily into marriages of convenience with the religious establishment. But in Begin's case there was more than cold political calculation. He truly believed that the survival of the Jewish people throughout history, the shaping of Jewish national will, and the nation's spiritual strength were inseparable from faith.

Before Sadat's visit to Jerusalem, Begin demanded not to violate the Sabbath in preparing for the visit. That same year he prided himself on the fact that a letter from President Carter was delivered to him after the Sabbath even though it had arrived the day before. He called upon all peoples to honor the Sabbath. In reply to an interjection by MK Yossi Sarid, he launched into a long monologue about the importance and uniqueness of the Sabbath in mankind's history.[54] In May 1982, he delivered another reflective speech about the Sabbath, in which he surveyed the civilizations of the world beginning with ancient Egypt and considered their attitude to the idea of a day of rest.[55]

During his premiership major revisions were made in legislation on religious issues such as the exemption of women from obligatory military service, work on Sabbath, sex segregation of beaches, autopsies, antimissionary activity, archaeological activity in holy places, and abortions. In no other period had religious Orthodoxy enjoyed such an increase in its strength: religious nationalist ideas were made an integral part of the state schools' curricula, there was a rise in the return to Orthodox, often ultra-Orthodox, religion, and support of religious institutions was increased. These were clear signs of a value change taking place in Israeli society in a climate of crisis.[56]

Begin struggled for decades to establish the rights of a political minority and to strengthen the status of the opposition. In foreign policy decisions that appeared to relate to historical right, Begin hovered near the edge of nonrecognition of the legitimacy of the government's policy. This became evident at historical turning-points, beginning with the 1947 UN partition plan. At a press conference in November 1948, Begin said that when the government faced critical decisions, it was the position of Herut that the public should be consulted through a public referendum.[57] That demand was raised again and again: with respect to the determination of the country's eastern boundary, German reparations, and the establishment of diplomatic ties with Germany.

Begin viewed the government's acquiescence to the Hashemite Kingdom's annexation of the West Bank as a temporary decision that would have to be reversed in the future.[58] In his view, the Alignment had never received authorization from the nation to repartition the Land of Israel. He challenged the legitimacy of any policy that was not compatible with the conception of Greater Israel.[59] When he went in the summer of 1974 to Sebastia, the site of an illegal settlement attempt by Gush Emunim, he said he did not understand how formal rights could be assigned greater force and validity than historical rights, "The foolish cries of 'putsch' will be of no avail." Faith and historical right were mighty enough to dissolve the law. Begin's tendency to locate the source of authority beyond the national institutions was a continuation of the Revisionist tradition. He believed that "the truth does not depend on strength, and rightness is not linked to the majority."[60]

For many years Begin was not able to establish the legitimacy of Herut as a potential ruling party and did not appreciably broaden its public backing. This continued up until the Six Day War. At that time political support for Herut began to expand following changes in political alliances and a rightward turn by the liberal middle class and the religious nationalists. The first accomplishment was a partnership in the mid-1960s with the Liberals. Then, before the Six Day War, Mapai was forced into a coalition partnership with Rafi and the Herut–Liberal bloc.

The legitimation of Herut as an alternative ruling party was inseparable from the political and moral decline of the labor movement and the increasing division within it. The demand for an alternative gained considerable ground after the Yom Kippur War, and the disenchantment it brought in the power and ability of the ruling party.

The rise and fall of great expectations

There were few who foresaw Begin's rise to power but in 1955, Zvi Levanon, the secretary of the Jerusalem Chamber of Commerce, wrote a book about it.[61] It opens with two members of a kibbutz in southern Israel discussing the incredible possibility of Begin becoming prime minister. Expressing their own deep disappointment with socialism, they state a conviction that the one person who will remain faithful to the path he set for himself, even after coming to power, is Begin. Begin's rise to power is envisaged in a Churchillian manner. The country is in deep crisis, the government resigns, the president invites Begin, as the man of destiny, to rescue the nation. In his first address to the Knesset as prime minister, he rescinds all the decisions of the previous government. Begin is not only prime minister but also foreign minister. The government he heads is the most efficient, daring, and resolute imaginable. Peace talks are held with

Lebanon and Egypt. The West Bank is conquered, and afterwards the East Bank as well. The United States and Britain, ultimately, support Israel.[62]

When Begin entered office in May 1977 he was sixty-four years old, a sick man, having suffered a severe heart attack. He told reporters that his illness would not affect his performance: "I intend to work day and night, and [I] pray to God that He give me the strength."[63] Reactions to his election that were not venomous or vindictive expressed a measure of anxiety, and in the best of instances, doubt. To many the victory looked more like defeat of the Labor party than victory for Herut. Fears were expressed about the fate of Israel's defense and foreign policy.

Begin now took pains to present a new image. He started with declarations on peace and to show an interest in affairs not directly concerned with Israel, his first act as prime minister was to offer asylum to Vietnamese boat refugees.[64] The search for partners, and the achievement of a broader legitimation swiftly gained momentum. One of the first steps Begin took was to appoint Moshe Dayan foreign minister, despite objections from the public and within the party.[65]

The new government's platform was as pretentious on domestic matters as it was ambitious in foreign affairs. In presenting his government, Begin stated that in its first session the Knesset would pass a state health insurance law, an arbitration law, a minimum wage law, and a state pension law. Violent crime would be uprooted, the young generation would be educated to love mankind, freedom, justice, and the homeland. The coalition agreement was especially far-reaching in the field of religion. For the first time the education portfolio was placed in the hands of a minority religious faction. It was a prominent manifestation of a new political alliance between the right and the religious parties that was to dominate Israeli politics in the coming years.

The coalition agreement stated that "The Jewish people has an eternal historical right to the Land of Israel, our incontestable patrimony." The government called upon the Arab countries to conduct direct negotiations with the aim of concluding peace treaties. As long as peace negotiations would be in process, he added, the cabinet would not exercise its right to extend Israeli law to the entire territory of the Land of Israel. That was an express condition laid down by Foreign Minister Moshe Dayan.[66]

Begin asked for a year's grace in which to correct the defects and imbalances of the past. During the first weeks, the press noted Begin's swift adjustment to the job and the efficiency with which he ran the government: discussions were concise and there were no leaks.[67] In contrast to preelection fears, government ministries were not purged of Alignment appointees. The area where real change was expected, apart from foreign policy, was the economy. Milton Friedman, the renowned conservative economist, was mentioned as a willing source of inspiration for the government's economic policy. The Likud promised to reduce inflation to 15 per cent, to increase capital investment, to streamline the bureaucracy and effect a tax reform. But despite these proclamations and external indications of direction, Begin actually came to the task of organizing his government unprepared.[68]

The pace of events during the first months of Begin's premiership, especially in the foreign policy area, was rapid. By the fall there was already talk, primarily among Begin's supporters, of his "ideological retrogression." Disputes within the government began to come to light, together with revelations about the cabinet's way of making decisions. The chances of a real reform of Israel's political, social, and economic life seemed dim.[69] From the government's very first days, it was hypersensitive about the media and distrustful of the pronouncements of intellectuals. As criticism of Begin mounted, these problems became more severe and the government's isolation intensified. By the beginning of 1978, Begin's prestige appeared to have been damaged.

During his first year in office, decisions made by Begin cast a shadow on his ability as a decisionmaker and on the moral validity of his political judgment. Among these was the pardon Begin granted, as acting justice minister, to Yehoshua Ben-Zion, a banker serving a prison term for the biggest embezzlement in the history of Israel's financial establishment. There were rumors about continued fundraising in the United States for the Herut movement's Tel Hai Fund. Finally, there was the naming of a completely unknown professor, Yitzhak Shaveh, as Begin's candidate for the presidency. Begin was not successful in arranging public support for his candidate and Herut Knesset members were compelled to vote for the Alignment candidate, Yitzhak Navon.[70]

In fact, Begin's premiership knew few balmy days. One of them, just a year and a half after he became prime minister, was his receipt of the Nobel peace prize, jointly with Anwar Sadat. Begin was then at the zenith of his power. On being informed that he had been awarded the prize, Begin asserted that it had been given to the Jewish people and that he was merely its addressee. Dayan, who was in the United States at the time, refused to convey the prime minister's congratulations to the Egyptian delegation with whom talks were being conducted. Sadat did not go to Oslo in December 1978 to accept the prize; Begin went with a large entourage. In Norway he delivered one of his most grandiloquent speeches. He opened by declaring: "I have come from the land of Zion and Jerusalem and here I stand before you humbly and with pride as one of the Jewish people, as a son of the generation of the Holocaust and of redemption."[71]

Eventually, senior cabinet officers, most of them not from Herut, left the government. Communications Minister Meir Amit resigned during the

Camp David talks. After the Camp David summit, distrust seeped into the relations between Begin and his two senior ministers – Weizman and Dayan. His views differed from theirs, and he thought he had lost control over their moves. After the peace agreement he reduced Dayan's status and curtailed his authority. With Weizman, a member of the Herut movement and a possible heir, he came to a total break.[72] By the end of the government's term in 1981, both Dayan and Weizman had resigned, as well as Finance Minister Yigal Horowitz.

Public opinion polls showed the Likud facing certain defeat at the elections. But in the course of one year, Begin was to succeed in temporarily reversing the situation and lifting himself out of a long period of personal decline. In the spring of 1981 he seemed to have freed himself of what had shackled him in the past and was now able to act according to his own light. In the preelection period he made the decision to bomb the nuclear reactor in Iraq, deepened Israel's involvement in Lebanon, and initiated an astonishing rhetorical attack against domestic opponents and world leaders.[73] In the May 1981 elections, Begin won a surprise victory. He then turned his sights northward. He immediately pushed the Golan Heights Law through the Knesset, and in June 1982 came the war in Lebanon. Hardly more than a year was to pass from the begining of the war and his resignation in August 1983. The lingering embroilment in Lebanon combined with a grave economic crisis, people close to him died – his wife, and deputy Prime Minister Simcha Erhlich – and the fall from the heights came suddenly.

During the election campaign of 1981 Begin had said that the hardest thing for him during his four years in office was the decision to evacuate the Rafah Salient. Veterans of the undregrounds likened the removal of the settlements to the policy of the British White Paper. Shmuel Katz wrote that Begin had never had a viable settlement policy. He had broken the momentum of Gush Emunim's settlement program and made a mockery of the idea of settling the Land of Israel.[74] Begin's supporters could not produce a satisfactory reponse. The prevailing view was that the prime minister was being outmaneuvered by his senior ministers, Dayan and Weizman. But this view clashed with the image of Begin as an authoritative leader, whose views are not challenged.

Within Herut itself no one dared oppose the leader of the movement. The new challenge came from a radical and fundamentalist force. At a cabinet meeting in May 1979, Begin fulminated that the supporters of Gush Emunim, "Messianists" who were "complex-ridden and arrogant." The idealists and political allies of the past were now "liars." He had already inveighed against them in late 1977, "We have no need for overseers of our loyalty to the Land of Israel."[75] The first skirmish took place in the fall of 1979. In October, the Supreme Court ruled that the settlement of

Eilon Moreh established by Gush Emunim was illegal, in that there was no vital military need for it. It was hinted that if Gush Emunim people tried to settle there again, Begin might consider handing in his resignation. At Anwar Sadat's funeral in October 1981 he told Secretary of State Haig that he might be forced to resign on the issue of vacating Yamit. In the spring of 1982 the Yamit settlers were evacuated after a bitter struggle with the army. The bulldozing of the city attested to a new brutalization in Israel's national life.[76]

Belief in the national will, rhetoric, and the importance of ideas were not adequate substitutes for facts and data, for careful, systematic preparation. Since the 1940s newspaper reading had been an obsession of Begin's, and this he regarded as a source of arguments and information to be used against opponents.[77] His choice of advisers and aides was not on the basis of expertise or talents. People were chosen on the basis of his personal inclinations, affection, and their relation to the "fighting family."

In May 1965, Begin had criticized Mapai politicians who were ferociously attacking Ben-Gurion for turning on him after seventeen years of "Byzantine flattery." But as leader of Herut, Begin himself was surrounded by people whose only merit was their loaylty to him. Aryeh Altman, the veteran Revisionist leader, once remarked that they had created an image of Begin as a man who never errs; the errors and failures were always attributed to others.[78] Nearing the end of his road, Begin found himself isolated and having to rely on unworthy advisers.

Begin did not meet the criteria he himself had set in his blistering criticisms of every government in Israel since the state was established. In 1976 he ferociously derided the bout of leaks from Rabin's government – stenographic records transmitted in a matter of minutes to the world's capitals. He complained further that appointments to official positions requiring special knowledge and talents were being made on the basis of political party and factional ties: "There isn't even one area of our national life about which it can be said that the government is functioning properly."[79]

When his government was still taking its first fledgling steps, Begin promised a comprehensive reform of its management. In fact the structure of the government was not revamped, and his control of the cabinet continuously deteriorated. Dayan wrote that, "not on all subjects did he invest study and thought." Dayan's sparse account of his government service is filled with the strains of such cynicism. Yigal Allon said in the Knesset, "We have returned to the style of high-sounding words versus real actions; of florid declarations versus actual realization; of verbal firing from the hip instead of well-considered, sober solutions that are rooted in reality."[80]

Shmuel Katz, who served the prime minister until the end of 1977, also left a portrait of Begin as inconsistent, easily influenced, lacking decision-making ability, and without the skills needed to assemble and conduct an orderly administration. He depicted him as the leader of a government that made no attempt to fulfill the social and economic planks of its platform, and which on the international plane, undermined the foundations of Israel's national security.[81] Katz had admired Begin as underground leader, but sharply criticized him as politician – the way he allowed himself to be dragged into Ben-Gurion's polemics, his retreat from principles at the first signs of resistance.[82] As time went by, wrote Katz, "the Byzantine climate" surrounding Begin grew denser and spread.[83]

Katz, who was supposed to manage an area to which Begin attached special importance, the field of information work, despaired of Begin's work style and of his defection from the fundamental positions of Herut. In the end he had a head-on clash with Begin, which ended, as did all manifestations of opposition within the Herut movement: on the last day of 1977, Katz submitted his resignation.[84]

Ezer Weizman described Begin as "weak, putting off decisions, and pushing problems under the rug."[85] Begin, Weizman claimed, treated his ministers like high school pupils who had to have morality preached to them. He was intolerant of opposing ideas, did not involve others in his decisions, and chose aides on the basis of their concurrence with his views. He was enthusiastic about the suggestion that IDF soldiers be required to wear berets again, and devoted more time to it than to dis-cussion of the air force's need for F-16 fighter planes. In his letter of resignation, Weizman wrote, "The more time passed, the more it became clear to me that the hopes that were pinned on us had no basis in reality."[86]

There were other decisions whose costly damage was revealed only too late. A conspicuous example was the decision to produce Israel's own jet plane, the Lavi. The decisionmaking process has been described by a lead-ing participant as a "theatre of absurd." It became evident that Begin, in the short period that he served as defense minister, lacked the competence and strategic knowledge for such a grave decision for the security of Israel. Army officers and bureaucrats shamelessly exploited his weakness for high ranking military men. In the autumn of 1987, the government was humili-atingly forced to abandon the prestigious project after spending over $1 billion.[87]

As leader of the opposition, Begin had consistently claimed that the prime minister is not empowered to decide on military and political issues of the highest order without prior approval of the government, and in certain circumstances of the Knesset. In practice, he often confronted his govern-ment with *faits accomplis*. The autonomy plan and the Camp David

Accords were submitted for cabinet and Knesset approval retroactively. The road that led to the war in Lebanon, and the conduct of the war itself, made a mockery of any rational decisionmaking process.

With characteristic euphemism, Begin called his failures in running the government "snags." Frequently the press reported that Begin had decided to put his government "in order": cabinet members would have to act according to the government's decisions and according to its timetable. He reprimanded Sharon, "There will be no more raising of voices around the cabinet table."[88] Nevertheless, breaches of discipline in the cabinet continued to be frequent occurrences.

Begin's weaknesses were part of his character, world view, and conception of leadership. His insistence on maintaining a façade of domineering leadership in fact gave cover to those who derided his authority but appearances were kept up so as not to undermine Begin's prestige. But behind the façade there were decisions and plans that were not examined in depth, or were decided without due cooperation among the relevant ministers. The cabinet did not hold a comprehensive discussion before Sadat came to Jerusalem. The twists and turns of the peace negotiations were not clear to the members of the government and Begin made no effort to clarify them, except to a few individuals. In the end, faults and weak points were found in the peace plan he proposed in 1977. Unnecessarily, in September 1978 at Camp David, and again in March 1979 before concluding the peace talks, Begin brought about a situation whereby he and the government had to make decisions under tight time pressures.

In the military realm, it is unlikely that Begin understood the system at his command, its operation, strengths, and limitations. The appointment of General Ariel Sharon as defense minister marked a downward turn in the government's ability to control the defense system. During the Lebanon War it was to become increasingly evident that the course of the war was not in Begin's control.

Menachem Begin's failure as prime minister and as national leader stemmed primarily from his faulty conception of reality. But above all, he failed fatally as a decisionmaker. A lack of logistical control was a recurring pattern with Begin ever since his days as commander of the Irgun. He was incapable of systematic operational planning. His ability was limited to his talents as a propagandist, political leader, and espouser of ideas. His failure as an executive exacted a high price. It sometimes led him to strategic compromise, and to concessions in matters of principle, or pushed him into a position from which there was no escape. In the end, his leadership was undermined.

That is the motif that unites the revolutionary on the beach at Kfar Vitkin and the prime minister in his office in Jerusalem. He allowed himself to be dragged along, more than he should have, by facts and situations created by his subordinates and ministers. Begin was a maximalist who lacked the organizational control that would have enabled him to achieve his objectives. Instead, he was moody, rising to the heights of exultation and sinking into deep depression.

14
The End of the Road

In the mid-1970s Begin said of Ze'ev Jabotinsky, the man he most admired: "He never knew defeat. He said instead, this is a gateway to victory. His spirit never fell when things took a downward turn. He declared instead, this is a sign of an upswing. Such is the soul of a fighter."[1] Begin the prime minister was not able to follow his example. In the fall of 1982, Begin entered a deep crisis. Since the late 1930s he had experienced similar crises after serious challenges to his leadership, defeat in elections, and on occasions when he held himself responsible for the deaths of others. The outward manifestations were clear: denial followed by apathy, melancholy, and in the end, facial blemishes.

In his later years Begin often seemed preoccupied with his physical condition. He began his letter to President Sadat in August 1980 with reflections about the human body: "And what in fact is the human heart? Simply, it's a pump ... What a cosmic wonder is the fragility of the human body ...!"[2] At the end of 1981, Begin slipped in his bathroom and broke his hip. His letter to journalist Yoel Marcus is a peculiarly detailed account of his fall, his helplessness, his cry for assistance, and his operation. He candidly discussed his heart attacks, the blockage in the cranial artery that affected his vision, and his worry that his only sister and his children would learn about his illness not from him but from someone else.[3]

At the end of 1982, Begin became more remote, indifferent, and depressed. The prime minister's physical and mental state became a topic of public discussion. When the subject had arisen earlier, it was usually met by a vigorous denial of the claims that the swings of Begin's moods were affecting his decision-making ability. But in his second term in office, the manifestations were such that such claims could not be dismissed as "malignant fictions."[4] In the summer of 1983 Begin came to the end of his road.

The question of Begin's resignation now constantly hovered in the air. At the time of the Independence Day holiday, he failed to send the customary letters to a number of bereaved families. In July 1983, referring to the war in Lebanon, he conceded for the first time that this is "a difficult hour for the nation." In August he did not celebrate his birthday. At the end of August, everything came to an end: "I can't any longer."[5]

In fact, Begin stepped down at the very time he had for years announced he would. At the last Herut convention before he came to power, he proclaimed that he would retire at the age of seventy and would write a three-volume work on "the generation of destruction and rebirth."[6] At a victory party after his reelection in 1981, he was less firm about that. He now told his supporters that if he remained healthy and the party wanted him, he would consider continuing as head of the Likud at the end of his four years in office. But one month later he declared that Churchill, Ben-Gurion, Golda Meir, and Moshe Dayan had not known how to retire in time; he himself intended to step down in 1983, as he had promised his wife.[7]

When Begin finally announced his resignation, his office witnessed a flurry of sycophancy as cabinet ministers and party members urged him to stay on. Begin stuck to his refusal. He told them, "I hoid no grudge, I don't blame anyone."[8] An attempt to organize a mass demonstration near his home sputtered out. Stupefaction was followed by slow acceptance. Yohanan Bader, familiar with Begin's previous escapes from duty, published a statement that he would not be surprised if Begin were to resume his responsibilities.[9] But his assessment was too hurried.

What did Begin's resignation signify – that beliefs had shattered against hard reality, flight from pangs of guilt, or the weariness of age and the betrayal of near ones? Shmuel Katz believed Begin was weighed down by a profound weariness and a sensitivity to losses, which he never had been able to bear.[10] Eldad thought that Begin had a "power of emotional restraint" that found no outlet, as well as an awareness of his responsibility.[11] Begin's daughter, Hassya, thought the main reason for his resignation was death of his beloved wife and lifetime confidante Aliza Begin, who had died on November 1982, while Begin was in the United States.[12] In October he had said his wife's condition would affect his decision as to whether to serve out his term. He may have felt guilty that he was not at her side in her final moments. It was a serious blow, and came at a bad time.[13]

Begin paid a high price for his self-control and the suppression of his emotions. Bader wrote, "He has the signs of raging, stormy temperament, but also manifests an iron inner discipline that binds the man's raging energy."[14] There may have been something compulsive about Begin's "heroic code", the rituals, the iron imperatives of behavior and the self-discipline he imposed on himself.[15] When he assumed the burden of supreme responsibility, reality would refute some of the inner world he had carefully constructed. When the readiness to admit error breached the tough outer façade, the personal consequences were severe.

It is easy to be misled by Begin's character. His personal characteristics seem so prominent and obvious that one might think that he can be understood merely from simple observation and reading what he said. But Begin's was a contradictory personality. He symbolized both the Jew from Brisk and the rebel and revolutionary; he was sensitive about casualties, unable to tolerate physical violence near him, a family man, a merciful leader. But he also had to contain within himself the rebel, stubborn opposer, and secessionist. Defeat and victory, it seems, were bound together for Begin – Holocaust and rebirth; fatal attack and rise to office; peace and war.

Israel after Begin will no longer be what it was. Values and basic patterns, the social and economic structure, the configurations of political association have all changed. Israel in 1977 was ripe for wide-ranging internal reform, yet despite congenial international and strategic circumstances Begin failed to meet his challenge and left a society in a state of economic bankruptcy, moral decline, without political stability, riven and divided. He himself was in deep personal crisis. Begin did not understand how the social and economic dimensions were related to the foreign policy and military objectives he had set. Instead of taking as his point of departure a small community seeking to preserve its existence and prosperity, he risked all for the sake of national glory. The vision of an undivided Greater Israel was not realized. As a leader and prime minister he was able to march only halfway on the road to the promised land.

The face of society changed. The bonds restraining hidden urges were loosened, even if not intentionally. Things that had never happened before in Israel and were believed impossible, did happen now: the rise of a racist party, political murder, and the growth of a Jewish terrorist underground. It became evident that democracy was not divisible; it was not possible to preserve it in one place and keep it out of another. Begin failed both in the improvement of the individual's lot and in social reform. He was a victim of what he did not believe: that history is a complex process and does not readily submit to singular events aimed at changing it in quantum leaps. Begin cast himself as the saviour of his nation but left behind him a nation divided and a legacy of distrust.

National will, historical right, and the voice of the invisible crowd were elements too frail to support the construction of a properly functioning society. Begin's historical romanticism never bowed before reality. When he obtained a political majority his belief in the justness of his course deepened and took on a measure of absoluteness. Begin did not base his government's policy on a stable social stratum. Nor did he mold a worthy political and institutional apparatus. He turned instead to the arsenal of the authoritarian leader – national unity, rhetoric, faith in his own ability, and populist incitement.

Begin left his party divided into fiefdoms, without an heir. In fact, it had already reached the point where a changing of the guard was imminent. The "fighting family" had withdrawn from the political scene even before Begin. Internal alignments did not reflect differences of view, but were the outcome of power struggles between new and ambitious faction leaders. There was no heir left from the ranks of the "fighting family." The party's old guard now rallied behind the former leader of a rival underground, Yitzhak Shamir.[16]

Begin did not take part in the 1984 elections. He apologized to his friends for not voting.[17] He was still chairman of the executive, which did not convene without his authorization. In the two years after he stepped down, the party experienced power struggles whose conduct was a source of shame. When the fifteenth convention of the Herut movement was convened in March 1986, it was called off overnight in total disarray, and the leaders of the contending factions were fearful to convene it again. Public opinion polls showed a decline in the Likud's strength and a rise in that of the radical right. Yet there were still feeble hints that Begin would yet return to public life.[18] He was still an irreplaceable, almost mystical presence for his party and supporters.

Begin was the commander of an underground whose achievements are the subject of a historical debate that will probably not be resolved. As an individual he was intellectually shallow. As a politician he was a tactician and leader of masses of no small skill. As a national leader he was a dilettante, but his self-confidence allowed him to overcome all difficulties and march the country toward its first peace treaty with an Arab country.

Begin began his life journey in Brisk and ended a recluse in his Jerusalem apartment. In the 1940s, in Vilna and in Palestine, he learned to stay for long periods in his house. Did he take on the character of a Hebrew king who, having sinned, sits in his house grieving and covered in shame? Was his the depression of a Jew who survived the Holocaust, or was it the heroic code of self-punishment of a Polish noble from the *szlachta*? Much along Begin's path was subject to noble or pitiful interpretation. Or perhaps that is history's way, to place the exalted and the ridiculous side by side.

Menachem Begin will continue to haunt rivals and staunch supporters alike for many years to come. The man in whose hands words were a weapon stepped down without a word to his people. With this refusal of accountability Begin assumed his final role: the culprit transforming himself to be the victim of history.

Notes

Bibliographical Note

All quotations and titles have been translated from the Hebrew. The original version, in most cases, is the authorized and inclusive one, preserving the omitted passages that sometimes are not included in the English translation. Spelling of Hebrew names has been in accordance with the practice of the persons in question. References are arranged according to the short-title method where the first reference to a book or journal gives full publication details.

Chapter 1 From Brisk to Jerusalem, 1913–1942

1 The date generally accepted as Begin's birth is August 16, 1913. His Polish passport bears the date July 13, 1913. An application he submitted for a life insurance policy gives August 31, 1913. Jabotinsky Institute Archives (henceforth JIA) P20/1(1).

2 Now the capital of Brest province, in the Bielorussian Republic of the Soviet Union. See also A. Golan, S. Nakdimon, *Begin* (Hebrew), (Edanim, Jerusalem, 1978), pp. 11–12; H. Canaan, *Ha'aretz*, June 17, 1977; R. P. Greenfield, I. A. Greenfield, *The Life Story of Menachem Begin* (Manor Books, New York, 1977), pp. 13–15; A. Edelberg, "History of the Jewish Community of Brisk," in *Encyclopedia of the Jewish Diaspora*, ed. E. Steinman (Hebrew), (Jerusalem and Tel Aviv, 1954), pp. 32–8.

3 Brest-Litovsk was also the seat of the Soloveitchik rabbinical dynasty.

4 M. Begin, "Three Things," in *Encyclopedia of the Jewish Diaspora*, pp. 249–52.

5 E. Haber, *Menachem Begin* (Delacorte Press, New York, 1978), pp. 13–18; E. Silver, *Begin: A Biography* (Weidenfeld and Nicolson, London, 1984), pp. 3–5; Golan, Nakdimon, *Begin*, pp. 13–15, 26–7.

6 L. Wolf, *The Passion of Israel* (Little, Brown and Company, Boston, 1970), pp. 254, 256.

7 See also, Haber, *Menachem Begin*, pp. 11–18; Silver, *Begin*, pp. 2–8; Golan, Nakdimon, *Begin*, pp. 12–28.

8 *Herut*, August 9, 1963.

9 Haber, *Menachem Begin*, p. 15; Silver, *Begin*, p. 3.

10 *Jewish Journal*, September 2, 1977.

11 Shmuel Shemer, interview with author.
12 M. Begin, *White Nights* (Hebrew), (Karni, Jerusalem, 1953), p. 32; for an English translation see M. Begin, *White Nights* (Steimatzky, Jerusalem, 1977). Begin recalls "learning while hungry." (Subsequent references are to the Hebrew version.)
13 JIA, P20/1(1). Curriculum vitae in Begin's handwriting; Haber, *Menachem Begin*, p. 20; Silver, *Begin*, pp. 6–7; Golan, Nakdimon, *Begin*, pp. 27, 35.
14 A. Dolav, *Ma'ariv*, June 10, 1977.
15 Begin, *White Nights*, p. 50. Begin records that he was a member of Hashomer Hatzair from the age of 10 to 13 (1923–6).
16 Ibid., p. 32.
17 The material relating to Betar during the 1930s is one of the less well-organized sections of the Jabotinsky Institute Archives. A thorough history of the movement has yet to be written.
18 See also ch. 4; Haber, *Menachem Begin*, pp. 27–8; Silver, *Begin*, pp. 15–20; Golan, Nakdimon, *Begin*, pp. 34–52; Y. Levi, *History of Betar Czechoslovakia* (Hebrew), (Betar CSR, Tel Aviv, 1960), pp. 106–16.
19 Begin, *White Nights*, p. 84; *Hamedina*, Sivan 16, 1939. Aliza Begin, seven years his junior, was born on March 25, 1920.
20 Y. Eldad, *First Tithe* (Hebrew), (Hadar, Tel Aviv, 1975), pp. 37–9; see also *At.*, November 1980.
21 Golan, Nakdimon, *Begin*, p. 54; Silver, *Begin*, p. 21. Eldad claims that Begin convened the Betar leadership to urge it to take part in the defense of Warsaw and behave as loyal citizens of Poland.
22 Golan, Nakdimon, *Begin*, p. 55. Rachel and Yehoshua Halperin fled to Brest-Litovsk, where they were interrogated about Begin by the NKVD. They were transported to Russia, where Begin met them after his release from the labor camp.
23 Begin, *White Nights*, p. 84.
24 See Haber, *Menachem Begin*, p. 57; Silver, *Begin*, p. 22.
25 Wolf, *Passion of Israel*, pp. 257–8; Haber, *Menachem Begin*, pp. 51–7; Golan, Nakdimon, *Begin*, pp. 55–6.
26 Eldad, *First Tithe*, pp. 35–42.
27 Shimshon Yuniczman personal archive. JIA, P106.
28 See also Silver, *Begin*, pp. 22–4. Eldad claimed that he does not know whether or not Begin was earnest about wanting to return to Warsaw.
29 JIA, P106.
30 Ibid.
31 Ibid., letter dated May 5, 1940.
32 Begin, *White Nights*, pp. 12, 150. Begin relates that he had pity for the agents following him, and observed their anxiety. It was not his first arrest. He had been detained briefly in mid-1939 after a demonstration outside the British embassy, following publication of the White Paper.
33 Ibid., p. 14.
34 *New York Times Magazine*, July 17, 1977.
35 Begin, *White Nights*, pp. 10–16; Eldad, *First Tithe*, pp. 42–6; Golan, Nakdimon, *Begin*, pp. 56–7; Silver, *Begin*, pp. 22–7.

36 Begin, *White Nights*, p. 150; *Hayarden* (June 11, 1941) published a report of Begin's arrest by the Soviet authorities. In addition, it printed a piece, lauding the imprisoned Begin and praising his skill in facing up to his interrogators.

37 At first sight, Begin's book resembles other works written at that time by intellectuals awakening from the spell cast by Communism like George Orwell and Arthur Koestler. But Begin's point of departure and his personal experiences are of a different sort.

38 Begin, *White Nights*, pp. 81–2; see also pp. 24, 50–1, 78.

39 Ibid. 77–8, 94; id., *The Revolt* (Hebrew), (Achiasaf, Tel Aviv, 1950), p. 15; for an English translation see M. Begin, *The Revolt* (W. H. Allen, London, 1979). (Subsequent references are to the Hebrew version.)

40 Id., *White Nights*, pp. 88–9, 128.

41 Ibid., pp. 108, 195. During his imprisonment, Begin had considered divorcing his wife; he particularly dreaded the possibility of her being summoned to interrogation. Later, he learned that she had emigrated to Palestine. He was reunited with her when he reached Palestine in May 1942. Begin's internment in a Soviet prison later gave rise to rumors that he was a Soviet agent. See JIA, P20/1(1).

42 See for an opposite view, Golan, Nakdimon, *Begin*, p. 61; Silver, *Begin*, p. 33.

43 Begin, *White Nights*, pp. 10, 102.

44 Ibid., pp. 166–75, 202–6.

45 Ibid., pp. 198, 217.

Chapter 2 Begin and Jabotinsky

1 Y. Halperin, "With Him in the Last Minutes," *Ha'umma*, 61–2 (1980), pp. 470–3; A. Propes, "His Last Minutes," ibid.; Joseph B. Schechtman, *Ze'ev Jabotinsky* (Hebrew) 3 vols. (Karni, Tel Aviv, 1957), vol. III, pp. 164–70. For an English translation see Joseph B. Schechtman, *Fighter and Prophet: The Vladimir Jabotinsky Story*, 2 vols. (T. Yoseloff, New York, 1956–61). (All references here are to the Hebrew version.)

2 *Herut*, July 8, 1964.

3 *Ma'ariv*, October 20, 1980.

4 See also Eldad, *First Tithe*, p. 117. Eldad writes that Begin said: "When I give an order, I sense the head of Betar standing at my back and commanding me to give the order."

5 M. Begin, "Ze'ev Jabotinsky," *Herut Hamoledet*, August 5, 1948.

6 Id., "What we Have Learned from Jabotinsky," *Ma'ariv*, July 30, 1976; See also interview with him in *Yediot Aharonot*, October 24, 1980.

7 M. Begin, "Herzl and Jabotinsky," July 25, 1944, in his *In the Underground* (Hebrew) 4 vols. (Hadar, Tel Aviv, 1977), vol. I, pp. 57–60; see also "Ze'ev Jabotinsky" (Av, 1943), in *Lehi Writings* (Hebrew), 2 vols. (Tel Aviv, 1959–1960), pp. 147–8. This article, which appears to have been written by Yisrael Eldad, gives a fairly guarded assessment of Jabotinsky's political achievements.

8 *Yediot Aharonot*, August 15, 1948, JIA, P106. Letter by S. Yuniczman, July 10, 1958; Golan, Nakdimon, *Begin*, p. 40. It should be noted that Eri Jabotinsky's

book about his father makes no mention of Begin; on Betar's second world convention in Cracow see B. Ben Yerucham, *Book of Betar* (Hebrew) 2 vols. (Jerusalem and Tel Aviv, 1973), vol. II, pp. 391–411.

9 Betar World Convention, Tel Aviv, May 16–22, 1949. Minutes of the meetings, JIA, B-3/1/6.

10 The historical lessons drawn from Garibaldi are themselves a topic worthy of thorough study. For all the pitfalls of historical analogy, there are some surprising points of similarity.

11 Z. Jabotinsky, "Mored Or", *Selected Writings* (Hebrew) 2 vols. (S. Zaltzman, Tel Aviv, 1936), vol. I, pp. 271–9. It greatly pleased Jabotinsky that Garibaldi supposedly met the Carbonari sailor who spoke to him of the need to unify Italy, in Odessa, his own native city. Jabotinsky's article was published in 1912.

12 Z. Jabotinsky, "The Kleizmer Coach," in *On the Road to the State* (Hebrew), (E. Jabotinsky, Jerusalem, 1963), p. 272; see also "Zion and Communism", ibid., p. 64.

13 M. Begin, "Their Wars and Our War," *Herut*, May 8, 1953.

14 Published in *Hazit Ha'am*, April 7, 1933.

15 Ben-Yerucham, *Book of Betar*, vol. I, p. 284. In the spring of 1931, when Propes wanted to resign, Jabotinsky wrote to him: "I shall never agree to the resignation of the man I regard as the creator of the entire Betar movement . . .;" Y. Shavit, *Open Season* (Hebrew), (Hadar, Tel Aviv, 1976), pp. 25, 41–2. The group supporting the amalgamation of Betar and the Irgun published a pamphlet "For the sake of the homeland." Issued in Tel Aviv in 1938, it called for "active resistance" on the part of the Revisionist party in Palestine. The signatories included Yellin-Mor and Begin.

16 *The Third World Convention of Betar*. Warsaw, September 11–16, 1938. (Hebrew), (Bucharest, 1940), (henceforth, Protocol); Stenogram, JIA, B2-4/1/6 (henceforth, Stenogram).

17 Protocol, pp. 45–6. Begin's speech on Tel-Hai fund.

18 Protocol, pp. 58–61; Stenogram, pp. 29–31. The Betar oath was composed by Jabotinsky in 1934 and approved by Betar's second world convention (Cracow, January 1935). It should be noted that the only sentence of Begin's quoted by Schechtman (*Jabotinsky*, vol. II, pp. 236–7), differs from the wording in the official minutes and from that in the stenographic record. Schechtman writes that in private conversation Jabotinsky agreed with Begin, but wished to avoid the erroneous impression that would be fostered by publicly conceding that there was no further point in diplomatic efforts. Schechtman's sole source is Menachem Begin.

19 M. Ben-Ze'ev [M. Begin], "Rescue Regime", *Hamadrikh*, 3 (November 1943). Here too, in an article written shortly before his proclamation of the revolt, Begin criticized the Revisionist policy of partnership with Britain.

20 Protocol, pp. 61–3.

21 Stenogram, pp. 31–3. Jabotinsky's words, as recorded in the official minutes, are almost identical with the stenographic notes.

22 Opening Address, First National Convention, Prague, January 31, 1938. JIA, C4-8/3, pp. 1–8.

23 Protocol, pp. 69–76. Jabotinsky wanted Ben-Yosef's name recalled "in the holy of holies," and not as an everyday matter. In the stenographic record, he spoke of "the cult of Ben-Yosef" (Stenogram, pp. 40–6).

24 D. Niv, *The Irgun Zva'i Leumi: Battle for Freedom* (Hebrew), 6 vols. (Hadar, Tel Aviv, 1965), vol. I, pp. 182–4. Begin was not seated on the platform at the opening of the convention. Betar's bi-weekly *Hamedina* was edited by Propes up to Begin's appointment, when the editor was replaced. The character of the journals now changed, with articles by Eldad and Begin appearing on a regular basis.

25 Protocol, pp. 99–112.

26 U. Halperin, "Platform for the Betar World Convention," JIA, B2-4/1/6.

27 See also id., *We Look for Power* (Hebrew), (Z. Schiff, Tel Aviv, 1938).

28 M. Begin, "The Father of the Hebrew Revolt" (Hebrew), in A. Remba (ed.), *Ze'ev Jabotinsky* (Shilton Betar, Tel Aviv, 1949), pp. 15–19; M. Begin, "The Revolt against British Rule in the Land of Israel," *Ha'umma*, 37 (1963), pp. 341–55.

29 See Y. Shavit, *The Mythologies of the Zionist Right Wing* (Hebrew), (The Sharett Institute, Bet Berl, Kfar Sava, 1987), pp. 85–127.

30 Z. Jabotinsky, "The Meaning of Avanturism," (Hebrew), *Hazit Ha'am*, August 5, 1932. Inter alia, he wrote: ". . . Due to the monism of means and tactics, it is forbidden to say anything and nothing shall be said." He maintained nevertheless that history is made by "the barefooted" – Lenin, Mussolini, and Hitler (in a letter to Dr. J. Freulich, Betar's *natziv* in Palestine, published in *Hazit Ha'am*, July 29, 1932). Jabotinsky reserved "forms of political warfare outside the bounds of law" for special circumstances, and on condition that they do not violate the sanctity of human life, or identify the perpetrator with a formal organization (in a letter to Yevin, August 9, 1932, JIA, A1/2/22/2). See also Ben-Yerucham, *Book of Betar*, vol. I, pp. 424–5. Jabotinsky elaborated upon the overt and democratic character of the Revisionist movement. Revolutionary action, "at a time of need and necessity" was possible, if committed at the instigation of the perpetrator alone, and if it did not flout "the moral law." See also, Schechtman, *Jabotinsky*, vol. III, pp. 212–18.

31 At a meeting held in May or June 1937 about the partition plan, and attended by several commanders of the Irgun, Jabotinsky requested that Irgun operations avoid harm to the civilian population. See A. Altman, Testimony, JIA, 71-13-2, p. 2; Niv, *The Irgun*, vol. II, p. 239; Schechtman, *Jabotinsky*, vol. III, pp. 219–49; *Hayarden*, July 12, 1936. The foundation of the Irgun, as of Betar, was not initiated by Jabotinsky. It was only on December 5, 1936 that he, as president of the NZO, took a hand in nominating the commander of the Irgun.

32 Z. Jabotinsky, "Amen," in *In the Storm* (Hebrew), (E. Jabotinsky, Jerusalem, 1953), pp. 211–18; Eldad, *First Tithe*, pp. 37–9; Niv, *The Irgun*, vol. II, p. 54.

33 The Plan for Revolt and Invasion, coded letters to David Raziel, JIA, 20, 4-1/13; Schechtman, *Jabotinsky*, vol. III, pp. 250–65. Jabotinsky was extremely hesitant with regard to the mode of operation. That year he said: "Please, give me a few months more; I think I begin to see prospects for a fundamental change in my views and actions." Even after publication of the 1939 White

Paper, Jabotinsky remained undecided. He was sharply critical of the independent action of the Irgun delegation to the 21st World Zionist Congress. To the end of his days, he appears to have been in doubt as to the ability of the Irgun to operate on a large scale. At all events, he never adopted the view that British rule constituted foreign occupation. See, Y. Nedava, "Jabotinsky's Contribution to Zionist Ideology," *Kivunim* (1981), pp. 59–60; E. Lankin, *The Story of Altalena* (Hebrew), (Hadar, Tel Aviv, 1967), p. 73; Y. Yellin-Mor, *Fighters for the Freedom of Israel* (Hebrew), (Shikmona, Jerusalem, 1974), pp. 47, 49, 53–6. Yellin-Mor writes that Jabotinsky's plan was a variation of Stern's "plan of the forty thousand," a grandiose and delusory plan that called for tens of thousands of immigrants to land all along the coast, from Rosh Hanikra to Gaza, to engage the British army and defeat it. Stern himself regarded Jabotinsky's plan as a spectacular flash in the pan that was likely to destroy the Irgun as a fighting force. See Eldad, *First Tithe*, pp. 32–5; Y. Ben-Ami, *Years of Wrath, Days of Glory* (R. Speller, New York, 1982), pp. 233–5.

34 Department of Oral Documentation, Institute of Contemporary Jewry, the Hebrew University of Jerusalem (henceforth ICJ). Testimonies by Y. Meridor, January 8, 1966, pp. 19–21; Y. Bader, March 3, 1968, pp. 3–6. In Meridor's view, Jabotinsky would have remained the Irgun's supreme commander, proclaimed the revolt, and become head of the provisional government. Meridor confirms, however, that Jabotinsky protested against attacks on women and children.

35 See also speech by Yermiyahu Halperin, fourth Betar world convention, Halperin related that Jabotinsky asked him to lobby for a Jewish battalion in the French army, but the British objected. His efforts to the same end in Canada and Norway were likewise fruitless. See Schechtman, *Jabotinsky*, vol. III, pp. 265–71. Early in September 1939, Jabotinsky wrote to the British prime minister declaring that the Jews of the world would stand by the democracies; see Z. Jabotinsky, *The Jewish War Front* (Hebrew), (T. Kopp, Jerusalem, 1940), p. 150; for an English translation see Z. Jabotinsky, *The Jewish War Front* (George Allen and Unwin, London, 1940). All references are to the Hebrew version.

36 Begin, *White Nights*, pp. 32, 54; Silver, *Begin*, p. 20; see also, Haber, *Menachem Begin*, p. 42. Begin spent some time with Jabotinsky during the turbulent election campaign of 1933 to the WZO; he also accompanied Jabotinsky when he met the mother of Abraham Stavsky, who was accused of assassinating Arlosoroff; see also, an interview with Begin, *Yediot Aharonot*, October 24, 1980.

37 Eldad, *First Tithe*, p. 21.

38 Id., "Between Reversal and Revolution" *Ha'umma*, 2/54 (1978), pp. 170–81; H. Canaan, *Ha'aretz*, August 2, 1978; A. Ben-Hurin, *Ha'aretz*, June 27, 1966. Ben Hurin criticized Begin's policy on Germany and wondered whether Jabotinsky would have led Herut "on the path followed by Menachem Begin and his colleagues all these years." He pointed out that of six members of the last world presidium of the NZO only two were members of Herut.

39 Y. Bader, *The Knesset and I* (Hebrew), (Edanim, Jerusalem, 1979), pp. 282–7.

According to Bader, in spite of Begin's efforts to emulate his mentor, the difference was very great. Begin's world was "narrower, more centralized, less variegated than Jabotinsky's spiritual world." At root, Jabotinsky was a rationalist, whereas "Begin's rationalism gives way to his profound, almost mystical, faith." In Bader's view, Jabotinsky's advocacy of individual freedom and individualism took preference over Begin's sense of order and duty.

40 Z. Jabotinsky, "Story of My Life" in *Autobiography* (Hebrew), (E. Jabotinsky, Jerusalem, 1958), pp. 18–21. On Jabotinsky's atheism, see E. Jabotinsky, *My Father, Ze'ev Jabotinsky* (Hebrew), (Steimatzky, Tel Aviv, 1980), pp. 29, 95–106. See also M. Begin, "Nationality and Nationalism," *Ma'ariv*, April 7, 1972; for Jabotinsky's will, see Z. Jabotinsky, *Memoirs of my Contemporaries* (Hebrew), (E. Jabotinsky and Amihai, Jerusalem, n.d). pp. 17–18.

41 R. Wohl, *The Generation of 1914* (Harvard University Press, Cambridge Mass., 1979).

42 See ch. 6.

43 Bader, *The Knesset and I*, pp. 282–3. Bader writes that to understand Begin it is necessary to recognize his profound wish to resemble Jabotinsky – as orator, writer and mentor of his generation, and also to be aware of the significance to him of the Betar oath. In the course of time, Bader writes, people gave up asking what Jabotinsky would have done, because "the answer would always be the answer of the questioner himself"; B. Akzin, "His Profile", *Ha'umma*, 61–2 (1980), p. 372. Akzin writes, referring to Begin that there are those who have made the concepts of chivalry and dignity absurd.

44 See A. A. Abrahams, "When Beneš Met Jabotinsky," p. 3, JIA P2, "He found a great difficulty in coming to the point at which one asked for something and concretized the discussion."

45 Jabotinsky, having been disarmed on Storrs' orders, undertook to present himself for detention as soon as he had completed a number of private matters. Begin, having learned that he was under surveillance, did not flee from Vilna. Jabotinsky, in refusing a pardon and insisting on complete exoneration before his release from prison, served as a model for Begin in his refusal to leave the Polish army and proclaim the revolt until his formal discharge.

46 Jabotinsky, "Story of my Life," pp. 41–3; in a similar vein, like most of the men who enlisted in the Jewish legion Jabotinsky regarded the experience as a splendid adventure. How different from the sentiments of his contemporaries who fought in the trenches. Jabotinsky's heroic view of history remained unaffected by the First World War.

47 Ibid., pp. 25, 36; Begin, *In the Underground*, vol. I, pp. 57–8.

48 See also Schechtman, *Jabotinsky*, vol. II, 292–301.

Chapter 3 The Revisionist Inheritance

1 See Y. Shavit, "Ze'ev Jabotinsky: Between Fire and Water" *Ha'umma*, 63/1 (1981), pp. 60–77.

2 Up until the end of the 1940s, *Hamashkif*, the Revisionist newspaper,

continued to carry the heading "With the permanent participation of Ze'ev Jabotinsky."

3 On the development of the rift between Paris and London, see J. B. Schechtman, Y. Benari, *History of the Revisionist Movement* (Hadar, Tel Aviv, 1970), pp. 249–52. See also A. Remba, *With Jabotinsky* (Hebrew), (Tel Aviv, 1943), pp. 122–39; B. Akzin, Testimony, ICJ, August 7, 1967.

4 Schechtman, *Jabotinsky*, vol. II, pp. 203–8.

5 Y. Weinshal (Testimony, ICJ, October 27, 1966) claims that the party in Palestine constantly pressed Jabotinsky to leave the WZO. B. Weinstein (Testimony, ICJ, April 22, 1977) claims that Jabotinsky was not acquainted with the political reality in Palestine and was fed second-hand information.

6 Schechtman, *Jabotinsky*, vol. II, p. 226. In the manifesto Jabotinsky proclaimed: "I, the President of the World Union of Zionist Revisionists, do announce that from this day on I personally assume the management of the union and of all the affairs of the world movement. The activities of the existing central institutions of the world movement are hereby ceased."

7 At the Eighteenth Zionist Congress, the balance of forces was 7 delegates for the moderate faction, 45 for the movement headed by Jabotinsky; see B. Lubotzky, *The Revisionist Zionist Organization and Betar* (Hebrew), (Hasifriya Hazionist Haqetana, Jerusalem, 1946), pp. 46–7. About 713,000 voters participated in a referendum among Zionist Revisionist members and in the elections for the founding congress of the NZO – about 450,000 in Poland, and only 26,000 in Palestine. Proportionally, the highest support for secession was in Palestine – about 98 percent; see Y. Shavit, *Revisionism in Zionism* (Hebrew), (Yariv and Hadar, Tel Aviv, 1978), p. 98; Ben-Yerucham, *Book of Betar*, vol. II, pp. 472–4.

8 See A. Propes, Testimony, ICJ, April 5, 1977, pp. 17–18; B. Weinstein, Testimony, ICJ, April 22, 1977, pp. 7, 21–2; Y. Weinshal, Testimony, ICJ, January 6, 1967, pp. 8–9. Weinshal reports that Jabotinsky faced the choice of losing the support of Betar and Brit Hahayal, who were the majority, or of remaining with the moderate faction headed by Grossman, who controlled the movement's organization and finances.

9 Lubotzky, *The Revisionist Zionist Organization*, pp. 15–16; Niv, *The Irgun*, vol. III, pp. 184, 193–4. See also *Ha'umma*, 2 (1974), pp. 199–206.

10 *Political Zionism* (Hebrew), (Netzivut Betar, Tel Aviv, 1939). The political principles of Revisionism are here given a bold and militant formulation.

11 See Z. Jabotinsky, "Call to Youth," *Ha'aretz*, November 3, 1926, also appears in: Y. Nedava, *Ze'ev Jabotinsky: The Man and his Teachings* (Hebrew), (Maarachot, Tel Aviv, 1980) pp. 121–6; the statement was made by Jonas Lesser (1932).

12 Z. Jabotinsky, "The Betar Idea" (Hebrew), in his *On the Road to the State*, pp. 307–8; Ben-Yerucham, *Book of Betar*, vol. I, pp. 8–37; Shavit, *Revisionism in Zionism*, pp. 106–11.

13 On the development of different tendencies within Betar and the debates about its status, see Ben-Yerucham, *Book of Betar*, vol. I, pp. 25–33, 115–24, 173–7, 233–7, 345–53, 438–9; Schechtman, Benari, *History of the Revisionist Movement*, pp. 338–46; Lubotzky, *The Revisionist Zionist Organization*, pp. 15–16. On the

beginnings of Betar's growth see A. Propes, Testimony, ICJ, April 5, 1977; also Ben Yerucham, *Book of Betar*, vol. I, pp. 136–45 and vol. II, 156–68; Shavit, *Revisionism in Zionism*, pp. 109–10; on the conflicting interests of Betar and the Irgun see H. Kook, Testimony, ICJ, September 26, 1968, p. 7. Begin, Yellin-Mor, and Epstein comprised a group that opposed Propes's leadership; see Eldad, *First Tithe*, p. 16; B. Lubotzky, Testimony, JIA, L-16. Lubotzky states that during his visit to Riga, Jabotinsky was highly critical of the Irgun's "only thus" symbol and slogan and contended that the Irgun and the party were conducting intrigues against him and were deceitful to him. If they didn't stop that, he said, "I'll beat them down like Grossman." See also E. J. Tavin, *The Second Front: The Irgun Zvai Leumi in Europe, 1946–1948* (Hebrew), (Ron, Tel Aviv, 1973), pp. 28, 80–3, 120–1. When the Irgun later set up the Diaspora Staff in Europe, disagreements between it and the Betar leadership came to the fore. These continued until the state was established and the Irgun dismantled. In the end, Betar was incorporated into the Herut movement; see also E. Jabotinsky, Testimony, ICJ, August 29, 1968, pp. 1–7.

14 A. Altman, Testimony, ICJ, December 18, 1966, p. 17; see also B. Weinstein, Testimony, ICJ, April 22, 1977, pp. 18–19; Shavit, *Revisionism in Zionism*, p. 97; E. Jabotinsky, *My Father, Ze'ev Jabotinsky*, pp. 141–4.

15 On the party in the Yishuv during the 1930s see: Shavit, *Revisionism in Zionism*, pp. 71, 82–6, 91–3, 115.

16 From the testimonies of the party leaders it seems there was a three-part structure composed of a moderate wing close to Altman and in part to the Hebrew State party headed by Grossman; a central faction, which up until the mid-1930s included most of the executive; and a radical wing headed by Abba Achimeir. Jabotinsky attached little importance to the party in Palestine and wanted it to serve primarily as a rear for diplomatic activity. See Y. Weinshal, Testimony, ICJ, October 27, 1966, pp. 2–3, 14 and January 6, 1967, pp. 1–6; A. Altman, Testimony, ICJ, January 14, 1966, pp. 1–2; *Hatzahar* (Hebrew), a one-issue Revisionist newspaper, July 22, 1940; Shavit, *Revisionism in Zionism*, pp. 71, 87–8.

17 Z. Jabotinsky, letter dated July 28, 1940, JIA, P 8 (A. Altman).

18 On the differences of view between New York and London, see the letter by Benyamin Akzin to A. Abrahams right after Jabotinsky's death (August 8, 1940, JIA, P 15, B. Akzin); also B. Akzin, Testimony, ICJ, August 30, 1967. Looking back, Akzin claimed that after Jabotinsky's death he saw no further point in the existence of the NZO and supported transfer of the center to Palestine. See further undated detailed document, JIA, P 2, A. Abrahams; S. Katz, *Day of Fire* (Hebrew), (Karni, Tel Aviv, 1966), pp. 128–9.

19 JIA, P 15, B. Akzin.

20 Schechtman, *Jabotinsky*, vol. III, pp. 163–4. In a cable to the committee of delegates on May 21, 1940, Jabotinsky wrote: "If the homeland enters veritable war conditions, let the majority bear responsibility and ensure the unity of the Yishuv except if the partition scheme is revived or actions are taken that are liable to harm the national future of the homeland."

21 *Hamashkif*, April 23, 1944; on the party's positions towards the end of the war and afterwards, see *Hamashkif*, August 27, 1944, memorandum sent by the

NZO to the conference of the Allies in New York; *Bulletin of the Central Executive* (Hebrew), issued by the Zionist Revisionist Union in Palestine, Passover 1947; the party platform at the Twenty-Second Zionist Congress and the program of the World Zionist Revisionist Union, Paris 1947, H. Merchavya, *A Homeland: A Collection of Documents* (Hebrew), (Levy, Jerusalem, 1949), pp. 448–55.

22 See Schechtman, *Jabotinsky*, vol. III, pp. 140–50, 160–5; B. Akzin, Testimony, ICJ, August 7, 1966, pp. 16–17. It appears that Jabotinsky refused to return to the WZO without preliminary conditions. He did, however, allow those close to him who opposed him on this to work for unification. Jabotinsky modified his positions after the Second World War erupted, and especially after the German assault on the West in May 1940. On May 18, 1940, he sent a telegram to Weizmann, Ben-Gurion, and Ruttenberg in which he called for joint consultations and the establishment of a united Jewish front.

23 On the agreement of December 20, 1940, see Lubotzky, *The Revisionist Zionist Organization*, pp. 66–9; A. Altman, Testimony, ICJ, November 14, 1966, p. 11; A. Shapira, *Berl* (Hebrew) 2 vols. (Am Oved, Tel Aviv, 1980), vol. II, pp. 586–612; Schechtman, *Jabotinsky*, vol. III, 248–9; Katz, *Day of Fire*, p. 138; B. Akzin, Testimony, ICJ, August 30, 1967.

24 A. Altman, Testimony, ICJ, November 14, 1966, pp. 22–3; December 4, 1966, pp. 6, 16–18; December 18, 1966, p. 4. Altman was for unification of all factions of the Revisionist right, a return to the WZO, and participation in a provisional government. See also id., JIA, P 8, hand-written document spelling out the reasons for returning to the WZO; testimony signed "Gera" (apparently Yellin-Mor), on a talk held with Altman (Testimony, JIA, A 3–13, A. Altman, under the heading "On the Future of the Movement"). Altman criticized the leaders of the undergrounds, especially Begin, for their unwillingness to cooperate in the unification of the movement. It should be noted that about 70 percent of the membership of the Zionist Revisionists voted for return to the WZO; Y. Weinshal, Testimony, ICJ, January 6, 1967, pp. 15, 18, 23, 25; April 26, 1967, p. 4. Weinshal was opposed to returning to the WZO. See also Niv, *The Irgun*, vol. III, pp. 62–5; *Bulletin of the Central Executive*, Union of Zionist Revisionists, August 1948.

25 On the Revisionist elite, see the comprehensive study by M. Lissak, *The Elites of the Jewish Community in Palestine* (Hebrew), (Am Oved, Tel Aviv, 1981).

26 See also Ben-Yerucham, *Book of Betar*, vol. I, pp. 136, 183, 409–10; Shavit, *Revisionism in Zionism*, pp. 17–19, 73, 79, 169, 197.

27 See *Days of Trial and Struggle* (Hebrew), (Tel Hai Fund Executive, Tel Aviv, 1945); also the announcement of the political office of the presidium of the NZO on October 13, 1944, and A. Altman's press conference on October 30, 1944, JIA, P 8.

28 Y. Berman, Testimony, ICJ, April 10, 1968, p. 12; Y. Weinshal, Testimony, ICJ, January 6, 1967, pp. 18–21, 26–7; A. Altman, Testimony, ICJ, October 9, 1966, p. 9.

29 A. Altman, Testimony, ICJ, October 9, 1966, pp. 1–4. Altman viewed the period of Raziel – whom he helped be selected as Irgun commander and

preferred to Stern – as the last period of satisfactory cooperation between the party and the Irgun; A. Altman, Testimony, ICJ, November 14, 1966, pp. 7–9, 15–16; id., Testimony, JIA, A 13-2. Altman claims that Jabotinsky ruled that decisions would be made jointly by the head of the committee of delegates, the commander of Betar, and the commander of the Irgun; id., Testimony, ICJ, December 4, 1966, pp. 4–5; H. Kook, Testimony, ICJ, September 26 and November 7, 1968. Kook called the Irgun a "national liberation movement with a military arm"; see also E. Jabotinsky, Testimony, ICJ, August 18, 1968, pp. 12–16.

30 See also S. Ben-Ami, "The Protocols of the Irgun Command" (Hebrew), *Hatzionut* (University of Tel Aviv and Hakibbutz Hameuhad, 1975), vol. IV, pp. 391–440; Katz, *Day of Fire*, pp. 165–6; Niv, *The Irgun*, vol. II, pp. 184–5; Schechtman, *Jabotinsky*, vol. III, p. 241. Jabotinsky denied that the Irgun was authorized to conduct political affairs, especially outside of Palestine.

31 Y. Meridor, Testimony, ICJ, September 1965, pp. 4–8; January 8, 1966, pp. 12–13; January 29, 1966, pp. 21–3; February 12, 1966, pp. 20–1; id., Testimony, JIA, M 4, February 8, 1966, p. 2. During the Meridor period, the party still had some control over the Irgun, especially on the financial plane. Meridor was forced to accept the establishment of a supervisory committee composed of representatives of the party, Betar, and the Irgun; see also Y. Bader, Testimony, ICJ, March 3, 1968, p. 5; E. Lankin, Testimony, ICJ, January 13, 1965, p. 7.

32 Also in this group were Schoffman, Yuniczman, Yutan, and Bukspan. See A. Altman, Testimony, ICJ, December 4, 1966, pp. 4–8; Y. Bader, Testimony, ICJ, December 16, 1967, p. 9; December 18, 1967, p. 13; February 28, 1968, p. 1; March 3, 1968, p. 3. Bader claims that he was coopted to the party center on Begin's initiative. Begin was interested in a link to the party, as long as the party was controlled by the activist wing.

33 Shavit, *Open Season*, pp. 43–6, 52–6. Between June and August 1940 most of the Irgun command headed by Stern left; E. Lankin, Testimony, ICJ, January 13, 1965, February 18, 1965; Lankin, *Altalena*, pp. 52–4, 71–7; Y. Meridor, Testimony, ICJ, February 12, 1966, pp. 1–14; January 29, 1966, pp. 5–17; October 1965, pp. 17–23; Testimony, JIA, M-4, pp. 1–2 (Meridor stresses the negative attitude towards Jabotinsky within Lehi); he was called, inter alia, "Hindenburg" and "Petain"). Y. Bader, Testimony, ICJ, March 3, 1968, p. 8; S. Katz, Testimony, JIA, K-1, p. 2.

34 See "Zionism of Construction, Political Zionism, and the Freedom Fight," Kislev 1944, *Lehi Writings*, vol. I, pp. 258–62, "Some Thoughts of a Hebrew Revolutionary," Adar 1944, ibid., pp. 477–9; Y. Meridor, Testimony, ICJ, September 1965, p. 19; Schechtman, *Jabotinsky*, vol. III, pp. 235–6.

35 See Niv, *The Irgun*, vol. I, pp. 168–9; Eldad, *First Tithe*, pp. 65, 103; A. Altman, Testimony, ICJ, October 9, 1966, pp. 3–12.

36 Eldad, *First Tithe*, pp. 115–18.

37 Yellin-Mor, *Fighters for the Freedom of Israel*, pp. 146, 177–8, 261–4.

38 Ibid., pp. 178–80, 230–45, 270–3. According to Yellin-Mor, Begin also wanted to replace the terms "foreign rule" and "British imperialism" with the neutral concept "reign of oppression." Speaking of Begin, Yellin-Mor said,

"From my long acquaintance with him, I know that he has a very high regard for his power of judgment, and that arguments of the other – especially in the political realm – penetrate his consciousness slowly and belatedly", see also the article by D. Margalit, *Ha'aretz*, February 11, 1983, which contains a fragment from Yellin-Mor's manuscript that was omitted from the book: "He [Begin] imagines himself standing on a high hill, carrying his utterances to those at its foot, whose eyes are uplifted to him. If they gaze at him with enthusiasm and admiration, he gives the one who so gazes a fatherly caress. He whose eyes express wonder or doubt, or even a sense of a bitter taste – that person is no longer his friend; and whoever is not his friend is considered an enemy."

39 Eldad, *First Tithe*, pp. 285–90.
40 Letter by Begin to the Lehi leadership, September 3, 1944, JIA, P 20 2/6; also his letter of June 11, 1946, K 18/2/2/1, to E. J. Tavin; Ben-Ami, The Protocols of the Irgun Command, meetings of September 19 and November 9. After the assassination of Lord Moyne, the Irgun command decided to end its contacts with Lehi; see Yellin-Mor, *Fighters for the Freedom of Israel*, pp. 148–50, 455–9; Eldad, *First Tithe*, pp. 326–7; N. Yellin-Mor, Testimony, ICJ, December 4, 1970; Y. Bader, Testimony, ICJ, December 16, 1967, p. 13; Tavin, *The Second Front*, pp. 132–3.
41 See E. Jabotinsky, Testimony, ICJ, August 29, 1968, pp. 11–12; Y. Ben-Ami, *Years of Wrath*, pp. 190–3.
42 See also Niv, *The Irgun*, vol. III, pp. 176–216; Tavin, *The Second Front*, pp. 78–9. Tavin was sent to Europe in part to reestablish contact with the HCNL and to see if it would accept the Irgun's authority. Beginning in November 1947 the Irgun's Diaspora Staff was headed by E. Lankin, and later by Y. Meridor.
43 Other central activists of the HCNL were Aryeh Ben-Eliezer, Yitzhak Ben-Ami, Eri Jabotinsky, and Yermiyahu Halperin. See Tavin, *The Second Front*, pp. 28–34; Niv, *The Irgun*, vol. IV, pp. 124–48, vol. V, 176–206, vol. VI, 164–70; Katz, *Day of Fire*, pp. 43–5, 161–4; E. Jabotinsky, *My Father, Ze'ev Jabotinsky*, p. 135; H. Kook, Testimony, ICJ, November 2, 1968, p. 2. It should be noted that the committee operated in the United States despite the objections of the Zionist Executive. For a nonflattering view of the HCNL see P. J. Barani, *The Department of State in the Middle East, 1919–1945* (University of Pennsylvania Press, Philadelphia, 1978), pp. 286–7; also J. Agassi, *Religion and Nationality* (Hebrew), (Papyrus, University of Tel Aviv, 1984), pp. 96–124.
44 JIA, H 4/1/1.
45 Proposal for the Creation of the Hebrew Republic of Palestine, October 23, 1947, JIA, H 4/1/7. See also Hillel Kook's letter of April 2, 1945 to Dr. Chaim Weizmann (JIA, H 4/1/7), in which he expresses a readiness for some cooperation with the Zionist Executive; *Answer*, May 2, November 28, December 5, 1947.
46 See Tavin, *The Second Front*, pp. 121–30; Katz, *Day of Fire*, pp. 232–40. The Irgun command wanted to send Katz to set up an Irgun representation to replace the HCNL. This was opposed by the Diaspora Staff. Tavin claims

that the Irgun received $30,000 directly from the HCNL. Merlin cites a
figure of $1 million as the HCNL's expenditure for the Irgun; see transcript
of HCNL's deliberations on May 8, 1944 (JIA, H 4/1/2); also H. Kook,
Testimony, ICJ, November 7, 1968, p. 11. According to Kook, when the
HCNL ceased its activities, there was $0.5 million in its coffers in
Switzerland. A breakdown listing of the HCNL expenses in 1946 shows that
more than half of its funds went for illegal immigration and the rescue of Jews,
and only a quarter for propaganda and activities on behalf of the Irgun.
According to Katz (Testimony, JIA, K-1, pp. 3–4), $450,000 was available to
the HCNL for arms procurements.
47 JIA, K 4-1/14.
48 JIA, K 18/2/2/1, 21 Shvat 1948.
49 JIA, K 18/2/2/1, June 6, 1947.
50 On relations between the Irgun and the HCNL see the exchange of letters
between the Diaspora Staff in Paris and Shmuel Merlin: letters to Merlin on
December 25, 30, 1947, and Merlin's letters on December 27, 1947 and
March 15, 1948, and a letter in April of that year, JIA, K 18/2/98. Merlin
complained that his mission was not defined and also about the manner of
his appointment in place of Kook. See also Y. Bader, Testimony, ICJ,
December 16, 1967, pp. 15–16; March 3, 1968, p. 12; E. Lankin,
Testimony, ICJ, February 18, 1965; S. Katz, Testimony, JIA, K-1, June 21,
1957. According to Katz, the HCNL's activity became crucial after 1946,
when the Irgun stepped up its operations and American journalists arrived
in Palestine. See also H. Kook, Testimony, ICJ, September 26, October 3,
November 2, 1968. According to Kook, he was sent by the Irgun to the
United States in 1939. Up until Jabotinsky's death it was feared that he
would not allow the Irgun to undertake independent activity; A. Ben-
Eliezer, Testimony, JIA, B-2 November 8, 1961, pp. 3–5; February 9, 1966,
pp. 1–3; Y. Weinshal, Testimony, ICJ, April 26, 1967, pp. 5–6, 14–15.
Weinshal backed Hillel Kook. In his view, Menachem Begin did not have
an overall political program and was opposed to the idea of a Jewish
government in exile.
51 JIA, K 4-1/14. See also Tavin, *The Second Front*, pp. 286–8.
52 Begin's letters of June 11, 1946 (JIA, K 18/2/2/1), June 14, 1946, and
May 24, 1946 (JIA, K 4-1/14).
53 JIA, K 18-2/8/10, December 4, 1947.
54 JIA, H 4-1/7. Letter to Chaim Weizmann, April 2, 1945, pp. 17–18. In this
letter Kook raised the possibility that Weizmann could head this body if he
were to cease being a British subject. See also JIA, K 18/2/2/1, letter dated
June 6, 1947, and H. Kook, Testimony, ICJ, November 7, 1968, p. 10.
55 JIA, K 18-1/8/10. Letters dated December 3 and 4, 1947.
56 See especially Lankin's letters from Paris to Hillel Kook, November 10,
December 27, 1947, January 5 1948. In a letter to Lankin in which Kook
clarified his positions, he wrote, "I can't be surprised any more by BD
[Begin]." see also Ben-Ami, *Years of Wrath*, pp. 468–77.
57 JIA, K 18-2/2/1, June 11, 1946 (apparently to E. J. Tavin); See also, Tavin,
The Second Front, pp. 110–13.

58 See Tavin, *The Second Front*, pp. 125–7; Begin's letter to Hillel Kook, 22 Tammuz 1947.

59 JIA, K 18-2/8/10, letter of December 4, 1947; see also Katz, *Day of Fire*, pp. 232–9; Niv, *The Irgun*, vol. V, pp. 206–7.

60 Tavin, *The Second Front*, pp. 116–20. Begin's letters to the Diaspora Staff, 7 Kislev, 1948; 24 Tevet, 1948; 11 Adar I, 1948.

61 See Tavin, *The Second Front*, pp. 236–40; Niv, *The Irgun*, vol. VI, pp. 174–6. In fact, most of the Irgun commanders were in Europe at this time.

62 See Tavin, *The Second Front*, pp. 242–50.

63 See Niv, *The Irgun*, vol. VI, pp. 172–6; A. Ben-Eliezer, Testimony, JIA, B-9, February 8, 1958; E. Jabotinsky, Testimony, ICJ, September 19, 1968, pp. 10–12. It was Eri Jabotinsky's view that Begin made a grave error in neglecting the struggle to take over the government and concentrating instead on ensuring his control of the Revisionist right.

64 *Herut*, October 20, 1948.

65 *Hamashkif*, May 17, 1948. In this speech Begin restricted his promise to "the boundaries of the independent Hebrew state," intending that the Irgun would continue its operations within Jerusalem.

66 The account that follows derives from *The Efforts to Unite Jabotinsky's Movement* (Hebrew), (World Executive, Zionist Revisionist Union, Tel Aviv, November 1948).

67 See JIA, P 20-2/1, Conclusions of the Political Committee.

68 See JIA, E 2/0/9. Urgent Consultation of the Temporary Center, August 30, 1948.

69 See JIA, P 20-2/1. Correspondence between the Herut Movement and the Zionist Revisionists. Letter to A. Abrahams, B. Weinstein, and S. Yuniczman, September 9, 1948 and Revisionists' reply on September 12, 1948; JIA, P 2 (A. Abrahams), draft without heading or date. The account is one of political usurpation by the Herut movement headed by Begin; see also Bader, *The Knesset and I*, pp. 17–21. Bader writes that the infrastructure of the new movement followed the structure of the Irgun. All the branch secretaries were from the appropriate regional division of the Irgun.

70 On the struggle between the Zionist Revisionists and the Herut movement, see the election campaign notices of the Zionist Revisionist Union, *Hamashkif*, January 24–25, 1949; *Hador*, September 28, 1949; JIA, P 59-5/9. M. Grossman, "The Revival and Continuation of the Zionist Revisionist Union," *Am U'medina*, no. 10, February 9, 1951. In a programatic article, Grossman attacked the ideological course of the Herut movement. See also the circular distributed by Grossman, JIA, P 59-5/4, *The Future of the Revisionist Movement*.

71 JIA, B/3/1/6 Betar Fourth World Convention, Tel Aviv, May 16–22, 1949.

72 JIA, E 2/0/9. Transcripts of sessions of the center and departments.

73 See Lecture by Menachem Begin at the Institute for the Study of Zionism, "From Underground to Party," November 28, 1974, JIA, P 20, Lectures 1948–1977; A. Altman, Testimony, ICJ, December 4 and 18, 1966, pp. 5–19. Altman accused Begin of thwarting the unification attempts. He also admits, however, that there was no room for two right-wing Revisionist parties.

Altman later joined Herut, Grossman joined the General Zionists; see Y. Bader, Testimony, ICJ, March 23, 1968, pp. 1–9; Y. Weinshal, Testimony, ICJ, April 26, 1967, pp. 8–10. Weinshal asserted that Begin wanted a monolithic party, and that from the outset he knew that Begin was not the man to continue Jabotinsky's line.

Chapter 4 Commander of the Irgun, 1943–1948

1 Begin, *White Nights*, pp. 223–4; Id., *The Revolt*, p. 33; Golan, Nakdimon, *Begin*, pp. 57–68; Silver, *Begin*, pp. 38–9; Y. Guttman, "Jews with the Anders Army in the Soviet Union," *Yad Vashem*, 12 (1972), pp. 171–213; N. Davies, *God's Playground: A History of Poland*, 2 vols. (Clarendon Press, Oxford, 1981), vol. II, pp. 484–7.

2 Begin, *The Revolt*, p. 33; an Interview by N. Bethell, December 20, 1978, *Israel State Archives* (henceforth, ISA), 16/72, P/A, 899.

3 JIA P 20/1 (1); Haber, *Menachem Begin*, p. 87.

4 Niv, *The Irgun*, vol. III, pp. 273–7.

5 Y. Meridor, Testimony, JIA M-4, February 8, 1966; Interview, *Yediot Aharonot*, January 5, 1979.

6 Id., Testimony, ICJ, January 8, 1966; Golan, Nakdimon, *Begin*, p. 67; D. Margalit, "Menachem Begin, Yesterday and Today," *Kol Ha'ir*, September 2, 1983.

7 Lev-Ami, The Protocols of the Irgun Command, pp. 407–8, n. 86; D. Margalit, "The Truth Has Not Yet Been Written," *Ha'aretz*, August 6, 1981; S. Nakdimon, "Members of the IZL, [Irgun] Command talk about the Commander." *Herut*, August 2, 1963.

8 Lankin, *Altalena*, pp. 64–6; id., Testimony, ICJ, January 1965.

9 Y. Bader, Testimony, ICJ, December 6, 1967; February 28, 1968.

10 A. Altman, Testimony, ICJ, November 14, 1966, pp. 19–20; December 4 and 18, 1966; Y. Weinshal, Testimony, ICJ, April 26, 1967, pp. 5–6.

11 S. Merlin, Testimony, JIA, M-17; H. Kook, Testimony, ICJ, September 26, 1968, pp. 17–19; E. Jabotinsky, Testimony, ICJ, September 19, 1968.

12 D. Engel, "The Futile Alliance: The Revisionist Movement and the Polish Government in Exile, 1939–1945" (Hebrew), in *Hatzionut* (University of Tel Aviv and Hakibbutz Hameuhad, 1986), vol. XI, pp. 333–59; Letter to the Polish Army requesting Begin's release from service, JIA, P 20, 1 (1); S. Korborsky "Unknown chapter in the Life of Menachem Begin and Irgun Zvai Leumi," *East European Quarterly*, 13 (1979), pp. 373–9.

13 A. Ben-Eliezer, JIA, P 33/4; id., Recollections of the Underground period, JIA, P 33/1; id., "Twenty Years Before," *Herut*, August 2, 1963. See also Golan, Nakdimon, *Begin*, pp. 67–8; Yellin-Mor, *Fighters for the Freedom of Israel*, pp. 175–6; Tavin, *The Second Front*, p. 33; Ben-Ami, *Years of Wrath*, pp. 302–12. Five regional commanders, including the commanders of Tel Aviv and Jerusalem, opposed Begin's appointment.

14 M. Begin, JIA, P 20 1 (1), Testimony, B-38; Golan, Nakdimon, *Begin*, p. 66; see also Begin, *The Revolt*, p. 101.

15 M. Begin, JIA P 20 1 (1). It is not clear what Begin means when he writes that "Yuniczman worked to get me released for the sake of activity in the legal movement; whereas Kahan and Ben-Eliezer did so to enable me to take command of the Irgun Zvai Leumi."

16 Eldad, *First Tithe*, pp. 14, 38.

17 Ben-Yerucham, *Book of Betar*, vol. I, pp. 280–2, 441–2; A. Propes, Testimony, ICJ, April 5, 1977.

18 *Report of Activities*, Betar Netzivut in Poland (Hebrew), June 1936 (JIA); Bader, *The Knesset and I*, p. 285; A. Propes, Testimony, ICJ, April 5, 1977, p. 26; Y. Bader, "What Motivated Begin," *Ma'ariv*, August 31, 1983.

19 Report by Shalom Rosenfeld to the Betar Command in London (Lodz, June 29, 1937), JIA.

20 See Y. Bader, Testimony, ICJ, December 18, 1967, p. 20.

21 On the characteristics of the fanatic revolutionary see M. Rejai, *The Strategy of Political Revolution* (Doubleday and Company, New York, 1973), pp. 29–30.

22 According to Jabotinsky's poem *Neder*, this included the imperatives of Zion, monism, Hebrew, enlistment, Legion, Hadar (dignity), and obedience.

23 Abraham Stern arrived earlier at a position where a break from the party seemed a necessity.

24 See Begin, *The Revolt*, p. 57.

25 This demand, which was central in the proclamation of the revolt, later became a bone of contention between the Irgun command and the HCNL.

26 M. Begin, P 20 1 (1) Testimony, JIA B-38. See also Ben-Ami, *Years of Wrath*, pp. 302–3; Begin, *The Revolt*, pp. 58, 101; Y. Meridor, Testimony, ICJ, January 8, 1966, pp. 11–12, 23–7; A. Lankin, Testimony, ICJ February 18, 1965, p. 15; Y. Bader, Testimony, ICJ, February 28, 1968, pp. 8–9; id., December 16, 1967, pp. 8–9; Tavin, *The Second Front*, p. 18; A. Even, "The Ideology Underlying the Irgun's Proclamation of Revolt and Its Confrontation With Reality," *Ha'umma* 2 (1974), p. 217.

27 See Begin, *The Revolt*, pp. 36–9, 63–3. On p. 53 he writes, "Certainly even without the blood-soaked events in Europe, even without the bloody 'consistency' of British policy in Palestine, one day or another, in one form or another, the Hebrew revolt against foreign rule in the Land of Israel would break out one day . . ." In 1942–3, Begin published a number of articles in *Hamadrikh* under the pen name M. Ben-Zeev in which he gave careful attention to some aspects of his conception that he thought might lead to revolt: M. Ben-Ze'ev [Begin] "The Main Question," 2 (April 14, 1943), pp. 224–6; "In Days of Perplexity," 3 (May 16, 1943), pp. 4–7; "Regime of Rescue," 3 (November 9, 1943), pp. 87–93; "Sketch of a Zionist Plan," 2 (October 1942). Begin surmised that the Second World War might end in 1944, and in the last of these articles he set the summer of 1943 as the final date for getting into action. See also Y. Shavit, "Begin's way to the Revolt (1938–1944)" in *The Mythologies of the Zionist Right*, pp. 125–52. Shavit's conclusion that Begin had not proposed a military revolt is implausible.

28 Begin, *The Revolt*, pp. 58, 98–9; id., "Their Wars and Our War," *Herut*, May 8, 1953.

29 See Begin, *In the Underground*, as follows: "We Shall Call For Revolt" vol. I,

pp. 81–98; "The Hebrew Liberation Army" (March 1947), vol. III, pp. 21–36; Broadcast, June 23, 1946, vol. II, pp. 151–4.

30 See Begin, *In the Underground*, as follows: "We Believe" (1944), vol. I, pp. 46, 48–9; "Herzl and Jabotinsky" (July 25, 1944), vol. I, pp. 57–60; "Ways of War and Underground Morality" (November 1946), vol. II, pp. 268–72; "Order of the Day for November 14" (November 12, 1947), vol. IV, pp. 62–3; "Terror and War" (December 1946), vol. II, pp. 304–5; "The Ethics of the War of Liberation" (April, 1945), vol. I, pp. 218–20. See also id., "Goal and Method in Revolutionary Warfare," *Ma'ariv*, March 16, 1972.

31 See Begin, *In the Underground*, as follows: "A Plan For the Fighting Nation" (July 18, 1946), vol. II, pp. 137–9; "Defeatists, Beat Your Breasts" (May 1947), vol. III, pp. 105–6; "Dangerous Haste" (October 1947), vol. IV, pp. 46–7. See also id., "The Strategy and Tactics of the Revolt," *Herut*, May 13, 1949.

32 Id., *The Revolt*, pp. 69, 72, 85; "Report by Moshe Sneh on His Talk With Menachem Begin," October 9, 1944, in *History of the Hagana* (Hebrew) 3 vols. (Am Oved, Tel Aviv, 1954–1972), vol. III, p. 1888.

33 Begin, *The Revolt*, pp. 63–75, 91–100.

34 H. Kook, Testimony, ICJ, October 3, 1968, pp. 22–4. Kook contends that a detailed conception of the revolt was formulated in the United States and brought to Begin's attention by Ben-Eliezer. He adds that there was no point in proclaiming the revolt in the United States.

35 See Y. Ratosh, *The Beginning of Days* (Hebrew), (Hadar, Tel Aviv, 1982), pp. 25–7.

36 Yellin-Mor, *The Fighter For the Freedom of Israel*, pp. 279–80.

37 Eldad, *First Tithe*, pp. 28, 38, 112, 255.

38 M. Begin, "Only a Nation That Fights Wins Independence," September 15, 1944, *In the Underground*, vol. I. pp. 110–16.

39 Begin, Lecture to the Institute for the Study of Zionism, November 28, 1974, pp. 1–2; Begin–Sneh talk, October 9, 1944, *History of the Hagana*; A. Paglin, Testimony, ICJ, November 27, 1970, pp. 22–3.

40 Begin, *The Revolt*, pp. 190–2. See also Shavit, *Open Season*, p. 68.

41 See Sneh–Begin talk, *History of the Hagana*, vol. III, pp. 1889, 1892; Begin, *The Revolt*, pp. 285–7; Lev-Ami, The Protocols of the Irgun Command, p. 437.

42 See *History of the Hagana*, vol. III, pp. 1540–58. At the beginning of the War of Independence, the Irgun numbered about 2,800 men, less than a quarter of them in combat units. According to a Hagana estimate, the Irgun had two mortars, 30 machine guns, 180 rifles, 100 submachine guns, 200 pistols and several hundred grenades and explosives; U. Milstein, "Etzel Against Begin," *Ha'aretz*, September 29, 1978; A. Paglin, Testimony, ICJ, November 27, 1970, pp. 1–2.

43 Begin, *The Revolt*, p. 94.

44 Lev-Ami, The Protocols of the Irgun Command.

45 Sneh–Begin talk, *History of the Hagana*, vol. III, pp. 1887–93; Lev-Ami, The Protocols of the Irgun Command, p. 421. At a meeting on September 19, 1944, Begin expressed a readiness to accept Ben-Gurion as head of a committee for national liberation.

46 J. G. Granados, *The Birth of Israel* (Hebrew), (Achiasaf, Jerusalem, 1949), pp. 157–62. M. Dayan, *Story of My Life* (Hebrew), (Edanim, Jerusalem, 1976), p. 55.

47 See also Katz, *Day of Fire*, pp. 256–7.

48 "On a Meeting Between Representatives of the United Nations Organization and a Delegation from the Irgun Zvai Leumi," 28 Sivan 1947; Begin believed that Britain wanted to retain Palestine as a military base. He denigrated the military strength of the Arab states; see Begin, *The Revolt*, pp. 200–2; Golan, Nakdimon, *Begin*, pp. 170–1.

49 *Herald Tribune*, July 5, 1946 (interview conducted on March 17, 1946.)

50 Begin, *The Revolt*, pp. 409, 415; Lecture at the Institute for the Study of Zionism, November 28, 1974, p. 9; Golan, Nakdimon, *Begin*, pp. 149–50; A. Paglin, Testimony, ICJ, November 27, 1970, p. 25.

51 Silver, *Begin*, pp. 47, 63 (interviews with Y. Galili and with E. Livni). See also Golan, Nakdimon, *Begin*, pp. 107–10; Katz, *Day of Fire*, pp. 181–2; Lankin, *Altalena*, pp. 66–71, and Lankin, Testimony, ICJ, February 18, 1965; Y. Meridor, Testimony, ICJ, January 8, 1966; Haber, *Menachem Begin*, p. 199.

52 Begin estimated that only about 40 people were fully engaged in underground affairs. The Irgun was comprised of two parts – the combat force and the propaganda force. The planned units of a "revolutionary army" and naval shock units were not established. Within the combat force there was an emergency "red section," which was a sort of underground within the underground.

53 Begin, *The Revolt*, pp. 100–88. See also Katz, *Day of Fire*, p. 196. Katz estimates that the number of British casualties from Irgun operations was about 200. Between 1945 and 1948 the British suffered 338 casualties at the hands of all the Jewish undergrounds combined.

54 Golan, Nakdimon, *Begin*, p. 134; Haber, *Menachem Begin*, pp. 107, 191; Begin, lecture at the Institute for the study of Zionism, November 28, 1974, p. 5. Begin may have drawn the idea of the importance of prestige from a remark by Col. Grey, Commander of the mandate police.

55 See Begin, *White Nights*, pp. 47, 130; Golan, Nakdimon, *Begin*, p. 109; see also the way Begin is addressed in letters to him by underground prisoners quoted by him in *The Revolt*; Haber, *Menachem Begin*, p. 153. Begin talked to rank-and-file soldiers only from behind a curtain.

56 Begin, *The Revolt*, pp. 436–7, 461.

57 Id., *The Revolt*, pp. 264–5; A. Paglin, Testimony, ICJ, November 1970, pp. 7–11.

58 Golan, Nakdimon, *Begin*, pp. 76–84, 150, 184; Haber, *Menachem Begin*, pp. 178, 186, 193. Begin was opposed to executing Y. Chylewicz and Heinrich Reinhold, even though their treason was clearly established. See also Katz, *Day of Fire*, p. 225.

59 M. Begin, "The Revolt Against British Rule in the Land of Israel," *Ha'umma*, 3 (7), (1963), p. 350; Silver, *Begin*, pp. 51–6. Y. Amrami estimates that nearly half the command was opposed to Begin's position.

60 Minutes of a Meeting Between Representatives of the Irgun and Representa-

tives of the Jewish Agency and the General Hagana, October 31, 1944. JIA, K4 19/12; Begin, *The Revolt*, pp. 199, 205–11.

61 Begin, *The Revolt*, p. 292; Shavit, *Open Season*, pp. 117–19; Golan, Nakdimon, *Begin*, pp. 82–106; Lev-Ami, The Protocols of the Irgun Command, meeting of November 9, 1944. It seems that the Irgun command did not believe the Hagana would act against them. Begin expected that the Hagana would announce the beginning of actions. See also Haber, *Menachem Begin*, pp. 132–47, 195.

62 Haber, ibid., pp. 174–5, 187–8; Silver, *Begin*, pp. 79–81. Some believed that Sergeant Martin's mother was Jewish; Y. Meridor, Testimony, ICJ, January 8, 1966; Golan, Nakdimon, *Begin*, pp. 171–3. Begin wrote that the humiliation of the beating of Jewish notables in Brisk in 1920 by the Polish army was etched in his memory for his entire lifetime; Begin, *The Revolt*, pp. 318–19, 345–51, 486–92; see also N. Levitzky, *Yediot Aharonot*, April 27, 1984; *Ha'olam Hazeh*, April 17, 1985. It is difficult to determine why the Irgun was so slow in coming to Gruner's rescue. Katz, *Day of Fire*, p. 260; Begin's interview with N. Bethell, April 2, 1976, ISA, 16/72, P/A, 899; Y. Ben-Hurin, "The Hanging of the Sergents: the End," *Ma'ariv*, August 28, 1987; N. Bethell, *The Palestine Triangle* (A. Deutsch, London, 1979), pp. 338–9.

63 Begin, *The Revolt*, pp. 294–311; Golan, Nakdimon, *Begin*, pp. 115–17. Begin learned of the casualty figures from the radio; Katz, *Day of Fire*, p. 197; Silver, *Begin*, pp. 68–9; Haber, *Menachem Begin*, pp. 162–5; Bethell, *The Palestine Triangle*, pp. 240–67; A. Bullock, *Ernest Bevin: Foreign Secretary* (Oxford University Press, New York, 1985), pp. 296–300.

64 Begin, *The Revolt*, Introduction and pp. 221–3; Niv, *The Irgun*, vol. VI, p. 78–94. Irgun and Lehi members participated in the attack on Deir Yassin on April 9, 1948; Golan, Nakdimon, *Begin*, pp. 178–9; Haber, *Menachem Begin*, pp. 208–9; Silver, *Begin*, pp. 88–96.

65 G. Cohen, "British Policy on the Eve of the War of Independence," in Y. Wallach (ed.), *We Were Dreamers* (Hebrew), (Massada, Tel-Aviv, 1985), pp. 13–177; M. J. Cohen, *Palestine and the Great Powers, 1945—1948* (Princeton University Press, Princeton, 1982), pp. 90–3, 249.

66 U. Brenner, *Altalena* (Hebrew), (Hakibbutz Hameuhad, Tel Aviv, 1978), p. 20; S. Nakdimon, *Altalena* (Hebrew), (Edanim, Jerusalem, 1978), pp. 37–48; Golan, Nakdimon, *Begin*, pp. 174–7.

67 Brenner, *Altalena*, pp. 41–2. At the beginning of June 1948, the Irgun had 3,660 members; *History of the Hagana*, vol. IIIb, p. 1541, vol. IIIc, p. 1808; M. Begin, Lecture to the Institute for the Study of Zionism, November 28, 1974, p. 19; Milstein, "Etzel Against Begin."

68 Begin, *The Revolt*, pp. 427–70; Katz, *Day of Fire*, pp. 373–5, 387. Begin was so proud that he showed visitors the Irgun positions in Jaffa.

69 Nakdimon, *Altalena*, pp. 113–16.

70 *Hamashkif*, May 17, 1948; see also the appeal to Begin by *Ma'ariv* editor A. Karlibach, *Ma'ariv*, May 17, 1948.

71 Brenner, *Altalena*, pp. 44–9; Nakdimon, *Altalena*, pp. 113–16.

72 Katz, *Day of Fire*, p. 394; Nakdimon, *Altalena*, pp. 34, 54–61, 121. See also

interview with Y. Meridor, *Yediot Aharonot*, January 12, 1979; A. Ben-Eliezer, Testimony, JIA, B-9, February 8, 1958.

73 Letters by H. Kook, December 3 and 4, 1947, JIA, K18/2/8/10. The plan is also mentioned in his letter of June 6, 1947. See also Nakdimon, *Altalena*, pp. 120–1.

74 Brenner, *Altalena*, pp. 70–92; Nakdimon, *Altalena*, p. 127. The arms on the *Altalena* were bought in France. The circumstances leading to cooperation between the French government and the Irgun are not sufficiently clear. A. Ben-Eliezer (Testimony, JIA, B-9, February 8, 1958), said that the *Altalena* was intended "to break the power of the Arab League which threatened us and French security in North Africa;" Tavin, *The Second Front*, pp. 157–67, 193–7.

75 Brenner, *Altalena*, pp. 99–104; Nakdimon, *Altalena*, pp. 133–40; Lankin, *Altalena*, pp. 15–23; Tavin, *The Second Front*, pp. 215–16. From Katz's letter of June 7, 1948, Begin could have deduced that the ship would sail in a few days time. Ben-Eliezer was opposed to informing the government of the ship's impending arrival (JIA B-9, February 8, 1958). In *The Revolt* the dates of the telegrams exchanged between the command and Paris are confused. Katz apparently did not know that he could simply cable the *Altalena* from a post office in Paris. See also M. Begin, "Secession, Saison, and Altalena," *Ma'ariv*, August 13, 1971; A. Ben-Eliezer, "Around Altalena," JIA, P 33/3.

76 Lankin, *Altalena*, pp. 303–16; Begin, "Secession, saison, and Altalena".

77 Nakdimon, *Altalena*, pp. 140–4, 158–62. Begin claimed that as far he remembered, he "took no part in discussions when they entered the stage of technical implementation"; Brenner, *Altalena*, pp. 26–33, 105–16; Brenner stated that the Irgun stretched out the negotiations with the government before June until the Diaspora Staff was able to assemble the arms and men for the sailing. See also Katz, *Day of Fire*, p. 386; "Minister Galili Answering Begin's Questions," *Ma'ariv*, August 20, 1971; Y. Kenyuk, "The Last Account," *Yediot Aharonot*, August 7, 1987. Kook claims that Begin confronted Galili with unreasonable conditions.

78 Nakdimon, *Altalena*, pp. 195–99; Brenner, *Altalena*, pp. 116–19, 124. Paglin differed with Begin during the *saison* and during the attack on Jaffa. He disagreed with Begin's strategy for the deployment of the Irgun, and wanted to expand the Irgun's strength in preparation for the decisive battles coming up on the domestic and external fronts. After the war, Paglin left the Herut Movement.

79 Brenner, *Altalena*, pp. 121–8, 134–9, 163–6.

80 Nakdimon, *Altalena*, pp. 229–40; Brenner, *Altalena*, pp. 163–6. According to Nakdimon, the consultation and the decision to board the ship preceded the opening of fire. That is also so in Brenner's account; Lankin, *Altalena*, pp. 316–19. According to Lankin the consultation took place after the muster was dispersed.

81 Y. Gruenbaum, Testimony, ICJ 4 (33) B (n.d.). At one stage Gruenbaum considered boarding the ship himself to talk to Begin; R. Frister, *No Compromise* (Hebrew), (Zmora, Bitan, Tel Aviv, 1987), pp. 350–63.

82 Katz, *Day of Fire*, pp. 411–15.
83 Interview with Y. Meridor, *Yediot Aharonot*, January 12, 1979.
84 Begin, *The Revolt*, pp. 211–18. Begin thought ten battalions could have been equipped with the arms aboard the *Altalena*.
85 Nakdimon, *Altalena*, pp. 253–98, 310–11; Brenner, *Altalena*, pp. 192–3, 202, 215–40; Lankin, *Altalena*, pp. 319–24.
86 Meeting of the Herut's Central Committee, February 28, 1949, JIA E 2/0/9; Begin's address, *Hamashkif*, June 23, 1948.
87 See Nakdimon, *Altalena*, pp. 318–25; Brenner, *Altalena*, pp. 251–65, 313, 323, 328–9, 335–8; M. Bar-Zohar, *Ben-Gurion* (Hebrew), 3 vols. (Am-Oved, Tel Aviv, 1977), vol. II, pp. 776–98.
88 Niv, *The Irgun*, vol. VI, 290–300. The Irgun command was hurt by the wording of the ultimatum, which declared that they had violated the laws of the state; Katz, *Day of Fire*, p. 396; Begin, *The Revolt*, pp. 243–4; Begin, Lecture to the Institute for the Study of Zionism, November 28, 1974, p. 17. There was opposition to dismantling the Irgun at the meeting of officers at which Begin announced he would no longer be commander; Brenner, *Altalena*, pp. 344–66; Nakdimon, *Altalena*, pp. 395–9.
89 See *Knesset Proceedings* (Hebrew), May 7, 1979, pp. 2477–88. One of the most unrestrained Knesset debates took place on December 1, 1959 (*Knesset Proceedings*, pp. 825–32). Ben-Gurion accused Begin of planning and organizing an armed rebellion. Begin accused Ben-Gurion of "secretly plotting to kill and destroy." See also D. Ben-Gurion, "The State and the Irgun," *Ma'ariv*, August 27, 1971; M. Begin, "Reply to Mr. Ben-Gurion and Cabinet Minister Galili," ibid., October 1, 1971; also articles by Begin in *Ma'ariv*, August 6, 13, 20, 1971; Y. Karuz, "Why Didn't Begin Tell the Government About the *Altalena* as Soon as It Sailed," *Yediot Aharonot*, February 25, 1972; Nakdimon, *Altalena*, pp. 467–72; Niv, *The Irgun*, vol. VI, pp. 251–78; Silver, *Begin*, pp. 97–108; Haber, *Menachem Begin*, pp. 217–23. Begin thought that the army would not dare attack the ship off the Tel Aviv shore.

Chapter 5 Leader of the Opposition, 1949–1977

1 Bader, *The Knesset and I*, pp. 17–22; Golan, Nakdimon, *Begin*, pp. 122–93; E. Jabotinsky, Testimony, ICJ, August 18, 1963.
2 The Herut Movement, Its Fundaments and Principles (Sivan, 1948), JIA, 7/7/9.
3 Menachem Begin's Programatic Lecture at the First Study Day, August 14, 1948, JIA, P 20
4 *Herut*, October 20, 22, 1948.
5 Bader, *The Knesset and I*, pp. 47–8.
6 See D. Dagan, *Ma'ariv*, December 24, 1972. The faction apparently also demanded that the party operate within the Histadrut.
7 Among those to leave were Abba Achimeir, Uri Zvi Greenberg, Wolfgang Von Weisl, and Abraham Weinshal; the Irgun commanders who left included

Amichai Paglin, Eitan Livni, Ya'acov Amrami (Yoel), Shlomo Levi, and Shmuel Katz.

8 Bader, *The Knesset and I*, pp. 47–9; Y. Bader, Testimony, ICJ, March 23, 1968; H. Canaan, "M. Begin, Leader Without Opposition," *Ha'aretz*, June 30, 1954; *Knesset Proceedings*, April 27, 1950; *Herut*, August 21, 1950; Golan, Nakdimon, *Begin*, pp. 193–223; E. Jabotinsky, Testimony, ICJ, August 8, 1963; D. Dagan, "All the Herut Splits Before the Begin–Weizman Showdown," *Ma'ariv*, December 24, 1972.

9 Herut Second National Convention, 26.2–1.3.1951, JIA, E1/27/9, E1/9/3/27; Bader, *The Knesset and I*, pp. 49–50; id., Testimony, ICJ, March 23, 1968. For the mood among Revisionist activists at that time, see the letter by A. Remba to S. Yuniczman, February 24, 1950, JIA, P 106.

10 Bader, *The Knesset and I*, pp. 56–8; id., Testimony, ICJ, March 23, 1968. Begin was depressed at the meeting with the secretary of the bar at which Bader asked to exempt him from the examinations. As far as is known, Begin was not admitted to the bar. See also Y. Sarna, "Chancellor in Sight," *Yediot Aharohot*, July 31, 1987.

11 Bader, *The Knesset and I*, pp. 101–2; Haber, *Menachem Begin*, p. 247.

12 Bader, *The Knesset and I*, pp. 89–90; M. Begin, Lecture to the Institute for the Study of Zionism, November 28, 1974, p. 14.

13 *Haboker*, April 9, 1958.

14 H. Canaan, *Ha'aretz*, June 30, 1954; A. Porat, "M. Begin: Head of the Herut Movement," *Yediot Aharonot*, February 5, 1964.

15 M. Begin, *Siege, Straits and Outlet* (Herut Movement, Tel Aviv, 1954), pp. 7–12.

16 *Herut*, February 1, 1963 (Begin's speech at the conclusion of the seventh national convention, January 22, 1963); *Haboker*, October 24, 1962, January 23, 1963; Bader, *The Knesset and I*, pp. 166–9.

17 *Herut*, December 20, 1955 (letter from Begin to Bernstein, the president of the General Zionist Federation); *Ha'aretz*, December 20, 1955.

18 *Herut*, June 2, 1957; Bader, *The Knesset and I*, pp. 109–13.

19 *Knesset Proceedings*, November 2, 1961, pp. 208.

20 *Herut*, April 6, 1961; *Haboker*, January 21, 1963; *Herut*, Oct. 18, 1964; see also A. Avneri, *The Liberal Connection* (Hebrew), (Zmora, Bitan, Tel Aviv, 1984), pp. 67–78, 84–7; *Ha'aretz*, September 26, 1982.

21 Herut Movement, platform for the fifth Knesset, 1961.

22 JIA 3/(7). "The Herut Movement–Liberal Party Bloc." Correspondence Between M. Begin and the Herut–Liberal Bloc Institutions; Y. Ben-Porat, "This is the Herut-Liberal Bloc," *Yediot Aharonot*, April 27, 1965.

23 M. Begin, "Reply to the Mapai Clown," *Herut*, November 20, 1959; *Knesset Proceedings*, February 24, 1960, pp. 720–1; May 13, 1963, pp. 1821–6, May 15, pp. 1859–60; *Haboker*, May 14, 1963; D. Horowitz, "Begin's Counterattack," *Davar*, May 16, 1963.

24 *Knesset Proceedings*, November 2, 1961; Bader, *The Knesset and I*, pp. 130–46.

25 *Knesset Proceedings*, January 12, 1966, p. 351.

26 *Herut*, Aug. 9, 1963.

27 On the crisis of 1966, see *Yediot Aharonot*, June 30, 1966; *Ha'aretz*, June 30,

1966; *Hayom*, July 3, 1966; *Ha'aretz*, September 4, 1966; *Yediot Aharonot*, September 4, 1966; Bader, *The Knesset and I*, pp. 186–90; Golan, Nakdimon, *Begin*, pp. 257–97; Avneri, *The Liberal Connection*, pp. 186–90.

28 See Silver, *Begin*, pp. 124–7; Haber, *Menachem Begin*, pp. 259–61.

29 *Ma'ariv*, March 1, 1967.

30 M. Begin, "Votes and Proposals at the UN," *Herut*, December 21, 1962.

31 Dayan, *Story of My Life*, pp. 411, 420; A. Eban, *An Autobiography* (Weidenfeld and Nicolson, London, 1984), pp. 387–8, 392, 487; Bader, *The Knesset and I*, pp. 197–8; Bar-Zohar, *Ben-Gurion*, Vol. III, 1519–47.

32 On this period, see Silver, *Begin*, pp. 130–41; Haber, *Menachem Begin*, pp. 262–85; S. Nakdimon, "What Begin is Doing in the Government," *Yediot Aharonot*, November 8, 1968; G. Cohen, "Why I Am In a National Unity Government," interview with M. Begin, *Ma'ariv*, June 20, 1969; S. Nakdimon, "The Scars of the Past Don't Affect the Present," *Yediot Aharonot*, June 12, 1969; *Ma'ariv*, May 9, 1975.

33 Y. Rabin, *Service Diary* (Hebrew), 2 vols. (Ma'ariv, Tel Aviv, 1979), vol. I, pp. 227–8.

34 Speech at a Gala Meeting of the Herut Movement and Liberal Party Centers, JIA P 20; Bader, *The Knesset and I*, pp. 198–218.

35 M. Begin, "The Wholeness of the Nation and the Wholeness of the Land," speech at the national council of the Herut movement, April 23, 1970; *Knesset Proceedings*, August 4, 1970; *Davar*, August 4, 1970; D. Margalit, "Begin's Mistake," *Ha'aretz*, August 17, 1972; Bader, *The Knesset and I*, pp. 225–7.

36 *Yediot Aharonot*, December 29, 1979.

37 E. Weizman, *The Battle for Peace* (Hebrew), (Edanim, Jerusalem, 1982), pp. 93–103; id., *Yours are the Heavens, Yours is the Earth* (Hebrew), (Ma'ariv, Tel Aviv, 1975), pp. 316, 322; Bader, *The Knesset and I*, pp. 220–1.

38 *Yediot Aharonot*, January 19, 1973; Bader, *The Knesset and I*, pp. 237–9.

39 *Ma'ariv*, *Yediot Aharonot*, December 24 and 25, 1972; *Davar*, *Ha'aretz*, December 25, 1972; *Ma'ariv*, *Yediot Aharonot*, *Ha'aretz*, December 28, 1972; *Yediot Aharonot* December 29, 1972.

40 A. Palgi, "The Mischief-Maker and the Cult," *Al Hamishmar*, December 29, 1972; M. Peled, *Ma'ariv*, December 29, 1972; M. Segal, "Begin Makes Things Easier for Labour," *Jerusalem Post*, December 26, 1972.

41 Bader, *The Knesset and I*, pp. 248–50; *Ma'ariv*, December 28, 1972.

42 Bader, *The Knesset and I*, p. 252; Haber, *Menachem Begin*, p. 292; E. Torgovnik, "Likud 1977–1981: The Consolidation of Power," in R. O. Freedman, *Israel in the Begin Era*, (Praeger, New York, 1982), pp. 7–27; U. Benziman, *Not Stopping at the Red Light* (Hebrew), (Adam, Tel Aviv, 1985), pp. 125–35; Avneri, *The Liberal Connection*, pp. 98–9.

43 Bader, *The Knesset and I*, pp. 256–7.

44 The eleventh council of the Herut Movement, September 29, 1974, JIA P 20; *Ma'ariv*, December 1, 1974; twelfth convention of the Herut Movement, January 13, 1975, JIA, P 20.

45 *Ma'ariv*, January 16, 1975.

46 M. Maisels, "Herut: It's a Long Way to Power," *Ma'ariv*, December 1, 1974; articles by Silvie Keshet in *Yediot Aharonot*, August 2, 1974, January 1, 1975.

47 *Yediot Aharonot*, April 23, 1976; January 12, 1979. Some of the creditors burst into Begin's apartment. Meridor believed that Begin's heart attack in 1977 was related to this scandal.
48 *Ma'ariv*, May 13, 1977; Haber, *Menachem Begin*, pp. 302–4.

Chapter 6 Conception of Reality

1 Begin, *White Nights*, p. 33; see also id., *The Revolt*, p. 10: "One almost entirely eliminates the objective reality within which the prisoner lives, and creates, within his soul, the unreal reality within which he wishes to live."
2 On the concepts of world view, ideology, and utopia see W. Dilthey, *Selected Writings* (Cambridge University Press, Cambridge, 1979); O. J. Harvey, "Conceptual Systems and Attitude Change," in G. W. Sherif, M. Sherif (eds.), *Attitude, Ego-Involvement and Change* (John Wiley, New York, 1967), pp. 201–26; M. Rokeach, *The Open and Closed Mind* (Basic Books, New York, 1960); B. Holzner, *Reality Construction in Society* (Schenkman, Cambridge Mass., 1968); K. Mannheim, *Ideology and Utopia* (Harcourt, Brace and World, New York, 1936), pp. 55–60, 71–8, 192–204.
3 Begin, *The Revolt*, p. 133.
4 *Hayom*, March 23, 1966; Begin, *In the Underground*, vol. I, pp. 57–8.
5 The 11th Council of the Herut Movement, September 29, 1974, JIA, P 20.
6 Begin, "We Shall Call for Revolt" (1944), *In the Underground*, vol. I, p. 87.
7 For Begin's "principle" of proof, see *White Nights*, p. 64; id., *In the Underground*, vol. I, pp. 63, 75. At times, Begin went to absurd lengths. In the case of the King David Hotel, he stated that by failing to comply with the warning to evacuate the building, the British army bore the blame for the terrible tragedy no less than its perpetrators; ibid., vol. II, pp. 161, 205. "(a) In the Land of Israel, there is a state of war. (b) In the Land of Israel there are two belligerent sides. (c) The rules of warfare permit – or, in our case, require – attacks on combat forces, and do not permit harm to civilian persons." See also, R. Kedar, *Al Ha'mishmar*. October 28, 1977: "He is permanently given over to a sophist world, a kind of metaphysical world which provides his mode of thought and action with a defence against the influence of the environment."
8 Begin, *In the Underground*, vol. I, pp. 247–51.
9 Ibid., vol. II, p. 103.
10 "Memorandum," June 1945. Ibid., vol. I, p. 267.
11 Ibid., vol. II, p. 190.
12 Rokeach, *The Open and Closed Mind*, pp. 51–2.
13 Such a conception of time is not untypical of Europe's radical right wing, or of persons displaying ideological dogmatism.
14 M. Begin, *World View and National Conception* (a draft with Begin's corrections). Lectures, 1948–77, JIA, P 20, pp. 30–1.
15 Among the more striking illustrations of Begin's symbolical attitude to realities are the episodes of the Western (Wailing) Wall and the British floggings of the 1940s. The Wall became "the symbol of the national revolt." The ban on blowing the *shofar* was a national humiliation, destroying the

national will "in the process of liquidating Zionism." Begin attached supreme importance to the Irgun's operation at the Western Wall. See: vol. I, Begin, *In the Underground*, pp. 122–33; vol. II, pp. 319–21. Begin's tendency to label phenomena or events with code-names appears to stem from this symbolistic view of reality.

16 On dogmatism see M. Rokeach, "The Nature and Meaning of Dogmatism," *Psychological Review*, 61 (1954), pp. 194–204; id., *The Open and Closed Mind*, pp. 182–4, 109–131. Begin's stereotypical view reflected a regression to the imaginary world of the small town in Eastern Europe (*shtetel*).

17 For a striking illustration of an absolute choice of options, see: Begin, *In the Underground* vol. II, p. 213. The choice was "either a war of liberation or extinction through betrayal"; "either a free homeland or a ghetto"; "either a popular uprising or a prolonged death agony"; "either a Hebrew government or a Judenrat".

18 See also, L. Festinger, H. W. Riecken, S. Shachter, *When Prophecy Fails* (University of Minnesota, Duluth, 1956), pp. 3–32.

Chapter 7 Historical Vista

1 Begin's letter to President Reagan, August 5, 1982 (trans. from the Hebrew version); on the limits of psycho-history see, S. Friedlander, *History and Psycho-Analysis* (Holmes and Meier, New York, 1978).

2 *Herut*, June 20, 1955, April 15, 1957; In an article verging on incitement, Begin attributed the main sequence of historical events, from Britain's decision to submit the Palestine issue to the United Nations, up to the British decision to leave the country, to the Irgun and its operations; M. Begin, "This is the chronology of betrayal and distortion," *Herut*, January 3, 1964. Begin unleashed a vicious attack upon the editorial board selected to write *Sefer Toldot Hahagana* (History of the Hagana). He accused Mapai of adopting the Orwellian tactic of rewriting history and of wanting "with all the force at their disposal during the days of [our] enslavement, to destroy us, to crush and eliminate us;" on the Commission of Inquiry see *Ma'ariv*, February 19, 26, 1982, March 10, 1982, June 5, 1985; *Yediot Aharonot*, February 19, 26, 1982, March 10, 19, 1982.

3 Quoted in *Ha'olam Hazeh* September 7, 1977.

4 M. Begin, "The Fourth Option" (January, 1948), in *In the Underground*, vol. IV, pp. 145–47.

5 Id., *White Nights*, p. 219.

6 *Herut*, May 5, 1949.

7 Begin, *In the Underground*, vol. I, pp. 42, 213–14, 257, 260–2; vol. II, pp. 35, 41, 79–81, 101.

8 Id., *The Revolt*, pp. 17, 122, 458; id., *White Nights*, pp. 102–3.

9 Id., *In the Underground*, vol. II, pp. 70, 113.

10 Id., "Voice of a Child," July 5, 1945, ibid., vol. I, pp. 251–6.

11 Id., *World View and National Conception*; id., "Nationality and Nationalism," *Ma'ariv*, April 7, 1972.

12 See also S. Nakdimon, *Yediot Aharonot*, July 17, 1977.
13 Begin, *The Revolt*, p. 55; see also *Ma'ariv*, July 30, 1976.
14 Begin, *In the Underground*, vol. I, pp. 28, 55, 96–7. In a single breath, Begin reeled off a list of historical leaders, from Judas Maccabaeus to De Valera, concluding with the rhetorical question: "[Were] they all fascists?"
15 Ibid., p. 266.
16 *Yediot Aharonot*, May 19, 1977.
17 *Herut*, January 16, 1949.
18 *Yediot Aharonot*, August 29, 1980.
19 Begin, *White Nights*, pp. 8–9; Interview, *Yediot Aharonot*, January 18, 1974.
20 As reflected in the Betar anthem, "to die or to conquer the mountain, / Yodfat, Massada, Betar," Garibaldi's original slogan appeared in various forms. In fact, most of Garibaldi's slogans referred to the Sicilian campaign. See G. M. Trevelyan, *Garibaldi and the Thousand* (Longmans, Green, London, 1948); G. M. Trevelyan, *Garibaldi and the Making of Italy* (Longmans, Green, London, 1948).
21 *Herut*, September 16, 1955; see also ibid., April 3, 1953.
22 M. Begin, "An Answer to Mr. Winston Churchill," November 1944, in, *In the Underground*, vol. I, pp. 189–95.
23 Id., "On the Greatest Statesman of Our Time," *Herut*, January 29, 1965.
24 *Knesset Proceedings*, August 4, 1970, p. 2765.
25 After the Lebanon War, it was said of Begin that he displayed "very great responsibility towards history, and shocking irresponsibility towards the present," D. Tamari, Interview, *Politika* (June,1985).
26 M. R. D. Foot, "Revolt, Rebellion, Revolution, Civil War: The Irish Experience," in M. Elliott-Bateman, J. Ellis, T. Bowden (eds), *Revolt to Revolution* (Rowman and Littlefield, Manchester University Press, 1974), pp. 161–85; T. P. Coogan, *Ireland Since the Rising* (Pall Mall Press, London, 1966); P. Johnson, *Ireland: Land of Troubles* (Holmes and Meier, New York, 1982), pp. 152–72; F. Martin, "The Evolution of a Myth", in E. Kamenka (ed.), *Nationalism, the Nature and Evolution of an Idea* (Canberra, 1973), pp. 57–800.
27 M. Ben Ze'ev [M. Begin], "1917–1942," *Hamadrikh* 2 (September, 1942).
28 Id., *In the Underground*, vol. I, pp. 87–96, 181.
29 Ben-Ami, The Protocols of the Irgun Command, p. 410.
30 *Knesset Proceedings*, May 3, 1950, p. 1248.
31 Ibid., May 22, 1967, p. 2221; see also M. Begin, "Taft, Korea, Israel," *Herut*, August 7, 1953.
32 *Knesset Proceedings*, October 16, 1973, pp. 4476–9.
33 Ibid., January 23, 1978, p. 1326.
34 Engel, *The Futile Alliance*, p. 359. The Irgun's symbol and its slogan "Only Thus" (*Tylko Tak*) were devised in Poland at the end of 1938. The Polish Military Organization (*Polska Organizacja Wojskowa*), the underground branch of the Polish legion in the First World War was apparently also a source of inspiration; see Y. Zehavi, "On the History of the Irgun in Poland", *Ha'umma* 2/64 (1981), p. 301; S. Sofer, "The Futility of Separation: Ideology and Foreign Policy," *Medina, Mimshal Vihasim Benleumiyyim*, 24 (1985), pp. 5–26;

A. Bromke, *Poland's Politics* (Harvard University Press, Cambridge, Mass., 1967), pp. 31–51.
35 A. Polonsky, *Politics in Independent Poland, 1921–1939* (Clarendon Press, Oxford, 1972); A. Walicki, *Philosophy and Romantic Nationalism: The Case of Poland* (Oxford University Press, Oxford, 1982); J. Szczepański, *Polish Society* (Random House, New York, 1970); R. F. Leslie, *The History of Poland* (Cambridge University Press, Cambridge, 1980), pp. 159–85; W. F. Penson, O. Halecki, R. Dyboski, *The Cambridge History of Poland* (Cambridge University Press, Cambridge, 1951), pp. 295–310, 365–86, 589–615.
36 Addressing historian Ya'acov Talmon, Begin said: "I am willing to learn history from you up to the First World War. With regard to what happened subsequently, I don't learn history from anybody." Quoted in A. Rubinstein, *Ha'aretz*, September 28, 1983. See also M. Begin, "Giving the Enemy His Due" *Ma'ariv*, September 22, 1970. Here, Begin argued with Talmon, contending that Czechoslovakia could have continued to exist with a large German minority.
37 M. Begin, "The Czech Example," November 26, 1944. In Begin, *In the Underground*, vol. I, pp. 184–6.
38 See, for example, *Knesset Proceedings*, July 27, 1970; November 23, 1971, p. 385; *Herut*, January 16, 1949; interview, *Yediot Aharonot*, January 18, 1974; M. Begin, "An Assault Against a Policy of Misery," *Ma'ariv*, May 10, 1974; speech, 12th Convention of the Herut Movement, January 13, 1975; *Ha'aretz*, *Yediot Aharonot*, *Ma'ariv*, July 27, 1970; M. Begin, "A Warning Against a Munich-Like Education," *Ma'ariv*, July 27, 1976.
39 M. Begin, "Real Dangers," *Herut*, July 25, 1958, where he called Nasser "the Arab Hitler"; id., "Facing Apeasement," *Herut*, December 11, 1959. For comparisons of the Palestinians to Nazis, see Begin's "The Arab Nazism against the Jewish Child," *Ma'ariv*, May 24, 1974; his address at a banquet in Secretary of State Cyrus Vance's honor, *Ma'ariv*, August 19, 1977; and his response to the coastal road bus massacre, *Yediot Aharonot*, March 13, 1978, see too his letter to President Sadat of August 18, 1980 (*Yediot Aharonot*, August 20, 1980).
40 Begin was always cautious in his Second Temple parallels, invariably referring to Modi'in rather than Massada. See Begin, *In the Undergound*, vol. I, pp. 109–10, pp. 169–73; *Herut*, November 16, 1952, April 19, 1963.

Chapter 8 Strategic Perspective

1 *Knesset Proceedings*, June 2, 1980. Begin felt himself maligned by an Alignment publication that said, "It is out of the question that a 'superstar' named Menachem Begin shall take all positions for himself." He said that he was at least as capable as Peres to handle security affairs, and that he was wakened at least once or twice a week by the hot line . . .
2 Z. Jabotinsky, *Samson* (E. Jabotinsky, Jerusalem, 1964), pp. 307–8; *Herut*, September 20, 1957. Addressing a gathering in Johannesburg, Begin spoke of

the might of the soldiers of the IDF and said, "In the heart of each of them is a drop of blood from the heart of Ze'ev Jabotinsky."

3 Haber, *Menachem Begin*, p. 54. Begin saw war dead for the first time in 1939, while he was fleeing from Warsaw.

4 M. Ben-Ze'ev [M. Begin], "1917–1942."

5 *Knesset Proceedings*, August 12, 1970, p. 2865.

6 Weizman, *The Battle For Peace*, p. 121.

7 M. Begin, "On Three Things," *Ma'ariv*, October 17, 1975.

8 Begin emphatically claimed that the revolt was guided by a defined diplomatic strategy. But when he mentioned Clausewitz's well-known statement that "war is the continuation of diplomacy by other means," he added, "Only a Prussian militarist could explain the meaning of war that way." He was unable to rid himself of hatred of everything German.

9 *Herut*, April 2, 1964; see also letter by M. Pa'il, *Ma'ariv*, November 18, 1984; this was no more an exaggeration than that of the description of the battle of Vittorio Veneto, by which the Italians concluded their part in the First World War, "the greatest victory in world history." D. Mack Smith, *Mussolini* (Weidenfeld and Nicolson, London, 1981) p. 31

10 The strategic arguments offered by Ze'ev Jabotinsky in support of his opposition to the partition plan of 1937 are the same as those Begin raised about Israel's narrow waist, which can be threatened from the mountains of Judaea and Samaria.

11 *Hamashkif*, August 6, 1948.

12 *Herut*, April 2, 1954.

13 For Begin's criticism see the following articles by him in *Herut*: "Perpetuation of War or Making of Peace," April 2, 1954; "Submission Invites Pressure," September 10, 1954; "Pressure Leading to Submission," September 24, 1954; "Moderation and Extremism," *Herut*, March 4, 1955. See also *Haboker*, August 31, 1954; *Knesset Proceedings*, February 28, 1955.

14 See Begin's contributions to *Herut*; November 6, 1955; "A Tactical and Strategic Consideration," December 16, 1955; "Where Are We Headed," June 1, 1955; "The Government that's Always Late," July 20, 1956. See also *Zemanim*, March 20, 1955. It seems that during the early 1950s, Begin had suggested that in the light of the grave military situation, Israel's children should be evacuated to South Africa.

15 M. Begin, "*Bituchen* or Security," *Herut*, December 24, 1954.

16 *Knesset Proceedings*, June 27, 1967. Begin liked to quote Tolstoy's saying, "morale is three times more important than material."

17 M. Begin, "Taft, Korea, Israel," *Herut*, August 7, 1953. Begin wrote that the Korean War ended in mutual defeat. Russia took the offensive for a defensive objective, and America took the defense for an offensive objective.

18 *Knesset Proceedings*, October 15, 1956, pp. 66–71.

19 Ibid., January 15, 1957, pp. 749–51; see also January 23, 1957, pp. 830–3.

20 Ibid., April 2, 1957, pp. 1660–4.

21 *HaYom*, May 19, 1967; *Knesset Proceedings*, May 22, 1967.

22 See *Ma'ariv*, January 22, 1971; M. Begin, "A Lesson From an Exercise in Offering Concessions," ibid., October 15, 1971.

23 M. Begin, "Two Schools and the Test of Reality," *Ma'ariv*, December 24, 1971; ibid., January 28, 1972.

24 *Knesset Proceedings*, November 13, 1973.

25 Ibid., October 16, 1973, pp. 4476–9.

26 *Davar*, January 20, 1974; *Knesset Proceedings*, January 22, 1974; M. Begin, "An Attack on a Miserable Policy," *Ma'ariv*, May 10, 1974; *Knesset Proceedings*, May 30, 1974, pp. 1467–70.

27 M. Begin, "Let's Look at the Facts," *Ma'ariv*, August 16, 1974.

28 See the following articles by Begin in *Ma'ariv*: "A Reply to Hypocrites at Home and Abroad," December 6, 1974; "Withdrawals Without Peace: An Advance Towards Peace?" January 3, 1975; "Kissinger's Pressure, Rabin's Announcement," February 14, 1975; "Where Concessionism Leads," January 31, 1975; "The Expectation of More Gestures," June 6, 1975; "To Submit or Not to Submit, That is the Question," July 4, 1975; "Persistence in Retreat and the Illusion of Rulers," July 18, 1975. See also *Knesset Proceedings*, March 24, 1975, p. 2309; June 15, 1976, 3024–7.

29 See interview by Y. Shavit, *Ma'ariv*, September 28, 1981; also *Ma'ariv*, September 27, 1981. When Alignment members M. Gur and D. Rosolio warned of the danger of mortgaging the IDF to American interests, Begin reminded them that Ben-Gurion had wanted to tie Israel into NATO.

30 *Herut*, February 27, 1951.

31 C. Vance, *Hard Choices* (Simon and Schuster, New York, 1983), p. 183.

32 *Ha'aretz*, September 3, 1978; *Yediot Aharonot*, April 25, 1980; *Davar*, September 30, 1980.

33 See M. Dayan, *Shall the Sword Devour Forever?* (Hebrew), (Edanim, Jerusalem, 1982), p. 69; Y. Marcus, *Camp David: The Path to Peace* (Hebrew), (Schocken, Tel Aviv, Jerusalem, 1979), p. 170; Z. Brzezinski, *Power and Principle* (Farrar, Strauss, Giroux, New York, 1983), pp. 92, 236. The attempts by Israel's supporters to raise Israel to the rank of an "ally," along the lines of Japan or the countries of West Europe, were rejected by the US administration. But in his pronouncements, President Carter intentionally wove in phrases such as "special relations," "ally," and "strategic asset."

34 *Yediot Aharonot*, October 5, 1980; *Ma'ariv*, September 10, 1982.

35 See *HaYom*, October 17, 1969; *Ma'ariv*, January 22, 1971; *Knesset Proceedings*, February 9, 1971, p. 1306; *Ma'ariv*, January 16, 1972.

36 *Davar*, December 23, 1973; *Ma'ariv*, February 15, 1974.

37 *Ha'aretz*, March 15, 1974; *Ma'ariv*, March 18, 1974.

38 See also E. Inbar, "Israeli Strategic Thinking after 1973," *Journal of Strategic Studies*, 6 (1983), pp. 36–59; *Ma'ariv*, January 16, 1980; *Yediot Aharonot*, April 25, 1980. After the Soviet invasion of Afghanistan, Begin contended that the positioning of Russian troops on the Afghan–Iranian border was extremely grave for Israel, though it is hard to see how it changed relations between Israel and the USSR.

39 *Jerusalem Post*, July 5, 1977, March 14, 1979; *Knesset Proceedings*, January 16, 1980, p. 1493.

40 *Ha'aretz*, November 14 and 17, 1980.

41 *Knesset Proceedings*, November 3, 1981, pp. 337, 340; *Ma'ariv*, November 20, 1981.
42 United States International Communications Agency, Tel Aviv, December 1, 1981.
43 *Knesset Proceedings*, December 14, 1981, pp. 778–9.
44 *Ma'ariv*, December 21, 1981.
45 Vance, *Hard Choices*, pp. 208–9; Inbar, *Israeli Strategic Thinking*, p. 49.
46 *Ma'ariv*, September 29, 1982; *Herut*, December 24, 1954; M. Begin, "Demilitarization of What, Agreement With Whom," *HaYom*, April 1, 1966; id., "Nuclear Capability and Its Curbing," ibid., March 11, 1966.
47 *Ha'aretz*, June 15, 1981; the announcement by Defense Minister Ariel Sharon spoke of a preventive doctrine that would form part of the defense policy of the 1980s. Government Press Office, December 15, 1981. See also Weizman, *The Battle for Peace*, pp. 84–5. It appears that Israel's nuclear option was one of Sadat's considerations in launching his peace initiative. The American response to the bombing of the reactor was ambivalent – the bombing had a detrimental effect on American policy of drawing close to Iraq, but on the other hand, the US stands opposed to nuclear proliferation.
48 S. Nakdimon, *Tammuz in Flames* (Hebrew), (Edanim, Jerusalem, 1986), pp. 80–3, 142–51, 165–9, 215–17.
49 Interview with the Prime Minister, June 8, 1981, Government Press Office; see also, Government Press Office, June 21, 1981. The government's announcement denounced the vote in the Security Council, especially that of the United States. See also S. Feldman, "The Bombing of Osiraq Revisited," *International Security*, 7 (1982), pp. 114–42; Silver, *Begin*, 218–20.

Chapter 9 Eretz Yisrael, The Palestinians, and the Idea of Autonomy

1 "On the Meeting Between Representatives of the UN Commission and a Delegation of the Irgun Zvai Leumi," 28 Sivan, 1947 (mimeograph).
2 For Begin's earlier views on the Arab question, see the following articles by him in *In the Underground*: "To Our Arab Neighbors" (September 15, 1944), vol. I pp. 116–18; "The Error and Its Price" (April 1946), vol. II, pp. 122–4; "Interview With UP Correspondent" (September 1947), vol. IV, pp. 12–16; "To Our Arab Neighbors" (December 3, 1947), ibid., 90–2; "From Defense to Counterattack' (December 7, 1947), ibid., 92–4, see also his *The Revolt*, pp. 64–8. The paradox of the Revisionist right's position on the Arab question was that, as compared to the Zionist left, their approach could in principle be free of all dogma and could range from absolute negation to a wholly liberal conception. The left, on the other hand, had to travel a circuitous route to reconcile its socialist beliefs, the demands of nationalism, and the reality of Palestine. The compromise achieved by the socialist Zionists was usually presented by the right as hypocrisy or as delusive and out of touch with political realities.
3 For Begin's Pan-Arab view, see his speech to the Eleventh Council of the Herut Movement, September 29, 1974, JIA, P2O. He also regarded pan-

Arabism as a form of imperialism that was seeking to undermine the foundations of the free world; *Ma'ariv*, January 9, 1978.

4 M. Begin, "Machiavellianism Exposing Itself," *Ma'ariv*, December 20, 1974; *Knesset Proceedings*, February 19, 1958, pp. 1010–11.

5 *Knesset Proceedings*, March 16, 1972, pp. 1843–5; at a mass rally in July 1982 in support of the government, he said that if a peace treaty was concluded with Lebanon, he would invite Hussein to meet with him and would propose "a free confederation of Western Land of Israel and Transjordan", *Ma'ariv*, July 18, 1982; Begin totally rejected the Saudi peace plan (known as the "Fahd initiative"). Its seventh paragraph spoke of "emphasis on the right of the states in the region to live in peace." He called the plan "the Saudi annihilation plan"; *Knesset Proceedings*, November 2, 1981, pp. 306–7.

6 *Knesset Proceedings*, May 7, 1979, p. 2436; December 14, 1981, pp. 763–5, 778–9.

7 Convention resolutions, September 1948, JIA; M. Begin, "Jerusalem," *Herut Umoledet*, July 29, 1948. On the fifth anniversary of the fall of the Old City of Jerusalem, Begin proclaimed that the nation's leadership had missed "the historic opportunity to arise and take possession of the entire land – the homeland was not liberated and we lost the City of David within the walls." *Herut*, May 3, 1953.

8 See *Knesset Proceedings*, June 15, 1949, p. 725; January 2, 1950, p. 384. Speaking of Ben-Gurion's "failure" in the War of Independence Begin wrote, "We have a small Hebrew state, with a large, and growing, Arab minority"; M. Begin, *On Foreign Policy* (Herut Center, Tel Aviv, 1953), pp. 16–17. He also wrote "Liberation of the homeland and peace are possible; peace without liberation of the homeland is not possible."

9 *Herut*, April 30, 1950; January 11, 1949; the editorial October 14, 1953 was entitled "To Jordan."

10 *Knesset Proceedings*, November 7, 1957, p. 202.

11 *HaYom*, June 28, 1966.

12 Ibid., January 8, 1969; see also remarks at the Herut Movement convention, May 26, 1958, pp. 16–17, JIA P 20 and a statement he made in July 1970, in Wolf, *The Passion of Israel*, pp. 264–5.

13 *Ma'ariv*, April 27, 1973; in 1978 Begin said that for the sake of peace he had agreed not to annex Judaea and Samaria. Ibid., May 5, 1978. See also: *Knesset Proceedings*, July 27, 1977, p. 467. After he was elected prime minister, Begin made an appeal to Hussein, but the king refused to meet him; see Silver, *Begin*, pp. 168–9.

14 *Knesset Proceedings*, April 4, 1949, pp. 289, 299–300; the *Herut* headline that day announced, "Heart of the Country Handed Over to Abd-Bevin, With Israel Government's Consent."

15 *Knesset Proceedings*, May 3, 1950, pp. 1282–5. Begin was in no way concerned with the efforts being made to win international legitimation for the boundaries of the new state.

16 Speech at a joint meeting of the Herut and Liberal party centers, November 20, 1968, JIA, P 20; M. Begin, "Partition as Principle and as Mockery of the Poor," *Ma'ariv*, July 7, 1973.

17 *Knesset Proceedings*, September 1, 1977, p. 753; *Yediot Aharonot*, February 20, 1980; *Ma'ariv*, September 29, 1980. See also *Knesset Proceedings*, June 11, 1969, p. 2995.

18 See S. Nakdimon, "The Map Crisis," *Yediot Aharonot*, March 19, 1971.

19 A typical ploy used by Begin to parry criticism from the right on the issue of settlement was to argue that Betar settlement groups had been the victims of intentional discrimination by the settlement authorities. That, however, was just the empty half of the historical truth. See *Knesset Proceedings*, November 2, 1970, p. 374.

20 Ibid., January 8, 1969, p. 1056; November 2, 1970, pp. 373–4.

21 Ibid., May 4, 1982. For a refutation of the existence of a demographic problem, see ibid., June 15, 1976, p. 3026.

22 See also S. Katz, *Neither Splendour Nor Courage* (Hebrew), (Dvir, Ma'ariv, Tel Aviv, 1981), pp. 113–15; *Knesset Proceedings*, February 1, 1983.

23 For Begin's remarks on historical rights, see, *inter alia*, *Knesset Proceedings*, November 2, 1970, p. 373; March 16, 1972, p. 1884; M. Begin, "Giving the Enemy his Due," *Ma'ariv*, September 22, 1972; Begin, speech to the Eleventh Council of the Herut Movement, September 29, 1974, JIA, P 20; *Yediot Aharonot*, May 13, 1975.

24 M. Begin, "The Right That Created Might," *Ma'ariv*, May 11, 1973.

25 Ibid., June 24, 1977; December 21, 1979.

26 *Ma'ariv*, *Ha'aretz*, March 31, 1980; *Yediot Aharonot*, April 27, 1982.

27 M. Begin, "A State for Israel, or a Colony for One and All," *Herut*, August 14, 1953.

28 Begin and Herut transformed Jabotinsky's poems into a hermeneutic code for interpreting political intentions. See Z. Jabotinsky, Songs of Zion in *Songs* (Hebrew), (E. Jabotinsky, Jerusalem, 1947).

29 M. Begin, "Facts Against Illusion and Deception," *Ma'ariv*, June 18, 1976.

30 *Knesset Proceedings*, December 16, 1959, p. 94; February 20, 1962, pp. 1320–2; Bader, *The Knesset and I*, p. 156. That same month, the Liberals, Herut and Mapam held a joint rally against the military administration.

31 *Knesset Proceedings*, October 10, 1963, pp. 7–8. Begin did not rescind the emergency regulations when he was prime minister. He often remarked that many times more houses were razed during the Alignment period than during the Likud period; *Yediot Aharonot*, November 23, 1981.

32 *Knesset Proceedings*, February 24, 1960, pp. 718–20.

33 *Ha'aretz*, July 25, 1977.

34 See the following articles by Begin in *Ma'ariv*: "Palestinians Are Upon You, Israel," October 30, 1970; "Sadat the Semite and Zionism," October 31, 1975; "Preparing the Ground for a Palestinian State," December 10, 1976. See also *Knesset Proceedings*, November 2, 1970; November 28, 1977, p. 519.

35 M. Begin, "Giving the Enemy His Due," *Ma'ariv*, September 22, 1972.

36 *Knesset Proceedings*, November 3, 1981, p. 339.

37 *Yediot Aharonot*, January 13, 1975; *Knesset Proceedings*, December 28, 1977; May 7, 1979, p. 2439.

38 See the following articles by Begin in *Ma'ariv*: "On Palestinism and Pragmatism," December 26, 1975; "Preparing the Ground for a Palestinian

State," December 10, 1976; "Rabin Waited for Rabat," *Ma'ariv*, November 1, 1974.

39 *Knesset Proceedings*, September 25, 1978, p. 4065.

40 Begin's speech at the Eleventh Council of the Herut Movement, September 29, 1974, p. 10, JIA. See also *Knesset Proceedings*, November 26, 1974, pp. 492–6; July 27, 1977, pp. 462–8; August 15, 1977, pp. 671–7; September 1, 1977, pp. 751–5; and *Newsweek*, August 22, 1977.

41 Wolf, *The Passion of Israel*, pp. 261–3.

42 *Knesset Proceedings*, November 26, 1974, p. 494; July 27, 1977, pp. 464–5.

43 *Yediot Aharonot*, October 24, 1984, Interview with Begin; Shmuel Katz remarked that the "interpolation of Jabotinsky's memory into Begin's autonomy plan . . . is desecration of the name." Katz, *Neither Splendour Nor Courage*, p. 150 n.

44 See also Walicki, *Philosophy and Romantic Nationalism*, pp. 64–85.

45 Jabotinsky, "The Story of My Life," p. 70; id., *Memoirs of My Contemporaries*, pp. 239–49.

46 Id., "Story of My Life", p. 71; see also J. Frankel, *Prophecy and Politics: Socialism, Nationalism and the Russian Jews, 1862–1917* (Cambridge University Press, Cambridge, 1984), pp. 161–6.

47 Jabotinsky, "Story of My Life,", p. 58.

48 Merchavia, *A Homeland*, pp. 397–9.

49 Jabotinsky's views may be deduced from the following articles and speeches: *Memories of My Contemporaries*, p. 297; "Story of My Life," pp. 62–72; "For the Creation of a Jewish Faction in the State *Duma*" (May, 1906), "Zionism and the Organization of the Jewish Nation in Russia" (Helsingfors, 1906). In, *Speeches* (Hebrew), (E. Jabotinsky, Jerusalem, 1947), pp. 15–28.

50 Z. Jabotinsky "Letter on Autonomism," in *Selected Writings*, vol. I, pp. 138–66.

51 Id., "Self-Rule of a National Minority," in *Nation and Society* (E. Jabotinsky, Jerusalem 1946), pp. 15–71. This was the dissertation Jabotinsky presented to Yaroslavl University in 1912 for the degree of master of law.

52 Ibid., pp. 70–1.

53 See also Y. Nedava, "Jabotinsky in Vienna," *Gesher*, 1/110 (1984), pp. 56–65. According to Nedava, Jabotinsky learned much about the issue of national minorities during his stay in Vienna in 1907–8; he especially noted the influence of Karl Renner (who also wrote under the name Rudolf Springer). Jabotinsky also tried to find out about the Ottoman *millet* system. Nedava contended however, that Begin's autonomy plan was not based on Jabotinsky's conception, and that in reality Israel's demand for sovereignty in the West Bank was hollow since resolution of the matter would have to depend on exogenous factors too.

54 JIA, C 4–8/3; *Jewish Herald*, March 4, 1938.

55 Z. Jabotinsky, "The Arab Question: Without Dramatic Excess," in Jabotinsky, *The Jewish War Front*, pp. 182–92.

56 Ibid., p. 183. The sources of Jabotinsky's thought remained more or less the same after the passing of a generation – Rudolf Springer, the Austrian Social Democratic Party, the Hungarian constitution of 1868, and the Turkish *millet*.

57 See M. Begin, "Equal Rights and Equal Rule," *Ma'ariv*, May 18, 1972.
58 Id; *In the Underground*, vol. III, p. 23.
59 Id., "Equal Rights and Equal Rule," *Ma'ariv*, May 18, 1972; id., "Land of Israel, Peace, and Citizenship," Ibid., November 17, 1972; *Yediot Aharonot*, June 11, 1973; *Ma'ariv*, March 18, 1974. The 12th convention of Herut once again approved the article about granting civic rights and "cultural autonomy"; *Yediot Aharonot*, January 13, 1975; *Ma'ariv*, January 17, 1975; *Yediot Aharonot*, June 6, 1975; In *Ma'ariv*, December 10, 1976 (M. Begin, "Preparing the Ground for a Palestinian State"), Begin spoke of "the Arab nationality in our land." He maintained that the demand for a "single ethnic" state was a "Nazi conception"; *Knesset Proceedings*, March 10, 1974, p. 540. Begin included in his plan, equality of rights, an option to choose either Israeli or Jordanian citizenship, and treatment of the refugee problem.
60 There are several versions as to how the autonomy plan came to be formulated. See U. Benziman, *Prime Minister Under Siege* (Hebrew), (Dvir, Tel Aviv, 1981), pp. 76–85, 267–71. The plan was brought before the ministerial defense committee, with the chief of staff in attendance. On December 13, 1977, Gen. Mordechai Gur expressed opposition to the plan, seeing it as the seed of a Palestinian state; E. Haber, E. Yaari, Z. Schiff, *Year of the Dove* (Hebrew), (Zmora, Bitan, Modan, Tel Aviv, 1980), pp. 172–81, 367; Marcus, *Camp David*, p. 156. Attorney-General Barak was the first person to whom Begin showed the plan; Weizman, *The Battle for Peace*, pp. 69, 92; Katz, *Neither Splendour Nor Courage*, pp. 143–4. Katz says that he received a copy of the plan from Barak. He was astonished; in Revisionism the idea of autonomy had always been related to the sovereign framework of a Jewish state; Silver, *Begin*, pp. 174–80.
61 Dayan, *Shall the Sword Devour Forever*, p. 64; Benziman, *Prime Minister Under Siege*, pp. 23–5; Vance, *Hard Choices* pp. 187–90; *Jerusalem Post*, July 6, 1977; the idea of self-administration had also been suggested by Moshe Dayan.
62 *Knesset Proceedings*, December 28, 1977, pp. 925–8.
63 Haber et al., *Year of the Dove*, p. 178; Katz, *Neither Splendour Nor Courage*, 149–59.
64 Weizman, *The Battle for Peace*, pp. 233–4; Dayan, *Shall the Sword Devour Forever*, pp. 93–4; Vance, *Hard Choices*, pp. 198–200; Brzezinski, *Power and Principle*, p. 120; J. Carter, *Keeping Faith* (Bantam Books, New York, 1982), pp. 300, 305.
65 *Knesset Proceedings*, March 29, 1978, pp. 2295–8.
66 Ibid., March 21, 1979, pp. 2081–5.
67 Ibid., January 16, 1980, pp. 1459–60.
68 Dayan. *Shall the Sword Devour Forever*, pp. 11–12, 16. Dayan refused to deal with matters related to the autonomy as foreign minister and ordered the staff of his ministry not to deal with them either.
69 Ibid., pp. 243–4.
70 Ibid., pp. 316–18.
71 C. P. Bradley, *The Camp David Peace Process* (Tompson and Rutter, Grantham, N. H., 1981), pp. 48–71.
72 *Knesset Proceedings*, May 7, 1959, pp. 2474–5; March 20, 1979, pp. 1884,

1891; Begin's speech to the fourteenth Convention of the Herut movement, June 3, 1979, pp. 3–4. Begin declared that there would never be a Palestinian state; *Knesset Proceedings*, September 19, 1979, p. 1034; *Ma'ariv*, March 19, 1980. Begin also claimed that Egypt was making demands that ran counter to the Camp David Accords; *Knesset Proceedings*, June 2, 1980, pp. 3114–15. Begin totally rejected the Egyptian proposals, especially their understanding of the significance of the legislative council; *Yediot Aharonot*, August 23, 1981; April 27, 1982, interview in the Egyptian weekly *Mayou*; *Knesset Proceedings*, May 3–4, 1982; *Yediot Aharonot*, September 30, 1982. Begin reportedly told the Knesset Foreign Affairs and Security Committee that it would be best if the autonomy were under Israeli sovereignty; *Knesset Proceedings*, October 18, 1982; "Text of report to American Jewry. Conference of Presidents of Major American Jewish Organizations. Washington," April 17, 1980, JIA, P 20.

73 *Ma'ariv*, May 22, 1979.

74 See Dayan, *Shall the Sword Devour Forever*, pp. 272–9; *The Peace Negotiations Between Israel and Egypt, September 1978—March 1979* (Hebrew), (Shiloah Institute, Tel Aviv University, 1979), pp. 19–28; Vance, *Hard Choices*, pp. 229–31; Silver, *Begin*, p. 204; R. A. Friedlander, "Autonomy, the Palestinians, and International Law: The Begin Legacy," in Freedman, *Israel in the Begin Era*, pp. 201–20; R. Lapidoth, "The Camp David Process and the New U.S. Plan for the Middle East: A legal Analysis," *USC Cites* (1982–1983), University of Southern California, pp. 17–26. In Lapidoth's view, autonomy is limited self-rule, but the difference between it and a state is qualitative and not a matter of degree.

75 *Knesset Proceedings*, March 20, 1979, p. 1815.

76 Eldad, "Between Reversal and Revolution;" p. 174; Benziman, *Prime Minister Under Siege*, pp. 228–9.

Chapter 10 International Orientation and Images of the World Order

1 See the following contributions to *In the Underground*: "Announcement" (February 27, 1944), vol. I, p. 31; "The Brigade and the Partition Plan" (September 24, 1944), vol. I, p. 119; "Recognition of the Jewish Agency: For What Purpose?" (December 3, 1944), vol. I, p. 201; "Policy and Illusion" (February 1946), vol. II, p. 77; here he wrote: "This Jerusalem, eternal and unvanquished, riveted the attention of the world only after the tommy gun was put to use in it." See also: M. Begin, "The Chief Factor" (May 1946), vol. II, p. 137.

2 M. Begin, "Elements of Policy," Central Seminar for Movement Activists, December 8, 1954, JIA, E1/9/6/6.

3 See M. Begin: "Outlines of Hebrew Foreign Policy," JIA p/20; id., *The Revolt*, p. 18; id., *On Foreign Policy*, pp. 22–6. Here Begin wrote: "If the Jew is not prepared to back his right with force, his cry is in vain. His right will be killed along with him."

4 M. Begin, "The Nation's Peace and the Land's Integrity," address to the National Council of the Herut Movement, April 23, 1970, Information

Division of the Herut Movement, p. 13; but to the same extent he regarded a concession made under pressure as a national disaster that has its roots in appeasement. See also his "Pressure Invites Surrender," *Herut*, September 24, 1954.

5 Speech at the First National Council of the Herut Movement, *Herut*, October 20, 1948.

6 M. Begin, "Without Nostalgia, Without Fear," *Ma'ariv*, November 12, 1976.

7 Id., "The Foreign Minister Makes an Admission," *Herut*, March 12, 1954.

8 For Begin's remarks on the importance of informational work as a component of foreign policy, see his speech at the 11th National Council of the Herut Movement, September 29, 1974, JIA, P 20; also his, "The Fundaments of Information Work Abroad," *Ma'ariv*, May 2, 1975; and "The Ten Senators of Mr. Eban," ibid., May 7, 1956; *Knesset Proceedings*, November 2, 1981, p. 307.

9 M. Begin, "The Mutuality Principle," *Herut*, April 15, 1960.

10 Id., "The Power of Prestige," ibid., October 26, 1956.

11 Id., "A Ripe Moment for Israel in America," *Ma'ariv*, April 18, 1975. On the Three Power declaration and the comments of Y. Meridor, see *Knesset Proceedings*, May 31, 1950, pp. 1574–6. See also Y. Bader, "The Danger of 'Guarantees'," *Herut*, May 17, 1963; Begin's remarks, *Knesset Proceedings*, February 9, 1971, pp. 1306–7; November 13, 1973, p. 4595; M. Begin, "Three-Sided or Four," *Herut*, April 8, 1960; interview with Begin, *Yediot Aharonot*, January 18, 1974.

12 *Knesset Proceedings*, October 21, 1963; M. Begin, *World View and National Conception*, p. 41.

13 Id., "*Bitukhen* or Security," *Herut*, December 12, 1954; Id., "Elements of Policy."

14 "From Defensive Posture to Diplomatic Offensive, From Lobbying for Guarantees to a Policy of Alliances," address at the National Council of the Herut Movement, December 26, 1957, pp. 7–10, JIA, P 20.

15 M. Begin, "Concepts and Problems of Foreign Policy," *Ha'umma*, 4 16 (1966), pp. 465–8.

16 Begin made extensive use of the rules of international law. See, e.g., inter alia, on how the new state is to be proclaimed, in *In the Underground*: "Special Announcement," June 13, 1944, vol. I, p. 80; on Britain's commitment to the mandate and the justification of action against Britain, "Warning Against Torture: Memorandum to the Allied Governments," July 9, 1944, vol. I, p. 35. Begin demanded that every Jew who declared that the Land of Israel is his homeland be recognized as a displaced citizen of Palestine; in that way the problem of majority and minority would be solved: "Majority and Minority," March, 1946, vol. II, 90–1. Another rule he made much use of in the 1970s, which was intended to tie the hands of the Alignment governments in taking diplomatic initiatives, was that if one side makes an offer and the other side does not accept it, the proposal is no longer binding; see: M. Begin, "Lesson From an Exercise in Making Concessions," *Ma'ariv*, October 15, 1971; also *Knesset Proceedings*, March 24, 1975, p. 2309. After the assassination of President Sadat, he noted that international treaties are binding on states regardless of changes in the political leadership; ibid., November 2, 1981,

p. 305. There is an interesting comment in the testimony of Y. Bader in ICJ, April 6, 1968, p. 13: "I think it is impossible to be both a lawyer and a statesman. These are different approaches."

17 *Yediot Aharonot*, December 24, 1973, and *Davar*, December 23, 1973. See also address to the National Council of the Herut Movement, December 26, 1957; address to Herut Council, October 23, 1967, JIA, P 20; address to the National Council of the Herut Movement, April 23, 1970, pp.20–1, JIA; M. Begin, "Jerusalem Is Not Pnom Penh," *Ma'ariv*, March 26, 1975; and Begin's reply to interpellation by Y. Tamir, *Knesset Proceedings*, June 11, 1969, p. 2994.

18 *Ma'ariv*, January 22, 1971; October 15, 1971; *Knesset Proceedings*, March 29, 1978, p. 2296.

19 Address to the Herut Movement Council, October 23, 1967, JIA, P 20; also published in *HaYom*, October 25–7, 1967.

20 *Knesset Proceedings*, August 4, 1970, pp. 2762–6. When he left the National Unity government, he went further and said that the government's consent to the Jarring initiative was a return to the formula Eduard Beneš had received from Great Britain in 1938. Begin argued that the rule of nonacquisition of territory through war applied only to wars of aggression. He added that another "great rule of international law" also gave support to Israel, "injustice does not create justice," or, in other words, the conquest of the Gaza Strip by Egypt and of the West Bank by Jordan were not recognized by international law and did not give them entitlement to those territories. See also *Knesset Proceedings*, August 12, 1970, pp. 2862–7; N. Feinberg, "Menachem Begin's Legal Interpretations," *Davar*, July 10, 1977; id., "The Legal Status of the West Bank," *Ha'aretz*, October 9, 1977; R. Lapidoth, "UN Resolution 242," *The Weiner Library Bulletin*, 26 (1982), p. 405. According to Lapidoth, the conquest of territories in self-defense is legitimate, up until the signing of a peace treaty. The preamble of the resolution does not denounce all military conquest, but nor does it contain anything decisive about sovereignty or that the occupation is legitimate for all time.

21 Begin, "Elements of Policy."

22 *Herut*, August 27, 1950. See also Begin, *In the Underground*, vol. I, pp. 245–7; vol. II, p. 56. In the 1940s Begin believed that if a world war was to break out it would also be a Jewish civil war, and that the Land of Israel would not be able to be neutral. He also maintained that the peace treaties do not establish a permanent state of affairs, only a short-range "period of atomic peace."

23 *Knesset Proceedings*, June 30, 1954, pp. 2085–6; October 15, 1956, pp. 67–8; M. Begin, "Foolish Diplomacy," *Herut*, July 16, 1954; id., "Israel's Foreign Policy, A Year's Review," *Herut Yearbook* (1955), pp. 67–8.

24 See M. Begin in *Herut*: "Changes in the World," January 17, 1958; "The Exodus From Egypt and Egypt's Exodus," July 30, 1954. Begin doubted Churchill's contention that nuclear arms had eliminated the strategic value of the Suez Canal. He believed the British had other reasons for withdrawing from the Canal.

25 Id., "Real Dangers," ibid., July 25, 1958.

26 Id., "How to Open," ibid., October 26, 1962.

27 See id., "Concepts and Problems of Foreign Policy," p. 463; *Knesset Proceedings*, July 15, 1964, p. 2364. In the early 1950s, Shmuel Katz expressed astonishment that Israel was included in the US aid program to Third World countries; ibid., January 23, 1951, pp. 860–1. See also Beign's ridicule of Ben-Gurion's visit to Burma, M. Begin, "Nu, Nu," *Herut*, January 5, 1962.

28 Begin, "Concepts and Problems of Foreign Policy," p. 464.

29 M. Begin, "Stupid Vote," *Herut*, December 1, 1961; *Knesset Proceedings*, November 12, 1962, p. 100; October 21, 1963, pp. 9–10; June 9, 1971, p. 2678. See also *Ma'ariv*, September 7, 1977; M. Brecher, *The Foreign Policy System of Israel* (Oxford University Press, Oxford, 1972), pp. 172–4.

30 See the following articles by Begin in *In the Underground*: "Factors Assisting Zionism" (November 26, 1944), vol. I, pp. 177–81; "Talks With Foreign Correspondents" (December, 1945), vol. II, p. 41; "The Hebrew Liberation Army" (March, 1947), vol. III, pp. 32–5; "A Reply to President Truman" (June 8, 1947), vol. III, pp. 112–13. See also id., "The Strategy and Tactics of the Revolt," *Herut*, May 13, 1949. Begin maintained that the revolt brought the conflicting interests of the British and the US to the surface, and created a common front of East and West that supported the establishment of the state.

31 Id., "Broadcast" (May 15, 1948), *In the Underground*, vol. IV, 326–33.

32 *Knesset Proceedings*, June 20, 1977, p. 15.

33 JIA P 20, Articles 1935–1950. It was supposed to appear in the IDF publication, *Bamahane*.

34 *Knesset Proceedings*, January 2, 1950, p. 387.

35 M. Begin, "Two Governments, One Regime," *Herut*, May 1, 1953.

36 *Knesset Proceedings*, January 23, 1951, p. 860; March 31, 1958, pp. 1757–60.

37 See M. Begin, Lecture at the First Study Day, August 14, 1948; id., "East or West," *Herut*, August 27, 1950; id., "Five Principles [from a speech in Tel Aviv]," *Hamashkif*, August 27, 1948; *Herut*, January 18, 1949; speech at the 2nd Convention of the Herut Movement, ibid., February 27, 1951.

38 *Herut*, April 6, 1961. Address to the Sixth National Convention of the Herut Movement. In fact, Begin divided the world into three. First was the "zone of freedoms," and opposing it stood "the realm of one-party class dictatorship under Communism" and "the region of non-Communist, personal, military, or sectarian dictatorships."

39 Begin frequently quoted Presidents Jefferson and Lincoln.

40 *Knesset Proceedings*, January 24, 1974, p. 1367.

41 Ibid., May 11, 1981, pp. 2628–30.

42 *Ha'aretz*, September 3, 1982.

43 See the reports towards the end of Samuel Lewis's term as ambassador to Israel, A. Shochat, *Ha'aretz*, November 9, 1984; E. Disenchik, *Ma'ariv*, June 7, 1985.

44 See M. Begin, *In the Underground*: "Statement" (November 8, 1945), vol. II, p. 21; id., "What Has Changed" (February 1946), ibid., p. 66.

45 Id., *On Foreign Policy*.

46 Id., in *Herut*: "The Surprised Surprise," June 5, 1953; "The Foreign Minister Makes an Admission," March 12, 1954.

47 Id., *American Arms to Israel's Enemies*, Herut Movement, May 1954.

48 See also id., in *Herut*: "Foolish Diplomacy," July 16, 1954; "One for the Gentile, One For the Jew," March 6, 1954.
49 *Knesset Proceedings*, August 30, 1954, pp. 2555–8.
50 *Herut*, October 22, 1954; M. Begin, "Submission Invites Pressure," ibid., September 10, 1954. Begin pointed to Pierre Mendès-France as an example of being able to stand up against the Americans. See also Begin, "Israel's Foreign Policy, A Year's Review," pp. 51–70.
51 *Knesset Proceedings*, February 28, 1955; June 6, 1957.
52 Ibid., October 18, 1955, pp. 88–91.
53 M. Begin, "Tactical and Strategic Considerations," *Herut*, December 16, 1955; *Knesset Proceedings*, January 2, 1956, pp. 681–2.
54 M. Begin, "An American Paradox," *Herut*, November 23, 1956.
55 See id., in *Ma'ariv*: "The Crisis in America and Us," April 9, 1971; "A Ripe Moment for Israel in America," April 18, 1975. Begin imagined that the Vietnam crisis would facilitate understanding of Israel's interests in holding onto the territories. See also ibid., his "Confrontation, With America?" June 4, 1971; "Don't Hurry, Mr. Sisco," July 30, 1971; and his speech to the National Council of the Herut Movement, November 17, 1971, JIA, P 20. In this speech he explained in detail his opposition to all the Israeli diplomatic initiatives since July 1970. He belittled Sadat's threats that he would go to war if a settlement was not reached: "We'll land blows on their heads as soon as they open fire that will be so heavy that they will hold their fire."
56 *New York Times*, May 19, 1977; *New York Post*, June 8, 1977; July 6, 1977; *Washington Star*, May 19, 1977; *Jerusalem Post*, June 10, 1977; see also Marvin Kalb's extensive report of his vist to Israel (CBS).
57 *Jerusalem Post*, June 22, 1977.
58 *Yediot Aharonot*, May 24, 1977.
59 Carter's and Begin's remarks as reported in *Yediot Aharonot*, July 22, 1977; for Begin's consent to the convening of a peace conference in Geneva in October, and for his visit to the United States, see: *New York Times*, July 18, 21, 1977; *Jerusalem Post*, July 15, 1977; *New York Post*, July 25, 1977; *Newsweek*, August 1, 1977.
60 *Ma'ariv*, July 26, 1977; *Jerusalem Post*, July 26, 1977. Begin solemnly noted the number of senators and congressmen with whom he met, and the number of hours he spent with the president. Among those he met was Henry Kissinger, who had been the butt of his attacks for many years.
61 *Knesset Proceedings*, July 27, 1977, pp. 462–70.
62 Ibid., p. 471; also August 15, 1977, pp. 671–2, for Allon's remarks on that subject; Rabin, *Service Diary*, vol. I, pp. 571–2.
63 For the president's reaction to the change in the settlements' status, see *New York Times*, July 29, 1977. On relations between the two countries, see *New York Times*, August 22, 1977, September 18, 1977; *New York Post*, August 22, 1977.
64 *Knesset Proceedings*, November 28, 1977, pp. 542–3; March 21, 1978, p. 2297; *Time*, September 11, 1978.
65 Benziman, *Prime Minister under Siege*, p. 112; Marcus, *Camp David*, pp. 242–3, 251. Bradley, *The Camp David Peace Process*, pp. 55–6. In February 1980 the

United States for the first time supported an Arab-sponsored resolution in the UN against Israel, after the establishment of settlements near Hebron. In the beginning of March, Carter retreated from that position.

66 *Yediot Aharonot*, September 10, 1981; *Ma'ariv*, September 13, 1981.

67 *Ma'ariv*, September 27, 1981; interview with Begin, ibid., September 28, 1981.

68 *Knesset Proceedings*, February 15, 1982.

69 Letters of the President and the Prime Minister, Government Press Office, February 16, 1982.

70 *Ma'ariv*, August 5, 1982.

71 *Davar*, September 5, 1982; *Knesset Proceedings*, September 8, 1982.

72 Begin, *White Nights*, pp. 21–3, 31, 210–12, 225–46.

73 Id., *In the Underground* (March 1946), vol. II, pp. 89–91.

74 See ibid., "The Soviet Union and the Return to Zion" (June, 1945), pp. 243–6, and "The Laws of Life Are Stronger Than the Will of Rulers" (March 1946), pp. 94–6. See also id., *The Revolt*, pp. 21, 276; memorial for Yuniczman, 1963, JIA, P 20. Begin said that Shimshon Yuniczman went to Teheran to meet with Russian representatives and proposed cooperation with them in return for "a certain technological invention." Nothing came of the plan. The articles Begin wrote in the 1940s about Russia may have been influenced by those of Nathan Yellin-Mor, which appeared at the same time.

75 M. Begin, "Slavery Imposed and Voluntary," *Herut*, November 24, 1961.

76 See id., in *Ma'ariv*: "For Leftism Everything's Permissible," March 24, 1972, and "Barbaric Leftism Hates Israel," June 16, 1972.

77 Id., "Elements of Policy."

78 M. Ben-Ze'ev [Begin], "The Comintern," *Hamadrikh*, 3 (June, 1943), pp. 52–8.

79 M. Begin, "Changes in the World," *Herut*, January 17, 1958. Begin distinguished between right-wing and left-wing dictatorships; see his "Real Dangers," ibid., July 25, 1958.

80 Id., "The Fight for Hegemony in the Communist World," ibid., July 12, 1963.

81 Id., "Paths of Policy Today," *Ha'umma*, 3–4/51–2 (1977), pp. 333–47.

82 M. Ben-Ze'ev [Begin], "Russia and Zionism," *Hamadrikh*, 2 (February, 1943), pp. 200–4.

83 *Knesset Proceedings*, November 25, 1952, pp. 157–9; M. Begin, "Astray on the Roads of Communism," *Herut*, January 10, 1958; id., "The Tragedy of the Historical Contradiction," *Ma'ariv*, November 19, 1971.

84 See id., in *Herut*: "They Always Exaggerate," July 24, 1953, "American Paradox," November 23, 1956; "Three-Sided or Four," April 8, 1960. See also *Ha'aretz*, November 18, 1956.

85 *Yediot Aharonot*, September 12, 1969; *Knesset Proceedings*, June 9, 1971, pp. 2674–5; M. Begin, "A Personal and Open Letter to Brezhnev," *Ma'ariv*, May 21, 1971.

86 *Knesset Proceedings*, November 2, 1961, p. 207; October 21, 1963, pp. 10–11; July 15, 1964, pp. 2364–5.

87 See R. O. Freedman, "Moscow, Jerusalem, and Washington in the Begin Era," in Freedman, *Israel in the Begin Era*, 151–99.

88 *Knesset Proceedings*, June 20, 1977; *Ma'ariv*, September 7, 1977.
89 *Knesset Proceedings*, January 16, 1980, pp. 1457–8; address to the Conference of Presidents of American Jewish Organizations, April 17, 1980, Washington, JIA, P 20.
90 *Knesset Proceedings*, April 1, 1983.
91 Ibid., October 16, 1973, p. 4478.
92 *Yediot Aharonot*, April 25, 1980; *Knesset Proceedings*, June 2, 1980, pp. 3073–9.
93 *Yediot Aharonot*, May 4, 1981; *Ma'ariv*, May 6, 1981.
94 Jabotinsky, too, addressed the British as "John Smith."
95 M. Begin, "Russia and Zionism," *Hamadrikh*, 2 (February, 1943), pp. 197–200; Interview by N. Bethell, April 2, 1976, ISA, 16/72, P/A 899.
96 Id., "Elements Supporting Zionism," (November 26, 1944), *In the Underground*, vol. I, pp. 177–81; ibid., pp. 233, 285; id., *The Revolt*, pp. 39–52, 85–91.
97 M. Begin, "Our Position," July 9, 1944, *In the Underground*, vol. I, 71–4. Begin, as always, had a historical parallel for his distinction between the British Empire and its mandate in Palestine to a Poland fought in World War I to reacquire its historical patrimony as far as Vilna and Lemberg, but did not want to fight against the Russian state proper; see also the talk between Begin and Moshe Sneh, *History of the Hagana*, vol. III, p. 1887.
98 M. Begin, "A Proclamation," *In the Underground*, vol. II, pp. 20–1.
99 Mack Smith, *Mussolini*, pp. 36, 194, 208.
100 *Knesset Proceedings*, January 2, 1950, pp. 387–9; *Zemanim*, August 31, 1954; Begin interview of March, 1954 reprinted in *Ha'olam Ha-Zeh*, September 7, 1979.
101 *Knesset Proceedings*, November 7, 1956, p. 202.
102 *Ma'ariv*, January 10, 1972; *Daily Telegraph*, *Guardian*, January 11, 1972. The headline of the *Daily Mail* was "The Return of a Nice Little Killer;" *Daily Telegraph*, *The Times*, *Guardian*, January 13–14, 1972; Silver, *Begin*, pp. 143–4.
103 *Yediot Aharonot*, May 29, 1977, December 4, 1977; speech at the Fourteenth Convention of the Herut Movement, June 3, 1979, p. 3, JIA, P 20.
104 *Yediot Aharonot*, November 6, 1981.
105 *Herut*, November 29, 1957.
106 See Lankin, *Altalena*, pp. 233–51; S. Merlin, Testimony, JIA, M–17.
107 See Tavin, *The Second Front*, pp. 152–66; Niv, *The Irgun*, vol. I, pp. 176–7; Y. Meridor, Testimony, ICJ, September, 1965, where he says of the agreement with France, without explaining, "according to sabotage plans that he drew up;" see also, Bar-Zohar, *Ben-Gurion*, vol. II, p. 777.
108 *Ha'aretz*, June 13, 1952; *Davar*, October 31, 1958.
109 M. Begin, "Told to the People of France," a speech before the French National Assembly, Paris, September, 1956. Herut Movement, September 1956; *Herut*, September 20, 1957.
110 *Knesset Proceedings*, November 7, 1956, pp. 201–3.
111 See *Lamerhav*, *Haboker*, *Ha'aretz*, June 2, 1957; address to the National Council of the Herut Movement, December 26, 1957, JIA, P 20; *Ha'aretz*, November 18, 1956; *Knesset Proceedings*, March 31, 1958, pp. 1759–60;

280 *Notes to Chapter 10*

M. Begin, "A Pact With France," *Herut*, January 23, 1959. Begin rejected the criticism that the opposition cannot undertake an autonomous diplomatic initiative; see also *Davar*, October 31, 1958; M. Begin, "The 'No'-Beckoners are Worried," *Herut*, February 13, 1959.

112 *Knesset Proceedings*, January 8, 1969, pp. 1057–8.

113 Ibid., July 15, 1964, p. 2367; *Hayom*, February 20, 1968; *Yediot Aharonot*, September 12, 1969.

114 *Knesset Proceedings*, August 15, 1977, p. 672.

115 *Ma'ariv*, January 12, 1978; Mitterrand visited Israel in 1982. Begin was not invited to a state visit to France.

116 *Ma'ariv*, October 7, 1980; September 28, 1981.

117 Begin, *The Revolt*, p. 9; *Herut*, February 27, 1951.

118 *Ha'aretz*, November 2, 1952. In giving his movement's greetings to de Gaulle, Begin called for Israel to join a world coalition of free nations against Germany; M. Begin, *Stress, Straits and Outlet*, The Third Convention of the Herut Movement, April 19, 1954 (Herut Movement, 1954). On that occasion he proposed that a world Jewish congress be convened in Paris to protest against Germany; on Clausewitz, M. Begin, "Paths in Policy Today," *Herut*, July 12, 1963 and "A Ripe and Ready Hour," ibid., August 27, 1954.

119 Ibid., January 6, 1952.

120 Ibid., January 8, 1952.

121 Ibid.

122 *Knesset Proceedings*, January 7, 1952, pp. 903–7.

123 Ibid., March 31, 1958, pp. 1758–9; June 29, 1959, pp. 2372–4. He invoked an image of Jews about to to be brought to the slaughter by German troops armed with Israeli weapons; M. Begin, "On Israel's Honor," *Herut*, January 8, 1960; *Knesset Proceedings*, October 24, 1960. Begin was disturbed by the fact that the government had ceased comparing Nasser to Hitler; ibid., November 2, 1961, pp. 207–8.

124 *Knesset Proceedings*, November 12, 1961; April 7, 1963, pp. 1742–3. Begin denounced the visit to Israel of Franz Strauss. He accused Shimon Peres of having allowed success to go to his head; see M. Begin, "The German Visitor and His Pronouncements," *Herut*, May 21, 1963; also *Knesset Proceedings*, October 21, 1963, pp. 8–11; July 15, 1964, pp. 2364–6.

125 *Knesset Proceedings*, February 15, 1965, pp. 1242–5.

126 Ibid., March 16, 1965, pp. 1541–5.

127 See ibid., May 17, 1965, pp. 1843–5, January 12, 1966, pp. 352–3, May 18, 1966, p. 1470; *Ha'aretz*, June 27, 1966.

128 *Ma'ariv*, September 7, 1977, May 22, 1978; *Yediot Aharonot*, May 26, 1981. Begin said, "The Chancellor served on the Eastern front with forces that conquered the city where my parents, my brother, and my sisters were slaughtered."

129 Speech at the Herut Movement Council, October 23, 1967, p. 17, JIA, P 20.

130 M. Begin, "How to Rescue" (February 6, 1944), *In the Underground*, vol. I, p. 28–9.

131 See M. Begin in *In the Underground*: "We Believe" (1944), vol. I, pp. 52–3; "What Else Has to Happen" (July 25, 1944), vol. I, p. 64; "To the Hebrew

Nation in Zion" (September 5, 1944), vol. I, p. 125. "Bearers of the Hope— Bearers of the Idea" (July 26, 1946), vol. II. See also *Herut*, July 30, 1954.

132 M. Begin, "What Are They Doing" (April 1945), *In the Underground*, vol. I, p. 217.

133 A. M. Haig, *Caveat: Realism, Reagan, and Foreign Policy* (Macmillan, New York, 1984), p. 173, "I myself," Begin said, "who lost my mother and my father and my brother and my two nephews, whose children never knew their grandparents, suffer from the Holocaust trauma. From the day I became prime minister, I swore that no one would shed Jewish blood with impunity."

134 *Yediot Aharonot*, August 27, 1982. Professor Shmuel Ettinger said, "No one has desecrated the memory of the Holocaust as has this prime minister."

135 See *Hamadrikh*, 3 (May 1943), p. 5. Among other things Begin wrote: "Maybe the arch-murderer was right when he said that the universal ideals of the Nazis will also be accepted by those who today are fighting against Germany."

136 See M. Begin in *In the Underground*: "One Decisive Front" (July 17, 1946), vol. II, pp. 185–7; "Political Outcomes" (October 31, 1944), vol. I, p. 155; "We Believe" (1944), vol. I, p. 43. See also id., *On Foreign Policy*, p. 23.

137 *Ma'ariv*, April 10, 1966.

138 *Yediot Aharonot*, January 13, 1975. The remarks were made at the Twelfth Convention of the Herut Movement, which was held at Hebron.

139 M. Begin, "*Bitukhen* or Security," *Herut*, December 24, 1954.

140 *Knesset Proceedings*, August 30, 1954, p. 2556.

141 Ibid., January 23, 1978, p. 1357; December, 14, 1981, p. 779.

142 M. Begin, "Universal Scope" (July, 1946), *In the Underground*, vol. II, p. 177.

143 M. Begin, "The Crisis in America and Us," *Ma'ariv*, April 9, 1971; *Yediot Aharonot*, May 15, 1975, interview with Begin; Marcus, *Camp David*, p. 246.

144 M. Begin, "Dialogue in New York," *Ma'ariv*, November 26, 1976; *Moment*, September, 1977.

145 *Yediot Aharonot*, January 13, 1975.

Chapter 11 The Diplomat

1 *Knesset Proceedings*, June 15, 1949, p. 725.

2 Ibid. p. 727.

3 M. Begin, "The Right that Created Might," *Ma'ariv*, May 11, 1973.

4 *Yediot Aharanot*, September 30, 1980; Marcus, *Camp David*, p. 186; *Ma'ariv*, July 15, 1981.

5 See M. Begin in *Herut*: "Foolish Diplomacy," July 16, 1954; "Between Rome and Jerusalem," January 10, 1964.

6 *Yediot Aharonot*, November 17, 1977; Haber et al., *Year of the Dove*, p. 144; Marcus, *Camp David*, p. 183.

7 M. Begin, "Beyond February 5," *Ma'ariv*, February 5, 1971.

8 Weizman, *The Battle for Peace*, pp. 179–80. Weizman wrote that Begin lived with the feeling that "he had absolute truth in his pocket," and would address those to whom he spoke like a teacher his pupils; *Yedior Aharonot*, October 6, 1985. Waldheim said that despite Begin's inflexibility, "I was surprised by his

self-restraint, even in highly emotional situations." For Boutros Ghali's assessment of Begin as negotiator, see Silver, *Begin*, pp. 181–2.

9 Carter, *Keeping Faith*, pp. 400–1; see also Haber et al., *Year of the Dove*, p. 200; Marcus, *Camp David*, p. 188.
10 H. J. Morgenthau, *Politics Among Nations* (Alfred A. Knopf, New York, 1973), p. 545.
11 Weizman, *The Battle for Peace*, p. 317; Marcus, *Camp David*, p. 125.
12 Dayan, *Shall the Sword Devour Forever*, pp. 94, 124–5. On the meeting in Ismailia, Dayan observed that "the entourage Begin took along was composed, as in the past, of 'cronies.'"
13 *Ma'ariv*, May 20, 1977; Katz, *Neither Splendour nor Courage*, pp. 89–90; *New York Times Magazine*, July 10, 1977; *Daily News*, June 3, 1977.
14 Katz, *Neither Splendour nor Courage*, pp. 9–10.
15 Ibid., pp. 46–8, 86–7.
16 *Ma'ariv*, December 21, 1981; *Yediot Aharonot*, May 13, 1981. Upon meeting the Dutch foreign minister, Begin reprimanded him for having met with Arafat. The minister appeared agitated and upset after that meeting; Silver, *Begin*, p. 245.
17 Z. Schiff, E. Yaari, *A War of Deception* (Schocken, Jerusalem and Tel Aviv, 1984), pp. 272–3, 288–91.
18 Dayan, *Shall the Sword Devour Forever*, p. 11.
19 M. Begin, "Nasser's Hostility and Bourguiba's Friendliness," *Herut*, April 16, 1965.
20 See *Knesset Proceedings*, November 16, 1970, pp. 178–80; M. Begin, "Mr. Dayan Requested a Reply," *Ma'ariv*, November 13, 1970; M. Bentov, "The Alternative: Eternal War," *Yediot Aharonot*, November 20, 1970.
21 See M. Begin in *Ma'ariv*: "Beyond February 5," February 5, 1971; "The Rogers and Jarring Initiatives," February 19, 1971. See also *Knesset Proceedings*, February 9, 1971.
22 *Knesset Proceedings*, March 16, 1971.
23 See M. Begin in *Ma'ariv*: "Don't Hurry, Mr. Sisco," July 30, 1971; "Confrontation with America?" June 4, 1971.
24 *Knesset Proceedings*, June 9, 1971, pp. 2673–8.
25 Ibid., November 23, 1971, pp. 384–6; June 5, 1972, pp. 2657–9; M. Begin, "A Principled Position, Please," *Ma'ariv*, May 5, 1972.
26 *Ma'ariv*, January 27, 1975. See also M. Begin in *Ma'ariv*: "The Decision to Believe the Arabs," July 5, 1974; "Kissinger's Pressure, Rabin's Announcement," February 14, 1975; "Between Dr. Kissinger and Israel's Ministers," March 22, 1974. See further *Yediot Aharonot*, April 7, 1975; M. Begin, "Realistic Foundations for a National Policy," *Ha'umma*, 1/42 (1974).
27 M. Begin, speech at the 11th National Council, September 29, 1974, JIA, P 20.
28 See *Yediot Aharonot*, January 13, 1975; M. Begin, speech at the National Council of Herut, December 26, 1957, JIA, P 70.
29 See M. Begin in *Ma'ariv*, "Sadat's Remarks and the Changing Lines," August 1, 1975; "Candid With Dr. Kissinger and With Ourselves," August 15, 1975.
30 *Knesset Proceedings*, September 3, 1975, pp. 4081–4. Begin assailed the

president of Egypt for his anti-Zionist and anti-Jewish views; see M. Begin, "Sadat the Semite and Zionism," *Ma'ariv*, October 31, 1975.

31 *Ha'aretz*, May 6, 1977; *Ma'ariv*, May 13, 1977.

32 *Ma'ariv*, May 24, July 8, and July 12, 1977; *Jerusalem Post*, July 6, 1977; *New York Times*, July 18, 1977. Begin boasted, "For the first time since the establishment of the state, we have drafted a proposal for a peace treaty." *Ha'aretz*, *Ma'ariv*, September 7, 1977; in an interview to Israel radio in mid-September, he said that the Arab countries are interested in peace, and that peace is inevitable.

33 On the recommendations of the Brookings Committee and the American position, see *Toward Peace in the Middle East* (The Brookings Institute, Washington, 1975).

34 Brzezinski, *Power and Principle*, pp. 83–122.

35 Carter, *Keeping Faith*, pp. 269–97.

36 Vance, *Hard Choices*, pp. 159–95.

37 Dayan, *Shall the Sword Devour Forever*, pp. 17–21; Marcus, *Camp David*, pp. 24–6; Benziman, *Prime Minister under Siege*, pp. 13–14; Haber et al., *Year of the Dove*, p. 14.

38 Weizman, *The Battle for Peace*, pp. 89–91.

39 Dayan, *Shall the Sword Devour Forever*, p. 19.

40 Ibid., pp. 23–7.

41 Vance, *Hard Choices*, p. 180.

42 Dayan, *Shall the Sword Devour Forever*, pp. 55–9; Benziman, *Prime Minister under Siege*, p. 15; Haber et al., *Year of the Dove*, p. 44; *Ma'ariv*, *Yediot Aharonot*, July 20, 1977.

43 Carter, *Keeping Faith*, pp. 290–1.

44 Brzezinski, *Power and Principle*, pp. 99–101; M. Begin, "Dialogue in New York," *Ma'ariv*, November 26, 1976.

45 Vance, *Hard Choices*, pp. 181–6; W. B. Quandt, *Camp David: Peacemaking and Politics* (The Brookings Institute, Washington, 1986), pp. 255–6. Quandt is of the opinion that Begin was the most talented negotiator at Camp David.

46 Dayan, *Shall the Sword Devour Forever*, pp. 28–37; Silver, *Begin*, pp. 168–9. Hussein refused to meet Begin.

47 On the contacts with Tuhami, see Dayan, *Shall the Sword Devour Forever*, pp. 38–49; for speculations about the purpose of Dayan's trip to Morocco in mid-September, see *New York Times*, September 19, 1977.

48 Marcus, *Camp David*, pp. 39–40; Benziman, *Prime Minister under Siege*, p. 18.

49 Dayan, *Shall the Sword Devour Forever*, pp. 61–8.

50 Ibid., pp. 69–75.

51 See Marcus, *Camp David*, pp. 42–3; Benziman, *Prime Minister under Siege*, pp. 20–31. The working paper included formulas on the Palestinian issue and for a separation between two agreements in the peace treaty, which played an important role at Camp David.

52 Vance, *Hard Choices*, p. 193.

53 Brzezinski, *Power and Principle*, pp. 109–11.

54 Carter, *Keeping Faith*, p. 295. A month before his visit to Jerusalem Carter sent

a personal letter to Sadat asking that he help by publicly expressing support for the Amenities policy.

55 Katz, *Neither Splendour nor Courage*, p. 136.
56 Dayan, *Shall the Sword Devour Forever*, pp. 86–90. In June 1979, Dayan tried to clarify with Sadat the reasons for his visit to Jerusalem. Dayan cites the reasons he gave, adding that Sadat's character was no less a determining factor than political calculations and considerations; Benziman, *Prime Minister under Siege*, pp. 33–47; Haber et al., *Year of the Dove*, p. 29; *Ma'ariv*, May 17, 1983, interview with Nicolae Ceauşescu, President of Roumania.
57 Vance, *Hard Choices*, p. 195.
58 *Knesset Proceedings*, November 15, 1977, pp. 403–4.
59 For Begin's reaction to Sadat's announcement and his words to the Egyptian people, see *Ma'ariv*, November 13, 1977.
60 See Weizman, *The Battle for Peace*, pp. 27–9, 55–7; Benziman, *Prime Minister under Seige*, pp. 35–7; Haber et al., *Year of the Dove*, pp. 54, 113, 119–20.
61 *Knesset Proceedings*, November 20, 1977, pp. 456–60.
62 Haber et al., *Year of the Dove*, pp. 134–5.
63 *Knesset Proceedings*, November 20, 1977, pp. 460–3.
64 Dayan, *Shall the Sword Devour Forever*, pp. 78–90.
65 Benziman, *Prime Minister under Siege*, p. 40; Haber et al., *Year of the Dove*, p. 127.
66 Dayan, *Shall the Sword Devour Forever*, pp. 49–50; Benziman, *Prime Minister under Siege*, pp. 44–5; Haber et al., *Year of the Dove*, p. 128.
67 Marcus, *Camp David*, pp. 50–2; Haber et al., *Year of the Dove*, pp. 241–2.
68 Benziman, *Prime Minister under Siege*, 96–7; Haber et al., *Year of the Dove*, pp. 161–5; Dayan, *Shall the Sword Devour Forever*, pp. 91–4.
69 Vance, *Hard Choices*, p. 189.
70 *Knesset Proceedings*, November 28, 1977, pp. 517–20, 542–6.
71 Benziman, *Prime Minister under Siege*, pp. 83–94; Dayan, *Shall the Sword Devour Forever*, pp. 91–4.
72 Dayan, *Shall the Sword Devour Forever*, pp. 94–6; Marcus, *Camp David*, pp. 61–4.
73 Benziman, *Prime Minister under Siege*, pp. 94–103; Haber et al., *Year of the Dove*, pp. 182–201.
74 *Knesset Proceedings*, December 28, 1977, pp. 927–8.
75 Brzezinski, *Power and Principle*, pp. 116–19. Before he left for Ismailia, Begin showed his autonomy plan to President Carter. Brzezinski advised the president to transform Begin's plan into a temporary settlement.
76 Carter, *Keeping Faith*, pp. 299–303; *The Peace Initiative: The Diplomatic Negotiations*, November 1977–July 1978 (Hebrew), (Shiloah Institute, Tel Aviv University, 1978), p. 13.
77 Dayan, *Shall the Sword Devour Forever*, p. 98.
78 Brzezinski, *Power and Principle*, pp. 240–3.
79 *Knesset Proceedings*, December 28, 1977, pp. 925–8.
80 *Yediot Aharonot*, January 9, 1978; Katz, *Neither Splendour nor Courage*, pp. 163–5.
81 Weizman, *The Battle for Peace*, pp. 237–8: Weizman had always thought that a

bilateral agreement with Egypt was preferable to American involvement in the peace process; Benziman, *Prime Minister under Siege*, pp. 106–8; Haber et al., *Year of the Dove*, pp. 243–7.

82 Dayan, *Shall the Sword Devour Forever*, pp. 97–118.
83 Vance, *Hard Choices*, 202–205.
84 *Knesset Proceedings*, January 23, 1978, pp. 1325–32, 1338.
85 Brzezinski, *Power and Principle*, pp. 245–9.
86 Dayan, *Shall the Sword Devour Forever*, pp. 110–11; Weizman, *The Battle for Peace*, pp. 263–4. Weizman writes that Begin emerged "bruised and battered" from the talks, which he described as "the most difficult of his life."
87 Carter, *Keeping Faith*, pp. 310–12.
88 Vance, *Hard Choices*, pp. 206–13.
89 Weizman, *The Battle for Peace*, pp. 268–77; Marcus, *Camp David*, pp. 55–60; Benziman, *Year of the Dove*, pp. 135–41.
90 See Haber et al., *Year of the Dove*, pp. 210–12; Marcus, *Camp David*, p. 54; Weizman, *The Battle for Peace*, pp. 121–5; *Yediot Aharonot*, September 27, 1985; Silver, *Begin*, p. 186; Benziman, *Not Stopping at the Red Light*, pp. 204–13.
91 Dayan, *Shall the Sword Devour Forever*, pp. 115–18.
92 *The Peace Initiative: The Diplomatic Negotiations*, p. 22.
93 Ibid., p. 25.
94 Weizman, *The Battle for Peace*, pp. 287–301.
95 *Knesset Proceedings*, July 24, 1978, pp. 3723–30.
96 *Yediot Aharonot*, July 20, 1978.
97 Dayan, *Shall the Sword Devour Forever*, pp. 119–25.
98 Vance, *Hard Choices*, pp. 215–19.
99 Brzezinski, *Power and Principle*, pp. 249–52.
100 Dayan, *Shall the Sword Devour Forever*, pp. 130–1.
101 Vance, *Hard Choices*, pp. 215–19.
102 Carter, *Keeping Faith*, pp. 320–7.
103 *Ma'ariv*, September 3, 1978.
104 Ibid., August 31, 1978.
105 *Knesset Proceedings*, November 2, 1981, p. 325; on Camp David see also S. Sofer, *Menachem Begin in Camp David: a chapter in the New Diplomacy* (Hebrew), (The Leonard Davis Institute for International Relations, the Hebrew University of Jerusalem, 1986).
106 See Marcus, *Camp David*, 88–91; Benziman, *Prime Minister under Siege*, p. 166.
107 Brzezinski, *Power and Principle*, p. 280.
108 Ibid., p. 261; Carter, *Keeping Faith*, p. 350. With American consent, the Israeli delegation conducted its debates and consultations during the talks in Hebrew, and later even in English. These debates usually ended in a change of the prime minister's tone, and sometimes also in a change of position.
109 Weizman, *The Battle for Peace*, pp. 319, 322.
110 Dayan, *Shall the Sword Devour Forever*, p. 132.
111 Carter, *Keeping Faith*, p. 383.
112 Ibid., pp. 330, 344.

113 Brzezinski, *Power and Principle*, p. 270.
114 Weizman, *The Battle for Peace*, pp. 345–7; Benziman, *Prime Minister under Siege*, pp. 194–7.
115 *Knesset Proceedings*, September 25, 1978, p. 4060.
116 For the Hebrew version, see *The Peace Negotiations between Israel and Egypt*, pp. 1–13; English version, Vance, *Hard Choices*, pp. 464–8.
117 *Yediot Aharonot*, October 1, 1978.
118 *Knesset Proceedings*, May 4, 1982; see also letter by Begin to Chief Rabbi Shlomo Goren, August 17, 1981, published in *Ma'ariv*, August 21, 1981.
119 *Knesset Proceedings*, September 25 and 27, 1978.
120 *Yediot Aharonot*, December 30, 1977; Eldad, "Between Reversal and Revolution," p. 173.
121 N. Yellin-Mor, "Without Thorns and Without Roses," *Ha'aretz*, September 25, 1978.
122 Katz, *Neither Splendour nor Courage*, pp. 200–13.
123 Vance, *Hard Choices*, pp. 227–9.
124 *Ma'ariv*, October 1, 1978; Dayan, *Shall the Sword Devour Forever*, pp. 154–6; Carter, *Keeping Faith*, p. 397.
125 Vance, *Hard Choices*, pp. 225, 228–9; *Knesset Proceedings*, September 27, 1978, p. 4066.
126 Carter, *Keeping Faith*, pp. 404–27.
127 Dayan, *Shall the Sword Devour Forever*, pp. 167–84.
128 On the discussions at Blair House and the atmosphere in the government, see Marcus, *Camp David*, pp. 190–217; Benziman, *Prime Minister under Siege*, pp. 209–26; Haber et al., *Year of the Dove*, pp. 359–64; Weizman, *The Battle for Peace*, pp. 234–5.
129 *Knesset Proceedings*, December 19, 1978, pp. 571–4.
130 See also the remarks by Foreign Minister Dayan in *Knesset Proceedings*, December 19, 1978, pp. 613–15.
131 Carter, *Keeping Faith*, p. 414; Vance, *Hard Choices*, pp. 243–4.
132 Brzezinski, *Power and Principle*, p. 279.
133 Carter, *Keeping Faith*, pp. 421–3.
134 *Knesset Proceedings*, March 12, 1979, pp. 1825–8.
135 Ibid., pp. 1828–35.
136 See Benziman, *Prime Minister under Siege*, pp. 249–60; Haber et al., *Year of the Dove*, pp. 374–84; Weizman, *The Battle for Peace*, pp. 360–2.
137 Dayan, *Shall the Sword Devour Forever*, pp. 217–28; Vance, *Hard Choices*, pp. 249–51.
138 *Knesset Proceedings*, March 20, 1979, pp. 1882–99.

Chapter 12   The War in Lebanon

1 *Ma'ariv*, August 14, 1983.
2 Ibid., March 16, 1973.
3 The most reliable account of the Lebanon war is that presented by Schiff, Yaari, *A War of Deception*; see also S. Schiffer, *Snow Ball: The Story behind the*

Lebanon War (Hebrew), (Edanim, Jerusalem, 1984); A. Naor, *A Government in War* (Hebrew), (Lahav, Tel Aviv, 1986).

4 M. Begin, speech at the Fourteenth Convention of the Herut Movement, June 3, 1979, p. 3; JIA, P 2. In the same period he said "We have abandoned the method of reprisal operations. We have taken the initiative out of the hands of the terrorists. It's in our hands."

5 *Ma'ariv*, August 20, 1982; see also: S. Peres, "Reply to Menachem Begin," ibid., August 27, 1982.

6 Begin shaped reality to his fixed historical parallels. In the gloom that followed the Yom Kippur War he said, "we must return to the primary, genuine meaning of 'there is no choice,' which proved itself in times of crisis and pressure." *Yediot Aharonot*, January 18, 1974, interview with Begin.

7 *Knesset Proceedings*, June 15, 1976, pp. 3022, 3027.

8 *Ha'aretz*, August 8, 1977; *Ma'ariv*, August 8 and 9, 1977.

9 *Ma'ariv*, September 3, 1978; Haber et al., *Year of the Dove*, pp. 306–7, 317–18; *Yediot Aharonot*, March 28, 1983; Carter, *Keeping Faith*, 352, 368–9.

10 *Knesset Proceedings*, May 7, 1979, pp. 2438–41; see also Begin's speech to the Fourteenth Convention of the Herut Movement, June 3, 1979; JIA, P 20; *Al Hamishmar*, April 7, 1981; *Yediot Aharonot*, April 29, 1981.

11 *Ma'ariv*, May 6, 1981, interview with Begin.

12 *Knesset Proceedings*, May 11, 1981, pp. 2623–31.

13 Ibid., May 12, 1981, pp. 2654–68.

14 Ibid., June 3, 1981, pp. 2883–5. Rabin spoke on the basis of an announcement by the Prime Minister's Office, May 24, 1981.

15 *Knesset Proceedings*, June 3, 1981, pp. 2885–8.

16 Ibid., p. 2891. See also D. Margalit, "A Version's Varieties," *Ha'aretz*, June 5, 1981, which points out the contradictions between the prime minister's Statements in the Knesset and before the Foreign Affairs and Defence Committee and the announcements of the Prime Minister's Office.

17 *Ma'ariv*, June 15, July 7, July 23, and August 17, 1981; *Ha'aretz*, July 14, 1981.

18 *Knesset Proceedings*, November 3, 1981; *Ha'aretz*, November 4, 1981.

19 *Yediot Aharonot*, February 10, 1982; in February 1982 Begin expressed his readiness to discuss the formation of a National Unity government; *Ma'ariv*, April 6, 1982; Press Statement, Prime Minister's Office, February 17, 1982. Deputy prime minister Simcha Ehrlich denied the accusations that he had leaked a plan to invade southern Lebanon.

20 *Ma'ariv*, February 27, 1980. Ibid., April 13, 1982, interview with Begin; *Yediot Aharonot*, April 13, 1982, interview with Begin; *Ma'ariv*, May 14, 1982.

21 Schiff, Yaari, *A War of Deception*, p. 38. The "grand plan" had grandiose objectives: not only to demolish the PLO as a political factor, but also to install the Falangists in Lebanon, expel the Syrian army, and finally, to undermine the stability of the Hashemite Kingdom and to achieve an agreement congenial to Israel with local leaders in the West Bank.

22 Israel Television broadcast, May 28, 1985. In effect, a debate about who should be the target of the opening blow continued right up to the opening of the war; A. Yaniv and R. J. Lieber, "Personal Whim or Strategic Imperative," *International Security*, 8 (1983), pp. 117–42. The article examines the military

options that were available to Israel and comes to the conclusion that a large-scale operation was the only available solution to the military problem faced by Israel in Lebanon; *Yediot Aharonot*, October 4, 1985, interview with M. Zippori.

23 In the prevailing description of the war, the general staff and the cabinet were cowed into following an operative plan which it was not their intention to follow. See: Schiff, Yaari, *A War of Deception*, pp. 93–124; Naor, *Government in War*, pp. 25–6; *Ma'ariv*, "The Unending War," June 3, 1983; *Yediot Aharonot*, "Three Years to the Lebanon War," May 31, 1985; Silver, *Begin*, pp. 222–40.

24 Schiff, Yaari, *A War of Deception*, p. 104. The ambassador in Washington, Moshe Arens, was convinced the war was unavoidable; on the attitude of the intelligence establishment, see also *Ma'ariv*, September 13, 1985. General Saguy, the head of the IDF Military Intelligence, regarded Chief of Staff Eitan's attitude to the Christians as a product of emotions, not of knowledge and facts. Begin usually went along with the chief of staff's assessments.

25 Y. Rabin, *The War in Lebanon* (Hebrew), (Am Oved, Tel Aviv, 1983), pp. 19–31; *Ma'ariv*, June 3, 1983, p. 9; Israel television broadcast, May 28, 1985. The Alignment leadership was apparently aware of the existence of two conceptions of the war. The party, it seems, did not want to appear in public as opposed to the war. Begin met with the heads of Alignment on April 6, 1982 and on May 16, 1982. From the questions they directed to defense minister Sharon at the second meeting, they learned that Sidon was included in the plan. It is also possible that when the war began they knew of the intention to go beyond the 40-kilometer line.

26 S. Nakdimon, "Sharon and Eight prime ministers," *Yediot Aharonot*, November 22, 1985; *Hadashot*, October 28, 1985; A. Haber, "Begin, For Those Who Don't Know Him," *Yediot Aharonot*, June 5, 1983; Benziman, *Not Stopping at the Red Light*, pp. 236–7.

27 *Knesset Proceedings*, September 8, 1982; see also Sharon's Lecture at Tel Aviv University, *Ma'ariv*, August 12, 1987.

28 Haig, *Caveat*, pp. 188, 326–7.

29 Schiff, Yaari, *A War of Deception*, pp. 77–92.

30 Interview with Ambassador Lewis, Israel Television, May 22, 1985; *Ha'aretz*, *Yediot Aharonot*, May 24, 1985; NBC, April 8, 1982; also worthy of note in *Ha'aretz* are the articles by Ze'ev Schiff and Yoel Marcus published before the war.

31 *Yediot Aharonot*, April 16, 1984.

32 Haig, *Caveat*, pp. 330, 333.

33 Schiff, Yaari, *A War of Deception*, pp. 11–20.

34 Government Press Office, June 6, 1982. In a letter to President Reagan, Begin confirmed that "The army has been instructed to drive back the terrorists to a distance of 40 kilometers to the north." The prime minister asked whether, facing a bloodthirsty aggressor, Israel is to be deprived of the natural right of self-defense; *Knesset Proceedings*, June 3, 1981, p. 2898; *Ma'ariv*, September 13, 1985.

35 See Schiff, Yaari, *A War of Deception*, pp. 144–62, 183–222; *Yediot Aharonot*, May 31, 1985; Haig, *Caveat*, p. 338.

36 *Ma'ariv*, June 3, 1983. There were those in the government who from the beginning thought that the outflanking operation was proposed by Sharon and Eitan in order to widen the scope of the war; see also Naor, *Government in War*, pp. 53–65.

37 *Knesset Proceedings*, June 8, 1982.

38 *Yediot Aharonot*, May 31, 1985.

39 Ibid., October 4, 1985.

40 Schiff, Yaari, *A War of Deception*, pp. 223–35; the cabinet secretary was forced to telephone the defense minister and the chief of staff to find out whether the IDF was or was not in the outskirts of Beirut. Finally, confirmation came from an operations officer in the Northern Command; see also Naor, *Government in War*, pp. 87–90, 129–30.

41 Schiff, Yaari, *A War of Deception*, p. 261; *Ma'ariv*, July 7, 1982.

42 *Knesset Proceedings*, July 28, 1982. Begin asked Geva, "Did you receive an order to kill children? So what are you complaining about?"; Schiff, Yaari, *A War of Deception*, pp. 265–6; R. Eitan, *Story of a Soldier* (Hebrew), (Ma'ariv, Tel Aviv, 1985), pp. 222–5, 282–4.

43 Schiff, Yaari, *A War of Deception*, pp. 276–9.

44 Ibid., p. 274; *Ma'ariv*, June 3, 1983; In the English-language version of their book (*Israel's Lebanon War* [Simon and Schuster, New York, 1984], p. 95), Schiff and Yaari write that at the beginning of the war Arafat sent a letter to Begin appealing to him to avoid a clash with the PLO forces. The message was passed on by Brian Urquhart, UN under-secretary general. It said, inter alia: "I have learned more from you as a resistance leader than from anyone else about how to combine politics and military tactics . . . You of all people must understand that it is not necessary to face me only on the battlefield. Do not send a military force against me. Do not try to break me in Lebanon. You will not succeed." See also General Y. Ben-Gal's version, *Ha'aretz*, June 2, 1987.

45 See Schiff, Yaari, *A War of Deception*, pp. 21–40.

46 Ibid., pp. 104–8, 125–43, 163–82, 270.

47 I do not deal with the question of whether the removal of the Palestinians from Lebanon was part of the war's master plan. The Falangists wanted the Palestinians expelled. During the war Begin may have ordered that reconstruction of the refugee camps in the south not be allowed. See Y. Sarid, *Politika*, June 1985; Schiff, Yaari, *A War of Deception*, pp. 259–60.

48 See Y. Shavit, *From Hebrew to Canaanite* (Hebrew), (Domino, Jerusalem, 1984), pp. 52–3; M. Sharett, *Sharett's Diary* (Hebrew), 8 vols. (Ma'ariv, Tel Aviv, 1978), vol. II, p. 377; A. Amir, "From Ashriki to Jumblatt," *Ha'umma*, 72 (1984), pp. 182–93.

49 Schiff, Yaari, *A War of Deception*, pp. 40–76.

50 Ibid., pp. 21–40.

51 Ibid., pp. 227–8, 241–4; *Yediot Aharonot*, February 10, 1984.

52 On events surrounding the conclusion of the agreement, see *Ma'ariv*, June 6, 1983.

53 *Yediot Aharonot*, January 18, 1974, interview with Begin.

54 See M. Begin in *Ma'ariv*: "Indeed, They Are All Guilty," November 30, 1973;

"The Agranat Commission Report and the Government's Responsibility," April 5, 1974.

55 *Knesset Proceedings*, April 11, 1974, pp. 1125–7.

56 See also Schiff, Yaari, *A War of Deception*, pp. 313–57; Report of the Inquiry Commission for the Investigation of the Events in the Refugee Camps in Beirut, 1983, pp. 78–81, ISA, 1–983–1–1.

57 Government Press Office, September 16, 1982; Schiff, Yaari, *A War of Deception*, pp. 345–6.

58 Government Press Office, September 20, 1982.

59 *Knesset Proceedings*, September 22, 1982; see also Begin's reaction to the reprisal operation in Qibya, *Herut Yearbook* (1955), pp. 51–5; and M. Begin, "The Crisis in America and Us," *Ma'ariv*, April 9, 1971. In the case of the Mai Lai massacre, Begin found it difficult to fix responsibility unambiguously. In any event, he did not absolve the high command.

60 "Testimony of Prime Minister Menachem Begin Before the Inquiry Commission," Government Press Office, November 8, 1982.

61 *Yediot Aharonot*, June 16, 1982; when the signal was given to launch the war, the head of the Mosad, Yitzhak Hofi, is reported to have said to Begin's aides, "This is going to be the Likud's Yom Kippur War", A. Haber, *Yediot Aharonot*, June 5, 1984.

62 See A. Bakhar, "Anatomy of Loneliness," *Yediot Aharonot*, December 23, 1983; A. Haber, "Begin, For Those who Don't Know Him," ibid., June 5, 1983; ibid., October 4, 1985. In reply to the argument that the government did not understand what was going on in the war, member of the cabinet Mordechai Zippori said, "Maybe someone doesn't know topography, but what's a road, what's a city, everyone understands. For that you don't have to be expert in strategy"; D. Horowitz, "Israel's War in Lebanon: New Patterns of Strategic Thinking and Civilian–Military Relations," in M. Lissak (ed.), *Israeli Society and Its Defense Establishment* (Frank Cass, London, 1984), pp. 83–102.

63 *Ma'ariv*, August 22, 1982.

Chapter 13 Leader and Prime Minister

1 Begin, *White Nights*, p. 243.

2 See his stand in the Aryeh Naor and Aharon Abuhatzeira affairs, *Ma'ariv*, September 28, 1981.

3 See also S. Aronson in *Ha'aretz*: "The Begin Syndrome," January 19, 1982; and "The Rebirth of the *Shtetl*," September 21, 1983.

4 *Ma'ariv*, April 9, 1976; see also Eldad, "Between Reversal and Revolution," pp. 170–81.

5 M. Begin, "What We Learned From Ze'ev Jabotinsky," *Ma'ariv*, July 30, 1976. See also id., "Where Are We Headed," *Herut*, June 1, 1956; id., "The Nation's Peace and the Wholeness of the Land," April 23, 1970 p. 9, JIA, P 20.

6 Id., Begin, *White Nights*, p. 32.

7 *Knesset Proceedings*, May 12, 1981, p. 2665; June 3, 1981, p. 2819.

8 These were when he presented his first government, on receiving the Nobel peace prize, and when presenting his peace plan in the United States. Before they appeared in print in Herut, he usually carefully reviewed the text of speeches he delivered, which were published in *Herut*. See M. Ben-Shachar, "The Man Behind the Headlines," *Ma'ariv*, October 10, 1983.

9 Begin, *The Revolt*, p. 122.

10 *Ma'ariv*, April 25, 1978; Marcus, *Camp David*, pp. 271–2. Marcus contends that the intention behind Begin's tough stance was to discover the furthest limit to which he could go. Shmuel Katz claims that his most assertive speeches usually signified that concessions had been or would be made.

11 Stenographic record, May 26, 1968, JIA, P 20; see also "Speech by Minister M. Begin Before the Western Wall," June 8, 1967, JIA, P 20.

12 Peace Treaty Signing Ceremony in Washington, March 26, 1979, JIA, P 20.

13 Speech by M. Begin at Memorial Ceremony for Yisrael Epstein, 1949, hand-written précis, JIA, P 20; eulogy for Aryeh Ben-Eliezer, 1969, JIA, P 20. "I had a brother. Just one. He is no longer. He was among the Jews brought to death. Over the years I came to have a second brother. That's Aryeh."

14 M. Begin, "Poet and Rebel," *Herut*, February 2, 1962.

15 *Knesset Proceedings*, February 25, 1980.

16 M. Begin, "My Opponent, Moshe Sneh," *Davar*, March 12, 1982.

17 Memorial for Shimshon Yuniczman, 1963, JIA, P 20; M. Begin, "Abba Achimeir: In Memoriam," *Herut*, July 6, 1962.

18 *Herut*, January 8, 1952.

19 See speech in Ramat Gan, August 7, 1961, JIA, P 20. On Begin's speech in Malkhei Yisrael Square, June 28, 1981, see the analysis by N. Gertz, "The Few Against the Many," *Jerusalem Quarterly*, 30 (1984), pp. 94–104.

20 Begin's use of such language goes back at least to the 1940s, when he referred to the leaders of Great Britain as "the spiritual midget, Attlee, and the great ignoramus Bevin," Begin, *In the Underground*, vol. II, p. 161. In a speech in Netanya (*Ma'ariv*, June 10, 1981) he cried "Assad, watch out. Yanush [Gen. Y. Ben-Gal] and Raful [Gen. R. Eitan] are ready." A few days later he attacked Helmut Schmidt and Valéry Giscard d'Estaing. At a cabinet meeting he spoke of Chaim Herzog's toadyism. Of Simcha Dinitz he said, "They took a minor paper shuffler, a bootlicker and toady who was a messenger boy for Golda, whom Dayan wanted to get rid of as ambassador to the US, and I let him stay on, and now he's ungrateful." At that same meeting he released a tirade against the television, its programs and staff, and even called President Yitzhak Navon, to task (*Yediot Aharonot*, May 4, 1981). In the Knesset he often saved his most blistering comments for his replies. For especially fierce debates, see *Knesset Proceedings*, May 7, 1979, pp. 2473–8; May 12, 1981, pp. 2655–68; June 3, 1981, pp. 2893–900.

21 See the beginning of the section entitled, "Homeland and Freedom", *The Herut Movement, Its Principles and Foundations*, Sivan 1948 JIA 9/7/7; Begin, *In the Underground*, vol. I, p. 170.

22 *Herut*, January 18, 1949.

23 M. Begin, "Perhaps We Will See It In Our Time," *Hamashkif*, August 13,

1948. Eliezer Livneh, member of a Mapai faction leaning to the right, fearing that the Irgun would proclaim the establishment of the state before May 14, met with Begin on his own initiative and only afterwards reported on the meeting to Ben-Gurion. E. Livneh, "Three Debates With Menachem Begin," *Herut*, August 8, 1963; Begin, *The Revolt*, pp. 425–6.

24 M. Begin, "Speech on July 6, 1967," JIA, P 20; *Ha Yom*, June 18, 1967.

25 *Knesset Proceedings*, July 4, 1976, pp. 3382–3.

26 The First National Convention in Prague, JIA C 4–8/3. Jabotinsky stressed the importance of "national unity," but also expressed his hope that the Zionist movement would not undergo what the United States had experienced eighty years ago, "but *mutatis mutandi*, we must be prepared for that possibility too."

27 M. Begin, *World View and National Conception*, 1949, mimeographed, with corrections by Begin, JIA, P 20.

28 Ibid., p. 21.

29 Ibid., pp. 25–31. The third element dealt with by Begin in the context of world view is the supremacy of law. Here he focused mainly on the principle of the separation of powers and expounded less on the rights of the citizen.

30 Ibid., p. 33.

31 See also id., "Outline for a Hebrew Domestic Policy," n.d., JIA P 20.

32 *Herut*, November 26, 1948.

33 Ibid., December 10, 1948.

34 *Ha'aretz*, January 8, 1982.

35 M. Begin, "Double Standard and Its Influence," *Ma'ariv*, July 7, 1973.

36 Ibid., October 24, 1969, January 17, 1975; *Knesset Proceedings*, March 10, 1974, pp. 587–91.

37 Weizman, *The Battle for Peace*, p. 282.

38 On domestic policy during the Begin era, see I. Sharkansky and A. Radian, "Changing Domestic Policy, 1977–1981," in Freedman, *Israel in the Begin Era*, pp. 57–75.

39 *Herut*, November 2, 1959. See also Haber, *Menachem Begin*, pp. 245–6.

40 *Herut*, September 17, 1959.

41 "Homeland and Freedom," August 5, 1948.

42 *Herut*, July 17, 1952; S. Ofer, "The Leader Who Goes to the Immigrant Camp," *Lamerhav*, April 29, 1955.

43 Ibid., June 24, 1956.

44 *Knesset Proceedings*, December 8, 1964.

45 M. Begin, "Around the President's Term," *Ma'ariv*, March 30, 1973; *Herut*, November 2, 1952.

46 Id., speech at the Fourteenth Convention of the Herut Movement, June 3, 1979, JIA, P 20.

47 *Knesset Proceedings*, November 2, 1981, p. 307; *Yediot Aharonot*, May 11, 1981; A. Elon, "Towards a New Society," *Ha'aretz*, November 9, 1981.

48 See "Transcript of Television Debate Between Prime Minister M. Begin and Labor Party Chairman S. Peres," June 25, 1981, Information Division, Herut. Begin still rebuffed Peres's attacks with selective use of statistical data, "we will increase exports, reduce inflation, develop the economy, approach

economic independence, we will build a Land of Israel beautiful in all its
length and breadth . . ."
49 On the political change in Israeli society, see A. Arian, "The Passing of
Dominance," *Jerusalem Quarterly*, 5 (1977), pp. 20–32; M. J. Aronoff, "The
Labor Party in Opposition," in Freedman, *Israel in the Begin Era*, pp. 76–101;
D. Horowitz, "More Than a Change in Government," *Jerusalem Quarterly*, 5
(1977), pp. 3–19; O. Seliktar, "Ethnic Stratification and Foreign Policy in
Israel: The Attitudes of Oriental Jews Towards the Arabs and the Arab–
Israeli Conflict," *The Middle East Journal*, 38 (1984), pp. 34–50; Y. Yishai,
"Israel's Right-Wing Jewish Proletariat, *The Jewish Journal of Sociology*, 24
(1982), pp. 87–98.
50 Begin, *White Nights*, pp. 45, 91–2.
51 Speech by Minister M. Begin at the Western Wall, June 8, 1967, JIA, P 20.
See also *Herut*, November 20, 1964.
52 M. Begin, "Nation, State, Religion," *Herut*, June 19, 1964; *Knesset Proceedings*,
December 1, 1958, pp. 375–7; February 9, 1970, pp. 731–5; Jabotinsky, *My
Father, Ze'ev Jabotinsky*, pp. 95–106.
53 *Ma'ariv*, September 28, 1981, interview with Begin; B. Kimmerling, *Zionism
and Economy* (Schenkman, Cambridge, Mass., 1983), pp. 137–9. Begin was
interested in religious symbols and rituals but did not display an interest in
the intellectual or theoretical aspects of the religion.
54 Haber et al., *Year of the Dove*, p. 119; *Knesset Proceedings*, November 28, 1977,
p. 518.
55 *Knesset Proceedings*, May 3, 1982.
56 See also D. E. Elazar, "Religious Parties and Politics in the Begin Era," in
Freedman, *Israel in the Begin Era*, pp. 102–120.
57 *Herut*, November 26, 1948.
58 *Knesset Proceedings*, April 4, 1949; May 3, 1950.
59 See M. Begin in *Ma'ariv*: "The Importance of Seriousness," February 2,
1973; "The Opposition Speaks For the Majority," May 9, 1974; "61: How
Then a Minority Government?", June 6, 1974. See also *Knesset Proceedings*,
January 22, 1974, p. 15.
60 M. Begin, "Settlement and the Cry of Putsch," *Ma'ariv*, August 2, 1974; id.,
"One for the Gentile, One for the Jew," *Herut*, August 6, 1954.
61 Yerubaal [Z. Levanon], *The Day Begin Rose to Power* (Hebrew), (Jerusalem,
1955).
62 After Begin was in fact elected prime minister, the known humorist Ephraim
Kishon wrote an article entitled "Waking from a Brainwashing," in which
Begin's victory seemed to be the triumph of the progressive conceptions of
the right and a victory of faithful adherence to principles. Kishon hoped that
Begin would succeed not only in foreign policy but also in overcoming the
tyranny of domestic bureaucracy. See *Ma'ariv*, July 29, 1977.
63 *New York Times*, May 19, 1977; *Yediot Aharonot*, June 22, 1977.
64 *New York Times*, May 18, 19, 22, 1977; *Jerusalem Post*, May 24, 1977; *Knesset
Proceedings*, June 20, 1977, p. 65.
65 Weizman, *The Battle for Peace*, p. 285; when Begin suffered a heart attack after
his electoral victory, the foreign minister already attempted to ensure his

position in the eventuality that the prime minister would not be able to continue in office; Benziman, *Prime Minister under Siege*, pp. 12–14; Marcus, *Camp David*, 24–7; *New York Times*, May 26, 1977; *Jerusalem Post*, June 7, 1977.

66 *Knesset Proceedings*, June 20, 1977, pp. 14–17; *Jerusalem Post*, June 21, 1977.

67 *New York Times*, June 14, 1977; *Jerusalem Post Magazine*, July 1, 1977.

68 I. Sharkansky, *What makes Israel Tick* (Nelson-Halls, Chicago, 1984), pp. 33–50.

69 *Jerusalem Post*, May 24, 1977; *New York Times*, June 26, 1977; July 3, 1977; July 17, 1977. E. Torgovnik, "Likud 1977–1981: The Consolidation of Power," in Freedman, *Israel in the Begin Era*, pp. 7–27; *Yediot Aharonot*, October 14, 1977.

70 *Ma'ariv*, August 22, 1977, on his relationship to Gen. (res.) Rehabaam Zeevi; *Yediot Aharonot*, September 11, 1977, on the Ben-Zion affair; *Davar*, December 6, 1978, on the Tel Hai Fund; Marcus, *Camp David*, p. 246; Avneri, *The Liberal connection*, pp. 248–32.

71 *Ma'ariv*, October 28, December 8, 11, 1978; Silver, *Begin*, pp. 206–7.

72 Weizman, *The Battle for Peace*, pp. 262, 358; Dayan, *Shall the Sword Devour Forever*, p. 100; Benziman, *Prime Minister under Siege*, pp. 155, 236; Katz, *Neither Splendour nor Courage*, pp. 122–3.

73 See also Y. Marcus, "The Man Who Went Out of His Political Mind," *Ha'aretz*, May 15, 1981; M. Begin, "Open Reply to Mr. Sternhell," ibid., August 4, 1981.

74 Katz, *Neither Splendour nor Courage*, pp. 196–9; *Ma'ariv*, September 27, 1978. In an advertisement placed by underground veterans, consent to the erection of American bases was likened to a restoration of foreign rule. They compared the removal of settlements to use of the "holy cannon" against the *Altalena*.

75 *Knesset Proceedings*, December 28, 1977, p. 992; *Yediot Aharonot*, May 7, 1979.

76 *Ma'ariv*, April 23, 1980; Haig, *Caveat*, p. 320. See also *Ma'ariv*, September 5, 1977, on Begin's visit to Maaleh Edumim; *Yediot Aharonot*, November 19, 1978. Zvi Shiloah wrote that "a leader who failed must go"; *Ma'ariv*, December 28, 1977, on the demonstrations by residents of Yamit and Kiryat Arba; see Y. Ben-Porat, *Yediot Aharonot*, December 30, 1977, on the change in Begin's views; *Ha'aretz*, April 6, 1979. On the demonostration in Yamit during Begin's visit; *Ma'ariv*, December 27, 1979, at the dedication of the yeshiva in Kiryat Arba Begin cut his speech short after shouts from the crowd of "traitor", "seller of the Land of Israel"; *Ha'aretz*, January 8, 1982, *Yediot Aharonot*, March 2, 1982, close to the evacuation of Yamit, Begin was quoted as saying, "Raful will be replaced if he doesn't do what we order him to."

77 Haber, *Menachem Begin*, pp. 300–1; Silver, *Begin*, p. 182.

78 M. Altman, Testimony, ICJ, December 18, 1966, p. 5.

79 M. Begin in *Ma'ariv*: "The Functioning of a Non-Government," October 29, 1976; "A Plague of Leaks and Over-Response," January 30, 1976.

80 Dayan, *Shall the Sword Devour Forever*, pp. 22–3. *Knesset Proceedings*, August 15, 1977, p. 672. See also: H. Rosenblum, "Close All Faucets Right Away," *Yediot Aharonot*, May 27, 1977; M. Golan, "Signs of Diminution in Begin's Leadership," *Ha'aretz*, August 5, 1977; U. Benziman, "Truth and Falsehood,

Overt and Covert – à la Begin," ibid., August 19, 1977; Y. Dror, "Fateful Decision In the Hands of One Man," *Yediot Aharonot*, January 4, 1978 and "Signs of Weakness," ibid., March 19, 1978.

81 Katz, *Neither Splendour nor Courage*, pp. 232–7.

82 When Herut had just been formed, Begin backed down on the issue of joining the Histadrut and of drawing up a proposal for a national constitution. See Bader, *The Knesset and I*, pp. 39–40; *Knesset Proceedings*, January 12, 1966, p. 353.

83 Katz, *Neither Splendour nor Courage*, pp. 10–12.

84 Ibid., pp. 160–8.

85 Weizman, *The Battle for Peace*, p. 303.

86 Ibid., pp. 168–71, 302–3, 402; Marcus, *Camp David*, p. 207; on the way Jabotinsky worked with his aides, see Schechtman, *Jabotinsky*, vol. II, pp. 292–8. Although Jabotinsky was tolerant and acted like a first among equals, he conducted disorderly meetings and was accused more than once of prevaricating and of not taking decisions. He said of himself, "I am a bad tactician."

87 S. Nakdimon, "Thus they have Decided 'Lavi'", *Yediot Aharonot*, August 21, 28, 1987; A. Avneri, "He knows", ibid., August 7, 1987. An event emblematic of Begin's style was his talk with Secretary of State Vance in early November 1978. The prime minister declared that Israel was not asking for a grant from the United States but a loan: "We'll give back every penny we receive." Vance announced that at a press conference and conveyed Begin's words to the president. The secretary of state responded sharply when Dayan told him that he wanted to correct the prime minister's announcement. Dayan knew how to leave the "grand gesture" to Begin, but this was going too far. Vance, *Hard Choices*, p. 236; Dayan, *Shall the Sword Devour Forever*, pp. 191–2.

88 *Yediot Aharonot*, March 8 and July 19, 1978.

Chapter 14 The End of the Road

1 M. Begin, "What We Learned From Ze'ev Jabotinsky," *Ma'ariv*, July 30, 1976.

2 Id., Letter of August 7, 1980, *Yediot Aharonot*, August 12, 1980.

3 Id., "His Policy On His Illness," *Ha'aretz*, December 4, 1981.

4 See on this Benziman, *Prime Minister under Siege*, pp. 146–52, 161; *Yediot Aharonot*, June 25, 1978, July 22, 1982; U. Benziman, "On Begin's Condition," *Ha'aretz*, June 2, 1978; ibid., August 8, 1983.

5 See *Yediot Aharonot*, December 23, 1982; television broadcast, May 28, 1985; A. Bakhar, "Anatomy of Loneliness," *Yediot Aharonot*, December 16, 1983.

6 H. Canaan, "I'll Retire At 70," *Ha'aretz*, January 6, 1977; *Yediot Aharonot*, October 1, 1978, interview with Begin; *Ma'ariv*, February 16, 1981; in July 1983, Begin proposed Shamir, Aridor, and Levy as a troika to replace him after he stepped down. Referring to Weizman, he said, "It's a pity. I loved Ezer;" *Yediot Aharonot*, July 8, 1981.

7 *Ma'ariv*, July 27, 1981; *Yediot Aharonot*, August 13, 1982.

8 *Ma'ariv*, August 30, 1983; Silver, *Begin*, pp. 241–52.

9 Bader, *The Knesset and I*, pp. 286–7; *Ha'aretz*, August 31, 1983; Y. Bader, "What Impelled Begin?" *Ma'ariv*, August 31, 1983.

10 S. Katz, "Reflections After the Resignation," *Ma'ariv*, September 16, 1983.

11 *Ha'aretz*, September 27, 1983.

12 *Yediot Aharonot*, June 21, 1985.

13 See *Ma'ariv*, October 19, 1982; Aliza Begin's funeral was on November 15, 1982. She was buried on the Mount of Olives. In keeping with the family's request, the funeral was not covered by the press. See also, A. Remba. *With Jabotinsky*, pp. 30, 36; Eldad, *First Tithe*, pp. 32–5. Begin's relationship with his wife had been deep and honest. In that he resembled Jabotinsky; one thing always able to lower Jabotinsky's spirits, was his wife's condition.

14 Bader, *The Knesset and I*, p. 285; id., "Anniversary of a Fighter," *Herut*, August 2, 1963.

15 On the importance of ritual for man's survival, see Begin, *White Nights*, p. 40.

16 S. Nakdimon, "Herut In the Post-Begin Era," *Yediot Aharonot*, May 18, 1984. In the 865-member Herut center, there were 160 members from the Irgun and 30 from Lehi. Aryeh Ben-Eliezer, the tolerant heir, died early. Ya'acov Meridor had destroyed his personal as well as his political credibility with his own hands. See also, D. Pollock, "Likud in Power: Divided We Stand," in, Freedman, *Israel in the Begin Era*, pp. 28–55.

17 *Ma'ariv*, July 23, 1984.

18 S. Nakdimon, "Begin: The Open Door of the Secluded Man," *Yediot Aharonot*, April 5, 1985; *Ma'ariv*, March 13, 1986.

Index